PERPETRATORS
VICTIMS
BYSTANDERS

Also by Raul Hilberg

The Destruction of the European Jews

PERPETRATORS

VICTIMS

BYSTANDERS

THE JEWISH
CATASTROPHE
1933–1945

RAUL HILBERG

HarperPerennial

A Division of HarperCollinsPublishers

Aaron Asher Books

A hardcover edition of this book was published in 1992 by HarperCollins Publishers.

PERPETRATORS VICTIMS BYSTANDERS. Copyright © 1992 by Raul Hilberg. All rights reserved. Printed in the United States of America. No part of this book may be used or reproduced in any manner whatsoever without written permission except in the case of brief quotations embodied in critical articles and reviews. For information, address HarperCollins Publishers, 195 Broadway, New York, NY 10007.

HarperCollins books may be purchased for educational, business, or sales promotional use. For information, please e-mail the Special Markets Department at SPsales@harpercollins.com.

First HarperPerennial edition published 1993.

Designed by Jessica Shatan

The Library of Congress has catalogued the hardcover edition as follows:

Hilberg, Raul, 1926–
    Perpetrators victims bystanders : the Jewish catastrophe,
1933–1945 / Raul Hilberg.
      p. cm.
    Includes index.
    ISBN 0-06-019035-3
    1. Holocaust, Jewish (1939–1945).   2. Holocaust, Jewish
(1939–1945)—Biography.   I. Title.
D804.3.H56   1992
940.53′18—dc20   92-52551

ISBN 0-06-099507-6 (pbk.)

17 18 19 20 AC/RRD 38 37 36 35 34 33 32 31

for
Gwendolyn

CONTENTS

Preface ix

PREFACE

The Jewish catastrophe during the years from 1933 to 1945 was a massive occurrence. It began in Germany and ultimately engulfed an area encompassing most of the European continent. It was also an event that was experienced by a variety of perpetrators, a multitude of victims, and a host of bystanders. These three groups were distinct from one another and they did not dissolve in their lifetime. Each saw what had happened from its own, special perspective, and each harbored a separate set of attitudes and reactions.

The perpetrators were people who played a specific role in the formulation or implementation of anti-Jewish measures. In most cases, a participant understood his function, and he ascribed it to his position and duties. What he did was impersonal. He had been empowered or instructed to carry out his mission. Moreover, no one man and no one organization was solely responsible for the destruction of the Jews. No single budget was allocated for this purpose. The work was diffused in a widespread bureaucracy, and each man could feel that his contribution was a small part of an immense undertaking. For these reasons, an administrator, clerk, or uniformed guard never referred to himself as a perpetrator. He realized, however, that the process of destruction was deliberate, and that once he had stepped into this maelstrom, his deed would be indelible. In this sense, he would always be what he had been, even if he remained reticent or silent about what he had done.

The first and foremost perpetrator was Adolf Hitler himself. He was the supreme architect of the operation; without him it would have been inconceivable. Hitler was always in the limelight, but most of the labor was carried out in the shadows by a vast establishment of familiar functionaries and ascending newcomers. In this conglomeration, some men displayed eagerness, while others had doubts. Within the leadership there were many professionals, including ubiquitous lawyers and indispensable physicians. When the process was extended to the four corners of Europe, the machinery of destruction became international as Germans were joined by governments in satellite states and by individual collaborators in occupied countries.

Unlike the perpetrators, the victims were perpetually exposed. They were identifiable and countable at every turn. To be defined as Jews, they only had to have had Jewish parents or grandparents. Discriminatory laws and regulations dealt in great detail with such problems as partners in mixed marriages, individuals with mixed parentage, and enterprises with mixed ownership. With each successive step, the gulf became wider. The Jews were marked with a star, and their contacts with non-Jews were minimized, formalized, or prohibited. Segregated in houses, ghettos, or labor camps, they were spatially isolated and concentrated. Beyond these barriers, the war cut off continental European Jewry from Jewish communities and Allied governments in the outside world.

The Jewish victims had leaders, and these individuals, occupying positions in hundreds of Jewish councils, have attracted much attention. The victims as a whole, however, have remained an amorphous mass. Millions of them suffered a common fate in front of pre-dug graves or in the darkness of hermetically sealed gas chambers. The death of these Jews has become their most important attribute. They are remembered mainly for what happened to them all, and for this reason there has been some inhibition about segmenting them systematically into component categories. Yet the impact of destruction was not simultaneously the same for everyone. There were, first of all, people who left in time—the refugees. The vast majority, who stayed or were trapped in place, included grown men and women, whose respective encounters with adversity were not identical. Some of the married Jews were in a special category, because they had non-Jewish partners. Jewish children had lives and afflictions all their own. The quandary for Christians of Jewish descent is a story in and of itself. The community as a whole was stratified from top to bottom in terms of wealth and income, and in many situations these material distinctions mattered a great deal. Even more significant were differences of personality traits. Whereas most victims adjusted themselves step by step to the increasing stringency of deprivation and loss, there was a minority, however small, that did not share the adaptations of the multitude. The inability or refusal to become reconciled to the assault gave rise to a variety of reactions, from suicides to open rebellion. Finally a remnant of persisters and resisters were found alive in the liberated camps and woods—survivors.

Most contemporaries of the Jewish catastrophe were neither perpetrators nor victims. Many people, however, saw or heard something of the event. Those of them who lived in Adolf Hitler's Europe would have described themselves, with few exceptions, as bystanders. They were not "involved," not willing to hurt the victims and not wishing to be hurt by the perpetrators. Yet the reality was not always so uncomplicated. Much depended on the relations of various continental European nations with the Germans and with the Jews. These bonds or fissures could facilitate or hinder action in one direction or another. Much was determined also by the character of the individual, particularly if it was an unusual or extraordinary character. In some areas, bystanders became perpetrators themselves. In many regions they took advantage of Jewish misfortunes and seized a profit, but there were also those who helped the hunted. Now and then, a messenger appeared and spread the news.

Outside the arena of destruction, an important group was faced with calls for rescue—the Jews of the United States, Britain, and Palestine. The Jewish leaders in these countries were not uncaring; in no sense did *they* view themselves as bystanders. They believed, however, that they were powerless, so much so that they became impotent in fact. The Allied governments, to which American and British Jewry appealed, did not lack power, but they were not about to go out of their way for the victims. The neutral countries on the European continent adopted a policy of not engaging in overt governmental actions that could be interpreted as taking sides. This self-limiting posture contributed to an abstention from assuming an active role also in the case of the Jewish plight. The churches, by contrast, embraced all humanity, but it was hard for them to extend their hand equally in every direction. For the Pontiff, this exercise was especially difficult and in the years after the war he has been labeled at times as the supreme bystander. Yet churchmen, Catholic as well as Protestant, were delineated by their nationality and temperament, much as all the inhabitants of Europe.

In this text, perpetrators, victims, and bystanders will appear separately. The twenty-four chapters, each dealing with a segment of one of the three groups, are written as modules. They are intended to be self-contained and may be read in any number and any order. No attempt has been made in this volume to cover everyone or everything. It is rather a book with brief descriptions and capsule portraits of people, known and unknown, who were once a part of this history.

I invested several years in research and writing. The time would have been longer, had it not been for the support I received from my friend and colleague, Alan Wertheimer, who chaired the Department of Political Science at the University of Vermont when I began the project. Through his efforts I obtained a fellowship grant from the John M. Olin Foundation, which paid for materials, trips, and, above all, free time. The foundation waited patiently while the work was interrupted, enlarged, and extended. I am profoundly grateful for this assistance. John G. Jewett, who was Dean of the College of Arts and Sciences, facilitated my study with a timely and supportive sabbatical leave. Finally I am indebted to archivists and librarians on three continents for their indispensable help. Without them the widely scattered sources would be lost, and names as well as events would remain unknown.

PART I

PERPETRATORS

"I was never cruel."

—Hermann Göring to prison psychologist
G. M. Gilbert in Nuremberg, 1946

1

ADOLF HITLER

ADOLF HITLER WAS BORN on April 20, 1889. His father Alois was a customs official of the Austro-Hungarian Empire in Braunau, on the border of Germany, and his mother Klara was much younger than Alois, who had already been widowed twice. Adolf was one of six children born to Klara, and one of only two who survived. Adolf's sister Paula remained obscure and unknown.

The family was not poor. Alois had worked himself up from humble beginnings, and when he died no one starved. Klara, to whom Adolf was close, died of cancer at the age of forty-seven. Her physician was a Jew.

When the adolescent Adolf Hitler went to school in the provincial cities of Linz and Steyr, he was not a good student. He received bad grades in mathematics, physics, and German, mediocre marks in religion and diligence, and excellent grades only in art and gymnastics. The length and quality of his schooling were nevertheless adequate and at least average for the standards of that time.[1]

Hitler was attracted to art, and in 1907 he arrived in the Austrian capital, Vienna, where he was to spend the next six years. There he had a close friend who was interested in music and it is there that Hitler listened to the operas of Richard Wagner, which abound with pre-Christian deities, muffled slow drumbeats, and arias that call for sheer power, especially the controlled escalation of the voice above a massive orchestra. Hitler failed to gain admission to the prestigious Vienna Art Academy. He was not faulted for his style, as the impressionists had been by the Paris Salon or the secessionists by the Viennese establishment. Hitler was traditional. He drew and painted buildings and landscapes. What he evidently lacked was sufficient ability to portray faces. Yet he did sketch his own face in a drawing tending slightly to caricature.

Although Hitler was rejected, he did not become a complete derelict. He lived in the twentieth district, which housed mainly workers and small traders. His room, in a house set aside for single men, was ordinary. Sometimes he may have lacked money for a coat or something else, but he subsisted on funds left by his family and on the proceeds from the sale of his pictures to art dealers. Apparently, two of these dealers were Jews.[2]

The Europe of 1907–1913 was drenched with doctrines that had lost much of their attractiveness by the end of the twentieth century: imperialism, racism, and anti-Semitism. Austria-Hungary had no overseas colonies, and its population was completely white, but it did have a sizable Jewish minority. In Vienna alone, there was a Jewish community of some 200,000, including many individuals who had recently arrived from eastern provinces, notably Galicia. Vienna was also a place where one could find an anti-Semitic movement that published literature ascribing destructive behavior to the Jews and asserting that Jews were a race, which could not and would not change. While Hitler resided in Vienna, he became acquainted with these ideas.

In Vienna, Hitler also became of military age. Like other countries of continental Europe, Austria-Hungary had peacetime conscription, in essence, the compulsory induction of able-bodied men for simple training and their placement in reserves that could be mobilized quickly for war. The years 1907–1913 were in fact characterized by increasing preparedness and an arms race pitting mainly Germany and Austria-Hungary against France and Russia. Hitler avoided the draft.

In 1913, he went to Munich and from there he made his peace with

the Austrian authorities. They examined him and found him physically too weak for military service. When Germany declared war in
August 1914, Hitler volunteered to enter the German army. He spent
the next four years on the Western Front, where he was wounded.
Promotions were denied him, because he was not considered a potential leader. On several occasions he was refused also the coveted
decoration of the Iron Cross First Class. Finally, he received it in
August 1918, after he had been recommended for it again. The successful sponsor was Lieutenant of the Reserves Gutmann, reportedly
a Jew.

Shortly before the end of the fighting, Hitler was gassed. Still
hospitalized at the time of the armistice, he remained in uniform after
his recuperation. Stationed in Bavaria, he could observe some of
Germany's postwar political upheavals, including a short-lived local
Communist regime that was swept away by the German army. Under the impact of democratization, the old military leadership could
no longer exclude political debates, but they were organized and
supervised. In the unit to which Hitler belonged, a soldier wanted to
know why Germany had lost the war. The company commander
assigned Hitler to write a reply.

Hitler's answer, dated September 16, 1919, is his first explicit
writing about the Jews. In this lengthy memorandum, he stated that
the Jews were exploiting nations, undermining their strength, and
infecting them with a racial tuberculosis. He went on to discuss
anti-Semitism, making a distinction between an anti-Semitism of
emotion, which could give rise only to temporary eruptions, or
pogroms, without leading to a solution of the Jewish problem, and
an anti-Semitism of reason, which would result in a series of legal
measures aimed at the eventual elimination of the Jews.[3]

Hitler's differentiation between forms of anti-Semitism was not
altogether commonplace and it could well have been the product of
his own contemplation. He referred to emotion (*Gefühl*) as momen-
tary. On the other hand, reason, the German *Vernunft*, is steady. He
wanted this steadiness for the attainment of his goal, the ambiguous,
yet total removal, disappearance, or elimination of the Jews, expressed in the German word *Entfernung*.

When Hitler wrote the letter, he was thirty years old. Its contents are unheralded by anything he had said or committed to paper in the past. Nothing in his earlier encounters with Jews accounts for his hostility. Because Dr. Eduard Bloch, the physician who had treated Hitler's mother, was a Jew, there has been speculation that in Hitler's mind Jewish doctors were dangerous to the health of the German people. Indeed, such a depiction emerged later on in crude Nazi propaganda, and Hitler as Führer did not want Jewish physicians to have German patients, but his reason was the *status* of doctors in society—they were models (*Vorbilder*) for everyone—and he did not want Jews to be a part of this elite.[4] The contacts with Jewish art dealers might also open questions about any old suppositions on his part that he was exploited or defrauded. Again, Hitler did decree the liquidation of Jewish commercial enterprises, yet he was never heard to complain about his own transactions with them. One man he castigated was his non-Jewish friend Reinhold Hanisch, who peddled Hitler's pictures for 50 percent of their price, and who may at one time have pocketed the whole amount. Hitler accused *this* man of embezzlement.[5] Finally, Hitler's life on or near the front lines from 1914 to 1918 is similarly barren, if one looks for clues to his preoccupation with Jewry. To be sure, he wanted no Jews in the German army after he had come to power, but as late as August 1938 he remarked to his entourage that "no matter what anyone said," there had been brave Jewish soldiers and even officers in the First World War.[6]

Hitler's fixation has its origins in Vienna, where he read anti-Jewish tracts and where, as he said later, he gradually began to hate the Jews. These printed words, or his glimpses in the Viennese streets of newly arrived Jewish migrants from the east, had not distorted his impressions of individual Jews he had met in Linz, Vienna, or the army. Rather, he developed an obsession with the Jews as a whole. He saw them as separate from the German nation, and he blamed them as a group for nothing less than the greatest loss of all: Germany's defeat. He must have been pondering this conclusion for a while, because his 1919 statement is neither hesitant nor tentative. It is the finished product of a man who was certain of his position.

After 1919, Hitler could not remain in the army, most of which had to be demobilized under the terms of the peace treaty. He did, however, enter into a new activity. During the remaining period of his military service, he had been sent out to investigate a small political group that called itself the German Labor party and that was suspected, if only because of its name, of leaning too far to the Left. Hitler joined that party as its 555th member and as the 7th member of its executive committee.[7] Soon he was given the top position, which he filled by virtue of his extraordinary ability to address an audience. The party became the National Socialist German Workers party, or in an acronym the Nazi party. In its program of February 20, 1920, several references were made to Jews, notably in proposals to revoke their citizenship rights, to remove them from positions in public employment, and to deport those of them who had entered Germany after the outbreak of the First World War. In no way, however, was this program a harbinger of what was to come.

Hitler decided in 1923 to take over the German government by a coup d'état. The idea was not novel. The Communists had seized control of Russia in November 1917; Benito Mussolini had climbed to power after a march on Rome in October 1922; and in Germany itself there were attempted takeovers, albeit unsuccessful ones, that could have served as an inspiration. Hitler's *Putsch,* as the Germans called such a coup, was carried out not in Berlin but in Munich, where important military officers supported it. Hitler marched with General Erich Ludendorff, the police opened fire, and the attempt failed. The incident, which took place on November 9, 1923, had been timed to assure a Nazi victory by November 11, the fifth anniversary of the armistice.

Following a trial for treason, Hitler spent a little more than a year in prison, where he started to write *Mein Kampf,* his polemical autobiography. His father Alois, according to this account, had not been anti-Semitic and had regarded anti-Jewish utterances as a sign of backwardness. The young Adolf himself had not noticed the Jews in Linz; they seemed not all that different from Germans. When he arrived in Vienna, he still did not recognize the Jews. Only after a while, did he become aware of their unheroic appearance, smell their unpleasant odors, and take note of their theatrical talk. From then on, he began to realize what the Jews were. They were middlemen who produced nothing, Marxists who took over trade unions, traders who controlled the stock exchange, scribblers of filth who contaminated German culture. They defiled German women with their blood. Clearly, Hitler took offense at the sight of Jews; they stood for ugliness, decay, repulsiveness, and syphilis.

After his release from prison, Hitler became legitimate. Still working on *Mein Kampf,* he settled in a modest apartment.[8] Shedding his Austrian citizenship, he took steps to become a German de jure, although his naturalization was not accomplished before 1932.[9]

His political life, however, was far from secure. The party work was full-time and with no job to fall back on, Hitler gambled everything on the small possibility of a victory. It was to be all or nothing, but at the end of 1928 the party, still small, counted only 108,717 members.[10]

Hitler's private financial life was a special problem. He had to borrow money. His only luxury, a Mercedes motorcar, which he loved but also needed for his expanding political work, attracted the attention of tax collectors, who questioned the completeness of his reported income figures and the size of his claimed deductions.[11]

By 1929 Hitler's royalties were substantial and he was finally well-to-do, living comfortably in much larger and better accommodations. He was known all over Germany, and more and more people flocked to his rallies. When the economic depression hit Germany with full force, Nazis and Communists alike drew increasing support, and after several elections Adolf Hitler was appointed Reich Chancellor on January 30, 1933.

He now reached the German people, not merely in print or at mass meetings, but in a powerful new medium: the radio. Oratory became identified with him. He would stand silently, motionless, before beginning slowly, in the voice of a baritone-basso, with the words "Volksgenossen, Volksgenossinen!"—a Nazi appellation meaning literally men and women who were comrades belonging to the same people. Gradually he would arrive at a crescendo, with the audience heard to go wild, shouting, "Sieg Heil!"—the Nazi German victory and salvation. Hitler's portrait could be seen everywhere; it showed a man in his forties, cold and penetrating. His associates spoke of him as hypnotic.

He understood the German language, understood the German people to the core. The prominent historian of Hitler in postwar Germany, Eberhard Jäckel, says that the German people loved him, held him inviolate, and pronounced him not responsible for "excesses," which they believed to have been perpetrated behind his back and without his knowledge. [12]

In his appearance, Hitler exemplified simplicity. He wore a plain uniform, without any unearned medals, but with his Iron Cross. He would refer to his wartime service as that of a simple soldier. After President Hindenburg's death, he declined to inherit Hindenburg's title, and eventually dropping the rank of Reich Chancellor, he remained only the leader, *Führer*. In this manner, he conveyed essence and totality.

There was little irony, subtlety, restraint, or understatement in his words, just as there were few instances of such usages in German discourse generally. Hitler did employ dichotomies. He played with opposites, especially the opposites of extremes. Everything he said publicly was designed to maintain the "yes" and the "no," and to deny exceptions, reservations, or compromises.

For Germany he wanted oneness. The popular slogan was "Ein Volk, ein Reich, ein Führer," which means one people, one Reich, one leader. The party was a "movement," and Germany marched in pulsating waves, "before us, with us, behind us."

His perspective, fashioned from a kernel of his Linz and Vienna youth, was architectural. It was not accident that he elevated a young architect, Albert Speer, to be the planner of Berlin and subsequently of war production. The public buildings were styled to be monumental, not modern or flat-roofed, and there was to be an expansion of enclosed space, as in the atrium of the Führerbau in Munich or in the sports arena of Nuremberg where the party rally of 1935 was held. But architecture was more than a matter of sites and structures. The entire Reich was to be visually unified by superhighways, the *Reichsautobahnen,* and for the people there was to be an aerodynamic car shaped like a beetle, the Nazi party's Volkswagen. Beyond even projects of engineering, the architectural idea pervaded administrative thought. The counterparts of architectural plans for buildings were the organization charts of new bureaucratic structures. New party offices, new SS and Police formations, new ministries with new functions were to come into being, and finally, alone above all the old and new power centers stood Adolf Hitler himself, the supreme architect of the Third Reich.[13]

Adolf Hitler and his followers were not missionaries seeking converts to Nazism among non-Germans, and Hitler neither embraced nor relied on a political theory. He did not even articulate distant goals. There was never a map to show what a German Europe would look like after a victorious war, and there was no blueprint to outline the destruction of the European Jews. What did exist were the stirring of a nation, the mobilization of its power, and the actualization of its threats. Germany moved, inexorably, on a path dictated by an inner logic, with less and less hesitation and more and more severity against its "foes."

In Hitler's eyes, the Jews were Germany's principal adversary. The battle he fought against them was a "defense." It was a settlement of accounts for all that Jewry had done. It was an answer to Jewry's laughter. Hitler was not going to be laughed at, belittled, or made the object of mockery. He saw the Jews as deriding everything that was sacred to a German. When he spoke on September 30, 1942, he said openly that the Jews would soon stop laughing everywhere. This much he prophesied.[14]

In the twelve years of his rule, the public figure Adolf Hitler stood as solitary leader, unchallengeable and untouchable. He uttered the words that reverberated in German ears and signed decrees in the Reich legal gazette. Everything else was hidden: his ailments, his female companion, his streaks of toleration and modesty.

Hitler was the sort of petit bourgeois man who invested in Mercedes stock certificates and who held on to his old rent receipts.[15] He did not allow portraits of himself wearing glasses. Just before he came to power he began to have stomach pains after a meal, sometimes while he was still eating. That this ailment could be noticed was as distressing to him as the pain itself. Thereafter he would forego meat dishes, and even pastries of which he was fond.[16] Unknown, like his discomforts, were also his private pleasures. Eva Braun joined her life to his and at the end, before they committed suicide together, he married her. No one outside his inner circle was aware of her existence until after the war. A military aide, Major

Gerhard Engel, who observed him closely between 1938 and 1943, recorded a number of small uncharacteristic incidents in Hitler's life. Thus, when the Commander of the Armed Forces, Colonel General Walter von Brauchitsch, underwent a divorce, Hitler, the liberal, was "magnanimous," offering financial support to satisfy the claims of Mrs. von Brauchitsch and insisting that in no event was the commander to be "burdened spiritually" after this tribulation. Once, when Hitler wanted to visit a coffeehouse, the Gestapo was about to evict a humorist, who was suspect by definition, from the premises. Hitler blocked the police, explaining that a humorist had to make jokes. With Engel, Hitler also paid a nocturnal visit to an art gallery to buy paintings.[17] One of his favorites, which he allowed to be photographed, was called *The Last Hand Grenade*.[18] His own artwork, however, was an embarrassment to him. In 1942, he instructed the Gestapo to obtain three of his paintings that were in private possession in Vienna and to destroy them.[19]

Hitler had revealed the hardships of his Vienna days, but he did not want publicity about his private life as Führer in Berlin. He shied away from allowing public knowledge of these aspects of his existence, precisely because they were the most normal. The image that he cultivated was that of a man who devoted all of his time to the German people and who was to be followed blindly. In actual fact, Hitler sometimes slept through half a morning, but generally he did allocate a full day to his work. To be alert, he began to take amphetamines, which were given to him at first in small doses, but which were increased when he acquired a tolerance for the drug. Gradually he became dependent on the injections and after the middle of 1942 his behavior started to change. No longer interested in people and cities, he withdrew to his headquarters. At conferences he would deal with small matters at length and repeat himself endlessly.[20] His efficiency was now impaired, but his absolutism remained.

Hitler did not decide everything himself. He did, however, have the power to issue orders at will. The scope of his decisions varied considerably. Often enough he concerned himself with minutiae, also in Jewish affairs, but Hitler is Hitler because of the enormous events he set in motion. When he came to a conclusion, he did not always do so rapidly, and when he announced it to someone, it was not necessarily self-explanatory. Yet these internal pronouncements were guidelines and inspirations, and meaning could be drawn even from his incomplete thoughts. Because Hitler stood above the bureaucracy, he was not the author—and seldom the editor—of laws or directives he signed. The administrative apparatus was in fact the source of a continuous flow of ideas and initiatives. Many major actions were taken without his express consent, and sometimes they were not reported to him. On occasion, he would have to arbitrate between contending potentates or factions. In these respects, Hitler was like all rulers in a complex society, but he never relinquished the prerogative to intervene, either to veto an action or, portentously, to bring it about. Finally, it must be said that Hitler could not have killed the Jews with his two hands and that he could not have accomplished anything without the men who staffed the far-flung organizational machine that carried out specialized functions of every kind. Yet to these men the extraordinary assault upon Jewry would have been inconceivable without him. He was, as they said repeatedly, indispensable.

All the characteristics of Hitler's decision making may be observed in the anti-Jewish operations between 1933 and 1945. His first intervention came about during the drafting of a law two months after he had become chancellor. In the highly charged atmosphere of these first months, the Nazi party organized a boycott of Jewish stores and Jewish judges were dragged out of courts. The ministries, working on a law about the civil service, considered the dismissal of non-Christian judges and prosecutors. At this point Hitler demanded the removal of all Jewish civil servants.[21] The aged Field Marshall Paul von Hindenburg, still president of Germany, protested to Hitler against the strong-arm methods employed by the party against Jewish judges who were disabled veterans of the First World War, and Hitler promised exemptions of several categories, including combat veterans.[22] On the other hand, the law was overarching enough to cover all "non-Aryans," that is to say any person, regardless of religion, who had at least one Jewish grandparent. Hitler also signed a number of corollary laws at that time to disbar Jewish lawyers and to dismiss patent agents and tax advisers.[23]

The civil service law covered professionals in universities and institutes, and the consequent loss of highly qualified Jewish physicists and chemists troubled the German academic establishment. In 1933, the German physicist Max Planck talked to Hitler about this problem. Planck mentioned Fritz Haber, the Jew who had synthesized ammonia by the fixation of nitrogen from the air. This feat, accomplished just before the outbreak of the First World War, had freed Germany from the need to import natural Chilean nitrates for the manufacture of explosives. Without this discovery, Planck explained, Germany would have lost the war at the outset. Hitler answered that he was not against Jews per se but against Jews as the supporters of Communism. When Planck tried to argue that, after all, there were valuable Jews as well as those who did not amount to anything, Hitler replied that a Jew was a Jew, that the Jews themselves did not make distinctions between one Jew and another, and now he was going to proceed against all of them. When Planck argued that the removal of Jews needed in science was tantamount to self-mutilation, Hitler said no, pointed to himself as a man of steel, slapped his knee, and became vehement. [24]

More than two years passed before Hitler ignited the anti-Jewish process again. By the beginning of 1935, the Jewish condition in Germany had stabilized and Jewish life was almost quiescent. Jewish civil servants, teachers, lawyers, artists, writers, and other professionals were losing their positions, and Jewish business establishments were the targets of takeover attempts by German firms, but there was still an economic base for most self-employed individuals and private employees. The emigration of the Jews was slackening and Jews still had not ceased to be Germans. Hitler, about to address the party rally in Nuremberg, wanted a change. He ordered the rapid drafting of a law depriving Jews of citizenship, and another law prohibiting the conclusion of marriages between Jews and non-Jews. The citizenship law was largely symbolic, inasmuch as the Jews still needed German passports to emigrate. The intermarriage prohibition was not going to affect mixed couples who had already sealed their union in a wedding ceremony, but the use of the word *Jew* in the text forced the Interior Ministry to define the term. Henceforth, Jews were persons with at least *two* Jewish grandparents, and if they were half-Jews they were included only if they belonged to the Jewish religion or were married to a Jewish partner. This formulation was less embracing than the term *non-Aryan*, yet for this reason harsher measures against Jews could be taken in the future with less reluctance or difficulty.[25]

From the definition decree to a host of other activities aimed at the Jews in the economic and social spheres, virtually everything consummated in the following few years was the work of underlings, functionaries, or entrepreneurs. Hitler adopted a passive mode, receiving suggestions and reacting to them. This pattern was most pronounced during the events of November 9 and 10, 1938.

An anti-Jewish outburst had been unleashed in cities all over Germany. It was a reaction to an occurrence in Paris, where a German diplomat had just died of wounds inflicted on him by a young Polish Jew. The pogrom was entirely a party idea, the brainchild of Propaganda Minister Josef Goebbels, and its first manifestation was the smashing of Jewish shop windows and the firing of synagogues. Such concerted action at a moment's notice was possible only because local party leaders had gathered in their hometowns to celebrate the anniversary of the aborted 1923 Putsch. The main celebration took place in Munich, but not everyone in the top ranks was present there. The festivities and dinner were not interrupted by the news from Paris, but Goebbels had the opportunity to talk to Hitler for about a half hour, and Hitler allowed the party to make its move.[26]

By the next day, the repercussions abroad and also at home were heard clearly, and Hermann Göring, the economic commander-in-chief who stood second in the hierarchy right under Hitler, berated Goebbels, forcing Hitler into the uncomfortable role of agreeing with Göring and defending Goebbels at the same time.[27] The damage and the arson had been inflicted by the party to demonstrate popular outrage against murderous Jewry, but it was the sort of act that Hitler had warned against, when he wrote his first anti-Jewish letter in 1919.

Correcting his course, Hitler ordered the liquidation of commercial Jewish enterprises and the compulsory transfer of Jewish industrial concerns to German ownership. In addition, he agreed to the levying of a heavy "fine" in the form of a property tax on the Jews. The tax was to be collected by the state, rather than the party, as Goebbels had wished. Even more significantly, Hitler was concerned enough about the possibility of renewed violence to veto a proposal to mark the Jews with a star at that time.[28]

The goal of mass emigration, which was pursued and intensified in 1938 and 1939, was feasible only for Germany and newly annexed Austria. It was no longer realistic, after the outbreak of war, for occupied western Poland, which held a much larger Jewish community. A major resettlement scheme, involving the movement of all the European Jews to the French island colony of Madagascar, was briefly considered by the Foreign Office and other agencies after the fall of France, but this plan could not materialize while Britain was still at war with Germany. Thus the two-year period after the beginning of the Second World War marks a period of uncertainty in the course of which additional measures, including ghettoization in Poland, were taken against the Jews in German-dominated Europe, but with only a nebulous conception of the ultimate purpose of these increasingly stringent steps. The ghettos in particular were unsightly and uneconomical devices. These high-density districts in poor sections of Polish cities and towns were packed with unemployed, starving, and disease-ridden Jews, and the German creators of this system considered it temporary from the start. Momentum was therefore joined with tension, as pressure developed for clarification of a truly "final" solution of the Jewish question.

Hitler made a number of critical decisions in his foreign policy between 1939 and 1941. He started a war, planned campaigns, and in 1940 instituted preparations for an invasion of the Soviet Union. In the realm of domestic affairs, he signed a directive in September 1939 for the killing of patients afflicted with hopeless mental diseases.[29] This piece of paper, with which the euthanasia program was inaugurated, did not spell out the word *mental*. It was, however, the product of arguments put forward by some physicians and party stalwarts to the effect that mental institutions were places in which people suffered for a long time without the possibility of a change for a better life. The asylums were costly to maintain, and the painless administration of some lethal agent to those of the inmates who could not even perform simple tasks was intended to provide relief for the patients and for the German people.

At the beginning of February 1941, during a meeting of old party comrades, Hitler was asked what he intended to do with the Jews. He replied reflexively, "Madagascar," and on being reminded that the island was far away, admitted that the project was not achievable. The Jews, he said, could be shipped off—after all, there were not that many—but he could not risk German vessels to British torpedoes. Now he had other thoughts, "less friendly."[30]

The next few months were crucial. Christopher Browning called them the "fateful months," the interval in which the pieces came together and in which a threshold was crossed.[31] The thrust was the culmination of a process that in retrospect had emerged from an inner logic not recognizable even to the perpetrators. It was primal, beyond rationality and irrationality. Like the invasion of the Soviet Union, which had the quality of an unlimited assault, it was a "reckoning." Because of that invasion, it seemed possible and, increasingly, imperative. If German men were going to die in this showdown, so would the Jews, those ancient adversaries who had survived all the wars and expulsions of the past.

Yet the decision was not a simple one, and it was not written and signed like the euthanasia order or the directive to invade the USSR. There is no particular moment or day that can be identified as the turning point in the interplay between preparations of scheming functionaries and Hitler's own utterances. We may assume a period of irresolution, followed by his cryptic intimations and predictions. We may also surmise that finally he articulated the unmistakable words that even his SS and Police chief Heinrich Himmler called frightful.[32] The words were not recorded, but they were alluded or referred to over and over. They were used repeatedly to counter arguments put forward by German and non-German authorities for exemptions or delays. The final solution was not evadable; it was the Führer's will.

Hitler was the supreme architect of the Jewish catastrophe. It is he who transformed the liquid ideas of 1940 into the hard reality of 1941. Hitler made this final step the inexorable outcome of all the anti-Jewish measures taken over the years, and he forged Germany's diverse and decentralized administrative apparatus into a network of organizations acting in unison to the end that shooting operations, deportations, and gassings could be implemented simultaneously.

The germination of the final solution may be traced to the first days of March 1941, when Hitler interjected a desire for an amendment in a draft directive dealing with the treatment of civilians in territories to be occupied in the USSR. He wanted the Jewish-Bolshevist intelligentsia to be eliminated and Bolshevist chieftains and commissars to be "rendered harmless." For this purpose he demanded the deployment of special organs of the SS and Police.[33] These organs, known as *Einsatzgruppen,* were formed by the Security Police just before the invasion and, together with some other SS and Police units, went into action soon after the battle was opened on June 22. Orders were passed down orally. After the war, several of the Security Police commanders insisted that they had been told to kill all the Jews in the path of the advance. The Jews, however, numbered in the millions and the killers were but thousands. To shoot a few commissars, the Einsatzgruppen were too big; for the total annihilation of Soviet Jewry they were, unaided, much too small. What was the meaning of the phrase "Jewish-Bolshevist intelligentsia"? Did this order comprise all the Jews? In June, July, and August 1941, the shootings were in fact confined to Jewish men and a relative handful of Communists. Yet it was clear soon enough that dead Jewish men were leaving behind live Jewish women and children who could not fend for themselves. Killing these utterly defenseless dependents was something new, another milestone fraught with a heavy psychological burden. By August and September, this totalization was mastered as well. The evolution of the process was complete and the shootings became routine.

European Jewry west of the line crossed on June 22, 1941, was not going to be spared. As early as March 25, 1941, Hitler promised his chieftain in the central portion of occupied Poland, Generalgouverneur Hans Frank, that the territory administered by Frank would be the first to be cleared of Jews.[34] On June 7, Hitler informed the Chief of the Reich Chancellery, Heinrich Lammers, that there would be no need for another decree defining the status of Jews in Germany, inasmuch as after the war, there would be no Jews left in Germany anyhow.[35] These remarks pointed to physical action against the Jews of Europe, but without a delineation of their ultimate fate. The bureaucrats continued to labor in the semi-dark. Reinhard Heydrich, the chief of the Reich Security Main Office, which had sent the Einsatzgruppen to the east, now sought to concentrate power in his hands. On July 31, 1941, he received authorization from Göring to prepare a final solution of the Jewish question in Europe.[36] But what kind of solution, precisely? Heydrich's specialist in Jewish affairs, Adolf Eichmann, noted in his memoirs after the war that Heydrich had heard from his superior, Himmler, of a decision by Hitler to annihilate the Jews physically. Eichmann, who had been called in by Heydrich to receive this news, thought that even Heydrich could not measure its import.[37]

Is this hearsay evidence to be credited? In his memoirs Eichmann mentions the incident several times. It is a marked, salient point in his recollections. More important, it is plausible. A clarification had been awaited with increasing urgency during the stagnation of the spring and early summer in 1941. By fall, however, there was motion everywhere. Trains were carrying Jews from Germany to regions in occupied Poland and cities in the occupied USSR; death camps were planned on Polish soil; and proposals were made to deport Jews from such distant places as Salonika, Greece, and Paris, France. Not Himmler, not Heydrich, not anyone could have moved with such rapidity on his own.[38] Moreover, when Heydrich provided a historical recapitulation of anti-Jewish actions to a conference of high-ranking bureaucrats, he referred to the "evacuation of the Jews to the east" as subject to the appropriate prior authorization of the Führer.[39]

Although Hitler had no fundamental afterthoughts about his act, he appears to have vetoed the killing of a thousand Jews on a transport that was on its way from Berlin to Riga on November 30, 1941.[40] Interestingly enough, the intervention on the afternoon of that day came too late. The Jews were killed on arrival and there is no record of a subsequent reaction by Hitler. Evidently the issue had been one of time, place, or manner, not of principle.[41]

Later, Hitler reinforced his decision on several occasions. In 1943, he told the Hungarian leader, Miklós Horthy, in no uncertain terms that he wanted the Hungarian Jews deported.[42] In 1944, he urged Josef Tiso, the President of Slovakia, to proceed against the remaining Slovak Jews.[43]

He preoccupied himself with vestiges of the Jewish presence in Germany. As of April 1940, he dismissed half-Jews, with certain exceptions, from the army, lest they assert a claim for immunity from any discrimination on the basis of their war record.[44] He forbade German soldiers to marry the widows of Jewish husbands.[45] At the end of 1944, he wanted the remaining civil servants with any Jewish ancestry or with Jewish wives to be dismissed. This measure was to be carried out by May 1, 1945.[46] He killed himself on that day after writing a testament in which he left no doubt that it was he who had prophesied the end of Jewry and that the Jews had indeed atoned for their sins.[47]

2

THE ESTABLISHMENT

THE DESTRUCTION OF THE JEWS was not centralized. No agency had been set up to deal with Jewish affairs and no fund was set aside for the destruction process. The anti-Jewish work was carried out in the civil service, the military, business, and the party. All components of German organized life were drawn into this undertaking. Every agency was a contributor; every specialization was utilized; and every stratum of society was represented in the envelopment of the victims.

The process of destruction was based on three premises. The first was an insistence not to exempt any segment of Jewry from the application of anti-Jewish measures. No Jew was to be overlooked in the dragnet. Hence, manifold and lengthy efforts were devoted to segregation and ghettoization, to diplomatic negotiations with satellite states for the surrender of their Jewish communities, to constant counting and guarding of concentrated Jews, and to relentless searches for Jewish escapees. Second, the complex relationships between Jews and non-Jews were to be severed with least harm to individual Germans and to the economy as a whole. From this maxim followed the careful attention paid to such problems as mixed marriages and their offspring, business enterprises with Jewish as

well as non-Jewish investors or managers, or debts and credits flow-
ing between Jews and non-Jews. Third, the killings had to be conducted in a manner that would limit psychological repercussions in
the ranks of the perpetrators, prevent unrest among the victims, and
preclude anxiety or protest in the non-Jewish population. To this end
relatively large numbers of indigenous collaborators were employed
in shooting operations in eastern Europe, and an elaborate system of
deportations was organized to transport Jews in sealed trains from
western and central European areas to secluded camps, equipped
with gas chambers, in occupied Polish territory.

All these preparations required the participation of functionaries in
a wide variety of offices. The following is a list of the principal
organizations and their special roles in the process of destruction.
They are arranged, somewhat in the order in which they became
involved in the process, to show how they furthered the operation
from stage to stage.

REICH CHANCELLERY	Coordination of laws and decrees
INTERIOR MINISTRY	Definition of the term *Jew* Prohibition of mixed marriages Decrees for compulsory names Dismissals from the civil service Deprivation of property
CHURCHES	Supply of proof of non-Jewish descent
JUSTICE MINISTRY	Elimination of Jewish lawyers Inheritance questions Divorce questions Regulation of names of enterprises
PARTY BOYCOTT COMMITTEE	Boycott of Jewish enterprises
PARTY CHANCELLERY	Participation in decisions involving the status of Jews

Reich Chamber of Culture	Dismissals of musicians, artists, and journalists and barring of writers
Education Ministry	Elimination of Jewish students, professors, and researchers
Propaganda Ministry	Suggestions to the press
Economy Ministry	Regulations for the acquisition of Jewish firms
Dresdner Bank and other banking concerns	Intermediaries in takeovers of Jewish firms
Various firms in retailing, wholesaling, manufacturing, and construction	Acquisitions of Jewish firms Dismissals of Jewish employees Utilization of Jewish forced labor in cities, ghettos, and camps Contracting for measures of destruction, such as supply of poison gas
Finance Ministry	Discriminatory taxes Blocked funds Confiscation of personal belongings Special budgetary allocations, such as clearing Warsaw Ghetto ruins
Foreign Office	Negotiations for deportations of Jews in foreign countries and of foreign Jews in the Reich
Transport Ministry	Transports to ghettos and camps Utilization of forced Jewish labor Acquisitions of Jewish personal property

ARMED FORCES	Logistic support of killing operations in the occupied USSR
	Direct killings in Serbia and the occupied USSR
	Ghettoization in the occupied USSR
	Discriminatory measures and deportations from France, Belgium, and Greece
	Regulation of forced Jewish labor in armament plants
	Employment of forced Jewish labor by army offices
	Transport questions
MUNICIPAL AUTHORITIES IN THE GREATER GERMAN REICH	Movement and housing restrictions
PROTEKTORAT ADMINISTRATION IN BOHEMIA AND MORAVIA	Anti-Jewish measures patterned on those of the Reich
GENERALGOUVERNEMENT IN OCCUPIED CENTRAL POLAND	Confiscations
	Ghettoization
	Forced labor
	Starvation measures
	Preparations for deportations
MINISTRY FOR EASTERN OCCUPIED TERRITORIES	Anti-Jewish measures patterned on those of the Reich
REICHSKOMMISSARIAT OF THE NETHERLANDS	Anti-Jewish measures patterned on those of the Reich
FÜHRER CHANCELLERY	Staffing of the Belzec, Sobibor, and Treblinka death camps

SS and Police

Reich Security Main Office	Marking of Jews in the Reich
	Supervision of the Jewish communities in the Reich and Protektorat
	Einsatzgruppen killings in the occupied USSR
	Preparations of European-wide deportations
Main Office Order Police	Guarding of ghettos, trains, and camps
	Participation in roundups and shootings
Economic-Administrative Main Office	Administration of Auschwitz and Maydanek (Lublin)
Higher SS and Police Leaders in occupied Poland	Deportations to death camps
	Administration of the Chelmno (Kulmhof), Belzec, Sobibor, and Treblinka death camps
Higher SS and Police Leaders in the occupied USSR	Shootings

One may note that each organization was responsible for a specific segment of the destruction process. Given the requirements of completeness, economy, and psychological security, each of these contributions was essential. At the same time, however, anti-Jewish work was only a portion of the administrative output of each of these agencies. The bureaucrat who dealt with Jews did so in a context that included all areas within his competence and jurisdiction. Thus an armament official might have been concerned with sabotage, shortages of materials, and withdrawals of Jewish labor. He would have mentioned all of these subjects in his monthly reports. A single conference of railroad officials might have been devoted to holiday trains for the Hitler Youth, the relocation of ethnic Germans, the transport of Russian workers, and the dispatch of Jews to death camps. Hence, the destruction of the Jews represented an expansion, always an added burden, but sometimes also a new challenge and an aggrandizement of power.

In several agencies the anti-Jewish work was large enough to justify the assignment of one or more functionaries to be specialists in Jewish affairs. Such officials could be found in the Interior Ministry, the Economy Ministry, the Finance Ministry, the Foreign Office, the Transport Ministry, the Ministry for Eastern Occupied Territories, and the Reich Security Main Office. Only one of them, Adolf Eichmann, who sat in the Reich Security Main Office, became well known as a symbol of virtually all the perpetrators at his trial in Jerusalem some time after the war. Eichmann had representatives in several satellite countries to "advise" these foreign governments in anti-Jewish legislation; his office supervised the Jewish communities in the Reich, Austria, and Bohemia-Moravia; and his men negotiated with the Transport Ministry for deportation trains. Caught by Israeli agents in Argentina, he was tried and hanged in Israel. Not every specialist had such a dramatic career. In the Interior Ministry Hans Globke drafted numerous decrees on such subjects as Jewish names, including the compulsory Jewish middle names of Israel and Sara, as well as technical decrees for the introduction of anti-Jewish measures in newly annexed regions. Globke was promoted after the war to the Federal Chancellor's Office, which he headed until 1963, and from which he was retired with honors to pursue his hobby of numismatics, particularly the collection of the coins of Axium and Armenia.[1]

Although the destructive work was largely embedded in administrative routines, much more was required of a bureaucrat than automatic implementation of anti-Jewish measures. Without his timely proposals and initiatives, the process would have been crippled, as various complicated steps against Jewry would inevitably have been postponed, dissipated, or aborted. Nor was innovation a function solely of the upper strata in the apparatus. Even while an official in the Justice Ministry pondered the inheritance problem resulting from deaths of Jews who had no wills, an SS noncommissioned officer in Auschwitz tried to figure out ways and means of burning bodies more rapidly. The task united men of diverse backgrounds, different occupations, and varying psychological dispositions. Segmented as they may have been at the start, they congealed into a massive machine.

The indispensability of every function in the destruction process and the interconnection of all the actions performed by the perpetrators were not obscure, opaque phenomena. The nature of the process could be recognized and understood by its lowest ranking practitioners. Werner Dubois was such an individual. He had served as a guard in the death camp Sobibor, where some two hundred thousand Jews had been gassed. A simple man who read the party's virulent anti-Jewish *Der Stürmer* without, however, being subjected to its influence, Dubois was in the camp when a Jewish revolt broke out there in October 1943. He was hit with axes and received a bullet through his lungs. On trial before a German court in the early 1960s, he made the following statement about the administrative role of a functionary:

> I am clear about the fact that annihilation camps were used for murder. What I did was aiding in murder. If I should be sentenced, I would consider that correct. Murder is murder. In weighing the guilt, one should not in my opinion consider the specific function in the camp. Wherever we were posted there: we were all equally guilty. The camp functioned in a chain of functions. If only one element in that chain is missing, the entire enterprise comes to a stop.[2]

3

OLD FUNCTIONARIES

THE MACHINERY OF DESTRUCTION consisted of old established as well as newly created organizations. Most of them were old. The traditional sector housed most of the leading officials, most of the ordinary personnel, most of the perpetrators in general. Here were the preexisting ministries, staffed by civil servants and containing such massive systems as the Order Police, which was conspicuously patrolling the city streets as well as the countryside, and the German railway, with its dense network of stations in all parts of Germany. There was no major purge in the ministries; the careerists remained at their posts and continued their daily work. Here were also the military, feverishly expanding for war, as officers rose in rank to command ever larger units. Finally, the old apparatus also contained business enterprises, largely self-governing and increasing in size as they moved from underutilized capacity to maximum production, and from conditions of widespread unemployment to acute labor shortages.

The functionaries in all these hierarchies also accelerated and intensified their activities against the Jews. Sometimes they did so in Berlin, refining anti-Jewish decrees, or writing discriminatory contracts, or making agreements to deport successively various groups of Jewish victims. Sometimes they operated in the field, at the scene of death, as in the case of Order Police engaged in shootings, or railway men driving trains filled with Jews into camp enclosures. Whether they were in command or lowly placed, in an office or outdoors, they all did their part, when the time came, with all the efficiency they could muster.

Lutz Graf Schwerin von Krosigk was such a man. Born in 1887, he studied law at several universities, including Oxford, where he was a Rhodes scholar. During the First World War, in which he lost two brothers, he served at the front and earned an Iron Cross First Class. After the war, he rose in the ranks of the Finance Ministry. He became Finance Minister in 1932 under Chancellor Franz von Papen and retained the post under von Papen's successors, Kurt von Schleicher and Adolf Hitler. In private life he was a simple man with a stable marriage and nine children. As minister, he oversaw a finance bureaucracy of 150,000 people. In the absence of a legislature, his ministry determined and levied the taxes, borrowed money for the German Reich, and allocated the public funds to civilian agencies and military forces. The ministry also collected additional taxes from Jews, including the fine imposed in 1938, and confiscated the remaining Jewish property of emigrated and deported Jews under decrees cosigned by von Krosigk. When he was placed on trial before a U.S. tribunal in Nuremberg after the war, he explained that he had always considered himself not a politician but an official and that as a civil servant he owed Germany his lifelong service. The court sentenced him to ten years of imprisonment, but the U.S. High Commissioner ordered his release on January 31, 1951. Von Krosigk retired to write books and died twenty-six years later in 1977.[1]

Franz Schlegelberger was one of the oldest officials. Born in 1875, he obtained a law degree in 1899, passed a higher examination in 1901, served as a judge in local courts of his native East Prussia, and then worked as an assistant judge of a court of appeals in Berlin. He went on to serve in the Justice Ministry, writing treatises about law and gradually rising in the hierarchy until he became a Staatssekretär, directly under Justice Minister Franz Gürtner. In 1938 he was informed that Hitler expected him to join the Nazi party. He did so without any apparent hesitation. When Gürtner died in 1941, Schlegelberger became the acting Minister of Justice.

The Justice Ministry expelled Jewish lawyers from the bar and concerned itself with the reduction of the rights of Jews in the courts. When Schlegelberger rose to the top position, the "final solution of the Jewish question" was in the offing. He participated in debates dealing with the vexing question of mixed marriages, the compulsory dissolution of which he opposed in alliance with the Propaganda Ministry, whose representatives specialized in matters of delicacy. With regard to a similar debate about half-Jews who did not belong to the Jewish religion and were not married to a Jewish person, he suggested a compromise between proponents favoring deportation and advocates of the status quo under which these people were subject only to a limited set of restrictions. Schlegelberger proposed that those of the non-Jewish half-Jews who were still single be sterilized. Ultimately, neither the divorces nor the sterilizations were adopted, and nothing more was done.

While Schlegelberger held the office of acting minister, he was also faced with a case in which a seventy-four-year-old Jew in the incorporated Polish region of Upper Silesia had been sentenced to two and a half years in prison for hoarding sixty-five thousand eggs in a lime pit. Some fifteen thousand of them had already spoiled. When Hitler read the report in the *Berliner Illustrierte,* he informed Schlegelberger through the Reich Chancellery that he wanted the culprit, Markus Luftglas, killed. The Führer's intervention was not the first of its kind, and three days after hearing from the Reich Chancellery, Schlegelberger reported that Luftglas had been handed over to the Gestapo for execution.

Schlegelberger retired after a year and a half as acting Justice Minister and received a gift of 100,000 reichsmarks from Hitler. In 1944 he obtained permission to buy a farm. This favor was special, because he was not a professional farmer.

Like Schwerin von Krosigk, Schlegelberger was a defendant before a U.S. tribunal in Nuremberg. In his final statement he expressed bitterness that he was rewarded for his hard struggle for justice by this moment of shame and misery. He was sentenced to life imprisonment by American judges who noted their own feelings toward defendants who had been judges themselves and who had sullied themselves in administering the law. Schlegelberger was released on medical probation in 1951. He died in 1970.[2]

Herbert Kühnemann, born in 1899, also was a lawyer and a young judge. He joined the Justice Ministry in 1932 as a Ministerialrat, a relatively high position for his age. On May 29, 1941, he chaired a conference of agency and industry representatives on the question of removing the names of Jewish enterprises that had been acquired by German purchasers. He wanted the names replaced as well, in order that the former Jewish presence in the economy be forgotten. The business representatives did not want to relinquish the old firm names, because these shields and letterheads were a valuable intangible property. Only the Party Chancellery supported the idea. Kühnemann lost his battle but gained a postwar career. In the nineteen fifties and sixties he was president of the German patent office.[3]

Generalleutnant (Major General) Adolf Herrgott commanded the prisoner of war camps in the Generalgouvernement. The position was of a type reserved for older officers, and Herrgott was indeed past his prime. Born in 1872, he had been a lieutenant colonel in the First World War and had earned the highest German medal given to an officer at that time, the *pour le mérite*. Separated from the army in 1923, he was recalled in 1939. In the course of the campaign against the USSR, which began in 1941, millions of Soviet prisoners were taken, and many of them were funneled through Herrgott's camps, where the death toll must have reached a figure in six digits. Jews among these prisoners were not supposed to survive at all. Those who were identified as Jews were subject to be shot by members of the SS and Police. Herrgott lived to be in his mid-eighties. A forgotten man, he died in 1957.[4]

The role in anti-Jewish activities of General der Infanterie (Lieutenant General) Otto von Stülpnagel was far more conspicuous. Like Herrgott, he was an older officer, born in 1878. Twice retired before the Second World War, he reentered the army in 1939, first to be the deputy commander of an army corps, and then to serve from October 1940 to February 1942 as the military commander in France. While in Paris he issued anti-Jewish ordinances on the installation of non-Jewish trustees in Jewish enterprises, the confiscation of radios in Jewish possession, and the exaction of a fine. At a very early stage of the final solution, on October 13, 1941, the Minister of Eastern Occupied [Soviet] Territories, Alfred Rosenberg, noted in a conversation with the Generalgouverneur in Poland, Hans Frank, that the military administration in France had already approached him with the wish to move the Jewish population of occupied France to the newly conquered regions in the USSR. Barely two months later, at the time of the imposition of the fine, von Stülpnagel wrote to General Quartermaster Eduard Wagner, requesting permission to deport a thousand Jews east. Hitler agreed, thus inaugurating the deportation program in France. After the war, von Stülpnagel, held in a French prison in Paris, committed suicide.[5]

One of the largest enterprises in Germany was the chemical combine I. G. Farben, which manufactured pharmaceuticals, photographic equipment, and many other products, including synthetic rubber. It operated dozens of plants, one of them in Leuna. The chief engineer at this plant from 1932 was Dr. Walter Dürrfeld. An ambitious man focused on his career, Dürrfeld joined the party in 1937. In 1941, when I. G. Farben looked for a site to erect a new plant near raw materials and a labor supply, Dürrfeld was appointed to build the structure. Its location was in Auschwitz, within the industrial part of the concentration camp. Dürrfeld spent several years as director of the plant. The inmates who worked on the construction site and in mines of I. G. Auschwitz died there by the thousands. When Dürrfeld was placed on trial in Nuremberg after the war, he told the tribunal that he had been the overseer of thirty thousand people, including employees and inmates, in a plant covering ten square miles. He could not have been everywhere at once. The court, however, sentenced him to eight years in recognition of the fact that anywhere in this plant Dürrfeld was still in Auschwitz.[6]

The family-owned firm J. A. Topf und Söhne, oven builders, was much smaller than I. G. Farben. It had only about one thousand employees, one of whom was Kurt Prüfer, the head of its crematoria division. Prüfer's career was uncovered by the French researcher Jean-Paul Pressac in the course of a research project exploring the history of crematory and gas chamber construction in Auschwitz. Born in 1891, Prüfer had a vocational education that encompassed some civil engineering. He joined Topf in 1911, fought in the First World War as a sergeant, pursued an additional year of engineering education, and rejoined Topf in 1920. Although threatened with the loss of his job when the economic depression of 1930 curtailed much of Topf's business, he managed to hold on and was prized as an engineer who knew much about crematories. After Hitler came to power, Topf crematories were built in the concentration camps Buchenwald, Mauthausen-Gusen, and Auschwitz. Prüfer traveled to Auschwitz repeatedly. He dealt there with the SS construction office and developed a close business relationship with his client. During his first visit in October 1941 the crematories, for which Prüfer received a commission, were intended only for inmates dead of disease, exposure, or starvation. From August 1942, however, Prüfer conferred in Auschwitz with the SS about the construction of four crematories that were to be equipped with gas chambers. During these conversations he made various suggestions for improving the efficiency of the gassings. In January, February, and March 1943 he was in Auschwitz again, this time dealing with problems as the buildings were completed. The Topf headquarters in Erfurt was captured by American troops on May 8, 1945. Prüfer was arrested, whereupon one of the owners, Ludwig Topf, Jr., committed suicide on May 31, 1945, but Prüfer was released and continued in his job, even after the Soviets took over Erfurt, which was in their zone. Finally he was taken into custody by Soviet authorities in March 1946, and his trail disappeared.[7]

Max Montua was a professional police officer. A farmer's son, born in 1886, Montua served at the front in the First World War and made his career in the Order Police. He was successful enough to become a Generalmajor (Brigadier General) of the Order Police by 1943, and he was briefly considered that year for an appointment to command German anti-partisan formations behind the lines in the central sector of the Eastern Front, a position denied him only because of his age. Montua had been the commander of the Order Police regiment assigned to Army Group Center from the beginning of the invasion of the USSR. His regiment was backup for any army units fighting pockets of Red Army soldiers or of partisans, and for detachments of Einsatzgruppen of the Security Police killing Jews.

On July 11, 1941, barely three weeks after the opening of the campaign, when the mission of the Einsatzgruppen had not yet been fully spelled out, Montua informed his battalion commanders of an order of the Higher SS and Police Leader in the rear area of Army Group Center that all Jewish men aged seventeen to forty-five had to be shot at once as "plunderers." Montua went on to specify that the shootings had to be carried out in remote locations. The graves had to be covered in such manner that they would not become places of pilgrimage. He forbade the photographing of executions and instructed his battalion and company commanders to take special care of the psychic needs of the men employed in these actions. Comradely evenings were to be organized to wipe out the impressions of the day, and the political necessity for these measures was to be explained to the men continually. [8]

Lieutenant of the Order Police Alois Häfele did not need explanations. Born in 1893 as the son of an agricultural laborer, Häfele attended only grade school. His mother died and the economic situation of the family was tight. In 1913 he joined the navy and during the First World War he took part in the naval battle of the Skagerrak on a cruiser. He was discharged with an Iron Cross Second Class when the war ended. After a short period as a baker's apprentice, he joined the police for economic security. His life became stable. He was married in 1922 and had two daughters. For many years he was stationed in a precinct in Karlsruhe, where he slowly rose in rank before being transferred to Freiburg in 1937. During the following year he took part in the march into Austria and in 1939 he went to the Polish city of Lodz, in a region that was annexed by Germany. A major ghetto was created in Lodz and many ghettos were set up in smaller cities nearby.

At the end of 1941, the Higher SS and Police Leader in the region, which was known as the Wartheland, established a death camp at the village of Kulmhof (Chelmno), which ultimately claimed more than 150,000 Jewish victims and several thousand Gypsies. The camp operated from December of that year to late summer of 1942 and was reopened briefly in 1944. During the 1941–1942 period the Jews were taken to a "castle," where gas vans pulled up to kill them.

Häfele arrived in Kulmhof from Lodz with a detachment of Order

Police on January 22, 1942, shortly after the camp had commenced its operations. In all, Kulmhof was run by ten to fifteen members of the Security Police and about eighty of the Order Police. The men of the Order Police served at an assembly point of arriving Jews, in the castle, and as guards on trains. In the castle the average strength of the Order Police was nine to twelve, half of them with twenty-four hours of duty and twenty-four hours off. There were also seven Polish prisoners, and sixty or more Jews, unloading the dead from the vans, and twenty, chained by their feet, in the castle. The Poles were permitted to have Jewish women for a night; the Germans obtained good pay and were informally allowed to take some Jewish property. Häfele, in the castle, helped himself to two watches.

Häfele's job was to receive the Jews in the castle and conduct them to one of the vans. He smiled in a friendly manner and sometimes assisted elderly persons and children. When there was a delay, he would shout from the ground floor to the cellar to accelerate the herding of the victims. According to some testimony, he killed a few people himself. Willing and eager in his work, he nevertheless asked for a transfer in the fall of 1942. When that request was refused, he stayed on during the liquidation of the first phase, when traces of the operation were obliterated. In 1943, he had leave to Karlsruhe, where he talked to an old superior, telling him that one got used to Kulmhof. Little men or little women, it was all the same, just like stepping on a beetle. As he talked, Häfele made a scraping motion with his foot on the floor.[9]

It is perhaps characteristic of less well educated men like Alois Häfele that when they expressed the truth they did so more plainly than intellectuals. He had accustomed himself to his task. So did the other eighty policemen at Kulmhof who had been drawn from the precincts of German cities, and so did Montua, Prüfer, Dürrfeld, Otto von Stülpnagel, Herrgott, Kühnemann, Schlegelberger, and Schwerin von Krosigk. Each had his career, most had families, and whether their anti-Jewish work was transitory or prolonged, peripheral or drastic, they did not flinch from the assignment.

The end of the Nazi regime on May 8, 1945, marked the beginning of anxiety for these incumbents, but in most cases the crisis was temporary. The functionaries could not be sure whether their positions would still be available under Allied occupation, or whether they would be retained in office, or whether their deeds would be discovered. Most of them survived this phase of their lives without severe mishaps. They were not wanton killers, after all. Whatever they did was, for most of them at least, a small part of their everyday activities. For a few who reestablished and furthered their professional or business lives, the wartime era was a relatively minor, if telling, gap in a paragraph written for *Wer ist Wer,* the *Who's Who* in Germany. It was not to be talked about in public, not even to be imparted to one's children. The new generation would not have understood these times in any case.

4

NEWCOMERS

Two categories of newcomers appeared on the scene: the party men and the new Germans. Both wanted a share of power. Of the two, the members of the Nazi party, notably those who joined it before 1933, were the earlier aspirants. The new Germans comprised the Austrians, Sudeten Germans, and ethnic Germans who became part of the German population as a result of annexations, conquests, and immigration after Hitler had come into office.

The party was very small at first, but from the beginning it was heterogeneous. When sixteen of the men who marched with Hitler in the abortive Putsch of November 9, 1923, in Munich were killed in the fracas, four of them were businessmen, three were bank clerks, three were engineers, and the rest were a judge, a retired captain, a blacksmith, a hatter, a headwaiter, and a valet.[1]

For its funding, the party depended on dues, paid by members, most of whom were of modest means, and contributions from well-to-do members and sympathizers. There were a few party owned business enterprises as well, but their income was not sufficient to sustain a major party apparatus. Even when the party had expanded in the early thirties, creating a multiplicity of offices, it could not replace, let alone duplicate, the existing power structure. Penetration of state agencies, even after 1933, was limited. Purges in the civil service were too minor to create many vacancies. A few of the top positions were, of course, captured by party men. The Interior Ministry was placed under Wilhelm Frick, the Economy Ministry somewhat later under Walter Funk, the Foreign Office eventually under Joachim von Ribbentrop, but relatively few of the posts ordinarily staffed by senior civil servants could be filled by party men even when opportunities arose as result of attrition. After all, the men in the lower and middle levels of the bureaucracy had to be able to look forward to promotion. Thus the Order Police was headed by Kurt Daluege, who was from the party, but every other Order Police general was a career man. The military and business sectors were particularly inhospitable to untrained, untried party protégés. As a result, the party had to build new organizations that could be funded by the Reich.

Several ministries were created, including Propaganda, under Josef Goebbels; Armaments, under Albert Speer; and Eastern Occupied Territories, for areas seized from the Soviet Union, under Alfred Rosenberg. In competition with the military, Heinrich Himmler built his SS, which he merged with the police. Hermann Göring had his Office of the Four Year Plan, as well as the Hermann Göring Works, an industrial combine that belonged to the Reich. A major portion of all the conquered areas was placed under old party men. Examples are Hans Frank, who ruled the Generalgouvernement in central Poland; Josef Terboven, who was in charge of Norway; and Reinhard Heydrich, who became the second Reichsprotektor in Bohemia and Moravia.

For the Austrians, there was continuity in the regional bureaucracy of Austria itself. Inasmuch as the small Austrian military was integrated into the German army, Austrians rose in rank and some of them obtained important commands. Austrian business expanded its influence in the Balkans. The Austrians also had territorial preserves in several parts of Germany's Europe. In the Netherlands, the Reichskommissar, Arthur Seyss-Inquart, and much of his entourage were Austrian. The military administration and garrison in Serbia contained many Austrians. In the Galician district of the Generalgouvernement, the Austrian Nazi Otto Wächter was Gouverneur.

Later on, he was chief of the military administration in Italy. Another Austrian Nazi, Odilo Globocnik, was the SS and Police Leader in the Lublin District. He was an organizer of deportations in his district, and in the Warsaw and Bialystok ghettos. In addition, he ran death camps. Most of his principal officers were also Austrian. Finally, the Austrian Ernst Kaltenbrunner was the last Chief of the Reich Security Main Office, which contained the Security Police (comprising Gestapo and Criminal Police) and the Security Service.

Ethnic Germans who migrated to Germany from regions occupied by the Soviet Union in 1939 and 1940 or who were placed under the umbrella of German authority when the German army moved into Eastern Europe and the Balkans were less common in leading roles. They were, however, active in occupied territories. Ethnic German businessmen took over a number of small Jewish firms in Yugoslavia. Among the users of forced Jewish labor, there were several ethnic German entrepreneurs in Poland and the USSR. Quite a few ethnic Germans were in the SS. An SS detachment drawn from ethnic German inhabitants of the Romanian-administered region between the Dnestr and the Bug killed tens of thousands of Soviet Jews in the region.[2] In Auschwitz, a sizable percentage of the guards was ethnic German.[3]

Inevitably there were tensions between many an oldtimer who had roots in his position from pre-Nazi times and the assortment of newcomers, including Austrians and ethnic Germans, who obtained appointments and advancement by the grace of the Nazi regime. To the practiced bureaucrat, the party men were inexperienced, opportunistic, and corrupt. To Hitler and his followers, the old organizational structure was laden with ossified jurists, vainglorious diplomats, and immobile generals. The old hierarchies were conscious of having tradition and recognition. The new men thought of themselves as a vanguard, defining Germany's mission.

One difference between the two groups was obvious to any observer. The newcomers were, on average, younger than their more established competitors. Any number of men in the new power centers were born in the twentieth century. At the top of the ladder, Generalgouverneur Frank, Reichsführer-SS und Polizei Himmler, and the Chief of the Party Chancellery Martin Bormann were all born in 1900. The Minister of War Production, Albert Speer, was born in 1905. The first chief of the Reich Security Main Office, Reinhard Heydrich, was born in 1904. In the apparatus of the Generalgouvernement, which was Frank's domain, youth was a salient feature. Thus, Frank's principal Staatssekretär, Josef Bühler, was born in 1904, and the directors of the Main Division Interior, in succession, Eberhard Westerkamp in 1903, Friedrich Siebert also in 1903, and Ludwig Losacker in 1906. In the Interior Main Division, the head of the Population and Welfare Division, which dealt with deportations, Lothar Weirauch, was born in 1908. Frank's first director of the Agriculture Main Division, Hellmut Körner, was born in 1904, his successor Karl Naumann in 1905. Main Division Labor was headed by Max Frauendorfer, born in 1909. Among the regional Gouverneure in the Generalgouvernement, Otto Wächter (first in Krakow, then in Galicia), was born in 1901, Karl Lasch of Radom in 1904, and Ludwig Fischer of Warsaw in 1905. Fischer's Amtschef (Chief of Staff) Herbert Hummel was born in 1907, and the Kommissar for the Warsaw Ghetto, Heinz Auerswald, in 1908. Such age cohorts were not uncommon in the newly formed agencies at home or in the conquered territories.[4] Within occupied regions particularly, the youthful newcomers contrasted sharply with their over-aged counterparts in the army and the police. At the same time, youth gave these men a cohesion no less potent than the seasoned age that united the older establishment.

The entrants into the new power structure may be differentiated in terms of three motivations. For some, particularly individuals with flexibility and ambition, a position in the new sector was an alternate, promising career created by circumstances. Others had struggled unsuccessfully in an occupation and found in the party or a party-dominated organization a concrete realization of their undiscovered talents. Still others were accomplished men who exchanged an attainment or profession for the new movement, because Nazism had become an all-consuming element in their lives.

In the first category were careerists who were least distinguishable from their colleagues in traditional positions. An example is Friedrich Vialon, born in 1905 and educated in the law, who was a young prosecutor before Hitler came to power and who then served in various posts within the judicial apparatus and the Finance Ministry. When a portion of the area wrested from the Soviet Union was placed under the Ministry for Eastern Occupied Territories, Vialon was given a post in the so-called Ostland, which comprised the Baltic region and western Byelorussia. There he engaged in much correspondence and also signed directives for the confiscation of Jewish property. After the war, he continued his career in Bonn, where he rose to be Staatssekretär, or second in command, of the Minister for Economic Cooperation.[5]

In the Generalgouvernement, the Interior Main Division's Westerkamp had been a Regierungsrat in the Prussian State Ministry in 1932 and a local official thereafter. He joined the party as late as 1937. The director of the Generalgouvernement's Main Division Economy, Walter Emmerich, was from the business sector and the Economy Ministry. He too joined the party in 1937. The most interesting case of a civil servant in new surroundings was Heinrich Müller. Born in 1900, he was a flyer in the First World War and then joined the Munich police, where he held a position in the Division Political Police. That office investigated Communists and Nazis alike, but Müller specialized in the Left. His expertise was recognized by Himmler and Heydrich, who employed him to build the one organization that has become a synonym for the Nazi regime: the Gestapo. Müller joined the Reich in 1939. He remained the Gestapo chief until the very end. Then he disappeared, never to be found.[6]

The second category consisted of party stalwarts who had made false starts in life and who were early failures or drifters in occupational pursuits. The SS in particular was a home for many of these people. Here they could find not only security, but if they had joined this organization early enough they could rise in rank and ascend in power with rapidity. Himmler himself is the prime illustration of such a career path. Although he was educated in a gymnasium and had taken courses at a technical college and the University of Munich, he was in a quandary during his early twenties, considering a variety of pursuits, including agriculture, and wondering whether he should emigrate. Nazism became for him an occupational choice and he embraced it to the limit. Notwithstanding his unmilitary appearance, let alone lack of combat experience, he was the lord of all SS units, the Security Police, the Order Police, and the concentration camps. He regarded himself as the executor of the hardest mission of all: the annihilation of the Jews. The prerequisites for such leadership were sheer will, persistence, and ruthlessness, coupled with unquestioning loyalty to Adolf Hitler and patronizing solicitude for his SS commanders and SS men. He had these qualifications to the hilt.[7]

Adolf Eichmann, who rose only to the rank of SS Obersturmbann-führer (Lieutenant Colonel), and who served under Müller in Heydrich's and Kaltenbrunner's Reich Security Main Office as the Gestapo specialist in Jewish affairs, was another example of a man who had found shelter in the party apparatus. Born in Solingen in 1906, he moved with his family to Austria. There he worked for an oil company, lost his job, and drifted into the Austrian Nazi movement. In 1934, after an abortive attempt to dislodge the Austrian government in a Putsch, he fled with other Nazis to Germany and began his career in Heydrich's growing security apparatus, first expediting Jewish emigration in accordance with the policy of 1938 and 1939, and then coordinating European-wide deportations to bring about the final solution. Although he had made an effort to study the Jews, visiting prewar Palestine and taking Hebrew lessons, he was no specialist in Judaism. His talents lay in the implementation of anti-Jewish policies. He was an organizer, manipulator, expediter, and overseer, and he developed the uncanny ability to make Jewish leaders themselves his assistants, even in the spring of 1944, when he convinced the Jewish leadership in Budapest that nothing would happen to the Hungarian Jews if only they followed his instructions. In the course of this destruction process, Eichmann came into his own, and in his negotiations with other agencies, the stationing of his representatives in German legations, the siphoning of funds from Jewish resources for deportations, and the procurement of transports from the railways, he scored success after success. He was a man who played the violin and a little chess, and who also drank at times. His private life was, in short, normal, but in the maze of the bureaucratic apparatus, Eichmann was a pathfinder and a supreme practitioner of destruction.[8]

To be sure, not everyone in the SS was a genius. Fritz Katzmann, the son of a miner, was born in 1906 and trained as a carpenter. He became a Nazi in 1927, joined the brown shirted SA the same year, and became a member of the SS in 1930. A brawler, he rose in the ranks, commanding a detachment of SS men who were mostly miners. In the nineteen thirties he was evaluated with such adjectives as "good" and "satisfactory" and judged to be strong willed, energetic, and knowledgeable within the limits of his education. He married, and his private financial life was orderly and unobjectionable. By early February 1941, Katzmann was the SS and Police Leader in the Radom District with the rank of Oberführer, a grade just above colonel. At that moment he was considered to be too young for promotion to Brigadeführer, which would have made him a general officer, but a few months later he did advance to that rank. As the SS and Police Leader in Galicia, which was taken from the USSR in June 1941, he was in charge of deporting or shooting hundreds of thousands of Jews. This operation was still in full swing when Katzmann, now a Gruppenführer, hungered for yet another promotion to Obergruppenführer and an appointment as the Higher SS and Police Leader in Danzig. The SS personnel chief Maximilian von Herff had some doubts about this move. He thought that Katzmann was a good organization man, but one who lost himself frequently in details. Katzmann was good enough when he could act in accordance with his own rules, but he was not a great diplomat or tactician. Von Herff believed that in Danzig Katzmann would not succeed. Katzmann was moved up nevertheless, and after the war he lived undetected in hiding.[9]

Katzmann's rise was meteoric, because he fit an ideal profile almost perfectly. Notwithstanding faults and drawbacks, he got things done, albeit in his own way. Carl Oberg was a bit different. Born in 1897 as the son of a physician, Oberg had more education than Katzmann and he was a veteran of the First World War. From the early postwar years he was a Free Corps fighter and a supporter of right wing causes. He was working for a banana firm, switched to a fruit import concern, and started a cigar store. In the SS his career was much more assured. In an evaluation of 1938, he was said to be conscious of his goals, certain in his demeanor, and capable of using the "correct" tone with subordinates. He had an "open" personality, although he was prone to pushing himself into the center for attention. Oberg replaced Katzmann as SS and Police Leader in Radom and was then promoted to Higher SS and Police Leader in France, where he managed the deportation of seventy-five thousand Jews. Whereas Katzmann had wiped out the Jews of Galicia, Oberg had seized only about a fourth of the Jews in France. To be sure, conditions were altogether different in the French arena, where the French bureaucracy had to be dealt with and where SS and Police forces were sparse. Himmler did not blame Oberg for the slow progress of the final solution in France, but in January 1943 he wrote him a scathing letter about two minor matters: four tanks and a failure to install a police colonel in a proper position under army jurisdiction in Marseilles. Oberg, said Himmler, was too comfortable in Paris and spent too much time in social affairs. He did not want Oberg to prolong his Christmas vacation. Himmler did not, however, remove Oberg, who stayed in France until the end and who was imprisoned there for some years after the war.[10]

The German journalist and former political prisoner in Buchenwald Eugen Kogon once referred to the personnel of the concentration camps as a negative elite. They were dregs who could do nothing but guard helpless inmates. Hermann Dolp, born in 1909, became a *Schutzhaftlagerführer,* that is, an SS officer in charge of all prisoners in a camp, in 1939. His camp was Sachsenhausen. The Inspector of Concentration Camps, Theodor Eicke, was utterly dissatisfied with the assignment of Dolp to his command and accused the SS Personnel Main Office of maintaining the view that the most stupid SS leaders were precisely the men to lead a concentration camp, with its complicated administrative machinery, responsibly. A month later, Eicke wrote again to point out that he knew Dolp very well and that he had expressed his reservations at the start. Dolp was willing and industrious, and it was not his fault that he was holding the high rank of Standartenführer (colonel) without requisite intellectual capabilities. But the "criminals" in Sachsenhausen did not fear him; they were leaning on their shovels and admiring the surroundings, while Dolp with his well meaning, almost stupid face was losing all authority. Eicke finally succeeded in his quest to get rid of him. Dolp was transferred to occupied Poland, but now he had real trouble. There were incidents involving drunkenness, a Polish woman, and alleged remarks by Dolp to the effect that he was master of life and death. He was reduced in rank to Sturmbannführer (major) and forbidden to touch alcohol for two years, but there was no possibility of dispensing with his services. Eicke's successor, Richard Glücks, had to build new camps and was forced to use experienced SS leaders, including those who were least praiseworthy. Dolp was sent as overseer of a camp complex of Jewish forced laborers in the Lublin District, where defensive positions were built at the demarcation line separating the Germans and the Russians. Subordinated to SS and Police Leader Globocnik, he was at last successful. Under primitive conditions, said Globocnik, without an adequate number of guards, and working with an inferior labor force consisting of Jews and Gypsies, he built the fortifications during early 1941. Much later, in 1944, Dolp was commended again, this time for leading a construction battalion in the 19th SS Grenadier Division with energy sometimes rising to "brutality."[11]

By comparison with Dolp and other SS men in the camps, the leading personnel of the Reich Security Main Office, its regional branches, and mobile units (the Einsatzgruppen) were intellectuals. Not a few of these men had status and prospects in society but chose Security Police work out of conviction. In doing so, several of them gave up their professions or attempted to pursue two careers. The officers of the Einsatzgruppen moving into the territories of the Soviet Union included a great many lawyers and other intellectuals. Otto Ohlendorf, chief of the Reich Security Main Office's inland intelligence, commanded Einsatzgruppe D in South Ukraine and the Caucasus. He had attended several universities, was an economist, and actually continued his career, after serving in the USSR, in the Economy Ministry.[12] The Weinmann brothers, Ernst and Erwin, were totally dedicated to the Security Police. Their father had been killed in the First World War, but they were not lost orphans. Ernst, born in 1907, was a dentist and closed his practice when, at the age of thirty-two, he became the mayor of Tübingen. An "uncompromising National Socialist," he spent several years in Belgrade, rising to Commander of Security Police in Serbia.[13] His younger brother Erwin, born 1909, was a physician who found his way to the Security Service. Promoted more rapidly than Ernst, he led a Kommando of Einsatzgruppe C in the shooting of Jews. He returned to the Reich Security Main Office and at the end of 1943 was posted as Commander of Security Police in Prague. He was now a Standartenführer and toward the end of the war was recommended for a further promotion to Oberführer.[14]

Max Thomas also was a physician. Born in 1891 and a veteran of the First World War with an Iron Cross First Class, he closed a successful practice to devote himself fully to the SS and Police. He was a widely educated man who had studied Greek, Latin, French, and English, and who had considered law before turning to medicine. His first love, however, was to be counter-intelligence work. His personnel record indicates that he was an enthusiastic Security Service man. The record is also filled with physical mishaps: In July 1943 he was wounded by a mine; in December 1943 his aircraft crashed; in March 1945 he was in a traffic accident. Himmler, who worried about him, wrote in January 1944 to urge him to stay in bed. It is always a mistake, said Himmler to Dr. Thomas, to rise from the sickbed prematurely. On his part, Thomas wrote encouragingly to Himmler in November 1944, enclosing two letters from his son Dietrich, who was an SS officer on the Eastern Front, and assuring Himmler that with men like Dietrich the war could not be lost.[15] When Germany did lose the war, Thomas committed suicide.

Thomas had been the commander of Einsatzgruppe C and Commander of Security Police and Security Service in the Ukraine from October 1941 to August 1943. The mass killing of Jews had begun under his predecessor, but there were still opportunities for shootings, some of which were conducted by one of his Kommando leaders, Ernst Weinmann.

Many of the new functionaries expressed their idealism primarily at their desks. Filling that description was a young man named Edinger Ancker. He was born into the middle class in 1909. His father was a manufacturer and his mother a descendant of a Saxon family of civil servants. Ancker studied law, preparing for a career in local government. By 1930, he had already joined the party. He became a lawyer, a bureaucrat, and an honorary member of the Security Service. He also served as a soldier, but in 1940 he was released from the army to join the staff of Reichskommissar Seyss-Inquart in the Netherlands. Ancker's assignment as deputy chief of the Reichskommissar's personnel office was the product of favorable comments about him in his party record: "clever," "open character," "steadfast," "carries out decisions ruthlessly," "compromise does not enter into consideration." While in the Netherlands he married a Dutch woman, Eleanora Walraven. The marriage did not pose a serious risk to Ancker's career, even after a ruling by Hitler in 1942 that men who had married women of an enemy nationality were not to be employed in responsible positions. Eleanora Walraven was well educated, could speak German, and came from a pro-German family. In 1941, her father, Cornelis-Christian Walraven, was the Dutch deputy police president of The Hague. Ancker's superiors had no reservations about this union. The couple had children, one of whom died in 1942.

By 1942, Ancker had in fact been transferred to the Party Chancellery, where he dealt with Jewish affairs. On March 6, 1942, he attended a conference with another Party Chancellery functionary. The meeting, chaired by Adolf Eichmann, dealt with the knotty problem of what to do with those half-Jews who were not of the Jewish faith and who were not married to a Jewish partner. Should they be left in peace? Should they be sterilized? Should they be equated with Jews so long as they had not married a German or were not the parent of a child whose other parent was German? The Party Chancellery representatives favored the radical solution that would have resulted in the deportation of all the unmarried half-Jews who did not have a three-quarter-German child, but this view did not prevail in the end.

Ancker, still young, was assigned to the Armed SS in 1944 and became an officer. Just before the German collapse, his wife wrote him a desperate letter from a town near Munich: "Edinger, Edinger, why have you forsaken me?" The enemy was advancing toward Nuremberg and bombers were overhead. Her father, who was with her, wanted to commit suicide.[16] Ancker survived the war. He was queried by the American prosecution in Nuremberg, but his record was too marginal for an indictment there.

The Austrian Otto Gustav Freiherr von Wächter was more prominent than Ancker. Born in 1901, he was the son of General Josef

Freiherr von Wächter, an Austrian Minister of the Army. The young Otto was active in sports, skiing, climbing mountains, and excelling as a rower in boat races. He learned Italian, became a lawyer, and practiced in Vienna. He also joined the Austrian Nazis and took a leading part in the futile Nazi attempt of July 1934 to seize power in Austria. Pursued by the Austrian government, he fled to Germany. There he dropped his title of nobility and became a German citizen. After the annexation of Austria, he served briefly in Vienna, and then as the Gouverneur of the Krakow District in Poland. When Galicia was added as a district to the Generalgouvernement, he moved with his Austrian entourage to Lvov, where he remained as Gouverneur until the Red Army dislodged the Germans from the region in 1944. Not yet out of work, he was appointed Chief of Military Administration in Italy, which had in the meantime been occupied by the Germans. Wächter presided over the ghettoization of the Jews in the Krakow and Galician districts, and over the deportations of Jews in Galicia and Italy. His heavy involvement was clear to him, and upon Germany's collapse, he fled again, hiding in Italy, physically separated from his wife and five children. He died there in 1949.[17]

The new agencies were carving out power, and in the course of their expansion they sometimes clashed with each other. One of these jurisdictional conflicts arose between two Nazi leaders, both of whom had been associated with the movement from its early days: Himmler and Frank. In this contest Frank was at a disadvantage. Himmler, in Berlin, was adding prerogatives to his office and pushing his SS and Police into the far corners of German-ruled Europe. Frank, in his capital, was limited to the boundaries of the Generalgouvernement, which were moved only once with the incorporation of Galicia. Himmler had stationed his SS and Police personnel in Frank's territory and had created numerous labor camps as well as death camps there. Frank defended his own concept of absolutism against any incursion, insisting that he was the sole lord in his house and demanding that the Higher SS and Police Leader, Friedrich Krüger, be clearly subordinated to him. In fact, however, Krüger and his surrogates thought of themselves as primary decision makers in a number of subject areas, including the crucial final solution. Theirs was the eventual triumph. The ultimate resolution was somewhat the reverse of the organization chart, for in the end Frank retained only in his subdivision Population and Welfare under Lothar Weirauch a veto power in the dissolution of ghettos and the deportation of their inmates.[18] There is no indication of a veto. The SS and Police took the initiative and pressed on with all the assistance that could be given by Frank's bureaucracy.

Yet much acid had been spilled by the two sides during their evolving confrontation. At a meeting on May 30, 1940, in which the police made a premature bid for control of the Jewish communities, Frank asserted the principle of the unity of administration and stated unambiguously that police were an enforcement arm of government—police had no purpose in themselves.[19] A few days later, Krüger wrote a letter to Himmler complaining about the elevation of Bühler to Staatssekretär. Bühler, who had been Frank's Chief of Staff in the German Academy of Law, said Krüger, was only thirty-five or thirty-six years old and the promotion placed him as deputy of Frank in a position to give orders to the Higher SS and Police Leader—a veritable demotion of Krüger and an intolerable situation. (Krüger was forty-four.)[20] In this matter, the SS recouped its position. Krüger became a Staatssekretär too.

In 1942, Himmler was on the offensive, raising the question of corruption in the Generalgouvernement, pointing explicitly to the Generalgouverneur's sister, Miss Frank, and to Gouverneur Lasch of Radom.[21] Shortly thereafter, Lasch was summarily shot.[22]

Frank did score occasional victories. In 1940, he succeeded in stemming the inflow of Poles and Jews who were expelled from the incorporated territories into the Generalgouvernement, and eventually the troublesome Krüger was replaced. Yet more and more Frank acquired the image of a follower rather than a leader. He agreed and acquiesced, insisting all the time that his was the final decisive voice. German residents of Galicia apparently saw him with all his splendor in a state of eclipse. As noted in a Security Service report, they called him "King Frank" and "Stanislaw the Latecomer."[23]

The joke was not without foundation. Frank acted like a monarch in his castle. He held court, entertaining composers and chess players. For more than two years, however, he had often taken the lead in the campaign against the Jews; he had hounded them, referring to

"Jews and lice" and driving the Jewish inhabitants from his "German" city of Krakow. He incarcerated them in ghettos, starving them there and causing the deaths of hundreds of thousands without the slightest attempt at mitigation. Then he made inquiries about the possibility of their rapid deportation to the "east." In a speech to his functionaries on December 16, 1941, he noted that in Berlin he had learned that the Jews could not be absorbed in the newly occupied Soviet territories. Berlin had told him, "Liquidate them yourselves." Frank went on to say that the Jews had to be annihilated "whenever we find them and whenever it is at all possible." He did not know how. "We cannot shoot" these Jews, "we cannot poison them," but something was going to be done to bring about their annihilation. [24]

Frank could not visualize the bullets and the gas, but he knew that he had burned his bridges behind him. In January 1943 he announced at a meeting that all those assembled there were on Mr. Roosevelt's war criminals list and that he had the honor of occupying first place on that list. [25]

In the meantime, his SS rivals had placed him on the defensive and were driving him into a corner. During a despondent moment on September 1, 1942, he noted for the record that a clique was trying to depose and to "eliminate" him. In undisguised language, he pointed to a new course adopted by Hitler that had led to the total destruction of security under law, to the concentration camp, and to the arbitrary will of the police. He had offered his resignation to Hitler, but Hitler had refused it. [26]

In 1944, after a sudden Soviet offensive ousted the Germans from Lublin, Frank heard about the death camp Lublin under its Polish name Maydanek. At that point, Bühler stated that nothing had been known about camps by the civil administration of the Generalgouvernement. [27] At his trial in Nuremberg, Frank asserted that he had confronted Krüger's successor, Wilhelm Koppe, with the words "Now we know." [28] At that trial, he also proclaimed Germany's guilt for what had happened, a guilt, he said, that would not be erased in a thousand years. [29]

Unlike the oldtimers, the newcomers could not easily extricate themselves from their pasts. The Allied occupation powers looked upon them as likely criminals, while the old bureaucrats in the traditional hierarchies were relieved that the prosecutorial attention paid to the former Nazi party and SS was becoming a fixation. The newcomers in turn argued, not entirely without justification, that they were not alone, that they had been singled out, that distinctions between the roles of the military and the SS were often arbitrary, that in Hans Frank's formulation, it was Germany's guilt. A few men, like Himmler, Globocnik, and Krüger, saw the handwriting on the wall and committed suicide to avoid trial. Some, like Müller and Katzmann, disappeared, in the case of Katzmann, under an assumed name. Others, like Higher SS and Police Leader Koppe, who lived in disguise manufacturing chocolates, were apprehended late enough in life to escape judicial judgment. A very few left a posthumous word for the family. Hugo Wittrock, the ethnic German Gebietskommissar of the City of Riga in Latvia who established a ghetto there, does not speak of this act in the text that was published after his death. Instead he explains with a mixture of self-satisfaction and self-justification that in those days Germany had reached its full potential, albeit not without excesses, such as the massacre of the ghetto's tens of thousands of Jews, carried out by the Higher SS and Police Leader Friedrich Jeckeln without Wittrock's participation.[30]

5

ZEALOTS, VULGARIANS, AND BEARERS OF BURDENS

THE PERSONALITY CHARACTERISTICS of the perpetrators did not fall into a single mold. The men who performed the destructive work varied not only in their backgrounds but also in their psychological attributes. As German domination of Jewry became more pronounced and complete, the perpetrators assumed their roles in noticeably different modes. Some of these men displayed eagerness, others "excess," while still others approached their task with reservations and misgivings.

Sheer zeal covered a number of categories. There were first of all the prime movers, who were certain that everything depended on them. Then there were volunteers who sought ways and means for participation in the anti-Jewish activities. Finally, there were the perfectionists, who set examples and standards for everyone.

The goal-driven, tireless expediters are typified by Adolf Eichmann, who would write memoranda, travel, and goad people unceasingly. The Austrian Hanns Rauter, who was the Higher SS and Police Leader in the Netherlands and whose reports were filled with statistics, was another achiever. Crediting himself with deftness, he succeeded in deporting over 100,000 of the 140,000 Jews in the Netherlands, the highest percentage in the western rim of Europe. [1] In the

Foreign Office, a party man, Martin Luther, intoxicated with power, threw himself into the strategy and tactics of deportations.[2] The party's race expert, Walter Gross, was excited with his idea of mating unmarried quarter-Jews in the expectation that some offspring of such unions might reveal a sufficient accumulation of Jewish traits to make them suitable for extermination.[3] The German railways had their idealists as well. Otto Stange, a sixty-year-old Amtsrat to whom Eichmann's section sent requests for allocation of transports, worked in his office alone, shouting into the telephone.[4] Bruno Klemm, a functionary in the Generalbetriebsleitung Ost, which set up programs of transports moving east, is said to have been a constant and insistent voice for finding rolling stock and time on tracks for Jewish transports to death camps.[5]

Some of the zealots were enthusiasts who looked for opportunities to inject themselves into the process. Generalleutnant (Major General) Otto Kohl, who controlled all railway movements in occupied Belgium and France, once received a low-ranking representative of Eichmann in Paris and, describing himself as an uncompromising opponent of Jewry and as a believer in a racial solution, invited the SS man to ask for trains, be it for ten thousand Jews or for twenty thousand. Kohl would deliver the equipment, even at the risk of having some people brand him as "raw."[6]

In the Einsatzgruppen, Sturmbannführer (SS Major) Bruno Müller commanded Sonderkommando 11b, which in 1941 operated in the extreme south, assigned to a Romanian army. When the Romanians captured the Black Sea port of Odessa, they began a major massacre of tens of thousands of Jews in the city. In this frenzy, which was the work of numerous Romanian military and gendarmerie units, Müller and his Kommando constituted an insignificant presence, but he could not let the moment pass without a contribution of his own. When he heard during the evening of October 22, 1941, that the Romanians had commenced shootings, he negotiated with them for some three hundred Jews who had already been seized and led the victims to a dried well, where he ordered them shot. The partially or wholly undressed bodies of the men, women, and children were then thrown into the well, and hand grenades were tossed in after the victims to kill the badly wounded.[7]

In the German city of Darmstadt, a relatively low-ranking official, Kriminalsekretär Georg Dengler, took over the section dealing with Jews in the local Gestapo office (Leitstelle) on January 15, 1943. By then, most of the Jewish residents had been deported, and by and large only Jews in mixed marriages remained. Dengler received a directive in accordance with which he could also request deportation of these people, but he had to have grounds other than the sole fact that the victim was Jewish. He took this authorization as an opportunity to deport a few old women, some of them particularly vulnerable because they were widows. One sixty-nine-year-old woman, whose German husband was still alive, had not listed herself with the compulsory middle name Sara. She used a soap coupon belonging to her daughter, who had the same first name. The woman's death occurred in Auschwitz, but the ashes were offered to her non-Jewish family. Another woman, widowed and aged seventy-six, who also had a daughter, had similarly omitted the Sara on a food ration card. Dengler turned to an assistant and said, "That is sufficient."[8]

Sturmbannführer Müller and Kriminalsekretär Dengler had relatively small roles in operations of massive proportions. The results of their actions were not commensurate with their eagerness; they would gladly have done more. The perfectionists, on the other hand, had enough work. Day by day, these zealots were the real pillars of the administrative apparatus. Their challenge was any matter that had been left undefined or unresolved, and their watchwords could have been precision and exhaustiveness. These bureaucrats could be found everywhere, in any agency. In the Food and Agriculture Ministry, they would concern themselves with such questions as the allocation of skimmed milk to Jewish workers exposed to poison. In the Finance Ministry they attempted to collect private pension payments that had been made to deported Jews. In the railroads they counted deportees and kilometers to bill the Security Police for transports of Jews going to killing centers. In Auschwitz they involved themselves with condemnation proceedings to widen the perimeter of the camp.

Unlike the zealots, whose work was always functional, there were men who deliberately brutalized the victims, or tortured them, or derived excitement or amusement from their fate. This kind of behavior was not particularly welcomed, but neither was it strictly prosecuted.

Most often, brutalization was an expression of impatience. It could be found among the veterans of killing operations, to whom the repeated roundups, shootings, or gassings had become a routine. Thus a German officer in the Generalgouvernement reported in August 1942 that SS and Police personnel were observed dealing body blows with rifle butts to pregnant women.[9] Guards standing in front of gas chamber doors would use whips or bayonets to drive the victims inside. Again and again, witnesses recalled that small children were thrown out of windows, or tossed like sacks into trucks, or dashed against walls, or hurled live into pyres of burning corpses.

In some instances, sadism was pristine. This form of conduct emerged in face to face contacts of those men who wanted to exhibit their mastery over Jews. Essentially these individuals played with their victims. In the early days, they handed toothbrushes to Jews to clean sidewalks. In newly occupied Polish towns, they cut the beards of pious Jews or used Jews as ponies for rides. In the permissive environment of a camp, they could make use of Jews for target practice, or they could select women as sexual slaves. In Auschwitz, the arch sadist Otto Moll promised life to an inmate if he could run barefoot twice across a ditch of burning corpses without collapsing.[10] The master of life and death syndrome also had its reverse side. An Auschwitz inmate was flogged for having unsuccessfully tried to commit suicide.[11]

The sadists were not especially innovative. They did not have the imagination of their counterparts in earlier centuries or their contemporaries in the ranks of the Romanians or Croatians. The predominant type of German sadism was somewhat predictable and virtually institutionalized. It even had a name, "to make sport," and often enough it took the form of staging "gladiatorial" fights among inmates or of commanding prisoners to carry heavy stones from one place where they were not needed to another place where they were not needed. That is not to say that the game was harmless. The gladiators and stone carriers would die, wounded or exhausted.

Some of the perpetrators liked to laugh at the Jews. The jokes, sometimes alloyed to sadistic practices, might consist of dressing up an inmate in a comic costume and stationing him in front of an Auschwitz latrine with instructions to allow prisoners in distress only one minute for their relief; or of affixing the Star of David on a gas building in Treblinka; or, in the more refined circles of the German railways, of sending transports to a death camp with the remark that soon there would be an additional consignment of soap.

Vulgarization was one product of increasingly destructive operations. Moral problems were another outcome. Clearly, the arena of destruction was not a place for questioning or hesitation. Yet there were people who could not cope easily with unexpected situations that spelled out the impending death of the victims. These doubters were not as self-assured as the unswerving zealots at their desks or the efficient, even barbarized, killers in the field. In the ranks of the bureaucracy, differences in fortitude were sensed immediately. The decisive functionaries were called "hard," the others "soft." The objectors, who were conscious of this characterization, would try to remove themselves from the scene or they would voice their dissent on the narrowest of grounds: not this unit, not at this site, not at this time, or not in this manner. Seldom, however, did they insist or persist. Most of the weakest among them were still capable of action.

Oberregierungsrat Hermann Keuter had qualms. As described in a Security Police investigative report in 1942, Keuter was born in 1899 and was a veteran of the First World War, in which he had served as a lieutenant. From 1922 he was employed as a civil servant by the finance administration in Düsseldorf. Before January 1933, when Hitler came to power, Keuter dealt with personnel matters, but because of his long membership in the Catholic Center party and his visible Catholicism, he was assigned to a less sensitive post. In May 1933, however, Keuter joined the Nazi party, and in 1937 he was transferred to the office of the highest regional financial official, the Oberfinanzpräsident. There he took over the direction of the real estate section in 1940. Promoted in August 1941, he then faced the requirement of having to deal with Jewish property in the course of the "evacuation" of the Jews. With "major inhibitions," he approached the Oberfinanzpräsident and requested to be released from this work. "Only" after the Oberfinanzpräsident reminded him of his oath and duties did he carry out the task.[12]

Ludwig Fischer was in no sense a man who could have been expected to express unease about any anti-Jewish policy. He was a lawyer who at the age of twenty-six in 1931 had risen to the position of deputy chief of the party's legal division. A ranking member of the Brown Shirts (SA) and a protégé of Hans Frank, he was Gouverneur of the Warsaw District from October 1939 to January 1945.[13]

The district contained Nazi Europe's largest ghetto in Warsaw. More than 400,000 Jews, many of them dispossessed and most of them jobless, subsisted there on meager food rations, insufficiently supplemented by black market supplies and some food parcels shipped in by relatives or foreign Jewish organizations from the outside. Six months after the ghetto's formation, Fischer, clad in civilian clothes and wearing boots, received the Jewish "Elder," Adam Czerniakow, to declare that starving the Jews was not his objective and that there was a possibility of increased official food allocations. At the same time Fischer demanded the removal of corpses lying in the ghetto streets. These bodies, he said, created a very bad impression.[14]

Notwithstanding Fischer's vaguely reassuring words, the food constriction continued, and during the following summer months the ghetto death rate climbed to 1½ percent a month. Fischer, who could not supply foodstuffs to the ghetto without the agreement of the Generalgouvernement's Main Division Food and Agriculture, was uncomfortable with the mortality figures. When Generalgouverneur Frank himself took part in a three-day conference about Warsaw District problems, Fischer made a lengthy presentation, in which he also discussed the Jews. Specifically, Fischer proposed that the following rations be guaranteed for each ghetto inhabitant: 1,050 grams of bread per week, 300 grams of sugar a month, an egg per month, 100 grams of marmalade a month, 50 grams of fat a month, a dozen potatoes a year, and fish and vegetables as available. Even these allotments, he said, were too low for sustenance and deaths were certain to increase in the winter. The contest in this war, he went on, was with Jewry as a whole, and what was to be expected in the event of a Jewish victory, he said, had pointedly been indicated in a publication by the "American Jew Kaufmann." The book to which Fischer referred was the work of an obscure author, Theodore

Kaufmann, that had been published that year by the Argyle Press in Newark, New Jersey. Kaufmann had indeed proposed the territorial dismemberment of Germany and the sterilization of the Germans. With this evidence of Jewish intent, Fischer stated his belief that "annihilating" blows to the "breeding herd of Jewry" in the Warsaw Ghetto might be "justified," but, unreconciled to the existing food supply, he recited in detail the higher food rations allowed for working and non-working Jews in the Lodz Ghetto.[15]

Fischer had put forward his suggestion for mitigation of the ghetto hunger with all due references to his Nazi convictions. There is no record of any subsequent intervention by the Gouverneur and it appears that the mass deportations of the Warsaw Ghetto Jews during the summer of 1942 took place without any challenge by him. After all, the deported Jews were not lying around in the street. They were out of sight. Nevertheless, Fischer's words in October 1941 are not without significance. He was not completely untroubled by the escalation of the destruction process in his domain, and he spoke when he might have kept silent altogether. To be sure, his request was turned down.

One of the reasons for closed ghettos, sealed boxcars, and secret death camps was the screening of the victims from the eyes of sensitive witnesses. Such precautions, however, could not be extended to the frontiers of action, where a physical confrontation of the perpetrator and the victim was unavoidable. A shooter had to keep his eyes open, and the experience could be unnerving.

The following story was noted by a Warsaw Ghetto resident in his personal diary. A fifty- or sixty-year-old policeman had shot a young girl in a ghetto street, possibly because of some observed transgression. The street emptied immediately, but one woman could not flee in time. The policeman, deathly pale, took her by the arm, pointed to the dead body, and ordered the blood to be washed away, all the while explaining that the shooting was not his fault and showing the woman a piece of paper that he said contained his orders.[16]

Psychological difficulties were noticed particularly among inexperienced shooters, some of whom stood trembling before their victims and occasionally failed to take deadly aim. Ideological explanations by commanders and military methods of execution did not help very much.[17] The men had to have practice.

At the beginning, during June and July 1941, before the orders had become entirely clear, the Einsatzkommandos, police battalions, and SS brigades would seize mainly Jewish men ranging in age from about fifteen to sixty. On August 1, however, this self-understood or self-imposed boundary was lifted by Heinrich Himmler himself. On that date, the mounted battalion of the 2nd Cavalry Regiment of the SS Cavalry Brigade noted the following instructions.

> Explicit order by RF-SS [Himmler]
> All Jews must be shot
> Jewish women are to be driven into the swamps[18]

The battalion commander, Sturmbannführer Franz Magill, had some difficulty with this order. "Driving women and children into the swamps," he reported, "did not have the success that it should have had, inasmuch as the swamps were not deep enough for complete immersion."[19]

Even in August 1941, the killers had not solved their problem. A city in which their difficulties surfaced conspicuously was Belaya Tserkov, about fifty miles south of Kiev. Belaya Tserkov had been captured in a rapid push by the Sixth Army. At the time, the commander of this army was Field Marshal Walter von Reichenau. The 295th Infantry Division, subordinated directly to Army Group South as a reserve, was located in the city during mid-August. A military government had been set up: a regional Feldkommandantur and a local Ortskommandantur. In the city were also small elements of Sonderkommando 4a, which was commanded by Standartenführer (Colonel) Paul Blobel, an architect. Blobel's local deputy was Obersturmführer (First Lieutenant) August Häfner. As observed by an army officer candidate, the Kommando was shooting eight hundred to nine hundred Jewish adults in small groups of nine. Two men would aim at each victim from a distance of about twenty feet. Sometimes the top of a skull flew off and the men were covered with blood.

On the morning of August 2, several soldiers alerted two military chaplains in the field hospital to a building in which some ninety Jewish children, ranging from small infants to age five, six, or seven, were kept with a few Jewish adults in two or three rooms, guarded by a Ukrainian. The children, who had been crying at night and had nothing to eat or drink for at least a day, were lying in their own filth. Some were licking the walls. The smallest looked comatose. The two clergymen, who suspected that Ukrainians had acted without German orders, called the attention of the divisional Catholic and Protestant chaplains to the discovery, and these officers in turn lost no time in approaching the 1st General Staff Officer of the division, Lieutenant Colonel Helmuth Groscurth.

Groscurth was a tall forty-two-year-old professional officer, who was the son of a Lutheran minister. Before his assignment to the 295th Division, he had served in the Armed Forces High Command under Intelligence Chief Admiral Wilhelm Canaris. A veteran of the First World War, in which he had been wounded and captured, Groscurth was profoundly pessimistic. Critical of ranking generals, suspicious of the Nazi regime, and disdainful of the SS, he wrote prolifically in diaries, letters, and memoranda. Within a half hour after the visit of the two divisional chaplains in Belaya Tserkov, Groscurth went to the house where the children were imprisoned and inspected the rooms himself. The very next day, he summarized what he had seen and done in a lucid, lengthy report.

The smell was insufferable. A member of the Sonderkommando told him that the families of the children had already been shot and that the children were also going to be eliminated. Groscurth demanded an explanation from the Ortskommandant, who declared himself incompetent and who suggested that Groscurth talk to the Feldkommandant, Lieutenant Colonel Riedl. This officer pointed out that the action was in the hands of an SS lieutenant who had orders from the highest authorities. The correctness and necessity of the orders, said Riedl, could not be doubted. Groscurth demanded that a continuation of the action be disallowed until a decision of Army Group South had been obtained. The General Staff Officer of the army group referred Groscurth to the Sixth Army. By 8:00 P.M., Groscurth succeeded in obtaining a delay from Field Marshal

Reichenau, and the Feldkommandantur shipped water and bread to the children.

On the following morning at 11:00 A.M., Groscurth, accompanied by a subordinate, met with Riedl, the army's counter-intelligence officer Captain Luley, Obersturmführer Häfner, and Blobel. As summarized in Groscurth's report, Luley declared that, even though he was an Evangelical (Lutheran) Christian himself, he would have preferred the clergy to have confined themselves to the care of the souls of the soldiers. Riedl became philosophical and said that the "extermination" of the Jewish women and children was urgently required, regardless of the form in which it was going to ensue, and that the division had unnecessarily delayed the elimination of the children for twenty-four hours. Blobel agreed, explaining that Reichenau understood the necessity of the action and suggesting that soldiers who snooped carry out the shootings themselves.

Groscurth was outnumbered. He had already been informed by the division intelligence officer that Blobel's description of Reichenau's attitude was accurate. Groscurth, falling back, said that the clergy had to suppose an inappropriate initiative by Ukrainian militia. As for the division, it had intervened solely because of the manner of implementation of the action. Concluding his report, Groscurth did not refrain from stating his position that "measures against women and children were involved, which were distinguished in no way from the atrocities of the enemy." He added that the entire action appeared to have been instigated by Lieutenant Colonel Riedl. The Feldkommandant had declared repeatedly that the Jewish herd had to be exterminated and that, once the adults had been shot, the children, especially infants, had to be eliminated as a matter of course.

Field Marshal von Reichenau had the last word. On August 28, 1941, he blamed the division for the "interruption" of the action and specifically rejected the contention that the measure was comparable to atrocities of the enemy. Such incorrect assertions did not belong in a report passing through many hands. The report as a whole, he stated, should not have been made in the first place.

The children were now shot, not by the German personnel of the Sonderkommando, but by Ukrainian militia borrowed from the army. The Ukrainians, said Obersturmführer Häfner after the war, had stood around trembling. Häfner himself was not spared some torment. A little girl took him by the hand before she was killed.[20]

The psychological obstacles in the path of Blobel's Sonderkommando were gradually overcome. After Blobel arrived in Kiev during the following month, he killed more than thirty-three thousand Jews in that city. For the individual perpetrator, however, there was always a first time, and that occasion was not necessarily a moment during the opening phase of the final solution. The time came for Major Franz Lechthaler, a fifty-one-year-old career police officer, in October 1941.[21]

Lechthaler did not have an outstanding record, and the 11th Reserve Police Battalion that he commanded was hardly an elite force in the police. There were reasons why his success was modest. Before the First World War, in which Lechthaler served as a sergeant, he was going to be a house painter. During the collapse of Germany in 1918, he was stationed in Kiev, where he was chosen to chair a newly formed soldiers' council of his regiment. The councils were a semi-revolutionary institution patterned after the Russian soviets. Here Lechthaler opposed an officer's speech to "persevere." When the German army was sharply reduced in size by the Versailles Treaty, Lechthaler was not retained as a soldier. In 1920 he joined the German police, where he rose to captain by 1932. Distrustful of Hitler, whom he called an Austrian, he told his men that he expected them to vote for Hindenburg and against Hitler in the presidential election that year. Given this background, Lechthaler's promotions came slowly under the Nazi regime. He was the last in his class to become a major and his application for membership in the Nazi party was held up for several years.

After German forces drove the Red Army from the Baltic region in the summer of 1941, Lechthaler and his battalion were stationed in the Lithuanian capital of Kaunas. He had only three companies, one of which was detailed to ghetto duty. At the beginning of October, he received orders to proceed with his battalion to the Byelorussian capital of Minsk immediately. He took the two companies not assigned to the ghetto, and three companies of Lithuanian auxiliary police.

In Minsk the newly formed 707th Infantry Division was responsible for military security of an area comprising the western portion of the occupied Byelorussian SSR (including territories that had been Polish before the war). The division was commanded by Generalmajor (Brigadier General) Gustav Freiherr von Mauchenheim genannt von Bechtolsheim, a fifty-two-year-old professional officer, who was the son of a Generalmajor and who had recently been promoted to his rank. Not destined for major military exploits, Bechtolsheim's division had only two regiments containing in all twenty-four infantry companies and some support troops.[22] The soldiers were somewhat overage and their equipment less than first rate. Bechtolsheim also had some Byelorussian helpers in two formations: an Order Service performing police duties and auxiliary guards for various installations.

In September partisans were already active in the divisional area and on October 2, Bechtolsheim reported that armed Jews had set fire to a tar factory. On the same day he noted that he had to transfer his Order Service to the SS and Police Leader in western Byelorussia.[23] Two days later, sixteen Jews who had derailed a fuel train were seized and shot by his own intelligence and reconnaissance company (the Secret Field Police).[24]

At this point, with his forces spread thin across Byelorussia, Bechtolsheim apparently asked for reinforcements. A German court trying Lechthaler after the war surmised that Bechtolsheim's immediate territorial superior in Riga, Generalleutnant (Major General) Walter Braemer, who had good relations with the SS, had requested help from the Higher SS and Police Leader, and that Lechthaler's battalion was the unit that had been sent for that purpose.

In his postwar statements before German prosecuting authorities, Lechthaler relates that on his way to divisional headquarters in Minsk, he was greeted with a public hanging of two very young men and a woman who, as hostages, were paying with their lives for an attempt on Bechtolsheim himself. The operations officer (Lieutenant Colonel Fritz-Wedig von der Osten) had a map in which were stuck little red flags, each of which represented an attack by partisans. Lechthaler was to conduct two raids against them. After the completion of these missions, he remembers having reported to the operations officer again. This time he was told to wipe out the Jews in the village of Smolevichi, just south of the Minsk-Borisov road. The operations officer explained that Jews and partisans were sleeping under the same blanket and that there would be no peace until the Jews were eliminated. When Lechthaler objected that he could not, after all, conduct such an operation on suspicion alone, the operations officer was adamant. Lechthaler asserts that he then sought out Bechtolsheim, who told him that the police battalion had been subordinated to the division and that Lechthaler had to carry out divisional orders.[25]

The extant orders prepared by the Operations Officer of the 707th Division and bearing the handwritten signature of Bechtolsheim reveal a clearly articulated policy. The order of October 10 states that Gypsies encountered by patrols were to be shot on the spot. The order of October 16 reiterates earlier instructions that Soviet soldiers, even if captured without arms, as well as escaped prisoners of war, were to be shot. In the October 16 order Bechtolsheim specifies that Jews without exception be removed from villages, which he considered to be the only shelters where partisans could hope to survive the winter. The annihilation of the Jews, he states, was therefore to be carried out ruthlessly. In the area of the 727th Regiment, which covered the western portion of the divisional territory, this mission against the Jews, he said, was to be carried out in the first instance by the Lithuanian companies.[26]

The orders also described some of the actions of the police battalion and its Lithuanian auxiliaries. On October 8, in the area of Uzlany-Rudensk, the Secret Field Police and Lechthaler's unit shot 641 people, including a Red Army man, a *politruk* (political officer of the Red Army), 9 partisans, and 630 suspicious elements, Communists, and Jews.[27] During the following three days, the same forces, augmented by divisional engineers, shot 800 partisans, Communists, "rabble," and Jews in Rudensk. On October 13–14 the police battalion was in Kliniki, where it shot 1,341 Communists, partisans, and Jews.[28]

At his trial Lechthaler did not discuss Uzlany, Rudensk, or Kliniki, but he did describe the action in Smolevichi. In that town, he said, he had made sure that only the Lithuanians were going to do the shooting. The indigenous village chief (*starosta*) was told to call out the Jews, and only the "dumb" ones appeared. There were no old people or children among them.

Smolevichi, however, was not the end. On October 26, according to Lechthaler, he was in division headquarters again. That day, the operations officer, reiterating that there would be no quiet until all the Jews had been eliminated, ordered Lechthaler to proceed to Slutsk. Referring to the map once more, the officer stated that the division was not overcoming the partisan menace and pointed to all the places where German soldiers had been killed or maimed. When Lechthaler objected that he could not allow German policemen to engage in such shootings, the operations officer suggested that he let the Lithuanians do this work. Lechthaler states that he went to Bechtolsheim again, but that this time the general did not listen. A day later, Lechthaler went to Slutsk without staying there to the end of the shootings. One of his company commanders, Willy Papenkort, remained at the scene.

The Slutsk massacre claimed Jewish men and their families. It was carried out with such brutality and with such inroads into the Jewish labor force that the local civilian Gebietskommissar, Heinrich Carl, an old party man, wrote a blunt letter of protest to the Generalkommissar in Minsk. One of the policemen recalled Papenkort as having said that the Lithuanians were swine.

Lechthaler was troubled enough to want to walk away from the operation. His pangs of conscience, however, were not so severe as to cause him to revolt. He completed the assignment, leaving flames and corpses, including those of children, behind him. Later on he was promoted and placed in charge of a police regiment.[29]

6

PHYSICIANS AND LAWYERS

THE MACHINERY OF DESTRUCTION included representatives of every occupation and profession. Many of these men contributed their expertise to one or another phase of the ongoing operation as a normal part of their daily activity. Accountants and bookkeepers, for example, could busy themselves with contracts that were products of pressure put on Jewish owners to sell their property without having to consider the propriety of such transactions. Engineers, architects, and builders could erect camps and gas chambers without having to be discomfited by the nature of these projects. The accountants could always say to themselves that acquisitions were acquisitions, and builders could reason that buildings were buildings. In some professions, however, participation in the destruction process was not so simple. A physician could not avoid the issue of whether the direct or indirect infliction of illness or death was compatible with the basic medical mission of reducing pain and prolonging life. He had to reconcile these contradictory objectives by telling himself that he was still practicing medicine in his new role. Robert Lifton called this transformation "medicalized killing."[1] Similarly a lawyer necessarily had to face at every turn the critical question of harmonizing peremptory measures against Jews with law. In fact this alignment was his principal task in the anti-Jewish work. Yet in the end lawyers, no less than physicians, mastered these mental somersaults.

From the first days of the Nazi regime, members of the medical and legal professions were preoccupied with the ouster of their Jewish colleagues. As of 1933, there were quite a few Jews in these occupations, and all the evidence indicates that their expulsion, which began almost immediately, was strongly supported by Germany's medical and legal establishments.

German physicians were highly Nazified, compared to other professionals, in terms of party membership, and the prevalent thought that there was a doctor surplus facilitated the ejection of Jewish practitioners, albeit in stages, from 1933 to 1938.[2] Jewish lawyers were similarly vulnerable. Some of them were disbarred as early as 1933.[3] The protected attorneys were those who had practiced on August 1, 1914, or who had been at the front during the war. Their continued presence irked the legal profession, which demanded their removal.[4] By 1938, the Jewish physicians and attorneys were restricted to Jewish patients and clients. Titles were also shrunk. Jewish doctors were henceforth "caretakers of the ill" and Jewish lawyers were "consultants." The field was now clear for further action.

"Medicalized" destruction was in essence a destruction of medicine. Only a handful of physicians, like Max Thomas, closed the doors to their offices to don an SS uniform and become killers par excellence. A somewhat larger number, however, became enmeshed in such activities as "race" categorizations, sterilizations, euthanasia, medical experiments, selections for gassings or shootings, and ghettoization. Depending on the particular program, the victims were Jews or non-Jews, including Germans. The postwar German geneticist Bruno Müller-Hill notes that originally there was to be a division of labor: anthropologists were to deal with Jews, Gypsies, Slavs, or Black people, and psychiatrists with Germans diagnosed as schizophrenics, epileptics, idiots, or psychopaths. Soon, however, physicians were on the front lines of all these campaigns. A psychiatrist who was also a psychologist, Robert Ritter, collected information about twenty thousand Gypsies and came to the conclusion that 90 percent of them were offspring of unions between Gypsies and "asocial" Germans. These Gypsy victims (insofar as they were not married to pure Germans) were loaded on deportation trains to death camps. A physician, Otmar Freiherr von Verschuer, took over the anthropological institute from the aging dean of Nazi anthropologists, Eugen Fischer, and busied himself with race research as well as determinations of whether Aryan or non-Aryan status should be attributed to individuals whose records were not conclusive about their descent.[5] Such verdicts had to be painstaking within the confines of Nazi racial conceptions, because a career or even a life could be at stake.[6]

Compulsory sterilizations had origins in a wider area of Europe and in America. The German program, which was carried out mainly before the outbreak of war, encompassed close to 400,000 people, most of whom were judged feebleminded, schizophrenic, epileptic, or alcoholic. The judgments were made in courts charged with determinations of hereditary illness. The sterilizations themselves required the services of physicians in gynecology and other medical specialties, as well as psychologists and companies furnishing medical supplies.[7] After the consummation of the program, a further possibility was considered. There was some hope that Slavic populations in German-occupied Europe could be brought to extinction by mass sterilizations. To this end, thousands of Jewish women and men in Auschwitz were sterilized in medical experiments designed to find an efficient method of performing the procedure quickly and without the knowledge of the victims.[8]

Euthanasia was brought about at the beginning of the war. This undertaking claimed the lives of about 100,000 people, the bulk of whom were Germans, but who also included Jews, Poles, and other Slavs farther to the east. The principal criterion for most of these killings was incurability. Although Hitler, who signed the order, did not specify mental illness, he meant incurable patients in mental institutions. If one counted beds, the mentally afflicted patients occupied a disproportionate share—possibly half—of all the spaces in the medical complex of hospitals, clinics, and asylums. This burden on health services was going to be reduced. Following a screening of records by psychiatrists, a total of 70,273 adolescent and adult patients were "disinfected" between the onset of the program and its conclusion on September 1, 1941. Another 258,108 remained under care in German hospitals. Cost savings, based on a projection of ten years, were 885,439,800 reichsmarks.[9] The economic consideration was not the only one. From the start, there was a notion that if only the afflicted men and women could understand the misery and worthlessness of their lives, they would not want to live. But euthanasia as a favor was applied only to Germans. The Jews, Poles, or Russians in any mental facility were not selected. Regardless of their condition, they were simply killed.

The euthanasia program was also the administrative precursor of the gassings in the camp network Belzec-Sobibor-Treblinka. One and a half million Jews were killed in these camps with carbon monoxide gas administered by a cadre whose German personnel were drawn from the euthanasia stations in which the incurable German mental patients had been killed. The first commander of Treblinka, Irmfried Eberl, had been a euthanasia physician.

A great many medical experiments were performed in concentration camps, which provided an ideal environment for such activities. By definition, inmates did not have a right to health or even life. If they were Jews, their existence in the camp was prolonged only for labor. Nevertheless, physicians requesting human beings for experiments would sometimes specify Jewish "criminals" or persons condemned to death as a kind of insurance against moral doubts. The experiments themselves could be pharmacological, to test drugs, or surgical, to improve techniques, but some procedures were designed with a view to future sterilizations on an assembly line. Robert Jay Lifton investigated the lives and experiences of some of the physicians who had served in Auschwitz. He discovered several types of individuals. Professor Carl Clauberg was a five-foot tyrant, with a history of violence toward women, who wanted to perfect sterilizations by means of injections. As a gynecologist Clauberg had made notable contributions in the treatment of infertility before the war, and now he had unlimited opportunities to pursue his research in the opposite direction. His Auschwitz experiments, however, were not crowned with a breakthrough. In Soviet captivity after the war, he was returned to Germany, apparently unrepentant. He died in German custody in 1957. Horst Schumann was a euthanasia veteran who also worked on sterilization techniques. His method used

X-rays. Reproductive organs were surgically removed from men and women to examine the damage. Schumann was not totally oblivious to what he had done, inasmuch as he spent years of selfless service in Khartum, Sudan, and Accra, Ghana, after the war, Lifton describes him as a kind of good samaritan in this period of his career. The young gynecologist Eduard Wirths was the chief camp doctor in Auschwitz. He made experiments to study pre-cancerous conditions of the cervix, using healthy inmates for his investigation. Wirths acquired a reputation for being kind to inmate doctors and other trusted inmates. At the same time, he organized the selection procedure at the ramp, where arriving Jews were sorted through superficial examination to step aside for labor or to go on to the gas chambers. For Wirths, says Lifton, "conscience gave way to conscientiousness." Caught after the war, he committed suicide immediately. [10]

Selections were conducted by several physicians at Auschwitz. Apparently they adapted themselves to this task in different ways. One survivor explained to Lifton that whereas one doctor, Josef Mengele, would stand at the ramp and partition the columns of new victims with "graceful and quick movements," another (Franz Lucas) would do so with evident reluctance, carefully and slowly. [11] In the final analysis, however, they were all there.

Although Auschwitz was in the postwar limelight, it was not the only camp in Nazi Europe where physicians selected people for death. In November 1941, the Security Police in the occupied USSR reported that the camp doctor of a prisoner of war enclosure in Borispol had handed over seventy-six wounded Jewish prisoners for shooting by Sonderkommando 4a. [12] The mention of this incident in the report was as casual as the act of the unnamed physician may have been.

The part that German doctors played in the ghettoization process in Poland was less direct than in sterilizations, euthanasia, experiments, or selections, but in the Polish cities their role had major consequences. Christopher Browning has shown to what extent ghetto formation, particularly in Warsaw, was cast as a health measure to protect not so much the Polish population as the German bureaucracy and military that were stationed there. [13] The danger was said to be typhus, a disease that was borne by lice and that was associated with the Jews.

The linkage of typhus with Jews was not new. When Warsaw was under German occupation during the First World War, the Germans observed an exceptional rise of typhus in the Jewish population of the city. Early in 1918, the German government banned the movement of Jewish workers from the eastern occupied area to the German Reich.[14] Much later, in 1973, the German epidemiologist Wilhelm Hagen, who had served as the physician of the German city administration in Warsaw during the Second World War, resurrected the statistics of 1917–1918 and pointed to the marked difference in the incidence of tuberculosis and typhus among Poles and Jews. The Jews, he said, had acquired much greater resistance to tuberculosis as a result of the "ruthless" selection in the medieval ghettos, but manifestly they were more prone to typhus.[15]

Ghettos were, of course, part of a larger SS vision for Polish Jewry. They were conceived in 1939 as a transitional concentration measure for a permanent solution not yet in view. For German doctors, however, ghettos were essentially quarantines. In the city of Warsaw, a "closed pestilence area" was established as early as the fall of 1939. The zone was simply a Jewish quarter, in which Poles were also living. The inhabitants could still come and go, but German personnel, especially military, were not supposed to enter these streets.[16] The walled ghetto in Warsaw, established a year later, was in a sense the final solidification of the quarantine idea.

Typhus did not spread in all of the ghettos. Its occurrence was relatively limited in Lodz or Radom, but in Warsaw it rose to epidemic proportions in 1941. Dr. Hagen, who was a Social Democrat by background, did what he could to help. He supported the Jewish plea for higher food rations—a request that was unsuccessfully repeated by Gouverneur Fischer himself—and at one point, when the German city planners wanted to cut off the southern half of the T-shaped ghetto, Hagen characterized the proposal as "insanity."[17] Later, he fought a battle with the Generalgouvernement's Population and Welfare chief Weirauch, whom he suspected of planning the killing of many Poles in the Lublin District.[18] Yet Hagen was also a German of his time. He never abandoned the coupling of Poles with

tuberculosis and Jews with typhus, and on July 7, 1941, he proposed
to Fischer, along with various disinfection measures, the following:

> Anyone leaving the Jewish quarter is to be given corporal punish-
> ment and, if in possession of means, also a heavy fine. Jews who
> become vagabonds are to be shot.[19]

Indeed, on October 15, 1941, a decree issued by the Generalgouvernement provided the death penalty for Jews apprehended outside
a ghetto.[20] In 1973, Hagen defended his proposal for shooting as an
unavoidable concession that was virtually meaningless inasmuch as
escaping Jews were already being shot before the decree. After the
war, he enjoyed another career as President of the Federal Health
Office. His antagonist, Lothar Weirauch, achieved a postwar triumph as well, when he became a Ministerialdirektor in the Federal
Ministry for All-German Questions.

Doctors served in a variety of offices and the programs in which
they were involved represent important developments in the process
of destruction. Lawyers were everywhere and their influence was
pervasive. Again and again, there was a need for legal justifications.
When the number two Nazi, Hermann Göring, suggested in the
course of a discussion at the end of 1938 that German travelers could
always kick Jewish passengers out of a crowded compartment on a
train, the Propaganda Minister, Josef Goebbels, replied: "I would
not say that. I do not believe in this. There has to be a law."[21]

The original tool for anchoring the destruction process in a legal
framework was the law or decree, that is to say, a measure drafted in
an agency, coordinated with other agencies insofar as their jurisdiction was touched by the proposed contents, and then published in a
legal gazette. So long as the principal agency was acting within its
traditional sphere of competence, there was no ceiling on what could
be done. Government, in short, was not limited. Often, however,
the decrees were written without a clear idea of their manifold applications. It is then that artful interpretations were employed.

An example of an unanticipated dilemma was the deportation of
Jews from German cities to the Lodz Ghetto, which was located in
Polish territory that had been incorporated into Germany. Under the

11th Ordinance to the Reich Citizenship Law, Jews "leaving" the country forfeited their property to the Reich, but since Lodz was *in* the Reich these Jews had not left the country. Staatssekretär Wilhelm Stuckart of the Interior Ministry saw that the 11th Ordinance could not be used in this situation, but there was a way out. Jews, after all, were commonly understood to be "enemies of the Reich" (even though these deportees were not nationals of an enemy state), and therefore their possessions could be confiscated under another law dealing with enemy property.[22]

A telling illustration of the manner in which the meaning of a law was expanded may be drawn from a series of court decisions construing the so-called Law for the Protection of German Blood and Honor, a measure that prohibited entry into a marriage as well as extramarital relations between Jews and Germans. Thus the courts ruled that sexual intercourse did not have to be consummated to trigger the criminal provisions of the law: sexual gratification of one of the persons in the presence of the other was sufficient. Touching or even looking might be enough. The reasoning in these cases was that the law covered not only blood but also honor, and a German, specifically a German woman, was dishonored if a Jew made advances toward her or exploited her sexually in any way. When a Czech who was a resident of the Protectorate of Bohemia and Moravia was indicted, his plea that, after all, he was not a German was turned down on the ground that Czechoslovakia had ceased to exist and that the status of Bohemia and Moravia as a protectorate made him a "protectee" of the Reich, to be likened to a German citizen. When a Jewish defendant argued that he was unaware of the German background of his partner and that therefore he lacked intent to violate the law, the court insisted that a Jew about to have relations with a German woman could not content himself with her assurances that she was of Jewish descent. He had to make a conscientious effort to obtain satisfactory documentary evidence of her status.[23]

Wide latitude of interpretation was also exercised for the severance of all kinds of contract obligations. The Jewish employee, for example, could be dismissed because he was disabled by reason of his

Jewishness. A Jewish tenant could be evicted because a lease was an instrument for a community of tenants to which a Jew could not belong. And so on, case after case.[24]

If a legal provision plainly fell short of covering a problem, one could sometimes resort to the analogy principle. A Jewish student could be deprived of his state fellowship, for example, inasmuch as a Jewish civil servant could be ousted from public employment.[25] Similarly, after the publication of the decree providing the death penalty for Jews fleeing from ghettos, a question arose whether one could apply this punishment to Jews escaping from labor detachments outside ghettos. The Kreishauptmann of Tomaschow, Karl Wilhelm Glehn, proposed that in such cases also the route to the work site and the place of work itself could be defined as a ghetto.[26]

As a last resort, the law could be used as a veneer. Increasingly the titles of decrees did not convey the content of their provisions. As the German historian Uwe Adam notes, there was a tendency to publish decrees as giving effect to anti-Jewish laws, whereas these decrees did not implement the laws at all.[27] Thus decrees in pursuance of the Reich Citizenship Law not only defined the concepts of "Jew" and "Jewish enterprise" but went on to deal with such topics as the dismissals of Jewish lawyers, the naming of a Jewish organization to which all Jews had to belong, and the confiscation of property belonging to emigrated or deported Jews.

In connection with confiscations, the term *trusteeship* was common. The custodial agency in these cases did not hold the property for the benefit of the Jews or their beneficiaries, but merely processed the absorption of the goods or assets into the budget of the Reich. Thus there were a Main Trusteeship Office East in the incorporated territories of Poland, a trusteeship office in the Generalgouvernement, and trusteeship offices in the areas controlled by the Reich Ministry for Eastern Occupied Territories, none of which acted as a genuine trustee. Still another label in the confiscatory process was the expression "Jewish estate." It was used with reference to the disposal of personal effects that had belonged to Jews killed in Byelorussia.[28]

The sheathing of anti-Jewish operations in the law took place even on the killing field. During the early days of the shootings, in the town of Dobromil, the Commander of Einsatzkommando 6, Erhard Kröger, a Baltic German from Riga who was trained and specialized in international law, confronted a group of Jews about to be killed and explained to them through an interpreter that they would now be executed in "retaliation" for numerous murders committed by the retreating Red Army among the civilian Ukrainian population.[29]

7

NON-GERMAN GOVERNMENTS

THE DESTRUCTION OF THE JEWS was European-wide. In a large area holding about 2 million Jews, a multiplicity of measures were taken by non-German authorities. Four countries that engaged in such action had joined Germany for the sake of conquest: Italy, Bulgaria, Romania, and Hungary. Two were satellite states that had been created by Germany: Slovakia and Croatia. Three others were occupied countries, which had fought against Germany, but in which collaborating governments or agencies were prepared to contribute anti-Jewish decrees or at least significant administrative assistance: Norway, France, and the Netherlands.

What Germany wanted from its allies was a cloning of the anti-Jewish regulations developed in Germany itself. It was hoped that steps would be implemented by friendly states in a proper order to make the Jews "ripe" for deportation. The sequence was to begin with a definition of the term *Jew* in accordance with the principle of descent; it was to continue with the expulsion of the Jews from any vital role in the economy; and it was to go on with devices for identification and concentration, notably the marking of the Jews with a star. Finally, help was welcomed in the form of roundups, rolling stock for transport, and payment to defray the costs of the deportations. To assure the accomplishment of these goals, the German Foreign Office and Adolf Eichmann's specialists in the field stood by with appropriate "advice."

Not everything worked out in the hoped for manner. Some countries wrote definitions of the concept of "Jew" which contained subtle deviations from the German formulation. Thus Italy exempted children of converts and Bulgaria spared all converts married to Bulgarians. Hungary and Slovakia changed definitions in response to tightening or relaxing German pressure. Romania dispensed with a single controlling definition altogether, preferring to specify a circle of victims in each decree.

Almost all of Germany's allies were avid expropriators. In societies that valued farmland and forests, as in the case of Romania and Hungary, Jewish agricultural properties, however few, were targeted immediately for takeover. The acquisition of Jewish industrial and commercial enterprises mattered in Slovakia, which wanted a stronger ethnic Slovak presence in these sectors. In Romania, where most industrial and many commercial holdings were foreign, similar considerations propelled the attempt to create a purely Romanian economic base. Both Slovakia and Romania, however, lacked capital and expertise. In Slovakia, some former Jewish owners remained as managers to operate their old firms under Slovak strawmen, and in Romania some Jewish companies simply remained in business.

The ouster of Jewish professionals and skilled laborers was pursued as a means of rewarding non-Jewish aspirants. Here too there were limits. In Hungary, Jewish physicians were still essential, and in Romania, gentile beginners stood as "doubles" next to Jewish craftsmen to learn a trade. Policies were quite different, of course, with respect to unskilled or unemployed Jews. France, Bulgaria, Romania, Slovakia, and Hungary drafted these people into labor companies, which were housed in camps and deployed in many outdoor projects. The Hungarian Jewish companies, which were the most numerous, were given such tasks as mining copper in Yugoslavia and clearing mine fields on the Eastern Front.

Concentration measures were sometimes adopted for pragmatic reasons. The housing shortage spurred the expulsion of thousands of Jewish families from the Slovak capital of Bratislava and the Bulgarian capital of Sofia. In Romania, there was a law allowing ethnic Romanians to claim Jewish apartments anywhere in the country. The Romanian city of Cernauti (Chernovtsy) had a long-lasting ghetto. In unoccupied France, impoverished foreign Jews were assigned by French authorities to "forced residence" in small towns.

The Germans placed particular emphasis on the introduction of a yellow identifying star that the Jews were to affix to their clothes, but the practice of collaborating governments in this undertaking was far from uniform. Croatia, which was created in 1941, imposed the emblem at once. Slovakia instituted the star with a proviso (removed later) that many working Jews and their families would not have to wear it. Hungary had no external identification, outside the labor companies, until the Germans occupied the country in 1944. Bulgaria mandated a plastic yellow button and then halted its production. Romania introduced a star in some provinces and subsequently voided the measure. In France, the German military government, but not its French collaborators, decreed the yellow patch. Italy had no star.

A crucial difference between German and non-German agencies surfaced in the course of deportations. Within Germany and territories occupied by Germany, the Jews were to be rooted out completely. Exceptions were made only for those living in mixed marriages and deferments were granted mainly to irreplaceable laborers. Non-German governments were much less compulsive in this regard, and they made distinctions in a more compromising manner.

In Slovakia and Croatia, some Jews were privileged. Even though Croatia killed almost half of its Jewish population in its own annihilation camps, it resembled Slovakia in exempting old established families, individuals needed in the economy, or people with various connections. Hungary ousted non-Hungarian Jews from newly annexed regions in the summer of 1941, delivering the victims to the German-occupied USSR, where they were killed, but Hungarian Jewry as a whole was not deported until the spring of 1944. Collaborationist France was often ready to intern or hand over stateless and foreign Jews but was reluctant to surrender Jews of French nationality. Bulgaria and Romania drew the line territorially. The Bulgarian government gave up the Jews of the freshly acquired regions in Macedonia, Thrace, and Pirot but resisted deportations from Old Bulgaria. Romania, which had lost Northern Bukovina and Bessarabia to the Soviet Union in 1940 and had recovered them in 1941, promptly expelled the Jews from these provinces. A year later, the Romanian government declined a German request to deport the Jews of Old Romania to Poland.

The unevenness of action in Germany's periphery was not an accident. Nowhere was the determination to implement the final solution so deep rooted as in Germany; nowhere was the issue so fundamental. Most of Germany's neighbors, whether allied or conquered nations, continually balanced a variety of considerations in their decision making. The result was a spectrum of reactions, from non-cooperation, to some forms of participation, to heavy involvement that nevertheless fell short in one aspect or another of reaching the German standard.

Two countries were unapproachable at any time. They were Finland, a German ally against the Soviet Union, and Denmark, wholly occupied by Germany, but with its prewar government still in place. Their small Jewish populations survived, in Finland, without a German foray, and in Denmark, after a largely abortive German attempt to act singlehandedly in a seizure operation.

Norway and the Netherlands had offered resistance to German invasions, and after they were overwhelmed, each was placed under a Reichskommissar. A Norwegian government in exile waited in London for an Allied victory, but in the meantime a puppet government under Vidkun Quisling in Norway pledged itself to support Germany. Although there were very few Jews in Norway, almost half of these few were rounded up for deportation with the help of old as well as newly established Norwegian police.[1]

Indigenous authority in the Netherlands was the product of a more complex situation. The Dutch cabinet had fled to London, but it had left behind the senior civil servants to run the country on a stable day by day basis under German rule. The principal functionaries in the Netherlands were four Secretaries General, one of them, Karl Johannes Frederiks, in charge of internal affairs, that is to say, general administration. The Dutch bureaucracy refrained from issuing any

regulations against the substantial Jewish community. All such measures were therefore exclusively German. The Reichskommissar,
however, did have Dutch assistance in the implementation of German policy, notably in the issuance of identification cards and in
registrations. When Jews were prohibited by a German ordinance of
September 15, 1941, from changing their residence without permission, the SS and Police wanted any violators to be apprehended by
the Dutch law enforcement machinery. The Mayor of Zutphen,
whom the Germans considered to be pro-Jewish, thereupon sought
a directive in this matter from the Dutch commissar of Gelderland
Province. The commissar replied that Dutch police were to abstain
from arresting any Jews who were not guilty of a punishable act,
and Secretary General Frederiks agreed with this opinion. It was
evident to the Germans that in the eyes of the Dutch administration, the disregard of a German anti-Jewish decree was not criminal
behavior.[2]

Notwithstanding this display of Dutch rectitude in the face of
German pressure, Dutch police participated in the large-scale roundups of Jews less than a year later.[3] The Amsterdam police were
injected into the operation at the end of August 1942. The Dutch
police chief of the city was Sybren Tulp, a man with no prior anti-
Jewish record, who had been an infantry officer in the Dutch colonial
army of the East Indies. Tulp was popular with his men. He wanted
them to be self-confident and he strove to shape them into a model
force. He also sought the goodwill of the Higher SS and Police
Leader Hanns Rauter, with whom he maintained regular contact by
telephone and correspondence. Tulp's police took on more and more
German features. Amsterdam had a newly formed police battalion,
most of whose members had been drawn from demobilized soldiers
of the Dutch army, and who were quartered in barracks. During the
summer of 1942, Tulp expanded his headquarters, forming a bureau
of Jewish affairs. Finally he led his men in the seizure of the Jews.
Only one of his officers refused duty. The mobile battalion, Tulp
reported, had acted with great dedication, looking for any Jews not
found at home in the general neighborhood.[4]

Not all Dutch police were so arduous. A Jewish survivor recalls
the arrest of his family in Apeldoorn on October 2, 1942. A member

of the German army's Field Police, accompanied by two Dutch policemen, appeared in the apartment. He ordered the family to prepare itself and left with one of the two Dutchmen. The Dutch policeman who was left alone with the Jews pleaded with them not to flee. Explaining that he was acting under orders, he said that he would be held accountable for their disappearance. The Jewish victims complied.[5]

The Dutch police would take the Jews to a concentration point, from which they would be sent to a railway station to board a train to a transit camp. In this shuttle, the Dutch railways, less visible than police in the streets, apparently cooperated with the Germans as a matter of course.[6]

When France approached defeat in 1940, a new government was formed, which asked for an armistice. Under the terms of this agreement, the northern part of the country, including Paris, and the entire Atlantic coast became a German-occupied area. The interior to the Mediterranean was unoccupied until November 1942. The French government had its capital in the small town of Vichy within the free zone. Its laws, decrees, and directives were also applicable in occupied territory, but there the German military administration could issue its own ordinances, preempting or overriding French enactments. Vichy remained independent in unoccupied France, where it was permitted to maintain a small army, and at the beginning it still controlled the French colonies. Yet in the French population on both sides of the demarcation line, there were feelings of humiliation, a sense of bewilderment over the sudden debacle, and the sheer pain caused by the burdens of the lost war. For these reasons, the Vichy regime emphasized old pride reflected primarily in the person of the aged Marshal Philippe Pétain; a new competence as represented in a corps of able leaders; and the necessity of facing reality in the form of an articulated policy of collaboration with Germany.

A comparison between Pétain and his German contemporary von Hindenburg is almost inescapable. Both men had triumphed in defensive battles during the First World War, Pétain at Verdun in 1916, Hindenburg against the Russians in 1914. Both had urged their governments to surrender, Hindenburg as Commander of the German army in 1918, Pétain as Vice Premier in 1940. Both served as heads of state in their eighties with full lucidity of mind. Pétain, however, was more than a symbolic ruler. He acquiesced, even though reluctantly, in anti-Jewish measures, and opposed, albeit indirectly, the deportation of Jews of French nationality. With these attitudes he incorporated the compromises of his regime.

The new professionalism was stressed in the military and civilian hierarchies. The armistice army weeded out older officers and attempted to become leaner like the 100,000-man German Reichswehr of the 1920s. At the same time, it dismissed, with a few exceptions, its Jewish officers and non-commissioned officers in order to be wholly "French."[7] Many Frenchmen were still prisoners of war, but only a few had joined General Charles de Gaulle in London. As Robert Paxton has shown, the Vichy army had retained the loyalty of the officers at home and in the overseas possessions. On several occasions, the military fought against British onslaughts against the French empire. A British naval attack was beaten back at Dakar in 1940, and a British invasion of Syria was resisted for a month in 1941. In the Syrian battle, there were thousands of casualties on each side, and when the French defenders were given a choice at the end of the fighting to go home or join de Gaulle's Free French forces, all but 5,668 of the 37,736 officers and men returned to France. A colonel who opted for de Gaulle was told by a major who kept his allegiance to Vichy: "Go to the Jews, then; they will pay you well."[8]

Within the civilian branches of the Vichy regime, there was an infusion of technocrats and careerists who, like Tulp in the Netherlands, thought of themselves as innovators. Several of these entrants were graduates of elite schools. One was François Lehideux, educated at the Ecole Libre des Sciences Politiques and a veteran of the Renault concern, who as Secrétaire d'Etat of Industrial Production signed a number of anti-Jewish decrees in the economic sphere. Another was Jean Bichelonne, trained at the Politechnique, who succeeded Lehideux and was also concerned with takeovers and liquidations of Jewish enterprises. Still another, Pierre Pucheu, was a product of the Ecole Normale Supérieure with experience in heavy industry who, as Minister of the Interior, signed a host of anti-Jewish measures leading to segregation and internments. Pucheu had been a member of the extremist right-wing Parti Populaire Français before the war, but his colleague, Justice Minister Joseph Barthélemy, another signer of decrees, had come into the office from the University of Paris, where he had been a respected professor of law. The chief of the Vichy government's police, René Bousquet, was a former prefect, and at the time of the deportations in 1942, he was only thirty-three. [9]

The Vichy regime had not only new men, but also a new agency: a Commissariat of Jewish Affairs. This office was headed by Xavier Vallat, a nationalist and militant Catholic, whose principal achievement was the creation of a Jewish council that would have to take orders from him. Vallat, however, was sufficiently hostile to Germany to be replaced by Louis Darquier de Pellepoix, who was more exclusively anti-Jewish. Son of a physician and a seventeen-year-old soldier of the First World War as well as an officer in the second, Darquier had studied and abandoned chemistry. During the 1930s he acquired his principal credentials by heading the Rassemblement anti-Juif de France. As Vallat's successor, Darquier dealt with property transfers and a host of other activities, but he was not always at the center of the action.

One man who played a pivotal role in the Vichy regime and who became the principal advocate of the policy of collaboration was Pierre Laval. Neither a modernizer nor an ideologist, Laval was a pragmatic politician. Born in a peasant family and trained as a lawyer, he was a man of high visibility long before the German invasion. Twice a premier in the 1930s and for a short period a foreign minister, he was co-author with Britain's Foreign Secretary Sir Samuel Hoare of a plan to appease Italy's appetite for Ethiopia by offering Benito Mussolini a few of Ethiopia's provinces. War seemed to him folly, and toward Britain and the Soviet Union, France's potential allies in a conflict with Germany and Italy, he harbored distrust. When France fell, he joined Pétain's cabinet but then lost his post in a palace coup. He returned as premier in March 1942, at a time when the deportation of the Jews of the occupied zone was imminent. Laval threw in his lot and that of France with Germany. Predicating his policy on a German victory, he was willing to make deals with the Germans. Thus he sought the release of French prisoners of war in exchange for an increase in the number of French laborers going to the Reich, and in the summer of 1942, he agreed to deport twenty thousand stateless Jews from the unoccupied zone as a concession to German demands. Among the victims were several thousand children who had not been expected by the SS and Police. In a gesture of largesse, Laval declared that the children did not interest him.[10]

Germany's southeastern allies, Bulgaria, Romania, and Hungary, were primarily interested in territory. All three had been territorial losers, and each was compensated under German patronage. As they drew nearer to Germany, they also commenced anti-Jewish activities.

Bulgaria's losses had occurred as a result of the Second Balkan War and the First World War. By spring 1941, Bulgaria controlled more land than it had ever had in the twentieth century. Yet the Bulgarian government was hesitant to be fully at Germany's disposal. Bulgarian troops did not fight on the Eastern Front and the Jews of Old Bulgaria were not deported. Anti-Jewish action was not omitted completely and something did happen to the Jews. The driving force in this campaign was Alexander Belev, the Commissar for Jewish Affairs. A prewar ultra nationalist, Belev was appointed to the newly formed commissariat by Interior Minister Peter Gabrovski in August 1942. A number of steps had already been taken against the Jews by that time, and Belev was to preside over the deportations. His path, however, was at least partially blocked. Foreign Minister Ivan Popov and Gabrovski himself became sensitive to internal counter-pressures and to the evolving changes in Germany's fortunes. Belev's success was therefore limited to the deportation of somewhat more than eleven thousand Jews from the newly annexed areas of Macedonia and Thrace.[11]

Romania's losses had occurred in the course of a few months in 1940. Territory had to be ceded to Hungary, Bulgaria, and the USSR. In 1941, Romania reacquired its eastern provinces from the Soviet Union and occupied a portion of Ukraine. Unlike Bulgaria, however, Romania had to commit its army in bitter fighting for these gains.

At the beginning of September 1940, immediately following the trauma of the three amputations, Romania acquired a dictator, General Ion Antonescu. A veteran of the First World War, when Romania had fought against Austria-Hungary and Germany, Antonescu was a Chief of Staff of the Romanian army in the 1930s. Openly right wing, he allied himself with the Iron Guard, a mystical religious-nationalist movement that was hostile not only to Romania's neighbors but to the three quarters of a million Jews who lived within Romania's pre-1940 boundaries. As one of the Iron Guard's intellectual spokesmen, Mircea Eliade, wrote in 1936: "[W]e are waiting for a nationalist Romania, frenzied and chauvinistic, armed and vigorous, pitiless and vengeful."[12]

The Iron Guard held several portfolios in Antonescu's initial cabinet, but in January 1941 it launched a revolt, in the process of which it also slaughtered Jews in and around Bucharest. The uprising failed, as Germany decided to trust Antonescu. Within months the frenzy came at the hands of Antonescu's army and gendarmerie.

A few days after Romania's entry into the war, violence engulfed the Jewish community of the city of Iasi, leaving several thousand dead. When Bukovina and Bessarabia were retaken, Antonescu ordered the expulsion of the Jews in these regions across the Dnestr River. This time the deaths were in the tens of thousands. After a Romanian general with his staff were killed in an explosion at their headquarters in the captured Soviet city of Odessa, Antonescu ordered a reprisal in the ratio of one to one hundred. The ensuing massacre of Jews was the largest in Europe. More mass dying of the expellees and more mass shootings of Soviet Jews followed in the wake of these events.

In the meantime, the Romanian bureaucracy imposed decree after decree on the Jewish population of Old Romania. A commissariat was established under a former newspaper correspondent of the Nazi party's *Völkischer Beobachter*, Radu Lecca. It is Lecca who was to hand over the remaining Romanian Jews to the Germans for deportation to Poland. At this point, however, the Romanian destruction process was frozen.

Antonescu was a man who had always had contacts with Jews and who never stopped arguing and talking with them. In an open letter to a Jewish leader, he attempted to justify the uprooting of Bukovinian and Bessarabian Jewry by claiming that during the one-year Soviet rule and in the course of the Soviet retreat, they had been loyal to the Soviet Union. Nevertheless, he subsequently received a two-man delegation and allowed himself to be convinced not to introduce the Jewish star. After the summer of 1942, he was no longer accessible to German demands for deportations, and in 1943 he explicitly forbade any German killing of Jews in Soviet areas under Romanian occupation. The war was being lost, and Romania's frenzy had spent itself.[13]

Compared to Romania, Hungary was more stable and controlled. Its long-time leader was the Prince Regent, Admiral Miklós Horthy. His rank stemmed from his service as Commander in Chief of the Austro-Hungarian navy. Hungary, which is landlocked, had no navy. Horthy came to prominence in the turmoil of 1919 and 1920, when a Hungarian Communist government under Béla Kun, a Jew, dissolved under the impact of a Romanian invasion, and Communists were hunted by counter-revolutionary forces. A self-proclaimed anti-Semite of the old school, Horthy could stare down any upstarts approaching him with extreme ideas. He knew the role that Jews played in Hungary's economy, and he was not about to surrender the country's material fortunes to incompetent, self-seeking opportunists. He did want to raise the Hungarian flag in neighboring territories inhabited by Hungarians, and in pursuance of this aim, Hungary rapidly enlarged itself between 1938 and 1941 at the expense of Czechoslovakia, Romania, and Yugoslavia. All of these acquisitions were made possible by Germany and soon enough the price for them was to be paid. Hungary entered the war against the Soviet Union, and Hungarian measures were instituted against the Jews. By German standards, however, both of these efforts were limited. Hungary stopped short of fighting all out, and beyond the broad sweep of its economic constriction of the Jews, it refused to deport them. In March 1944, the Germans occupied Hungary and from May to July deported 450,000 Jews with matchless efficiency. Horthy, who was smarting under the German intervention, heard the protests of Allied and neutral governments. Before the deportations reached Budapest, he stopped them. A few months later, the Germans replaced him with an extremist. By then the transport of Jews to Auschwitz was no longer feasible.[14]

Laval, Antonescu, and Horthy were not political extremists and there was comparatively little room in their governments for such people. Too many of the revolutionaries on the ideological Right lacked the credibility of traditional leadership. The movements of the ultraists were either imitations of Nazism or were assumed to be Germany's tools. Only in Slovakia and Croatia did extremists monopolize governmental power from the start, but these countries were German products. Germany needed the nationalists of the Hlinka party in Slovakia and the Ustasha movement in Croatia, and to these groups in turn Germany presented the only chance of survival. Hence they aligned themselves with Germany fully, contributing soldiers to the campaign against the USSR and moving against their Jews. Croatia struck out at its Jewish inhabitants with heavy shootings, while Slovakia was the pliant satellite falling into step with Germany's expectations. The only independence they manifested in Jewish affairs was in their protection of favored Jews.

After three years of war, the situation gradually changed in all of Germany's domains. In France during November 1942, Italy in September 1943, Slovakia in August 1944, and Hungary during the following November, German forces intervened physically to prevent a further deterioration of Germany's position. The indigenous bureaucracies still functioned, still collaborated, but they were no longer relied on as before. To round up the remaining Jews, the Germans were increasingly dependent on ultra parties and their motley crews of helpers.

8

NON-GERMAN VOLUNTEERS

WHEN GERMANY MOVED north, west, south, and east to occupy territories, German civilian personnel, army garrisons, and police in these regions were spread thin. The occupation regime could be an overseer, and it could provide a core of the enforcement mechanisms, but it could seldom act alone to maintain basic services and public order. Still less could it rely wholly on its own resources for such tasks as the confiscation of harvests, the impressment of labor, the combating of partisans, and the guarding or killing of Jews. For all these missions, German agencies employed local mayors, indigenous police, and assorted militia. The non-German helpers were approved holdovers, or newly recruited, or, sometimes, self-organized. Not unexpectedly, they also varied in their motivations. Some of these men wanted to avoid hard physical labor; others wanted privileges or prestige; still others were inspired by conviction; but in essence they all served voluntarily.

In France, a number of ideologically based organizations furnished French manpower for the Nazi crusade. Thus a group of right-wing organizers led by Eugene Deloncle in occupied Paris formed the Légion des Volontaires Français Contre le Bolchevisme shortly after the German invasion of the Soviet Union. The legion, eventually a regiment of the German army, was to participate in the campaign on the Eastern Front,[1] but in December 1942, French legionnaires training in the Radom District at Kruszyna in occupied Poland had an opportunity to kill Polish Jews. By that time, most of the Jewish inhabitants of the area had already been deported, and clusters of remaining Jews, kept in labor camps, were gradually thinned out as well. According to a German gendarmerie lieutenant, Jewish police had caused anxiety among the 552 Jewish laborers in Kruszyna by telling them that they were "next." The lieutenant had only two German gendarmes and eight men of the French legion lent to him by the German army, when he was attacked by Jews who tore his coat and scratched him. The Jews attempted to escape and the French opened fire on their own. With subsequent reinforcements of twenty-five Ukrainians and a larger number of French legionnaires, the Jewish breakout attempt was contained and 113 Jewish men lay dead in a wide circle around the encampment. "With special ardor," reported the lieutenant, "the Frenchmen charged solely with guard duty participated in finishing off the Jewish wounded."[2]

Militarized formations that remained in the French homeland offered their services in roundups during deportations, thereby providing backup for regular German and French police. One of these organizations was the Parti Populaire Français (PPF), established in 1936 by Jacques Doriot. Until 1934, Doriot had been an active Communist. When Marshal Pétain led French forces in support of Spanish troops in a campaign against Moroccan rebels in the early 1920s, Doriot handed out anti-war leaflets. Later he staged a Communist demonstration in the Place de la République in Paris. As a right-wing politician during the German occupation, Doriot had a number of followers in the Pétain administration, although—given his background—he did not have the trust of the Marshal himself. In occupied Paris, his party attracted more than a few adolescents, and when the first major roundup of Paris Jews was conducted in July 1942, some three hundred to four hundred Doriot youths in blue shirts with PPF armbands volunteered to assist in the seizures.[3] After German forces occupied the free zone in November 1942, the southern branch of the party, which consisted of congeries of ideologues, underworld characters, and individuals who wanted to avoid labor service in Germany, assisted the undermanned German and French police in tracking down Jews.[4]

Yet another militarized formation in France was the *milice*. Commanded by an adventurer who was also a First World War hero, Joseph Darnand, this organization was consecrated as an official body on January 30, 1943, after Vichy France was forced to demobilize its armistice army. The *milice* was now, as the French historian Jean-Pierre Azéma called it, the government's praetorian guard, fighting increasing numbers of French resisters. It also hunted down Jews trying to escape from the German dragnet in the former free zone.[5]

The French exremists had their counterparts in Italy. There the overthrow of Mussolini in the summer of 1943 and the subsequent surrender to the Allies by the government of Pietro Badoglio resulted in the occupation of northern and central Italy by the Germans and the reestablishment of a remnant Fascist regime with a relatively unreliable Italian police force. The skeletal SS and Police did, however, have the assistance of small, organized Fascist legions operating principally in Rome, Milan, and Florence, and partially supported by the Interior Ministry; a Milizia volontaria set up by the Fascist party and placed under the direction of an old Fascist, Renato Ricci; and finally uniformed Fascist party members formed into Black Brigades under Fascist Party Secretary Alessandro Pavolini.[6] In occupied Italy, only about a fifth of the more than forty thousand Jews were caught, but several thousand of them were arrested by Italians.[7]

Extremists were active also in Hungary. When Berlin no longer trusted Admiral Horthy to keep Hungary in the war, the German military, SS, and legation overthrew the aged Hungarian leader in October 1944. By then, the sole candidate who could completely satisfy German needs was the ultra-right-wing Arrow Cross leader Ferenc Szalasi. Most Jews had already been deported. Only the Jewish labor companies in the Hungarian army and the Jewish community in Budapest were still intact. It was too late for renewed deportations to Auschwitz, but not for death marches of Jewish laborers and for roving Arrow Crossists in Budapest, who shot thousands of Jews on the banks of the Danube and threw them into the icy river.[8]

In Slovakia, a revolt broke out in the summer of 1944. Fearing defections, German forces disarmed the Slovak army and went on to crush the insurgents. Thousands of Jews who had been bypassed as essential or privileged during the 1942 deportations were rounded up with the help of Slovak police and militarized units of the Hlinka party. For the Hlinka guards, this occasion was not a debut. They had been volunteers for seizures of Jews in 1942, and there is nothing to indicate that they failed to perform their assignment two years later. In these twilight hours of the war, the German Security Service did notice, however, that corrosion had reached the core of the last Slovak loyalists. One of these collaborators, Josef Nemsilla, was overheard to say in the air-raid shelter that the Allied bombs raining on innocent Slovaks should rather have been aimed at Hitler and all those Germans who had brought about this situation.[9]

The native auxiliaries in occupied France, Italy, Hungary, or Slovakia, who donned a uniform to fight partisans or join in the hunt for Jews, had emerged in the wake of weakened or collapsing governments. In Polish and Soviet territories, the setting was totally different. Here no satellite states were permitted to exist and, apart from indigenous central offices with limited functions in each of the three prewar Baltic republics, the highest echelon of non-German administration was a mayor or a rural chief. These local authorities were closely supervised by German military or civilian organs.

Polish municipalities, which were located in the Warsaw, Lublin, Radom, and Krakow districts of the Generalgouvernement, played only a peripheral role in the establishment and maintenance of ghettos. During the time of ghettoization, Polish mayors and chairmen of Jewish councils were both placed under direct German control in administratively parallel as well as separate positions. Polish mayors were concerned with ghettos mainly in financial questions and certain residual functions, such as public utilities. The nature of the official city-ghetto relationship in Warsaw is discernible from the diary of Adam Czerniakow, Chairman of the Jewish council in the ghetto. Mayor Julian Kulski rebated to Czerniakow fees collected from Jews, and at one point, when the question of reducing the size of the ghetto arose, he told Czerniakow that he would support him in arguments against such a change.[10]

Mayors in occupied Ukrainian territory were chosen by military government officers, sometimes in consultation with the Security Police. The appointments were not always successful. In Mariupol the mayor had to be replaced after it was discovered that he was married to a Jewish woman.[11] The mayor of Kremenchug was actually shot by the Security Police for protecting Jews.[12] In several cities, however, the mayors were assigned a variety of tasks in Jewish matters. After the Jewish population was shot in Nikolaev, the mayor was ordered to reserve Jewish furniture for the military and Jewish apartments for ethnic Germans who had lost the roofs over their heads.[13] In Kharkov, the municipality was charged with the registration of the entire population. The census was to be conducted street by street in December 1941. The names and addresses of Jews were written down on separate yellow sheets.[14] Shortly after this procedure was completed, the Jews were removed from their apartments and placed in a tractor factory from which they were taken out in batches to be shot.[15]

In the Byelorussian city of Borisov, which was under military administration, the local mayor was Stanislav Stankevich. According to an ethnic German whom Stankevich had recommended for the job of commanding the indigenous city police, a banquet was held on November 8, 1941, for about two hundred German and native policemen who had been pulled together from Borisov and other locations. The occasion was a planned action against the ghetto. With their food and drink, the men were treated to speeches by German army officers, representatives of the police, and Stankevich. On the next day, eight thousand Jews were shot. Stankevich transported the clothing of the dead from the grave site to the city for delivery to White Russian Self-Help, a welfare organization.[16]

In Lithuania, the German invasion of the USSR triggered an uprising by the Lithuanian Activist Front. Local Lithuanians fought the retreating Red Army in the Lithuanian capital of Kaunas, seizing the radio station and hoisting the Lithuanian flag hours before the vanguard of the German army reached the city on June 24, 1941. Two days later, a Lithuanian pogrom, instigated by the newly arrived German Security Police, resulted in the death of several thousand

Jews. At the beginning of July, a committee of Jews was summoned by the Security Police to be informed that the Jewish population would have to move into a ghetto. The measure was presented to the Jews as a means to preclude further violence against them. By that time, the Lithuanian Activist Front had established a rudimentary governmental structure, including a mayor's office in Kaunas. On July 10, the mayor, Kazys Palciauskas, issued an order for the ghetto's formation. His act was confirmed by the newly appointed German civilian Stadtkommissar, Hans Cramer, on July 31. The deadline for moving into the ghetto was August 15. Some thirty thousand Jews were to be squeezed into the Viliajampole quarter, a section without running water then housing about twelve thousand people. The Jewish Committee for the Transfer of the Jews to Viliajampole vainly appealed to the Germans and the Lithuanians for more space and time. Several meetings were held with Lithuanian municipal officials. After one of these talks, a Jewish negotiator, Anatolijus Rozenbliumas, characterized the conversation as overtly friendly, but he added that there was an undertone of pressure. The Lithuanians had insisted that the handling of the transfer would be even more stringent if the Jews did not comply with all demands.[17]

The Lithuanian municipality of Vilnius was busy with the orderly storage of furniture abandoned by Jews who had to move into two adjacent ghettos within the city. The warehouses of the city administration were not roomy enough to hold all these pieces, and Mayor Dabulevicius requested permission to use the synagogues outside the ghetto boundaries for the overflow.[18]

Agencies and units of indigenous police were a second tool in the hands of German occupation authorities in the east. The police were uniformed and armed, and their drastic activities were more direct than those of the mayoral offices, but they existed, like the municipal administrations, because they were needed by their German rulers.

Of all the native police forces in occupied Eastern Europe, those of Poland were least involved in anti-Jewish actions. Territorially, Polish police were confined in the main to the four original districts of the Generalgouvernement, where they numbered about fourteen thousand.[19] The Germans could not view them as collaborators, for in German eyes they were not even worthy of that role. They in turn could not join the Germans in major operations against Jews or Polish resistors, lest they be considered traitors by virtually every Polish onlooker. Their task in the destruction of the Jews was there-fore limited. In Warsaw, two policemen, one German and one Pol-ish, would stand outside a ghetto gate, and a Jewish policeman inside. In the countryside, where no photographs were taken, Polish police tracked down Jewish escapees.[20]

Within the territories wrested from the Soviet Union, the Ger-mans used police auxiliaries more freely. German disdain for local populations was not as great there as in Poland, and local reticence to collaborate with Germany was not as universal as that of the Poles. In a region ranging from the outskirts of Leningrad to the mountains of the Caucasus, new police forces came into being with rapidity. At first these eastern helpers were either self-organized or recruited by the army or the Security Police. Heinrich Himmler, who as chief of the SS and Police was an empire builder, seized the opportunity to bring a large number of them under his jurisdiction.[21]

The Security Police employed only a small percentage of these auxiliaries. The great bulk of the helpers, eventually hundreds of thousands, were placed under the command of the Order Police. Native personnel augmenting the Order Police were designated the *Schutzmannschaft*. Mirroring the organization of the Order Police in Germany, the Schutzmannschaft could be found in cities, rural districts, and battalions. The stationary component of the Schutz-mannschaft included Ukrainians, Byelorussians, Russians, Eston-ians, Lithuanians, and Latvians. The battalions, which were orga-nized by nationality, did not contain "Russians" but did include "Cossacks." Each battalion had an authorized strength of about five hundred and could be moved, sometimes far from its point of origin, to fight partisans or to kill Jews.

The multiplication of Schutzmannschaft battalions gave pause to Hitler himself. He did not want combat units of Ukrainians or Balts that could back claims for independence of their countries.[22] The momentum, however, could not be broken. In the final phase of the development, after most Jews in the area were already dead, a Ukrai-nian SS division was raised in Galicia, two Latvian divisions were fighting in the SS on the front, an Estonian SS division had been raised, Lithuanian police battalions were in action, and Russians were added to the German army.

In the lineup of nationalities under German control, the Ukrainian population was most numerous. Its size as of 1939 was 36,000,000, and the Ukrainian SSR as a whole was occupied by the Germans by 1942.[23]

The district of Galicia, which had been a part of Poland before the war, was incorporated into the Generalgouvernement in 1941. Because most of the inhabitants of Galicia were Ukrainian,[24] the SS and Police Leader of the district, Katzmann, envisaged a Ukrainian police of sixty-three officers and twenty-nine hundred men for his area. Given the history of Galicia under twenty years of Polish rule and two years of the Soviet flag, he did not have a trained reservoir of acceptable Ukrainians in such numbers. Accordingly he established a police school for Ukrainians in Lvov.[25] Less than a year later, Ukrainian police in Galicia were used extensively for roundups of Jews destined for the death camp Belzec, as well as for some shootings.[26]

East of Galicia, the initial Ukrainian police was a militia formed under the patronage of the German army. Generally the Ukrainian mayors were given the responsibility of organizing this force, assuring its political reliability, and paying for it out of local budgets.[27] German military government was not altogether at ease with the militia, and rules were laid down to limit its size and weapons.[28] Soon enough, the Order Police stepped in to take over these Ukrainians. Henceforth they were under stricter control and their salaries were paid by the German Reich.[29] As of July 1, 1942, Ukrainian police and firemen in stationary posts numbered 5,631 in the cities and 31,027 in rural areas.[30] As in the case of Galicia to the west, very few of these men were officers or even non-commissioned officers.[31] Everywhere, however, they far outnumbered German personnel. Typically, in the Brest-Litovsk area of Volhynia, German gendarmerie totaled 26 men and Ukrainian gendarmerie 308.[32]

Almost all the Jews left behind by the retreating Red Army in Ukrainian territory were killed. Einsatzgruppen composed of German Security Police, Order Police, and SS moved from city to city, shooting the victims or gassing them in vans. Almost from the beginning, Ukrainian militia were used in these killings as helpers. In

Zhitomir, for example, Ukrainians surrounded the Jewish quarter for the registration and killing of 3,145 Jews.[33] In Korosten, they drove 238 Jews into a building in preparation for an action.[34] In Kherson, a Ukrainian *Selbstschutz*, or "self-protection," group set up by Sonderkommando 11a helped seal off "execution" sites.[35] In Radomyshl, German Security Police shot 1,107 Jewish adults and Ukrainian militia shot 561 Jewish "youths."[36] In Kakhovka, a "cleansing" was conducted by a Ukrainian militia detachment consisting of twelve men under the command of an ethnic German, Oskar Ruf.[37] In Uman, there was an unplanned pogrom by Ukrainian militia and German soldiers, in the course of which Jewish apartments were demolished. This action displeased the Security Police, because it caused Jews to go into hiding.[38] Generally, however, the Security Police welcomed the presence of militia during killing operations, not only as auxiliaries, but as a means of involving at least a part of the Ukrainian population in the anti-Jewish measures.[39]

In Ukrainian areas quickly traversed in 1941 there was a second wave of shootings in 1942. This sequel was most intense in Volhynia, where hundreds of thousands of Jews were living in small ghettos. For the renewed killings, all available SS and Police forces were deployed along with the stationary Ukrainian police, now organized as a Schutzmannschaft.[40]

There were also Ukrainian Schutzmannschaft battalions, eighteen and a half of them by July 1, 1942.[41] In addition, the first three battalions set up in Byelorussia, and variously labeled as Ukrainian or White Ruthenian, were in fact staffed mostly by Ukrainians recruited in prisoner of war camps. In October 1941, when only a few members of the advancing Einsatzkommando 8 had been left behind in the Byelorussian capital of Minsk, the commander of this rear detachment, Sturmbannführer (Major) Hans-Hermann Remmers, received instructions to begin killing the local Jews in the Minsk Ghetto, inasmuch as room had to be created for German Jews who were going to be taken there. Remmers approached the SS and Police Leader, Brigadeführer (Brigadier General) Carl Zenner, and pointed out that he could not ask his handful of men to undertake such a morally burdensome task. Zenner promised indigenous help and Remmers, relieved, returned to his men to tell them: "Thank God, we are no longer going to have to do the shooting, the Ukrainians are doing it!"[42]

Still more Ukrainian prisoners of war who volunteered for service with the SS and Police were sent to a training camp at Trawniki in the Lublin District. The graduates of this camp became guards of ghettos and camps in the Generalgouvernement. They were the major component of the guard forces in the death camps of Belzec, Sobibor, and Treblinka, where one and a half million Jews were killed.[43] In the spring of 1943, a Trawniki training battalion was thrown into the battle of the Warsaw Ghetto. There, while shooting at the Jews, they suffered some casualties of their own.[44]

The Byelorussian population was not nearly as large as the Ukrainian, and the Byelorussian Schutzmannschaft numbered in the single thousands during 1942.[45] A single ethnically Byelorussian battalion was set up later. Yet the local Byelorussian police was used just as much as the Ukrainian. In the rural district of Baranovichi, which contained several ghettos, the gendarmerie forces in posts included 73 Germans and 816 native auxiliaries.[46] The gendarmerie commander of this district, Lieutenant Max Eibner, was instructed by the Gebietskommissar in charge of the district, Rudolf Werner, to "liberate" the countryside from the Jewish population so far as possible. For this purpose Eibner was to use the men at his disposal.[47] In compliance with the order, Eibner organized several shootings, for which he deployed his German gendarmerie and his Byelorussian Schutzmannschaft.[48]

A major role in the east was played by Baltic police. This fact is remarkable, because the Baltic population was rather small. As of 1939, the number of Estonians, Latvians, and Lithuanians was less than five million all together.[49] The history, however, of the Baltic nations differed from that of their neighbors. They had had twenty years of independence, followed by a single year of Soviet rule. Officers and men who had served in the armed forces of the three countries, students and graduates of national universities, as well as members of nationalist movements and organizations were still on the scene when the German invasion began. Their anti-Soviet feelings were intense and to Germany they looked for deliverance and restoration of their independence. In German eyes, these men were a ready made auxiliary.[50] The Reich did not permit the formation of Baltic governments or autonomous Baltic armies, but it encouraged the growth of the indigenous police, which equaled in size the Ukrainian and which had three times as many officers as the Ukrainian Schutzmannschaft.[51] Moreover, Balts were not only in the Order Police but served under the aegis of the Security Police as well. During the first weeks of the German occupation, Baltic volunteers took the initiative, striking out at Jews and suspected Communists to such an extent that the commander of the rear area of Army Group North ordered the cessation of all their self-empowered arrests and shootings. From now on, he decreed, they would have to confine themselves to actions authorized by German offices or an indigenous judicial arrest warrant.[52]

The smallest Baltic population, little more than a million, was the Estonian. The prewar Jewish inhabitants of Estonia numbered only some four thousand, and because the German army did not reach northern Estonia for a while, most were able to flee. The first Estonian police collaborators were called Okamaitse, literally "self-defense," or Selbstschutz. Although subordinated to the German army, they were available to Sturmbannführer Martin Sandberger, Commander of Einsatzkommando 1, whose force was only about a hundred. The Selbstschutz rounded up a thousand Jews in Tallin, Dorpat, and various towns. Between September 26 and 29, 1941, the Einsatzkommando and its Estonian helpers shot 440 Jewish men, sparing the Jewish council members and physicians. (The women and children were subsequently transferred from a camp in Harku, near Tallin, to the Russian city of Pskov, outside Estonia, where they were shot.)[53]

Although the Jews of Estonia were gone, Estonian police were still in the killing business. By 1942, Sandberger had his own Estonian Security Police, organized under the Estonian Major Ain-Ervin Mere, with criminal police and political police components. When a transport from the Theresienstadt Ghetto in Bohemia-Moravia arrived in Raasiku, Estonia, on September 5, 1942, with a thousand

Jews, almost all the deportees were shot, mainly by Estonian Security Police posted to the camp Jägala. The same fate was meted out to a Berlin transport that came a week later.[54]

In 1943 and 1944, there was a regular concentration camp in Estonia: the Vaivara complex. Commanded by Hauptsturmführer Hans Aumeier and staffed by German and Estonian guards, Vaivara received several thousand Jewish workers for shale oil production from the remnant ghettos of Kaunas and Vilnius. When the Red Army suddenly appeared at the subcamp of Klooga in September 1944, two thousand inmates were shot. The Soviet vanguard found bodies still burning.[55]

The 2 million Lithuanians constituted the largest Baltic population. The Jews of Lithuania were also the most numerous in the region. Prior to the German invasion, more than 250,000 Jews lived in the Lithuanian SSR, which included most of the territory of pre-war independent Lithuania and the newly attached area of Vilnius.[56] About 90 percent of the Jews, unable to escape, remained behind in June 1941.

In the old Lithuanian heartland, many of the police collaborators were drawn from partisans who started an anti-Soviet uprising under the umbrella of the Lithuanian National Front during the first hours of the German invasion. One group, specifically mentioned by the German Security Police, consisted of about six hundred laborers under the command of a journalist, Jonas Klimaitis.[57] With Security Police encouragement, this group killed about thirty-eight hundred Jews in Kaunas and twelve hundred in other towns.[58] The partisans in the Kaunas area were soon disbanded by the military. "Reliable" men were selected from their ranks and formed into five police companies. Two of the companies were assigned to Sonderkommando 1b, which used them immediately for major shootings in Kaunas.[59] Lithuanian helpers also made themselves useful in smaller cities. As early as July 1941, the Lithuanian police of Mariyampole (Kapsukas) prepared lists of "Jews" and "Lithuanians."[60] Inside and outside Kaunas, the killings were continued by Einsatzkommando 3, which noted on September 19, 1941, that a total of 46,692 people, the overwhelming majority of whom were Jews, had been shot with the help of Lithuanian partisans.[61] The killings inundated dozens of localities through the rest of the year. In many of these towns, local Lithuanian police and instant volunteers pitched in, seizing the Jews, holding them for the arrival of a detachment of the Einsatzkommando, and joining in the shootings.[62]

In the Vilnius region, where Lithuanians were only about 6 percent of the population, the German army found 3,600 deserters from the 29th (Lithuanian) Territorial Corps of the Red Army, already assembled and ready for an assignment.[63] By the beginning of July, 150 Lithuanians in Vilnius were employed by Einsatzkommando 9 to round up and shoot 500 Jews a day.[64] When the Jews of Vilnius were subjected to ghettoization two months later, Lithuanian police and freelancing "Selbstschutz" in the city lent a hand. At 6:00 A.M. on September 6, 1941, the police conducted the Jews to the ghetto site and the Selbstschutz formed a cordon around the ghetto to prevent escapes.[65]

When Lithuanian Schutzmannschaft battalions were set up, many of these units were sent out from their homeland to other regions. The first of the border crossers were the Lithuanian companies of Major Lechthaler's 11th Reserve Police Battalion, which killed thousands of Jews in Byelorussia. During August and September 1942, two Lithuanian battalions took part in "Operation Swamp Fever," which covered the marshes of Byelorussia and Ukraine. In this expedition, more than eighty-three hundred Jews were killed.[66] Two other battalions were posted in succession to the death camp of Maydanek (Lublin).[67] Lithuanian battalions ranged all the way to the southern Ukraine, eight hundred miles from the Lithuanian frontier, where they guarded Jewish laborers.

On a per capita basis, the Latvians, numbering some 1,600,000, were represented as heavily as any nation in the destruction of the Jews. As soon as German forces reached the Latvian capital of Riga on July 1, 1941, volunteers banded together with German approval. Among the entrants into the new auxiliary were officers and soldiers who had served in the army of independent Latvia; soldiers who had been discharged or who had deserted from the 24th (Latvian) Territorial Rifle Corps of the Red Army; former members of the *Aiszargi*, the civil guard, which had been maintained by the prewar Latvian state; members and sympathizers of the Perkonkrust, a right-wing movement that was extreme enough to have been outlawed while Latvia was still independent; university graduates who had belonged to fraternities; athletes and gymnastics teachers; relatives of Latvians deported by the Soviets; and assorted youths.[68] Not prevalent in this conglomeration were professional policemen, many of whom had been purged and arrested by the Soviet regime. Only 10 percent of the old police force served in the Latvian police under German rule.[69]

During July and August 1941, the principal German actors on the Latvian scene were the Security Police and the armed forces. The Chief of Security Police's Einsatzgruppe A, Walter Stahlecker, wanted to unleash some local violence against the Latvian Jews, who numbered seventy thousand when the Germans arrived. As early as July 1, the Einsatzgruppe was in contact with Latvian personalities, notably Viktors Arajs, a young man of humble background born in a small town in 1910 who had attended the University of Riga, where he had managed to join the "aristocratic" Lettonia fraternity. He had received a law degree in March 1941, when Latvia was under Soviet rule, but he had also defended Latvian peasants threatened with expropriation by Soviet authorities, and he had gone into hiding before the German invasion. During the summer and fall 1941, Arajs gathered a few hundred men. They served the Einsatzgruppe and did its work.[70]

The German armed forces, which included a naval command in the port city of Liepaja and army Kommandanturen in the interior, had jurisdiction over a much larger, albeit more amorphous indigenous police force, which was called Hilfspolizei or Selbstschutz. The organizers of this force were two officers of the old Latvian army, Lieutenant Colonel Voldermars Veiss and his deputy, Lieutenant Colonel Roberts Osis. One of the territorial commanders of the Selbstschutz was Lieutenant Colonel Karlis Lobe in the Ventspils area. After civil administration was established in Latvia at the beginning of September, the Selbstschutz was pruned and transformed into a Schutzmannschaft with stationary components and battalions.

The pogrom-like violence envisaged by Stahlecker was slow to start. In Riga, the toll was 400.[71] In Liepaja, Latvian "civilians" with armbands and rifles drove Jews in trucks to an area near the beach, where the victims were shot.[72] In Daugavpils, in the southeast of the country, where Latvians were only about a third of the population among Russians, Poles, and Jews, the Latvian residents hesitated to organize themselves and "confront" the Jewish inhabitants.[73] To be sure, this situation was soon remedied and the Latvian Selbstschutz there was engaged in massive shootings.[74] In Jelgava, south of the capital, the Security Police observed a similar lethargy but reported with satisfaction that finally the "population" had killed all the 1,550 Jews in the city and its environs.[75]

If, in the early days, Latvians appeared to be less spontaneous than their Estonian and Lithuanian neighbors, their efficiency increased over time. In Riga, the police prefecture and the central prison were used as holding pens for Jewish men whom the Arajs Kommando removed in batches to a shooting site in the woods. In a number of towns, Arajs men arrived in blue buses to shoot the Jews concentrated by local Latvian police. By mid-October, more than thirty thousand Latvian Jews had been killed by German and Latvian police forces.[76] Most of the remainder were shoved into a ghetto in Riga.

The sojourn of the survivors in the Riga Ghetto was brief. Transports of German Jews were due in the city, and to make room for the deportees, Higher SS and Police Leader Friedrich Jeckeln struck at the ghetto at the end of November and the beginning of December, killing another 27,800 Jews.[77] All available forces were thrown into this action: German police, a Schutzmannschaft battalion, Arajs men, Riga precinct police, and Riga harbor police.[78] At the conclusion of the operation, Lieutenant Alberts Danskops of the Arajs Kommando was observed with a mandolin, playing Chopin's funeral march, as he led a group of 450 Jews dragged out of hiding to the old cemetery, where they were shot.[79]

By 1942, Latvian police battalions made their appearance in Ukraine, Byelorussia, and the Generalgouvernement. In Byelorussia they assisted in shootings of Jews.[80] In Warsaw two battalions helped in the roundup of 300,000 Jews, who were sent from the ghetto to the death camp of Treblinka.[81] Gradually, more than 100,000 Latvians wore a German uniform. Thirteen thousand of them were casualties by July 1, 1944, among them Colonel Veiss, killed as a regimental commander in the 19th (Latvian) SS Grenadier Division.[82] Viktors Arajs fought as a battalion commander, first in the 15th, then in the 19th Latvian SS divisions. Years later he was tried in a German court and sentenced to life imprisonment.

On February 24, 1942, a small incident occurred in the 19th (Latvian) Schutzmannschaft battalion. A young recruit in the battalion approached his commanding officer, Lieutenant Colonel Roberts Osis, with a request for a transfer to the Security Police. In the presence of a fellow lieutenant colonel, Carlis Lobe, Osis asked the young man whether he would prefer shooting Jews to service in a regular unit among true warriors. When the recruit said that he wanted to go to the front, Osis replied that no one in the Security Police was fighting there. Then Osis told him that he was too young to shoot Jews. If Osis was going to let him have his wish, what would this young man do ten years later, when he would see the dead bodies of Jews in his dreams? The young man launched an official complaint, reciting disparaging remarks by Osis and Lobe about the Security Police. The accusation was read by the two ranking German Security Police and Order Police commanders in the Baltic-Byelorussian area. Lobe, defending himself, pointed out that the complainant was seventeen or eighteen years old, that he had wanted to shoot Jews, and that Lobe had told him that he was unfit. As to Lobe's own experience, he only had to point to his record: During the previous year he had personally led the "cleansing action" in the area of Ventspils and Kuldiga.[83]

PART II

VICTIMS

9

THE JEWISH LEADERS

A UBIQUITOUS FEATURE of Nazi domination of the Jewish communities was the system of *Judenräte*, or Jewish councils. These governing bodies were established under law or decree, or simply in pursuance of oral instructions. The councils were designed to serve two purposes. Primarily they were to be conduits for regulations imposed upon the Jews, but they were also intended to be the principal or exclusive channel for petitions or appeals from the captive victims to the perpetrators. The Germans did not want to deal with the Jews individually.

The role of the councils was consequently different from the activity of their peacetime predecessors. In prewar times, the various Jewish community organizations were essentially caretakers of synagogues, cemeteries, religious schools, and hospitals. The councils, on the other hand, were faced with massive Jewish unemployment, crowding, hunger, and epidemics. Long before Hitler came to power, Jewish leaders were concerned about improving the Jewish situation; now they pleaded for mitigations or postponements of harsh restrictions and impositions. In earlier days, the Jewish communities would employ administrators, bookkeepers, and clerks to run community institutions; the new councils also established a regulatory bureaucracy, and in the east, where they were ghetto governments, they maintained a standing Jewish police force as well. Once, the Jewish leaders had carried out only a Jewish mission, but as members or functionaries of councils they were expected to enforce a multitude of peremptory demands of "the authorities," be it the supply of statistical information, the surrender of Jewish belongings, the recruitment of forced laborers, or the seizure of people for deportation. As one German official summarized the new system, "Jews who disobey instructions of the Jewish council are to be treated as saboteurs."[1]

The aggregate membership of the councils is numbered in the many thousands. The principal reason for this high figure is geographic. Only in Central and Western Europe were councils set up on a country by country basis. In the east they were placed in charge of local communities city by city and town by town. It is true that there were more Jews in the Warsaw Ghetto than in France, more in the Lodz Ghetto than in Belgium, but most of the hundreds of ghettos in the east had relatively small populations, and in each of these communities there was a council burdened with problems as crushing as any. The size of the councils could vary. Twenty-four members was the rule for countries or cities, twelve or fewer for towns. In some regions or localities no councils were formed. They were dispensed with where killing began immediately, as in Croatia and Serbia or the cities of Dnepropetrovsk and Kiev in the occupied USSR. Councils were absent also in Denmark and Italy, two countries that had resisted German pressure. No council came into being in Athens, after local Jewish leaders decided with Greek backing to disappear in the mountains. By and large, however, councils covered the German-dominated continent.

Ordinarily, German agencies made no attempt to find out who was who in a Jewish community. The appointment process in a newly occupied city would often consist of a short search for a recognizable Jewish leader who would be told to fill a council with the requisite number of men. There were no specific rules for eligibility. Typically, an order by Security Police Chief Reinhard Heydrich to his mobile units operating behind the lines of German armies invading Poland in 1939 stated that councils were made up "so far as possible" of the "remaining suitable personalities" and rabbis.[2] Not stated but self-explanatory was the requirement that council chairmen and key council members would be fluent in German.

Who then served on the councils? The appointments were overwhelmingly conventional. Choices had to be made quickly and the candidates were people who could be called upon on short notice. In the main, they were businessmen, professionals, religious figures, or prewar Jewish community officials. Younger men were elevated primarily in smaller towns.[3] Women in leadership positions were rare. It would not have occurred to anyone to suggest a Communist or, for that matter, an ultra-religious Jew, whose garments and earlocks would have given offense to the Germans.[4]

The first chairman of a Jewish council was Rabbi Leo Baeck. By background and appearance he was ideal for the post. The son of a rabbi who had written books, Baeck himself became a rabbi who wrote books. He belonged to the liberal branch of Judaism, while remaining traditional in his practice of the religion. Not a Zionist, he did not condemn the Zionist movement. When the First World War broke out, he volunteered to be "field rabbi," a position that did not make him a chaplain, inasmuch as the German army accorded this status only to Protestant and Catholic clergymen, but that did allow him to wear a German uniform and to pray publicly for the Emperor and for Germany.

Tall and bearded, Baeck was married to a rabbi's daughter, who was his perfect wife until her death in 1937. He had a pulpit and a teaching position in a liberal Jewish seminary. At home his private library was located in a room equipped with a ladder on wheels running along the bookshelves.[5] During the 1920s Baeck was also active in Jewish community politics, and in 1933 he was hoisted by his supporters into the top position of the newly formed Reich Representation of Jewish Land Federations.[6]

Between 1933 and 1939, the Nazi regime gradually impoverished the Jews and called for their emigration. At this point the Jewish community organizations increased their welfare work and tried to facilitate the departure of families, children, and adolescents. By 1938 this machinery was taken over by the Gestapo. Baeck, still at the helm, was sixty-five years old. Having turned down all opportunities for emigration, he was determined to stay at his post as long as ten Jews were left in Germany. Baeck projected reliability and respectability to the remaining Jews, and together with his associates he also presented to the community a constellation of reassuring familiar faces.

After the outbreak of war, however, the Reichsvereinigung, as the Jewish council was called in Germany, was drawn into such activities as pushing Jewish families into Jewish apartment houses and preparing victims for transport to the east. Under orders of the Gestapo, Baeck's subordinates assigned space, resources, and personnel for the efficient conduct of the deportations. Baeck himself presided at meetings of the Reichsvereinigung during these twilight hours of German Jewry, but the protocols reveal only a shadowy figure who did not speak. In January 1943, Baeck was sent to the "Old People's Ghetto" of Theresiendstadt. More than ten Jews were left in Germany, but they were a small fraction of the Jewish population before 1933.[7]

In Austria, which was annexed in March 1938, almost all the Jews lived in Vienna. The Jewish community leaders in the city were immediately placed under arrest, and the SS brought in a "practitioner" who would know what to do with them. The practitioner was Adolf Eichmann. His first move was to reject the president of the Jewish community, Dr. Desider Friedmann, perhaps because Friedmann had been a member of a lodge or because he had accompanied the last Austrian chancellor on an economic mission. Instead Eichmann selected Dr. Josef Löwenherz, who was the vice president of the prewar community and also a veteran Zionist, but who was managerial and considered non-partisan in intra-Jewish politics. At the first meeting of Eichmann and Löwenherz, the thirty-two-year-old SS lieutenant slapped the stately Jewish leader, who was twenty years his senior, and gave him his instructions.[8] As Eichmann wrote to a friend in the SS: He had the Jewish leaders trotting along and working diligently.[9] Löwenherz in fact worked in Vienna until the Red Army occupied the city seven years later. Most of Austria's Jews emigrated in 1938 and 1939, but the large majority of the remainder were deported in 1941 and 1942, with the diligent assistance of the community machinery.

Continuity was also common in occupied Poland. The Lublin

Judenrat was virtually in its entirety the prewar Jewish leadership. In Warsaw, the peacetime president of the Jewish community had fled and his place was taken by his fifty-nine-year-old deputy, Adam Czerniakow. An engineer, Czerniakow had been trained in Germany before the First World War and had held administrative posts in Poland between the wars. As chairman of the Warsaw Jewish Council he had harsh words for Jewish leaders who had fled or emigrated right after the German invasion. He considered them deserters.[10]

A deputy of another kind was Chaim Rumkowski, the Jewish "Elder" of Lodz. In that city, the prewar president was also gone, the vice president moved to the top post, and Rumkowski became the new vice president. Early during the occupation most of the new council members were shot and Rumkowski was chosen as the Jewish leader by the German overlords. Tall, blue-eyed, silver-haired, and clean-shaven, he was sixty-two years old. He did not have much education, and as a merchant before and after the First World War he experienced one or two business failures, but he attempted to discharge his debts. A Zionist, he involved himself in community affairs and managed several orphanages with devotion. Widowed and childless, he became a dedicated autocrat in the ghetto. He was able to act alone, because the fear-stricken men who had replaced the murdered councilmen were merely his advisory board.

Increasingly self-assured, Rumkowski accustomed himself to power. Now he could reward friends and intimidate adversaries. With every step he focused attention on his unique position. When he married again, he chose a woman less than half his age. When bank notes were printed in the ghetto, they bore his likeness. Frequently he made speeches with phrases like "I do not like to waste words," "My plan is based on sound logic," "I have decided," "I ordered," "I forbid," and "My Jews." Rumkowski presided over his community through periods of starvation and deportations for almost five years.[11]

In Bialystok, power was given by the council to an engineer, Ephraim Barasz, because the council chairman, Rabbi Gedalia Rosenman, was too feeble to hold the office in more than a titular way. Barasz, like many major Jewish leaders in Poland, was a Zionist. Born in a smaller town nearby, he moved to Bialystok in 1934 and became the genuine manager of the community organization. Between 1939 and 1941 the city was under Soviet rule. When the Germans occupied Bialystok, Barasz became the vice chairman of the council. He was forty-nine. Although the council met periodically under Rosenman, Barasz was clearly the man in charge. At a meeting of June 29, 1942, a council member effusively praised Barasz. The council, he said, had become a government and Barasz its prime minister, "as well as the minister of the interior, minister of industry, because in the ghetto everything must be concentrated in one hand."[12]

Control was also solidified in one man in Vilnius, but there the process took longer and it was the outcome of massive upheavals and dire insecurity in the Jewish community. Like Bialystok, Vilnius was incorporated to the USSR from 1939 to 1941, but unlike the Bialystok Jews, the community in Vilnius lost more than half of its residents in several waves of shootings during the initial months of the German occupation. A Judenrat was formed immediately upon orders of the military commander, but most of its members, including the chairman, were killed after a brief period. Following this massacre, two ghettos were established, each with its own Judenrat. Soon there was a partial exchange of population. Old people, the ill, orphans, and the unemployed were sent to Ghetto No. 2. Artisans and holders of work permits were moved to Ghetto No. 1. Ghetto No. 2 was doomed and during the following year, Ghetto No. 1 became a disciplined, tightly run community. The prime mover of this militarization was the ghetto's police chief, Jacob Gens. By the middle of 1942, he was named by the German overseers as the "Ghetto Representative," and the Judenrat chairman, Anatol Fried, became his deputy in an outright switch of positions.[13]

Gens was thirty-nine nears old when he took over the reins of the Vilnius ghetto. In his youth he pursued academic studies, which he interrupted to join the newly formed Lithuanian army at the age of sixteen. There he rose to the rank of Senior Lieutenant and married a non-Jewish Lithuanian woman who was also well educated. He wanted a transfer from the infantry to the nascent Lithuanian air force, but the air arm accepted only bachelors. Gens then continued his studies at the university, remaining a reserve officer. He taught languages, literature, and physical education in a Jewish high school, moved to Kaunas with his wife and baby daughter, and eventually worked for the Shell Oil Corporation. Gens was a Lithuanian patriot who made anti-Soviet speeches, but he was also a conscious Jew who followed the right-wing militant Zionist movement, known as the Revisionists and led by Vladimir Jabotinsky. This man, who died in 1940, had preached that if Jews would not liquidate the Diaspora, the Diaspora would liquidate the Jews. Gens, working hard, stayed in Lithuania. Under the gathering war clouds of the late 1930s he was called back into the army, attended staff officers school, and was promoted to captain. When the Soviets arrived, he lost his job and was in danger of being purged. He found refuge in Vilnius.

As police chief of Ghetto No. 1, Gens appointed several Revisionists to key positions in his department. When some of the inhabitants of Ghetto No. 2 tried to slip into his ghetto, he opposed the infiltration on the ground that the ill, the old, and the unskilled would add to the vulnerability of people who were healthier, younger, and more capable. Later, as Representative, he mobilized all the resources of the ghetto to make it a workshop, staking everything on its survivability until the moment of liberation. Like all Jews, Gens was subject to ghettoization, but as a practical matter, he did not have to be in the ghetto at all. He probably could have found refuge with the help of former Lithuanian army associates, and that of his wife, who was living at his insistence outside the ghetto. Alternatively he might have escaped to fight with Jewish partisans, who would have welcomed him as a trained military officer. But he chose to remain and be judged by history.

In emphasizing a policy of accommodation and production, Gens did not differ from other ghetto potentates. The Vilnius Ghetto, however, had a Jewish resistance movement, which he tolerated, but with which he was in competition. He was going to join it if all else failed; in the meantime he held it in check. Gens, sure of himself, persisted in his course, even while the resisters were in a quandary over the question of risking severe German retaliation for a chance to fight. In this contest Gens prevailed. He drove a wedge between the organizers of resistance and the ghetto community. The people followed *him*.[14]

*   *   *

From the examples of Baeck, Löwenherz, Czerniakow, Rumkowski, Barasz, and Gens, one can see a spectrum of leaders and types of leadership, from old officeholders to emerging crisis managers, and from a traditional superintendency to the aggressive and internally unhampered decision making of a dictator. What had not occurred in Germany, Austria, or the principal cities in Poland was a major argument about whether there should be a Jewish council at all. Such debates did take place in the Netherlands, France, and Romania.

The discussion in the Netherlands was relatively short. A suspended Supreme Court judge, Lodewijk Ernst Visser, opposed the council, and a classics professor, David Cohen, asserted that idealists like Visser could always look down on those who adopted a realistic path, but that realism was inevitable. Visser died very soon after expressing his view, and Cohen, together with the diamond merchant Abraham Asscher, served in the council as co-chairmen.[15]

In France and Romania the outcome was not the clear ascendancy of one faction over another, but a divided power center, with challenges and tensions. The Jewish council in France (the Union générale des Israelites de France, abbreviated UGIF) was formed after a lengthy deliberation at the end of 1941. Its creation was a demand of the French Vichy regime, and thus the UGIF was to be answerable to a government that was itself subject to German control, completely so in the occupied north, and after November 1942 also in the south. Those who by reason of their activities or prominence had been suggested by Vichy to become members of the new body had a choice. They could accept or refuse, although in the latter case someone else might be named.

One who dropped out was René Mayer, born in 1895, veteran of the First World War, lawyer, chef-de-cabinet of a minister, Pierre Laval, in 1925, and active in management positions involving transportation and utilities. When France faced defeat in 1940, he was in London but made his way back to Paris. Early in 1941, he wanted the Vichy government to urge foreign Jews to leave France. His reservations about the UGIF were based not only on the fact that it was going to be a Judenrat but also on the fear that it would be a device to reduce the rights of French Jews to the level of Jewish immigrants. After his refusal to join the UGIF, he escaped to North Africa and joined Free French forces on the side of Britain.[16]

One of the candidates who did accept an appointment to the UGIF was Raymond-Raoul Lambert, born in 1894, veteran of the First World War, *chevalier de la légion d'honneur*, editor of a French Jewish weekly, and administrator of a committee assisting Jewish refugees from Germany. When the Second World War broke out, he returned to the army with the rank of captain. After his demobilization, he toyed with the idea of leaving France with his family, if only to spare his children the painful experience of discrimination against Jews, but he remained and took over the UGIF in the Southern Zone.[17]

Unlike Germany and other countries, where an old Jewish community organization was not allowed to coexist with a new Judenrat, France still had its peacetime Jewish Consistoire Central. In 1940, it was headed by the sixty-seven-year-old elder statesman Jacques-Edouard Helbronner, holder of the *croix de guerre* and cousin of two Rothschilds. He went to law school with Paul Gerlier (later a cardinal), served on the staff of War Minister Paul Painlevé in the First World War, and knew Marshal Philippe Pétain. When the UGIF was formed, he declined to accept its presidency or serve it as a member. He is reported to have opposed the idea of a protest by Cardinal Gerlier against the treatment of foreign Jews, lest French Jews be endangered. After German forces entered the Southern Zone, Lambert asked Helbronner to make an appeal to Premier Laval. Helbronner refused.[18]

In Romania the contrasting figures were Wilhelm Filderman and Nandor Gingold. Filderman, born in 1882, was an attorney. During the First World War he had been an officer in the Romanian army and by 1923 he became the president of the Romanian Jewish community organization, which in the 1930s became the Federation of Romanian Jews. The dangers facing the Jews of Romania prompted Filderman to address persistent appeals and protests to Romanian authorities. He wrote to Marshal Antonescu after the Jews of Bessarabia and Bukovina were pushed across the Dnestr. He went to the Marshal to have the Jewish star decree voided in Romania, and later he asked for mitigations in the exaction of special taxes and forced loans. For the deportees languishing in ghettos under Romanian control between the Dnestr and Bug rivers, he pledged his personal funds, albeit with the condition that American or other foreign Jewish organizations deposit in Swiss banks an equivalent sum for his personal use after the war.[19] The Romanian government was annoyed with Filderman, and once it arrested him, but the Romanians wavered enough to give him answers or even concessions.

Filderman and Gingold were opposites in almost every respect, but they were not opponents. As the de facto head of Romania's Judenrat, the Centrala, Gingold was insecure enough to meet with Filderman on occasion and to recruit a variety of assistants, including some Filderman supporters. Gingold did accept responsibility for publishing anti-Jewish regulations and handing over Jewish assets to the Romanian government. He was in his mid-thirties when he took the helm of the Centrala. Trained as a physician and a recent convert to Catholicism, he remained a patriotic Romanian even while Romanian army and gendarmerie units killed Bessarabian, Bukovinian, and Ukrainian Jews en masse. The Jews of Old Romania, he reasoned, did not have to fight at the front for Romania. Their contributions of property and labor were a substitute under the circumstances for the sacrifices demanded of a nation in a war. The government for its part was not impressed with Gingold, even though he did its work. He labored, unloved by Jews and unappreciated by the Romanians, in his Bucharest ivory tower, cut off from the world.[20]

The large majority of the Jewish leaders were convinced that on their own they could not reverse the process of destruction. Their single objective was stability. Change, which was welcomed at one time as a step toward betterment, was dreaded now, because it meant deterioration and harm. That is why these leaders tried to retard the downward trend, to save at least some people, or as a last resort to make the lot of everyone more bearable. In this struggle for postponements, exceptions, and mitigations, any pause was a respite, and even a new low would be turned into a foundation for new hope. The crowded disease-ridden ghetto as such had become the promise of a haven, and the imposition of forced labor a lifeline to survival.

In making their appeals, the Jewish leaders varied only in style.

When Filderman addressed Antonescu in protest against the deportations of the Bessarabian and Bukovinian Jews, he wrote the word:
"This is death, death, death." Seldom, however, was the Jewish
leadership so blunt. One did not mention the unmentionable, and
most often petitions were designed to achieve limited goals. Czerniakow in Warsaw appealed for the privilege of buying unrationed
foodstuffs for the ghetto. The Jewish leaders in Berlin asked for milk
to be sent along with children about to be deported. Barasz in Bialystok tried to lower a deportation quota, and the Hungarian Jewish
council, accepting deportation as a given, wanted it only to be carried out in a humane spirit. All of these particular petitions were
unsuccessful, as were most of the others, but pleas could never be
dispensed with. For the Jewish leadership, they were the only conceivable mode of dealing with the perpetrators.

In their internal deliberations, the leaders had two watchwords.
One was preserving the substance, the other salvation through work.
In Helbronner's mind, the substance was the old established French
Jewry. For Gens, it was the young and healthy part of the Jewish
population. In a crisis it did not include the elderly, the incapacitated,
or the "criminals." Once, when Gens sent his police from Vilnius to
the neighboring small ghetto of Oszmiania, he sacrificed people who
could not work anymore, preserving the remainder. Gens made it a
principle not to surrender young women and children. He did not in
any case have many of the latter.[21]

The exhortation to work had its basis in a fundamental principle.
Inasmuch as the ghettos were economic units, they had to trade
something for the meager supply of food and fuel, and to the extent
that ghetto production was essential to the Germans, it might save
the inmates from destruction. Not surprisingly, therefore,
Rumkowski and Gens strove to turn their ghettos into factories,
while Barasz voiced concern that the number of Jews working in the
Bialystok Ghetto was too small. This is what Barasz said in an extraordinary session of the Jewish council on October 11, 1942:

> Today we have called into the meeting all those who share with
> us the heavy burden of the ghetto in order to state quite openly
> where we stand in the world. Most recently the danger to the

district and city of Bialystok has come palpably close. That is why
we must try to avert it or push it into the future or at least reduce
its extent. Unfortunately, Bialystok had recently become the
second-largest ghetto after Lodz and therein lies the big danger.
The gaze of our enemies bores through us and only exceptional
circumstances can preserve us from disaster. The fire is lapping
from east to west and has almost reached our district. In order that
this fire does not spread further, we have to take exceptional measures in Bialystok itself. . . .

The crux of the danger lies in the percentage of 14,000 workers
among the 35,000 ghetto inhabitants. Even if the authorities did not
ask us for labor, we would have to attempt with all our strength to
penetrate the economy; so that, if one wished to annihilate us, a gap
would be created in the economy, and for this reason we would be
spared. Only then is there any hope for us; we cannot expect
mercy. . . .[22]

The Jewish leaders were in the cauldron themselves. They too
were victims. How, in these circumstances, did they judge their own
positions? The fewest of them would speak of wielding power, although they were conscious of knowing more than the Jewish multitude and of making decisions for the whole community. They did
not think that they enjoyed undeserved privileges, even though they
were aware that they ate better and were housed more spaciously
than most other Jews. They believed that their service was an obligation, and they were convinced with absolute certainty that they
carried the entire burden of caring for the Jewish population. In this
respect, even Rumkowski fits the mold. As he said at one time, "I
am no politician but just a work horse in heavy harness, pulling a
wagon loaded with 170,000 human lives."[23]

The Jewish leaders were, in short, remarkably similar in their
self-perception to rulers all over the world, but their role was not
normal and for most of them neither was their fate. The survivors
among them came mainly from the west. Leo Baeck of Berlin was
found in 1945, a prominent inmate of Theresienstadt. Remembered
by a large number of refugees who had left Germany before the war,
he was repeatedly honored and an institute was named after him. His

counterpart in Vienna, Josef Löwenherz, quietly took up residence in New York. He received no adulation at all. Löwenherz had an efficient assistant in Vienna, Rabbi Benjamin Murmelstein, who was heavily involved in deportations and who finally presided as the Elder in the Theresienstadt Ghetto. Murmelstein prudently chose a life of anonymity in Rome, where he was engaged in business activity. After his death in 1989, the Jewish Community of Rome refused to bury him near his wife, but allowed him a plot at the edge of the cemetery. The proconsuls of the Netherlands Community, Cohen and Asscher, were placed on trial before a Jewish court of honor, at which Asscher refused to appear. He died shortly afterward. Cohen was indicted by the Dutch government, but the charges were dropped. In Romania, Filderman resumed his old post as chief of the Jewish community but later left, pursued by the Communist government. Nandor Gingold of the Centrala had resigned his post before Romania's surrender upon his promotion to the status of an assimilated Romanian in 1944. In 1945, he was placed on trial for spoliation, sentenced to life imprisonment, but released to practice medicine for many years in a Bucharest clinic. René Mayer, who did not want to join the UGIF, became a cabinet member and premier in postwar France. Raymond-Raoul Lambert, the leader of the UGIF in the Southern Zone, was seized in 1942 and transported to Auschwitz, where he was gassed with his family. Lambert's opponent, the old, distinguished Jacques Helbronner, was arrested a few months later. He too was killed in Auschwitz. In Poland, the overwhelming majority of the Jewish leaders died with their communities. Adam Czerniakow in Warsaw committed suicide when the deportations began and when he realized that he could not save the Jewish orphans. Jacob Gens lost his battle for the survival of the Vilnius Ghetto. Called by the Germans one day and probably suspecting that this was his end, he went anyway and was greeted by a bullet. Barasz was killed in 1943 when the Bialystok Ghetto was liquidated, and Rumkowski boarded one of the last trains from Lodz to Auschwitz.

10

THE REFUGEES

A HALF MILLION JEWS left Germany, and countries that imitated German discriminatory measures, before the onset of the final solution. Although they were among the first victims of anti-Jewish actions, they did not experience the full impact of the catastrophe. They had lost their homes but did not move into a ghetto. Some of them had seen the inside of a concentration camp, but not Auschwitz. Very few wrote memoirs, and none of them referred to themselves as refugees for long. The term was not a badge of attainment or honor; it was felt to the bone as a diminution of status as soon as one crossed into another country or stepped off a ship.

Numerically, refugees were a majority of the Jews who had lived in Germany, Austria, and Danzig before the war; a relatively small portion of the Jews in Bohemia and Moravia; and even smaller percentages of the Jews in Italy and Hungary. Emigration was not a group affair. Each prospective refugee family had to find a place of refuge and had to make its own decision to leave.

Among those who departed early were people with money, some foreign Jews, Zionists for whom the time had come to go to Palestine, the artists, teachers, professors, and other intellectuals who had lost their positions under decrees issued at the beginning of the Nazi regime, as well as students for whom education and economic advancement were no longer guaranteed or possible. During the first five years, however, many Jews regarded the rule of Adolf Hitler as a temporary phenomenon that one had to live through, or a setback to which one could adjust, or at worst the threat of a narrowing life that was nevertheless more bearable than the uncertainties of exile. For entrepreneurs, serious retarding factors were the loss of capital upon the sale or liquidation of a business coupled with the imposition of flight taxes and the freezing of one's remaining cash in the event of emigration. Those who depended on salaries or wages faced the external barriers erected by immigration countries suffering from high unemployment rates. The retired, disabled, or chronically impoverished Jews were in a particularly disadvantaged position, a point not lost on the Nazi leadership, which held discussions more than once about the real possibility that well-to-do and productive people would leave, while the "rabble" would stay behind.

In fact, the refugee outflow decreased year by year from 1933 through 1937, and it moved up sharply only in 1938 and 1939.[1] Several developments accounted for the sudden upward thrust. One was the annexation of Austria in March 1938. Another was the precipitous outbreak of violence on November 10, 1938. For twenty-four hours, from midnight to midnight, synagogues were burned down, shop windows of Jewish stores were smashed, and Jewish families were forcibly evicted from their apartments. Over twenty-five thousand Jewish men were delivered to the concentration camps Dachau, Buchenwald, and Sachsenhausen, where most of them were held for a period of weeks or months. Shortly after this upheaval, a series of decrees spelled out the end of all Jewish enterprises and the concomitant loss of jobs in the Jewish labor force of these firms. It is then that the Jews sought any haven, be it Cuba, Japanese-occupied Shanghai, or a neighboring country with porous borders, like Belgium, France, and Italy, which could be entered with a temporary visa or illegally. Not a few of these refugees were penniless, and when they reached their first destination they turned to soup kitchens financed by American or other free Jewish communities.

Yet on the whole, the refugees were younger and less incapacitated than the Jews who remained behind. Even if destitute, many of the emigrants had abilities and ambitions. A small but significant segment of the departing population consisted of professionals or of youngsters oriented toward the professions. The pool contained individuals with recognized or potential intellectual achievements. In the sciences especially, the migration represented an extraordinary transfer of talent from Central Europe to Anglo-Saxon countries.[2]

Six Jewish Nobel laureates left Germany after Hitler's rise to power. They were James Franck in physics; Fritz Haber and Richard Willstätter in chemistry; Otto Warburg, Otto Meyerhof, and Otto Loewi in medicine.[3] In addition, sixteen Jewish refugees from Germany, Austria, Italy, and Hungary received Nobel Prizes in the sciences after their emigration: Otto Stern, Max Born, Felix Bloch, Dennis Gabor, Emilio Segré, Arno Penzias, and Jack Steinberger in physics; Georg de Hevesy, Max Perutz, and Gerhard Herzberg in chemistry; Fritz Lipmann, E. Boris Chain, Hans Krebs, Salvador Luria, Konrad Bloch, and Bernard Katz in medicine. Most of the future laureates left when their positions were threatened or terminated in Germany. Among the others Max Perutz, stranded in Britain when Austria was annexed, did not go back. Similarly Fritz Lipmann could not return from Denmark. When Felix Bloch, in Switzerland, received an inquiry from the German physicist Werner Heisenberg about his plans, he replied on August 13, 1933, that he did not wish to return to his post at the University of Leipzig or accept a similar position in any other German university.[4] The Italian Salvador Luria fled from France in 1940, and the Hungarian Georg de Hevesy, who had moved from Freiburg to Copenhagen, escaped from there in a fishing boat in 1943.

In the social sciences and humanities, entire schools of thought were transplanted. The aged Sigmund Freud left Vienna for Britain. Bruno Bettelheim arrived in the United States after incarceration in Dachau and Buchenwald. The Gestalt psychologist Kurt Lewin visited the United States in 1932 and stayed there when Hitler was appointed Chancellor. The anthropologist Claude Lévi-Strauss went to the United States from France in 1940. The jurist Hans Kelsen made his move to the United States from Vienna. Economists Ludwig von Mises and Franco Modigliani became emigrants, von Mises in Switzerland when his native Vienna was annexed and Modigliani when he left Italy for the United States. Both were subsequent recipients of the Nobel Prize in economics. An adolescent refugee from Germany, who was trained as a political scientist in the United States, became a towering Secretary of State: Henry Kissinger.

In architecture the refugees included Erich Mendelsohn, known for his wide windows, and Marcel Breuer, who is associated with tubular chairs. Among the sculptors were Jacques Lipschitz and Ossip Zadkine. The French painter Marc Chagall was a refugee during the war and the American-born painter Lyonel Feininger was a resident in Germany when he was forced to leave. An army of writers and musicians was exiled. Some of the literary figures were Stefan Zweig, Arthur Koestler, and Franz Werfel.

Two of the composers were Arnold Schoenberg and Darius Milhaud. Pianist Artur Schnabel, harpsichordist Wanda Landowska, cellist Emanuel Feuermann, and conductors Bruno Walter, Otto Klemperer, Georg Solti, George Szell, Erich Leinsdorf, Maurice Abravanel, and Paul Kletzki were all refugees.

It should be noted that immigrants did not stand out in every field of endeavor. The record of the intellectuals was not duplicated in the business world. The occasional manager in a large enterprise, such as W. Michael Blumenthal, who came to the United States via Shanghai as a young man and who rose to be Secretary of the Treasury, was a rare exception. Robert Maxwell, a publishing magnate in Britain, built a conglomerate that collapsed after his death. Nine days before the end of his life, he spoke at a public dinner about the Jewish catastrophe, asking how many of the younger victims would have become not tycoons but Nobel laureates.

The boundary of major successes must be drawn also geographically. They were much more limited in Palestine and subsequently in Israel than in the West. The reason for this difference is primarily a matter of size and development. Palestine could not attract or support more than a handful of those immigrants who sought or needed a large and complex economic structure in which to pursue their work.

Even in the developed countries, the intellectuals and artists had their difficulties. Scientists Otto Frisch and Edward Teller were denied Rockefeller grants on the ground that they could not return to Germany. The political scientist Hans Morgenthau could not become an assistant professor at Brooklyn College before he was a deity at the University of Chicago. The economist Alexander Gerschenkron is reported to have worked as a longshoreman before he was a Harvard professor. Franco Modigliani managed a book center for imported Italian books before he did the work for which he received the economics Nobel Prize. The composer Arnold Schoenberg, an Austrian patriot and convert to Christianity who reverted to Judaism after his emigration, struggled in the United States to the end of his life. He taught for a modest salary at the University of California at Los Angeles and retired with a tiny pension, giving music lessons to support himself. The tenor Josef Schmidt, in Belgium during the German invasion, fled to Switzerland and died in a Swiss internment camp at the age of thirty-eight after his admission to a hospital was refused.

Medicine was Jewry's portable profession par excellence. Yet physicians were not generally welcomed in the United States, where economic competition for patients was fierce. In the State of New York, the former director of Neurological Institute at the University of Vienna, who was the author of two hundred papers, attempted to avail himself of a New York law permitting the practice of medicine without an examination by physicians of "conceded eminence and authority." Despite attestations by American physicians describing him the "most prominent" or the "leading" neuropathologist in Europe, the highest New York court ruled that the refusal by the state to grant the dispensation was not arbitrary, unfair, or capricious.[5] When a husband and a wife, both ordinary physicians, arrived in New York from Frankfurt, the wife worked in menial jobs while the husband studied English. In the end she never practiced. Widowed, she lived in a modest apartment, an old woman like many others.[6] In Britain several hundred physicians were unable to practice before they attained citizenship. A historian of this scene reports: "A surgeon secretly washed corpses in a morgue, a radiologist repaired radios and a bacteriologist peddled baking soda."[7] Mathematicians do not have to take licensing examinations, but those of them who migrated to the United States found themselves in a market that could not even employ all the native-born Americans with doctorates.[8]

Unlike doctors or mathematicians, lawyers could not, without extensive retraining, practice their craft at all, unless they took up restitution or indemnification cases in Germany after the war. Poets and novelists were trapped in the German language. Not many could appeal to new audiences. Franz Werfel did so with his saccharine *The Song of Bernadette*, which featured Catholicism, and Arthur Koestler with his unsparing *Darkness at Noon*, about Communism in the Soviet Union, but the novelist Stefan Zweig and his wife committed suicide in Brazil, and the satirist Kurt Tucholsky killed himself in Sweden at the age of forty-five.[9]

The vast majority of the refugees were not scientists, physicians, lawyers, or artists. They had no profession or valuable skills, and if they were no longer of school age, they had to think in terms of starting a very small business without much capital or of obtaining a job at the bottom of the ladder. For many of them the experience was painful and degrading. Down was a woman alone in Britain, struggling to obtain a work permit, unable to pay her rent, and finding a position as a domestic helper with a non-Jewish refugee household where she was allowed to share a room with two dogs. She was hungry enough to eat the dogs' food.[10] Down was also a family in which father and son tried to sell perfume door to door in Panama, "getting doors slammed in their faces." After arriving in New York, the father committed suicide and the mother worked as a fur finisher for the rest of her life.[11]

Almost all of the refugees who entered English-speaking countries went through a stage of economic and psychological shock. That was the time they might have had to rely on local relatives for money to pay for the initial rent and groceries. They might have had to sell personal possessions they had taken along, including cameras, china, stamp collections, or fur coats. During this initial period they were told at every turn that they were lucky, that they would have to work hard, and that they should learn English right away. Invariably the adults would speak the new language with a foreign accent that they could not shed. They were informed that everything in their past was inferior to what they would encounter now, and they were expected to agree. In America, they were instructed, as listeners of Johann Sebastian Bach and as readers of Johann Wolfgang von Goethe, that Victor Herbert was a great composer and Washington Irving a great writer. Accustomed to friendship, which to them was a lifelong tie to people of similar thought and philosophy, they could not find this institution in America, where casual acquaintances one hardly knew were often called friends. The United States seemed isolated as well as isolationist, a vast nation of individuals who did not ponder the meaning of life or understand the world around them.

After the end of 1941 the economy and mood of the United States changed rapidly. The country had been attacked. Unemployment gave way to labor shortages, and refugees joined or were inducted into the armed forces. In the abnormality of war, life for the refugees became more normal. The opposite, however, was the fate of thousands of emigrants in France and Britain who were interned as security risks. A large group in Britain was condemned to a barracks existence on the British-ruled Indian Ocean island of Mauritius. The refugees in Shanghai were constricted by the Japanese to the Hongkew quarter of the city from 1943 to the end of the war. About 100,000 refugees in countries surrounding Germany were subsequently trapped by German armies. Exposed and vulnerable, these Jews were ideal victims during the first roundups to death camps.

Not all the refugees in the West originated in the nineteen thirties. When Germany launched its western offensive in May 1940, thousands of Jews moved south from the Netherlands and Luxembourg, tens of thousands fled from Belgium, and more tens of thousands abandoned their homes in Paris for the unoccupied zone. Some of these refugees boarded ships in Marseille while there was still time, and some attempted to enter Switzerland or Spain.

Another, more massive flow began in an eastward direction when the Germans invaded Poland in 1939. It was extended farther to the east with the German assault on the USSR in 1941. Many Jews saved themselves in this flight; uncounted others succumbed to hardships. The Polish Jews were allowed to move to the western zones of occupied Germany after the war, where they became irrepatriable displaced persons, waiting for several additional years in camps until they could find a final home in Palestine or the United States.

11

MEN AND WOMEN

THE FINAL SOLUTION was intended by its creators to ensure the annihilation of all Jews. Most often, men and women were rounded up simultaneously for transport to a death camp or to be shot in front of a ditch. Their bodies were burned in the same crematory or buried in the same mass grave. They had been taken into the same arena of destruction, because the Nazi vision encompassed a Europe from which the Jews had to disappear in their entirety.

Yet the road to annihilation was marked by events that specifically affected men as men and women as women. First there were changes of roles. Then there occurred transformations of relationships. Finally there were differences in stresses and trauma.

At the outset skills and occupations were those of men or those of women, and these patterns did not vanish. Men were still physicians, traders, tailors, shoemakers, bakers, painters, and porters. Women remained nurses, cooks, seamstresses, and cleaners. Mothers at home might have had to assume the whole burden of caring for the children, guarding the weekly ration of bread. In time, however, the impoverishment of the Jews ground down the men and ushered in a new equality. As Jewish shops were closed and men lost their jobs, they could no longer make family decisions about where one should live or what one could afford. The newly isolated community consisted of men without power and women without support. In Berlin, a wife turned to her husband and asked, "Are you a rabbi? Are you a man?"[1] A great many men were unemployed and others were drawn to forced or semi-forced manual labor, most of it in labor companies or work camps, for road building, railway construction, river regulation, mining, and fortification work. Women were still barred by tradition from most key positions in leadership, but more and more of them took their places in the factory.

Under intensified constrictions, men and women could be thrown together or pulled apart. In the Minsk Ghetto, deportees from Germany reportedly engaged in much sexual activity,[2] whereas in distant Shanghai, where women were engaged in weary physical labor, divorces increased.[3] When the ghetto in Vilnius was thinned out until only workers and their immediate families were allowed to stay, new marriages—most of them fictitious—were formed with great rapidity.[4] By contrast a deportation order in the Lodz Ghetto resulted in divorces. There the Jewish administrators were required to draw up lists. The inclusion of names posed a moral difficulty and led to a search for justifications. It was decided to punish men who in the past had not volunteered for labor outside the ghetto and who had been forcibly assigned to these projects. The penalty was to be the deportation of the families of these men. In the wake of this development, many of the wives applied for a dissolution of their marriages.[5]

Women were a majority in the Jewish population of German-dominated Europe. In Poland before the war (1931), 52.08 percent of the Jews were female. In Byelorussia (January 1939) the figure was 53.25, in Ukraine (January 1939) 53.70, in Lithuania (1923) 52.08, in Latvia (1930) 53.68, in Hungary (1930) 52.08, in Czechoslovakia (1930) 50.81, in the Netherlands (1919) 51.90, in Germany (1933) 52.24, and after emigration within the old boundaries (1939) 58.16.[6] In the final tally, women were most probably more than half of the dead, but men died more rapidly.

The greater acceleration of deaths among men is visible in the ghettos. It must be assumed that in Warsaw Ghetto, the population was predominantly female, yet in 1941 deaths of adults totaled 22,978 men and 16,246 women.[7] In the Lodz Ghetto, where people were shipped in and out, women were a substantial majority, ranging from 54 to 57 percent during January 1, 1941, to June 30, 1942. On average their number was about 56 percent. Yet deaths were 13,729 men and 8,981 women, a statistic that may be translated into a death rate of men that was nearly twice as high as that of the women. Examining every listed cause of death that accounted for at least 1 percent of the fatalities in the Lodz Ghetto in 1941 and the first half of 1942, one may then see that men succumbed in greater number than women to every one of these causes, save "diseases of old age" and cancer. For the three leading causes, the raw figures are the following[8]:

	MALE DEATHS	FEMALE DEATHS
Heart Disease	3,715	2,572
Malnutrition	3,200	1,745
Lung Tuberculosis	2,946	1,601

Starvation was not only a primary cause of death but in many cases contributed to the deterioration of patients suffering from other diseases. Did men eat less than women in the Lodz Ghetto? The rationing system was skewed in favor of functionaries and laborers. Were women exempted from heavy labor? There is a photograph of two young women in the ghetto harnessed like horses to a flat cart loaded with a large drum of excrement.[9] Without a doubt, however, many more men than women were engaged in the most strenuous occupations. The supplemental food allocations did not compensate the individual for the energy expended in the work, and if a laborer became ill without recovering for a week, the additional rations were taken away.[10] Noteworthy is the fact that in the age group twenty to twenty-five the death rate of the Lodz Ghetto men was three and a half times that of the women.[11]

The comparative advantage afforded to women was limited to the labor recruitment and expansion drives of 1940, 1941, and 1942. With the onset of deportations there was a reversal of fortunes. Labor became numerically the most important reason for deferment or exemption during roundups. More women than men could now be considered "surplus." At least 80 percent of the Warsaw Ghetto Jews were deported during the summer of 1942. On the eve of the deportation, the ghetto had 368,902 inhabitants, of whom 211, 292, or 57.28 percent, were women. After the deportations, about half of the remaining Jews were hiding and 35,633 were registered. In this counted half, only 15,696, or 44.05 percent, were women.[12]

The Lodz Ghetto was thinned out in several deportations. The first wave was implemented during January–May 1942. As of December 31, 1941, the ghetto had 162,681 inmates, including new arrivals from Germany. Women of all ages numbered 92,703, or 56.98 percent, and men 69,978, or 43.02 percent. The transports to May encompassed 54,990 deportees, including 34,223 women and 20,767 men, a reduction of the women by 36.92 percent and of the men by 29.68 percent, ignoring the ghetto deaths while the deportations were in progress.[13]

The phenomenon of men dying first was not confined to the ghettos. The shootings in the occupied USSR began with the killing of men. The same procedure was followed in Serbia. Both of these operations were started in 1941, and in both the perpetrators were groping their way. In the Soviet territories as well as in Serbia, there was a need to rationalize the infliction of death, and it was easier to do so when the victims were men. For the police reservists in the east and the army in Serbia killing men was burdensome enough. But women could not be left alive very long after the breadwinners were gone, and as soon as native collaborators could be mobilized in the Soviet territories and SS personnel became available in Serbia, it was the turn of the Jewish women and children.

Men in the Hungarian labor service companies were among the first casualties from Hungary. "Labor" in the east was the German explanation for deportations from France, and the first six transports from that country consisted almost wholly of men. A subsequent action in Paris during July 1942 resulted in the seizure mainly of women, some of whom were the wives of previously arrested men, and of the children of these couples. Not much later thirteen consecutive transports were once again filled with more men than women. These deportees included thousands of French soldiers who had been demobilized for service in labor camps and who were easy targets.[14]

In the death camps, a reprieve was exceptional. It was granted to those who could perform work, some of it skilled and much of it heavy, to the extent that it was needed. In this selection, fewer women than men were spared from immediate gassing. Possibly a third of the Jews who survived Auschwitz were women. In the other camps, where inmate forces were small and survivors mere handfuls, women disappeared. Only a few escaped from Treblinka and Sobibor. None emerged from Belzec and Kulmhof.[15]

12

MIXED MARRIAGES

WHEN THE JEWS were emancipated in Europe, they began to enter into mixed marriages. Before the Second World War, such marriages were still rare in Poland, the Baltic states, and Romania. Their rate had been rising for two decades in the Soviet Union. Their increase was both earlier and higher in Germany, Austria, Hungary, Bohemia, Moravia, and the Netherlands. They had become common in Denmark and Italy.[1]

Nazi Germany and its allies did not dissolve mixed marriages by decree. The non-Jewish partner in these marriages was not going to be treated as a Jewish person, lest gentile family members and churches protest in chorus, nor could the Jewish partner be subjected to the full barrage of anti-Jewish decrees, lest the non-Jewish spouse be hurt. Moreover, not many mixed marriages were dissolved as a result of a court action initiated by the non-Jewish partner. Divorce was not yet a style of life in the first half of the century and the intermarried Jews were not going to be deserted in large numbers by their husbands or wives. By and large, therefore, these Jews were safe from destruction. This is not to say, however, that they were going to have a peaceful life or that none of them was going to be caught in the net. In Germany particularly, they were constantly watched and in the German bureaucracy they were repeatedly a subject of discussion. They could never be sure of what might happen to them next.

Already during the nineteen thirties, many intermarried Jewish men lost jobs and livelihood. When the concentration of Jews into Jewish houses began in Germany, mixed unions were divided into two groups, privileged and unprivileged. A marriage was privileged if its offspring had not been raised as Jews. In such cases, the Jewish partner remained privileged even if the marriage no longer existed and even if an only son had been killed in action during the Second World War. Also privileged was the childless wife of a German husband for the duration of the marriage. The exemption was applied not only to housing but also to the wearing of the Jewish star. It was not plenary, however. In France, hundreds of intermarried Jews were concentrated in the transit camp Drancy, from which they were sent off to the Channel Islands for fortification work.[2] Heavy work schedules were also in store for Jews in mixed marriages living in Vienna and Frankfurt.[3]

The principal worry of the intermarried Jews was the ever present possibility that they would be deported. Capitalizing on this anxiety, the German administration in the Netherlands induced some men whose non-Jewish wives were still capable of having children to undergo sterilization in exchange for immunity.[4] In some areas, the Jewish man in a mixed marriage was simply seized. During a sudden roundup in Berlin factories at the end of February 1943, such Jews were caught alongside other Jews while at work. The intermarried men were segregated after their arrest and placed in a separate building on the Rosenstrasse, where their future fate was in doubt. For the next several days, the German wives demonstrated in the open street for the release of their husbands, who were then freed.[5] In Italy, however, the SS rode roughshod over their Italian collaborators to dispatch 140 to 150 Jewish men and women in mixed marriages to Auschwitz.[6] In Lithuania during 1942, the Security Police arrested 12 Jews, all in mixed marriages and all converts to Catholicism, who had remained with their wives at home because they did not think they had to move into a ghetto. The Lithuanian wives were being pressured to divorce their husbands.[7]

In Slovakia the wife of a Hungarian-speaking resident was taken away. The incensed Hungarian addressed a letter to the volunteer corps (FS) of the German party, pointing out that he was a Hungarian Christian married to a baptized Jewish woman who had now been deported. "I am not sorry," he wrote, "at least I am rid of her," but these impudent Germans with their 100 percent Jewish wives, why were those women not transported as well? He went on to give the name and address of a man whose Jewish wife was allowed to remain because, he said, her husband was a member of the German party. "You are going to pay," he wrote, "because precisely those Jews who stay are going to drink your blood."[8]

In the occupied USSR the physical absence of the non-Jewish husband could be hazardous for the Jewish wife left behind. A survivor of a massacre in Mariupol notes that the Jewish wives whose non-Jewish husbands had remained in the city were spared, but that intermarried Jewish women whose husbands had been inducted into the Red Army or evacuated by the Soviet government were seized with their children and shot. The Jewish husband in a mixed marriage had to report to the Germans in any case, but his wife and children had the option of staying at home.[9]

The most serious situation for intermarried Jews arose upon the dissolution of their marriage. There were cases in Germany of divorces resulting from political or societal pressure that were not intended by either partner to bring about a termination of the relationship. Even before the deportations, however, those men who maintained physical contact with their former wives were guilty of "race pollution," and by 1940 a number of such "polluters" were quartered in a barracks of the Sachsenhausen concentration camp. There they were subjected to special torture and death, such as suffocation in a broom closet or exposure to streams of cold water directed with hoses to the heart.[10]

When a marriage was not peaceful because of antagonism, the Jewish partner could be endangered. The following is the story of the long life of a mixed couple in Hamburg. In 1908, Amalie S., who was born in 1882, married a Christian man, P., who was born in 1881. Her father was a leather manufacturer who also had an investment in a furniture factory. P. worked in the furniture plant as a manager, and soon the couple had a daughter, who remained an only child. During the First World War P. served at the front and received decorations. By the nineteen twenties, he had his own jewelry manufacturing business and Amalie, who had commercial training, helped him.

The marriage was happy and harmonious until 1928, a year when Amalie, then forty-six, changed radically. Without provocation she became jealous, accusing her husband of infidelity, and in 1929 or 1930 she denounced him at the health office, claiming that he had venereal disease. P. was not infected. Amalie went on to pawn belongings without financial necessity and declared that she was not going to be happy until P. was in his grave. When P. could no longer endure her behavior, he would move out for some periods of time. In 1934, he decided to divorce her, but when she asked him for forgiveness he changed his mind. For a while they lived peacefully, but then she resumed her outbursts, accusing him of consorting with whores.

At the end of 1943, P.'s younger sister moved into their apartment. The sister, divorced from her husband, had two sons, both soldiers. One had been killed in 1941, and she herself had been bombed out. Amalie now began a new line: the revenge of the Jews would begin soon; lists were already being prepared for this revenge; the German soldiers were all murderers; the German children killed in air raids had been murdered by Hitler; Germany had lost the war. The sisters-in-law had continual arguments and on February 18, 1944, while P. was not present, Amalie asked her husband's sister to leave. The sister-in-law began to pack and in her agitation talked to a woman in the apartment house. The woman passed on the sister-in-law's complaints to a minor party official, who advised P. to divorce his wife. The same party man talked to his superior, saying that the quarrel seemed to be a domestic affair that had spilled over into the political arena.

When the party did nothing, Amalie's sister-in-law inquired about the address of the Gestapo. P. and his sister then visited the specialist in Jewish matters at the Hamburg Gestapo office and asked what would happen to Amalie after a divorce. The Gestapo man said that she would go to a Jewish home but added that false accusations against her would be punishable. The sister-in-law was taken aback by this answer, but as the situation in the apartment deteriorated, both she and her brother decided to "get rid of" Amalie. The sister-in-law prepared a statement against the "Jewess," and the Gestapo asked P. whether he was prepared to sign it too. He did so. On March 22, 1944, P. instituted divorce proceedings and two days later Amalie was arrested. The divorce was granted on April 5, 1944, with the specifications that Amalie was at fault. While Amalie was held in prison, P. and his sister sent her clothing and other necessities. In July, Amalie was transported to Auschwitz and did not return.[11]

The divorced or widowed Jewish partner of a mixed marriage could be in a precarious situation, even with children who had not been raised in the Jewish religion. In the Netherlands, the Jewish journalist Philip Mechanicus, who was divorced from his Dutch wife and who was the father of two grown daughters, was kept in a transit camp for an entire year. Then he was shipped to Auschwitz, where he died.[12] Also in the Netherlands, a widowed refugee from Germany, Hermann Rosenbaum, asked for an exemption from wearing the Jewish star (and hence also from deportation), pointing out that his deceased wife had been an Aryan, and that he had two children, one of whom, a seventeen-year-old *Mischling*, had been drafted into the German army. Moreover, Rosenbaum himself had been a front-line soldier between 1916 and 1918. The case was handled by Gertrud Slottke of the German Security Police in The Hague. She recommended to Hauptsturmführer Zoepf that the request be denied on the ground that the petitioner had been widowed since 1937 and that he had not done anything special for Germany. Zoepf agreed.[13]

If a child was adopted, there was no immunity at all. The historian H. G. Adler tells the story of the widowed Arthur von Weinberg, a major on the front line during the First World War and a prominent figure in Germany's chemical industry thereafter. Weinberg had married a German widow in 1909 and had adopted her two daughters, both of whom subsequently married noblemen. Following his arrest in the home of one of his adopted daughters in June 1942, the Plenipotentiary of the Chemical Industry, Karl Krauch, wrote a lengthy letter to the Chief of Himmler's Personal Staff, Karl Wolff. Despite this high-level intervention, Weinberg was transported at the age of eighty-one to the Theresienstadt Ghetto, where he died.[14]

Adler also recounts the case of a German physician in Kissingen, Dr. Oswald Eller, who was married to a Jewish woman. The couple had no children. On May 1, 1942, Dr. Eller sent a letter to interior Minister Frick, in which he stated that he had married Ella Anschütz in 1904 and that he was near seventy now and filled with worry about the fate of his wife if he should die. The marriage was childless only because of a physical impairment that was his alone from birth. During the marriage his wife had adopted a completely German attitude in accord with the political views of her husband and had joined the German National party. Both had voted for Adolf Hitler before 1933. The three brothers of his Jewish wife had been soldiers in the First World War and one had become an officer because of bravery. For thirty-eight years his wife had stood by his side. Hence he was asking for assurances, while he was still alive, that his wife would not be forced to wear the Jewish star after his death and that she would not be subjected to the further consequences, such as "resettlement to Poland, etc." The petition was pushed down to Eichmann's office, the Gestapo in Nuremberg, and the Gestapo in Würzburg. It was finally denied. Adler believes that in view of the absence of additional correspondence in the folder, the couple survived the war.[15]

Unlike Dr. Eller, the merchant Max Wagner in Solingen had divorced his Jewish wife in 1934. Denied the protection of a mixed marriage, she was deported to the Lodz Ghetto in October 1941. For Wagner, this turn of events was a disaster, because his two sons, one born in 1925 and the other in 1931, were deported with her. At the time of the divorce, his children, who belonged to the Jewish religion, stayed with their mother, because he could no longer maintain a household of his own. He had sent a letter to the Jewish Community in Düsseldorf to declare that his sons were no longer to be considered members of the Jewish religion, but in the absence of a prescribed court procedure, this simple notification was, as he discovered later, insufficient to remove their Jewish status. Wagner remarried in November 1941 and immediately instituted proceedings to gain full custody of his sons. In a letter to Interior Minister

Frick he petitioned for their return from Lodz, setting forth his relationship with them and adding that he had been a volunteer in the
First World War, in which he suffered a 30 percent disability. In
December 1942 he was informed orally by the local Gestapo that his
sons Arthur and Egon were deceased. They had been shipped "farther to the East for labor and had died during transport." Wagner
then stated that he had corresponded with his sons and had sent them
money, but that he had not heard from them or obtained any receipts
after September 1942. He could not understand how his younger
son, aged eleven, could have been sent out for labor and he wanted
to know *how* his children had died. He was told that there were no
death certificates and that there was no information about the causes
of their deaths.[16]

Max Wagner could not shield his children, because officially they
were still categorized as members of the Jewish religion and they no
longer lived in his household at the time of their deportation.[17] Neither could the German husband of a Jewish wife confer immunity on
her Jewish child in his home, if that child was not his. In 1931, a
devout Protestant, Jochen Klepper, then twenty-eight, had married
a Jewish woman who was thirteen years older and who had two
Jewish daughters from a prior marriage. The elder emigrated before
the war, but the younger one remained with her mother and Klepper
in Berlin. Klepper, a troubled man, was a writer whose major novel,
Der Vater, about the Prussian soldier-king Frederick William I, appeared in 1937. It was lauded in Nazi circles, where the king was
regarded as a major German hero. Interior Minister Frick even gave
copies of the book as presents. Although Klepper had to count his
money, he lived a middle-class life. He bought Baroque furniture
and his social circle included nobility who were beholden to him for
his novel. After the outbreak of war, his wife worked at Siemens.
Denied children of his own because of her age, he hoped that she and
her daughter would convert to his faith. His wish was granted and all
three celebrated Christmas 1940 as a Christian family. His wife had
given him a Baroque dove symbolizing the Holy Ghost and Klepper
was supremely happy.

Between January and October 1941, Klepper was away in the
German army, but while he was in Poltava, Ukraine, he was dis-

charged because of his mixed marriage. When he returned, the Jews of Germany were threatened with deportation. His wife said to him that if there was going to be a compulsory divorce, she would consider suicide—under the circumstances not an unforgivable sin. Klepper rejected the idea as a defiance of God. Desperately he tried to obtain from the Swedish legation a visa for his wife's twenty-year-old daughter, and from Frick permission for her emigration. The Interior Minister received him on December 6, 1942, but in this conversation also brought up the safety of Klepper's wife, pointing out that there were attempts to draft a compulsory divorce decree. "I cannot shield your wife," said Frick, "I cannot shield any Jew. In their very nature, such things cannot, after all, be done in secret. They will reach the attention of the Führer and then we will have an awful scene." That day Klepper, his wife, and her daughter talked about committing suicide together. On December 9, Eichmann received Klepper, refusing to give his final yes to the daughter's emigration, but reassuring Klepper that the decision would probably be positive. Apparently, however, the outcome was negative, and on December 10, Jochen Klepper, his wife, and her daughter killed themselves.[18]

13

CHILDREN

THE FATE OF THE CHILDREN may be charted in four consecutive situations. The first was the early regime of restrictions. The second was life in the ghetto. Then came selections for deportations or shootings. Finally children were killed.

There were comparatively fewer children in the Jewish community than in the surrounding non-Jewish population. The Jewish birthrate was declining more rapidly than that of non-Jews, and in Prussia, Austria, Bohemia-Moravia, Hungary, and Italy, it had fallen below the replacement level.[1] Nine months of anti-Jewish measures in German-controlled regions or in countries allied with Germany had the effect of depressing the rate even more. In areas where the process of pauperization and segregation took some time, not only infants but also small children were fewer. That is not to say that these children did not suffer.

During the phase of economic and social discrimination, the fortunes of children were those of their fathers and mothers. They lost space in housing when their parents were driven out of apartments, and their freedom of movement was reduced when all Jews were deprived of such freedom. They no longer had the old quantity or variety of food, when supplementary rations were cut or shopping hours shortened for Jews. They were specifically targeted as students in schools, somewhat analogously to adults dismissed from jobs. If they could not emigrate—and outside Germany and Austria the vast majority had no prospect of leaving—their lives were sober and somber. Like their elders, with whom they were trapped, they had little to look forward to and much to be anxious about.

In Eastern Europe, ghettoization, with its privations and constrictions, introduced a question of life and death. Here one may see a large magnification of death rates, with the smallest children suffering first and the most.

The most complete statistics for a larger ghetto come from Lodz, where the Jewish council prepared a detailed report for the period May 1940 to June 1942.[2] After the ghetto gates were closed on April 30, 1940, the Jewish population was 163,777. Tens of thousands of Jews were subsequently transported in from the countryside and from cities in Germany, Luxembourg, and Bohemia-Moravia, but this augmentation was outweighed by deaths and deportations. As of June 30, 1942, the count was only 102,546. The ghetto was wiped out in 1944.

In Lodz, as elsewhere, the birthrate of the Jewish population was plunging under German rule. From age distribution data in the report, it appears that during the 1930s, the average annual birthrates must have been around 16 per 1,000. The May–December 1940 rate was about 8 per 1,000 on an annual basis. The 1941 rate was 4 per 1,000.

At the beginning of the ghetto period in Lodz, disaster struck the infants. From May 1, 1940, to the end of 1941 there were 1,390 ghetto births. A total of 416 children died in this group during their first year of life by December 31, 1941. More than a third of these deaths were attributed to premature birth, and the following five of the identified causes were lung disease, diseases of the digestive system, food poisoning, malnutrition, and dysentery.

For the period May 1, 1940, to June 30, 1942, the total number of infants who died was 1,150, including 610 who had been born before the ghetto's formation, the 416 born in the ghetto whose death as infants occurred by the end of 1941, and 124 more ghetto born or newly arrived infants who died during the first half of 1942. So rapid was this attrition that 872 of these 1,150 children had already died in 1940.

The increasing mortality rate of children past infancy was roughly proportional to the steeply rising death rate of the adults. The report does not specify causes of death for children aged one to fourteen, but if premature births, heart disease, and diseases of old age are subtracted from a list compiled for the entire ghetto community, the major remaining causes were, in 1940, dysentery, lung diseases, and diseases of the digestive system, and in 1941 and 1942, tuberculosis and starvation.

The Lodz Ghetto had an elaborate organization of social services, including orphanages, children's "colonies," a children's sanatorium, a tuberculosis station for children, and a dental clinic for children.[3] The services in the tuberculosis station were free. During the first month of its operation in March 1941, 501 children were treated there; by January 1942, the number was 5,275. The station had its own X-ray apparatus. It administered injections and operated a referral system under which 1,681 children were transferred in the course of the first year to hospitals, children's colonies, and an orphanage designed for prevention. The report does not state how many children infected with tuberculosis died in these places.

Starvation was the other major cause of death. The rationing system in the Lodz Ghetto was geared to keep workers working. By mid-1942, about 70 percent of the ghetto population was receiving a laborer's allocation, that is, the ordinary ration and an additional 150

TABLE A: MORTALITY OF CHILDREN
IN THE LODZ GHETTO

	Deaths per 1,000 of		
	ALL LODZ JEWS	CHILDREN AGED 1–8	CHILDREN AGED 8–14
1938	10.7	[2–3]	[1–2]
May–December 1940	65.1	19	6.1
1941	75.8	18	8.5
January–June 1942	182.2	26	23.2

Note: Only whole numbers can be calculated for the age group 1–8 years.

grams of bread and 40 grams of sausage a day. The remaining 30 percent were by and large the elderly, the sick, and the children.[4]

A palliative for children was a milk kitchen. During September–December 1940, the quantity of "milk mixtures" in the kitchen was an average of 99 liters a day. In 1941 it was 262 liters, and during the first four months of 1942 it was 318 liters. The parents had to pay for the milk.

In Lodz most children lived in households and shared the food that was eaten there. Families in ultra-poor homes sold slightly better rations to acquire a larger bulk of the most basic, sometimes barely edible food. The upper stratum in turn bought the more desirable items for money. In the wage-earning middle, the working parents could pool their rations with the sparse one of the child, but the Elder of the Lodz Ghetto, Rumkowski, was not happy with such sharing. The father who used the coupon meant only for him to feed his child would lose physical strength and be unable to work at maximum capacity. Accordingly, in 1943 Rumkowski altered the system to provide food for workers on work premises. For four thousand homeless children, he said, there were shelters where each child received "good soup" twice a day.[5]

The Warsaw Ghetto statistics are not nearly as detailed as those of the Lodz Ghetto, but they are sufficient for a crude comparison between the two communities. The Warsaw Ghetto was formed in November 1940 and it was subjected to mass deportations that began in July 1942. During this period the ghetto population averaged somewhat over 400,000, as people were shipped in from surrounding areas and 69,000 inhabitants died. The available mortality rates show that the overall death rate in the Warsaw and Lodz ghettos reached approximately the same peak, and that the children in the two ghettos suffered similar proportional losses.

What did the Warsaw Ghetto do for its children? The major institutional benefit consisted of "midday" meals, made from oats, groats, or noodles mixed with some vegetables and fat and distributed to specially designated groups. During the second half of 1941, such meals were received by an average of 31,740 children.[6] The Warsaw Ghetto, unlike Lodz, was under a ban against elementary schools. Informal instruction was offered by "house committees."

TABLE B: MORTALITY OF CHILDREN IN THE WARSAW AND LODZ GHETTOS

	Death rate of all Warsaw Jews	Deaths of all Warsaw Jews	Deaths of all children to age 15 in Warsaw Ghetto	Children as % of all Warsaw Ghetto deaths	Children to 14 in Lodz Ghetto as % of Lodz Ghetto deaths
November 1938–June 1939	[12]	3,175			
November 1939–June 1940	[33]	8,695			
May–December 1940					18.83
January–July 1941	91.7	19,251	1,596 Deaths of all children to age 13	8.29	5.77
August–December 1941	174.9	23,998	2,419	10.08	
January–June 1942	144.0	26,355	3,060	11.72	5.23

Note: The Warsaw figures for 1939–1940 are contained in a letter by Adam Czerniakow to the World Jewish Congress, September 1, 1940, American Jewish Archives/World Jewish Congress Collection, Alphabetical Series—Poland 204 A-2. Warsaw Ghetto data for 1941 are in the statistical report by Czerniakow to Ghetto Kommissar Auerswald, February 6, 1942, Zentrale Stelle der Landesjustizverwaltungen, Akten Auerswald, 365 e. The 1942 data are in subsequent monthly reports by Czerniakow to Auerswald, Zentrale Stelle, Collection Polen, Red Numbers 365 e and d. Warsaw had a somewhat smaller prewar Jewish birthrate than Lodz. See the Warsaw rates in Liebman Hersch, "Jewish Population Trends in Europe," in Jewish Encyclopedic Handbooks, *The Jewish People Past and Present* (New York, 1955), vol. 2, p. 11. On the other hand, Lodz received relatively childless Western Jews, whereas the Warsaw Ghetto had several augmentations of poor Jews from nearby, probably with more children on average.

When the ban was lifted at the beginning of September 1941, schools were organized for children up to the age of eleven.[7] As of January 1942, 3,000 students attended the schools; by July there were 6,700. An important service of the school system was breakfast. In January, most of the school children received it.[8] Occasionally, there were special rations for children. In February 1942, the ghetto's Provisioning Authority included two eggs (price: 0.70 zloty apiece) on the children's coupon.[9] Council chairman Czerniakow tried to carve out a partial or temporary benefit whenever possible. He organized fund drives for children, cleared space for playgrounds, and raided luxury food stores and restaurants laden with black market merchandise to distribute the goods to children in orphanages and in the street.[10]

Even though there were orphanages and hospitals in the Warsaw Ghetto, these underfunded institutions were dependent on private donations (some from abroad). Often they did not have enough beds, food, or fuel or the barest medicines. In March 1941 a woman took an enfeebled and gasping child to the children's hospital. The physician on duty examined the child and as a condition for admission demanded 15 zlotys from the mother for burial costs. When the woman screamed that she was a refugee who had been deported four times before arriving in the ghetto and that she did not have the money, the physician walked away.[11]

In the shelters for refugees who had been moved to the ghetto from the countryside, conditions were grave. During the winter months, lice-infested children without coats or shoes could stay warm in their unheated rooms only by staying in bed.[12] In January 1942, at a single collecting point for refugees at 9 Dzika Street, 63 of 128 children died. The figure for four refugee shelters was 215 dead children, or 37 percent of all the ghetto children who died that month.[13]

Finally Jewish children in Warsaw were increasingly on their own. Some were engaged in the ghetto's extensive black market trade with the outside world. When they were intercepted with small quantities of potatoes or carrots, they were sometimes beaten and their food was confiscated. Some poorer parents allowed their children to steal across the ghetto boundary for just a meal provided by a charitable Polish family. Yet more and more children became beggars within the ghetto itself. They would circle market stalls to pick up any rotted vegetable, or sing to attract the attention of pedestrians, or only stand with frostbitten legs and cry.[14] In 1941, 152 of them died in the street.[15] By 1942, many no longer had a home, and homeless they were helpless. Czerniakow wanted to rebuild ruined houses to shelter at least five thousand.[16] It never came to that.

The ghetto not only affected the material conditions of the child, but also transformed its psyche. Many of the smaller children had no memory of freedom. The ghetto was the norm. Czerniakow quotes one such child in his ghetto: "I do not yet wear the armband, but when I grow up I will wear one."[17] The historian of the Theresienstadt Ghetto, H. G. Adler, describes the children there as "shadowed," "always nervous," and "exceptionally awake." They saw their parents deprived of rights and respect and subjected to a regime of indignities, themselves reduced to the impotence of children. Roving in groups, they often chose their own anarchic paths.[18] Nor was this scene confined to Theresienstadt. Gangs of roaming orphans aged nine to fifteen were also noted in the ghetto of Vilnius.[19] In many ghettos, the older boys in particular were forced into adult roles, be it as beggars, smugglers, apprentices, workers, or simply members of the legion of unemployed.

When the deportations began, children were caught in the maelstrom. Most often they were moved out with their families. This procedure was generally easier for German perpetrators and Jewish councils alike. In Slovak internment camps, the Jewish resettlement staff prided itself on making up lists of an even one thousand deportees, comprising men and women and divided into older people, a middle group, and children.[20] In Berlin, where the SS rounded up Jews in factories at the beginning of 1943, the Jewish housing office together with other Jewish functionaries and nurses were looking for women and children to "reunite" the families.[21] There were, however, situations in which children departed after their parents, as well as occasions when they went first.

France presents the primary case of leftover children. In 1942, stateless families were to be arrested without their children, because of the German desire to preserve the legend that Jews were going to the east to work. French police, on the other hand, found it more expedient to seize children aged two or more and actually resisted the idea of having the children released, lest they would have to find a place for the children and then arrest more adults to fill the trains. The dilemma resulted in a compromise in the course of which parents were moved out of the internment camps, to be followed with Eichmann's agreement by the children. On subsequent transports children were mixed with other adults and some trains were composed primarily of children.[22] By 1943 and 1944 Jewish organizations succeeded in placing more and more children in Catholic orphanages and boarding schools or spiriting them across the French frontier. In southern France, particularly, where a French directive specified an exemption of unaccompanied children over the age of five, Jewish welfare workers persuaded arrested Jews to abandon their children, in order to spare them from deportation.[23] Dispersal, however, was not always fast enough and some children were seized. In the end, about 11.9 percent of the deportees from France were children up to the age of fifteen.[24] In Belgium the comparable figure was 19.7 percent.[25]

In the work ghettos of Eastern Europe children were allowed to stay primarily for the purpose of maintaining the morale and productivity of their parents. Sometimes, however, this concession was withdrawn. Dr. Aharon Peretz, who was a physician in the Kaunas Ghetto, testified about such an event. At the end of March 1944, when the people of the ghetto expected no disruption of their routine, the Jewish police were ordered to assemble on the pretext that they would receive air raid instructions. The police were detained and when a German in a loudspeaker truck warned the Jews that anyone caught in the street would be killed, some mothers intuitively screamed "Children!" Frantically children were hidden in boarded-up cellars, and to some Dr. Peretz gave an injection so that they would sleep. Outside, children were loaded on trucks and cars. One mother ran after her three small children, who had already been placed in a vehicle. Heedlessly she shouted at a German, "Give me the children!" He answered, "You may have one."[26]

In Lodz, where the ghetto was thinned out by deportations during the first months of 1942, the remaining community was still diverse enough to worry Ghetto Elder Rumkowski. Now he was going to redouble his effort to convert the ghetto into a factory. Fearful that anyone not working would be in jeopardy, he wanted all children over ten to work.[27] Then something happened. On the evening of August 31, 1942, the Germans demanded that fifty members of the Jewish police assemble at 5:00 A.M. Before dawn on September 1, the Germans arrived to clear out the hospitals, one of them the children's hospital. On September 4, Rumkowski made a speech in which he announced that "by order of the authorities," all Jews under the age of ten and over sixty-five had to be "resettled." Standing before a crowd, a "broken Jew," he said, "In my old age I must stretch out my hands and beg: Brothers and sisters, hand them to me, give me your children!" Working in two twelve-hour shifts, the statistical division of the Council's Registration and Records Department prepared lists, but the Germans were impatient. Relying on visual identification, they proceeded with Jewish police and firemen from block to block to seize the victims. The cooperation of the policeman and firefighters was bought with a promise to spare their children.[28]

For the Jewish leadership, children were a special subject of concern. Every leader in the European Jewish community knew that children were the biological guarantors of its future. Jacob Gens in Vilnius would not surrender them. Wilhelm Filderman in Romania wrote letters to save orphans languishing across the Dnestr River. Raymond-Raoul Lambert, already awaiting his own deportation in an internment camp near Paris, urged that children be scattered while there was still time. When Adam Czerniakow in the Warsaw Ghetto could not obtain assurances from the German resettlement staff about the ghetto orphans, he took a poison pill.

Rarely could adults escape from ghettos with children, although in the woods of Byelorussia there were some camps in which Jewish partisans tried to protect young families. A few attempts were also made to place children with gentile hosts. The following story is told in a judgment of a United States court. In the small town of Lisets (Lysiece), located in the Galician region and inhabited at the time by a mixed population of Ukrainians, Poles, and Jews, a Jewish physician managed to leave his small daughter with Polish friends before the Jewish community of Lisets was bodily transferred to the ghetto of Stanislawow. The little girl was passed on to a gentile Polish woman, Jadwiga Spilarewicz. When Mrs. Spilarewicz heard that a Polish family had been arrested for harboring Jews, she decided to take the child to Krakow and stopped in Lisets to obtain money from a relative for the trip. Two Ukrainian policemen immediately arrested her and she was held for several weeks. The child was also seized. One of the policemen, Bohdan Kozij, was observed dragging her to the courtyard behind the police station. As the child was pleading to be spared, Kozij shot her at point-blank range. Her body was seen at the Jewish cemetery. [29]

Very few children could survive in camps. Of 4,918 children to age fifteen, who were deported to Auschwitz from Belgium, 53 came back. [30] Adolescents could sometimes pretend to be older. When Elie Wiesel arrived in Auschwitz, he was fifteen. A prisoner walked up to him to ask how old he was. Fifteen, was the reply. No, eighteen, the older prisoner corrected him. But he was fifteen, Wiesel said again. Not satisfied, the stranger told him to listen to his advice. When Wiesel was confronted by an SS officer who selected people for the gas chamber, he was asked about his age again. Eighteen, was the answer. [31]

In the pure death camps of Treblinka, Sobibor, Belzec, and Kulmhof, there was no chance for children at all. In Kulmhof, Simon Srebnik was thirteen. The German guards kept him as a mascot. When the camp was broken up, they shot him and left him for dead. He lived to tell his story. [32]

In areas where shooting operations were conducted, children were swept up as well. Only at the beginning, when men were selected, did children remain with their mothers. It was a short reprieve. [33] After a while the remaining children became aware of what was happening. Dr. Peretz observed them in the Kaunas Ghetto playing grave digging, execution, and funeral. [34]

During the summer and fall of 1942, several hundred thousand Jews were massacred in the Volhynian-Podolian region. When the Germans entered a small ghetto and lined up its Jews, a little girl asked: "Mother, why did you make me wear the Shabbat dress; we are being taken out to be shot." The shooting site was on a hill about two miles away, and the mother, carrying the child, was forced to run this distance after a truck already filled with victims. Standing near the dugout half-filled with bodies, the child said: "Mother, why are we waiting, let us run!" Some of the people who attempted to escape were caught immediately and shot on the spot. The mother stood there facing the grave. A German walked up to the woman and asked: "Whom shall I shoot first?" When she did not answer, he tore her daughter from her hands. The child cried out and was killed.[35]

14

CHRISTIAN JEWS

AT FIRST GLANCE the notion of "Christian Jews" is a contradiction in terms. During the Nazi era, however, there was a sizable group of people who were Christian by religion and Jews by decree. These individuals were also victims.

The official concept of "Jew" evolved in two stages. In 1933, the phrase "non-Aryan" was introduced to cover every person, Jewish or Christian, who had at least one Jewish grandparent. Two years later those non-Aryans who had at least three Jewish grandparents were classified as Jews. Thus the definition of 1935 embraced converts to Christianity, as well the child of two converts, even if baptized at birth. Only the half-Jews were classified on the basis of their own religion. They were not considered Jewish if they did not belong to the Jewish religion on the date of the decree and were not married then or later to a Jewish partner.

The formulation of 1935 was applied not only in Germany, but also in territories under German control, including Austria, Bohemia-Moravia, Poland, the Netherlands, Belgium, France, Serbia, Salonika, and areas wrested from the USSR, with modifications made only for the date on which a half-Jew had to be free of the Jewish religion and not married to a Jewish person. Furthermore, the

German concept became a model for states allied with Germany, although there one may observe various deviations that reveal the influence of the churches.

The largest concentration of Christian Jews was probably that of Greater Hungary, where the estimate for 1941 was about 62,000. Germany as of 1933 had about 40,000, Austria at the time of its annexation in March 1938 up to 25,000, Bohemia-Moravia in 1939 up to 10,000, truncated Romania in 1942 close to 5,000, the Netherlands in 1942 over 2,500, Slovakia in 1939 over 2,000, Italy several thousand.[1] In Poland the figure was at least in the thousands.

A substantial percentage of all these people, if not quite half of them, were protected by reason of intermarriage. The descendants of converts could sometimes escape detection, if their records, especially in occupied territories, were not easily traceable.[2] In the Netherlands, Evangelical Protestants were shielded from deportation as a concession to the Protestant churches,[3] but in the main such exemptions were not granted, lest the whole idea of defining Jews in accordance with their ancestry be defeated. Jew, as the Nazis said, remains Jew.

Notwithstanding the emphasis on descent in the decrees, thousands of Jews, driven by panic, adopted Christianity as a talisman. They did so especially in countries where churches were believed to have some political strength. An observer of the German Security Service in Slovakia reported that Jews were gathering "in swarms" around the baptismal font. In one provincial town, he said, some Jews were going to the synagogue on Saturday and an Eastern Orthodox church on Sunday.[4]

Longtime converts and individuals actually born as Christians were in a difficult psychological position. They had resigned from or had never been a part of Jewry. For many of them the Christian religion was a means or extension of their emancipation. They were the antithesis of those Orthodox Jews who always expected persecution and who would not, even in time of danger, place a child in a Christian institution for safekeeping or contemplate a life of disguise with forged baptismal certificates. Even the non-observant assimilated Jews were still conscious of being Jews. When to their dismay Germandom or, in other countries, another status was denied them, they still had the ancient, often half-forgotten Jewish culture, with a language, a literature, and a liturgy, that belonged to them alone. And in addition, they had retained their bonds with each other. The Christian Jews, on the other hand, were now the complete outsiders, abandoned by the host country and distanced from the Jewish community, which they themselves had left behind.

The first Christians of Jewish descent to feel this predicament were those of Germany. Only two and a half months after the concept of "non-Aryans" was promulgated, Christian non-Aryans created an organization with the long title Reich Association of Christian German Citizens of non-Aryan or Not Purely Aryan Descent. The founders emphasized their "German thinking," "Christian sentiment," "national principles," and the "Führer idea." They considered themselves as representing an interest community numbering, with Aryan family members, in the "millions." In 1935, however, when a new law declared that Jews could not be citizens, they had to restyle themselves the Reich Association of Non-Aryan Christians, and still later, emphasizing that the apostle Paul had been a Jew, they became the Paulus Federation—Reich Association of non-Aryan Christians. With a great many professionals in its national and local leadership, the organization provided its members with legal consultation, employment referrals, and educational advice. By 1937, it was also a forum for lectures about emigration, but at that point it received official word that it could no longer include individuals classified as Jews. The remaining members now were Christian half-Jews and quarter-Jews, the so-called *Mischlinge,* and the title of the organization was discreetly changed to Association 1937. In its news bulletin, the Association dealt at length with the Mischling concept and its legal implications. As non-Aryans the Mischlinge had long been barred from public employment, but they learned to their great relief that Mischling enterprises had not been defined as Jewish. As limited but identified victims, they were not allowed to change their names and they were hemmed in when they wanted to marry. The Christian half-Jew who married a Jewish person became Jewish by definition, but at the same time marriage to a German required special permission. The Mischlinge turned inward and advertised for mates in their own news bulletin. In 1939, just before the outbreak of war, their organization was dissolved.[5] Atomized, they tried to survive, severed from one another.

The Christian Jews, who were thrown back into the Jewish fold, were not returnees. By and large, they held on to their Christianity, even while they were subject to the Jewish fate. The prevailing Jewish attitude toward these converts is illustrated by a small incident in Warsaw, where a Jew had who taken the rare step of severing his membership in the Jewish community to affirm his atheism was mistakenly classified as a Christian in the labor files of the Jewish Council. Writing to protest, he explained that he had left the Jewish community in 1933 to be without any religion. "To list me," he said, "as a baptized Jew—a category which I myself look down upon, identifying me with that group—is a grievous moral wrong." The chairman of the council, Czerniakow, included the entire letter in his diary.[6]

The Jewish community could forgive conversion to Christianity under pressure of persecution, and in some cases it made allowances also for greatness, placing in its pantheon men like Benjamin Disraeli, the Jew whose conversion enabled him to become a much admired British Prime Minister, or the poet Heinrich Heine, whose adoption of the Protestant religion in a vain pursuit of an academic or bureaucratic career did not diminish the attraction of his Jewish themes or the magnetism of his ironic, melancholy style. Such solicitude, however, was not extended to ordinary individuals, who did not possess the saving grace of luminosity, but who nevertheless became Christians, as Rabbi Alexandre Safran of Romania put it, of their "own free will."[7]

The converts, on their part, were not ready for a reunion. Most often, they attempted to maintain the maximum separation from the Jewish community. They had become in the fullest sense involuntary Jews. During the German occupation of Hungary, the Christian Jew Sandor Török served for two months in the nine-man Hungarian Jewish Council. In July 1944, after the deportation of the Jews from the provinces outside Budapest, the Christians of Jewish origin, who were numerous in the capital, succeeded in forming their own council,[8] and when a ghetto was formed in the city later that year, the Christians in the quarter were allowed to mark their houses with a cross instead of a star.[9]

The converts appealed for protection to governments and churches. They hoped for help from non-Jewish relatives, friends, acquaintances, and associates. There were a few situations, however, when they played significant roles in the Jewish community.

One such example is Romania, where two young Christian Jews offer a contrast of attitudes and of deeds. Nandor Gingold, the physician, acted as the head of the Jewish Council with abject subservience to the Romanian government. Franz von Neumann, on the other hand, used his considerable financial and political resources as an industrialist to help sway the Romanian authorities from a decision to deport the Jewish community of Southern Transylvania.[10] What von Neumann did was a major act with a major result.

The Warsaw Ghetto offers a particularly noteworthy scene of Christian Jews in conspicuous positions. As of January 1, 1941, the ghetto contained 1,761 persons who belonged to non-Jewish denominations.[11] During the following month, a group of baptized Jews consisting of intellectuals and former officials arrived with their families in the ghetto. These latecomers had been protected by an agreement between the Germans and Count Adam Ronikier, chairman of a relief council made up of Polish, Ukrainian, and Jewish components. The German side had broken the agreement.[12] The converts lived near the two churches in the ghetto, had the use of one of the presbyteries for some living quarters, and obtained help in the form of money and soup from the Catholic welfare organization Caritas. They also demanded two seats on the Jewish Council. One was granted to them. It was occupied by Lucjan Altberg, legal counsel of the Polish Industrial and Commercial Association before the war. In the ghetto he also held a number of administrative posts. During the 1942 deportations he was able to cross the wall into Polish Warsaw.[13]

One of the prominent converts was Ludwik Hirszfeld, who had directed the Division of Bacteriology and Experimental Medicine and the Section of Serum Research in the Polish State Institute of Hygiene in prewar times. In the ghetto he was Chairman of the Health Council, organized a laboratory in the Jewish hospital, and helped teach illegal courses in medicine. One of his lectures was devoted to blood and race. During the deportations he was saved with his family through the efforts of a Polish acquaintance and other

Poles. After the war he founded the Institute of Immunology in Wroclaw.[14]

The convert Jozef Stein was the Director of the Jewish hospital. He was a tireless worker, besieging Council Chairman Czerniakow for money and inaugurating the lecture series with a talk about life and death. He was also a co-author of a study made by Jewish physicians in the ghetto on the medical consequences of starvation. Unlike Hirszfeld, Stein did not survive. He perished with his family in the death camp of Treblinka in 1943.[15]

Converts in the Jewish police—or Order Service, as it was called—were much more controversial. One was the experienced criminal lawyer Miecyslaw (Adam) Ettinger, who filled the position of disciplinary magistrate in the force. His appointment resulted in a four-and-a-half-hour discussion in the council. Opponents argued that a magistrate at such a tragic time had to represent the highest ethics of the Jewish people, and that a man who had been baptized for opportunistic reasons could not qualify. Ettinger, apparently incorruptible, retained the office.[16]

The case that became most notorious was the appointment of the convert Jozef Szerynski as chief of the Warsaw Ghetto's Jewish police. Szerynski, whose original name was Szynkman, had a prewar career as lieutenant colonel in the Polish police. According to Stanislaw Adler, who served in the ghetto police as a lawyer concerned with organizational measures, Szerynski had tried to obliterate not only his Jewish name but also his entire Jewish background, even developing a "decidedly anti-Semitic" attitude. When the German occupation began, Szerynski was under arrest for several months, and upon his release he faced financial difficulties and unemployment. In Warsaw, the Jewish community had no one who could take charge of a two-thousand-man police force, and when Szerynski's name was mentioned, he obtained the job. With Czerniakow, Szerynski developed a symbiotic relationship. The chairman and the police chief saw each other frequently, rode in the council's car to see German officials, or spent a weekend day in the more pleasant surroundings in the Jewish mental hospital of Otwock outside the ghetto. At a time when the stressful financial situation of the council left the police without a budget for regular pay, allowing and forcing the police to obtain contributions or engage in business activity, Czerniakow would worry about funding the police, whereas Szerynski seemed satisfied to have secured a decent salary for himself. The police chief also gave in to a craving for food, which he received with the help of a trusted adjutant and which shortly made him obese.

Szerynski did not side with the Germans. He tried to keep up his relations with Polish police officers and hoped for his reemployment in the Polish police after the war. When a Jewish rival in the ghetto organized a control office, which was widely perceived to be an intelligence network for the SS, Szerynski and Czerniakow succeeded in having it abolished.

On May 1, 1942, Szerynski was arrested by the Gestapo for having stored furs, confiscated from Jews, with a Polish police officer. Czerniakow made repeated attempts to have him released, but the German suspicion of fur smuggling was so strong that Czerniakow was told not to expect Szerynski's return. Nevertheless, Szerynski was reinstated late in July. He was needed for the great roundup of the ghetto population. A Jewish labor official relates a story of Jewish porters approaching Szerynski in the middle of the deportations with a plan to resist. Szerynski convinced them that Treblinka did not mean death. Shortly thereafter, Szerynski was wounded in the jaw by a member of the incipient Jewish underground. Disfigured, his face appeared to be frozen in laughter. Again he took command and helped the Germans conduct smaller deportations from the remnant ghetto during January 18–21. A few days later, he killed himself.[17]

Many Christian Jews were not doctors or functionaries, and bereft of all connections, they found themselves alone. One of these victims was Cordelia Edvardson.

Cordelia was born in Germany a few years before Hitler came to power. She was the daughter of a single parent, the half-Jewish Catholic novelist Elisabeth Langgässer. Her father, a Jew, did not marry her mother, because he was already married and did not want to leave his family. Elisabeth Langgässer eventually married a German and Cordelia was brought up as a Catholic in this household. Cordelia's Jewish background was kept a secret from everyone, and as a nine-year-old she even danced with an SS officer at a wedding. At one point she wanted to join the female counterpart of the Hitler

Youth—the Bund Deutscher Mädchen (BDM). Out of the question, her mother and stepfather informed her curtly. The cocoon disappeared totally with the introduction of the Jewish star, which she had to wear. She was now asked to leave the association of Catholic girls to which she belonged. Its motto was "One for all and all for one."

Her stepfather was an academic man who had entertained hopes for a successful academic career. He was cut off from his own family, because he had married a half-Jewish woman with an illegitimate child. For days on end he was silent. He would protect his stepdaughter but also shout at her. Soon she had to move out of the apartment, lest it would have to be marked with a Jewish star on the door to note her presence. She stayed with other Jews and obtained—since she was still a minor—a Jewish guardian. Her mother, increasingly worried, approached an officer of the Spanish Blue Division, which had been sent to the Russian front, and asked him whether he would marry Cordelia to give her protection. He agreed, but the marriage could not take place, because Cordelia was only fourteen. Her mother then succeeded in having her adopted by an old Spanish couple, and Cordelia actually received Spanish citizenship.

Then one day the Gestapo asked her to report. The notice was sent to her mother's and stepfather's apartment, and Cordelia received a message that said she should visit them, no matter how late in the day it was. She found them on the wide sofa, which was their bed, under a four-foot portrait of Christ. Her mother had already decided to accompany her to the Gestapo office. There a man in civilian clothes explained that Cordelia would never receive an exit permit. The grant of Spanish citizenship was not in question, but he wanted Cordelia to sign a piece of paper declaring that she voluntarily agreed to be subject to all the German laws, including the racial laws. When Cordelia balked, he pointed out that her refusal to sign would result in action against her mother for having arranged the Spanish adoption to evade German law. Cordelia signed.

Berlin had already been emptied of all but a remnant of Jews, and before long Cordelia was sent to the Jewish hospital, which served as the collecting point for Jews arrested for deportation. She was sent to Theresienstadt and from there to Auschwitz. Because she was young and strong, she was given a number and survived the experience, although just barely. She recuperated in Sweden, where some Polish and Hungarian Jewish women called her a German swine. Her mother, still in touch with her, wanted details about Auschwitz for a novel she planned to write. Seeking roots, Cordelia stayed in Sweden. She married a non-Jewish Swede and had children of her own. Yet she was still troubled, especially about her children. Obsessed by Goethe's poem *Der Erlkönig*, she thought of the poem's last line: In his arms the child was dead. Her older son died. After many years she went to an old priest to leave the Catholic Church. She had no objection to the crucified Christ; it was the resurrected Christ in triumph whom she did not know and did not want to know. In 1974 she arrived in Jerusalem, home at last.[18]

15

THE ADVANTAGED,
THE STRUGGLERS,
AND THE DISPOSSESSED

AT ANY ONE MOMENT during the Nazi years, and in any given place within the German power sphere, there was inequality in the Jewish community. While some Jews would salvage comforts, others staved off hunger, and still others lingered at the door of death. Although the German destruction process was a massive leveler, it did not obliterate long-standing distinctions. Indeed it sometimes fostered or created new ones. Through waves of upheavals, the phenomenon of stratification reappeared in ghettos and even in camps. The differences, however, had acquired a new meaning. They were no longer a time-honored measurement of attainment, but a telling indicator on a scale of vulnerabilities. Now the upper strata consisted of people who had gained or retained advantages with which to endure the German assault. The middle had to struggle day by day, and at the bottom men, women, and children could no longer stay alive without the meager assistance of Jewish organizations or of impoverished, enfeebled fellow Jews.

Jewry went down like a ship. Even the nicest apartment in a ghetto was still a ghetto apartment, and the armband made of silk was still an emblem of subjugation. Yet suffering was not rationed, nor was death altogether random. For some individuals, deprivations were lessened or slowed. There were several ways in which one could be a part of this advantaged group. One was status.

The distinguishing characteristic of status is that the individual had to have it already. In peacetime it might have been devoid of all significance, but during ghettoization, deportations, or shootings, it could have decisive importance. An example might be foreign nationality. The nationality had to be that of a neutral country that could protect the victim, or of an enemy state that could retaliate against Germany or one of its allies. It would not do to have Luxembourg citizenship in France, inasmuch as Luxembourg had disappeared in the Nazi scheme of things. Another, if somewhat more precarious, mantle than an effective foreign nationality was marriage to a non-Jew. Yet another source of privilege was military service in the First World War. During the early days of the Nazi regime, veterans could hold on a little longer in the German civil service, and later on those who were decorated or disabled were sometimes favored with a transport to the "Old People's Ghetto" of Theresienstadt instead of a direct trip to a shooting site or a death camp. Service, however, had to be rendered in the right army. Germany did not recognize the veterans of armies it had fought, like the French or Russian. Conversely, Romania—an ally of France and Russia in the earlier war and an ally of Germany in the second—made no concessions to veterans who had fought in 1914–1918 for Austria-Hungary. Old people in the Greater German Reich also had some status. German agencies involved in the deportations could not pretend that the elderly were fit for the hard labor supposedly performed by people "resettled" in the "east." Hence the older men and women were taken to Theresienstadt, where a small number were still alive at the end of the war. Finally there were small groups who raised successful questions about their Jewish descent, such as the Karaites in Eastern Europe and the so-called Portuguese Jews in the Netherlands.

A second source of advantage was a privileged position, notably on Jewish councils or in the Jewish bureaucracy that grew and proliferated under council rule. The survival rate of council members was not spectacular. Some councils were wiped out in the early stages of ghettoization. Others were kept as long as needed. Overall, however, the Jewish council members were spared intense deprivations of crowding, cold, and gnawing hunger. After all, they were supposed to be able to do their work, and that reasoning applied also to council employees.

The Jewish bureaucracy was larger than it had been before the war. Part of the expansion stemmed from the increase of burdens and functions assumed by the Jewish leadership. Depending on the extent of ghettoization, the councils were given such new tasks as housing allocation, labor recruitment, food distribution, public order, and even production of goods. A significant upper layer of functionaries owed their livelihood to these activities. With the growing scarcity of food in the ghettos, the possibility of obtaining increased rations or subsidized lunches also became an important factor for clerks, so much so that positions were sought even without a salary.[1]

The Jewish police were a special component of the ghetto's administrative structure. Not provided with firearms and frequently unfunded, they were even bereft of the designation "police." Officially they were called the "Order Service." Nevertheless, volunteers were plentiful. There were two thousand Order Service men in the Warsaw Ghetto, some six hundred in Lodz, five hundred in Lvov, five hundred in Lublin, and so forth. Of course, the Jewish police were afforded certain benefits. Stanislaw Adler, who served as a lawyer in the Order Service of the Warsaw Ghetto until the moment of the deportations, describes the situation of the force in great detail. From the start, he states, "The displays of rank and higher education, the saluting and street marches stirred up ridicule and aversion in the starving people." The Order Servicemen were regarded as useless drones. On their part, the police reciprocated the resentment. Soon, discipline deteriorated. Lack of pay resulted in absenteeism and abandonment of posts. The Order Service command, with the cooperation of the council, obtained additional rations for its men, but allocations of special foods not sufficient in quantity for the entire force were shared only in the upper echelons. To increase the meager salary base of the Order Service, a special tax was instituted. It was collected directly house by house under threat of blockade. Inside the Order Service, social cleavages began to surface. The guards assigned to the wall to prevent smuggling were despised in view of their violent behavior and their use of opportunities for profit. At headquarters, by contrast, clean-cut young men from families that had been privileged before the war performed clean clerical and messenger duties. Before long, idealism died off in the Order Service. Once, when Stanislaw Adler complained to the council member Bernard Zundelewicz about money squandered by top Jewish police officials in drinking bouts with Polish police, Zundelewicz told him that "in times like these" everyone was looking out for himself. "And you, colleague," he said to Adler, "you are in the Order Service only to save your life."[2]

Adler drew a major line between police service before and during deportations. The major roundup in the Warsaw Ghetto was conducted by an SS and Police Resettlement Staff geographically, section by section, and the Jewish Order Service was deployed in these seizures. A number of Jewish policemen were themselves deported to the Treblinka death camp during a subsequent action in January 1943. In one of the barracks, an inmate is said to have told a story that the Order Service men had tossed out their caps as their train moved from the Treblinka station into the camp, fearful of what might await them there at the hands of people they had arrested.[3]

During the deportation phase, a deferment afforded by a position was closely monitored by German agencies. In the course of the very orderly transports from Germany and the Netherlands, the Security Police requested data about personnel in the community machinery and demanded reductions in proportion to the shrinkage of the remaining Jewish population.[4] Martha Mosse, in charge of housing referrals in the Jewish community of Berlin, protested to her Jewish superiors against inroads into her own staff. Her trump card: She was now involved in preparing transports. For this task she had only ninety-five employees, including sixteen former members of a cultural association placed in her division. She could not spare anyone, because she was responsible for questionnaires presented to deportees and for comparisons of the tentative transport lists of the community with the final ones of the Gestapo. Both her registration section and her list section were overburdened. Thus the list section also determined the order in which individuals were to be deported, and so forth.[5] Arthur Lilienthal, board member of the Jewish Reichsvereinigung, which administered all the Jewish communities within the prewar borders of Germany, was unimpressed. Writing to his fellow board member Paul Eppstein, he pointed out that other communities, such as Munich, had already given up employees and that Berlin would have to get along with fewer of them as well.[6]

When the deportations in Germany had run their course, even the most privileged members of the Reichsvereinigung were privileged no more. Erich Simon, born in 1880, widower of an Aryan woman and a former Regierungsrat in Prussia, was the statistician for the Reichsvereinigung, a position in which he supplied the SS with materials about the disappearing Jewish community. The SS statistician Richard Korherr, who valued and respected Simon, was going to rely on him for an historical overview. He had exacted a promise from the Berlin Gestapo that Simon would not be deported. In June 1943, however, Simon was detained at a collecting point for Jews about to be transported. Korherr could not extract him. When Simon was sent to Theresienstadt, Korherr could not get him back.[7]

Status or position was highly prized in the Jewish community, but there was also an advantage in having a special skill, occupation, or profession. Two requisites, however, had to be met. The specialization had to be in demand, and it had to be the product of long training. There was not much room for writers or musicians, in short anyone who was not essential to the perpetrators or to the physical survival of the community and who, in the final analysis, would have to be supported with dwindling Jewish resources. An example of such a special group in difficulty within the walls of the Warsaw Ghetto was a body of about two thousand Orthodox Jews, half of them children, engaged in full-time religious study.[8]

Favored were people who could make something: carpenters, furriers, shoemakers. Diamond cutters in Amsterdam and watchmakers in Galicia were an elite. Jewish managers of industrial or other enterprises, at first thought dispensable, could also be needed, especially if there were no efficient replacements in the local economy. Even traders with specialized knowledge could be utilized at times, like a small number of raw material experts who made purchases for the Office of the Four-Year Plan on the Dutch black market. Jews were not supposed to be used as translators in the interest of security, but they held such jobs in German offices in the eastern territories.

Among the professionals, the most important category were doctors and nurses. Jewish physicians were relatively numerous throughout Europe. In some areas there were also a large percentage of doctors in various medical specialties. As a result they were among the last Jews to be deported in Bulgarian-held Macedonia as well as in Hungarian cities. A German Security officer noted in a report from Slovakia that after the main deportations of 1942, Jewish doctors were still treating Slovaks. The Jews, he said, knew how to influence and change the attitudes of the Slovak population by serving patients for small fees or no money at all.[9] Exceptions for physicians were sometimes made in occupied territory by the Germans themselves. In Kremenchug, Ukraine, the army exempted two doctors to assure care of Ukrainians.[10] In the Baranowicze Gebiet (or Baranovichi area) comprising eight *rayons,* the total of 120 physicians included 68 Jews. The city of Baranowicze had 51 physicians, 32 of them Jews. Only nine of the city's Jewish physicians were in the local ghetto. To be sure, this need for Jewish doctors was watched carefully by the German regional medical superviser, Dr. Gerhard Wiechmann, who would rule that Jewish doctor so-and-so was superfluous or that so-and-so could be "eliminated."[11]

Physicians stood on the upper rung of the ladder in the ghettos, even if their numbers there were somewhat heavy. Probably no ghetto could equal Theresienstadt, whose population reached a high of fifty-eight thousand in September 1942, and which had 363 practicing physicians.[12] But only in the smallest ghettos might there have been a shortage or lack of doctors. At the same time, the physicians had to have a feeling of impotence in the rising tide of illness. They lacked drugs, alcohol, even bandages. Eyeglasses has to be collected from those who had died. Above all, there was not enough food, and they could not cure starvation. The patients, trusting and grasping, came to them again and again. In this pressing situation, physicians made a few discoveries. In Theresienstadt, for example, they found out that the intestinal diseases of enteritis and colitis were seldom serious in young people, even without any medical help, but that the same ailments were often fatal in older men and women, notwithstanding the administration of scarce sulfa drugs.[13]

Now and then, there were reactions against physicians in the ghetto community, just as there were resentments against other favored groups. A diarist in the Warsaw Ghetto noted on May 27, 1942, that an order, which he attributed to Ghetto Kommissar Auerswald, had prohibited special armbands. Up to now, said the diarist, various Jewish officials and also certain professionals, such as doctors and dentists, had devised armbands showing not only the compulsory Jewish star but also their specialization. "These special armbands," he wrote, "were intended to announce: we are not simple, ordinary Jews, we are carrying out important duties and therefore should have special privileges." Now, he noted, there would be "just one great mass of Jews," and Hitler's thugs on the ghetto street "will not have to stop and consider if they should also bash in the head of the Jew who is a doctor."[14]

At the time of the mass deportations in Warsaw, only a few physicians, including heads of hospital wards and some of their helpers, were permitted to stay. The ward chiefs were exempted "automatically," and they in turn selected others from their staff for retention. One of the health professionals was a medical student who had not finished her studies before the outbreak of war and who was employed as a practitioner in pediatrics in the ghetto hospital. When the roundups began, the children crowded around her and asked her to stay with them "until the end." She promised to do so. Soon thereafter, she found out that she would be spared from deportation. She definitely wanted to live. As panic spread, she was approached by a young woman with a plea to give a lethal injection to that woman's bedridden mother, lest the Germans shoot the mother in bed. She complied with this request and went on to treat several more people in the same way. Then it occurred to her how she could escape from the ghetto without breaking her promise to the children. In the presence of a senior physician she put morphine into the mouths of infants. After this act she told the older children that she would give them medicine that would take away their pain and asked them to swallow a dose that was sufficient to kill them. She did not wait to observe the outcome.[15]

Physicians also had favored positions in camps. Hospitals and dispensaries in concentration camps or killing centers were often only facades. Patients who did not recover quickly enough were put to death by the camp administration with an injection, a bullet, or the gas chamber. Robert Lifton notes the irony, not lost on inmate doctors, that the camp hospitals offered a more secure shelter to the physicians than to the patients.[16] Moreover, in some hospital huts the help that the doctors could render with their primitive tools was offset, if that is the word, by the practice imposed by the SS on inmate physicians to select the weakest patients for gassing. Once, a trio of women physicians was given the assignment of handing over such patients. The two younger women hid and left the older one to do the job herself. Angry, the older woman accused her younger colleagues of lacking solidarity.[17]

Status, position, and an occupational skill were three modes of acquiring an advantage. Money was the fourth. In the 1930s it facilitated emigration. At the time when Jewish forced labor columns were organized in Warsaw and Lublin, relatively well-to-do Jews could buy their freedom for a monthly fee, the proceeds of which were used to support the families of the laborers.[18] Labor exemption certificates could also be purchased in Romania.[19] When ghettos were formed in Poland, Jews in roomy apartments outside the projected ghetto boundaries could exchange their living quarters for the best available space within the newly delimited ghetto quarters. In Old Romania, where Jews by the tens of thousands were ejected from frontier areas and rural districts, but where ghettos were not established, the market determined who could move into an adequate apartment in the interior cities. Accumulated money lost much of its value in the Lodz and Theresienstadt ghettos, which had their own currencies, or in the dozens of "colonies" formed for expelled Jews from Bukovina and Old Romania in the area between the Dnestr and Bug rivers, where a special currency had been instituted as well, but in the Warsaw Ghetto money was crucial if one wanted to eat. In Warsaw, there were in fact two groups of people with money: those who had possessed it before the war and had been able to retain some of it, outside frozen bank accounts, in cash or jewelry, and the "new rich" who obtained their resources either because they could take advantage of the attempted industrialization of the ghetto or because they were smugglers. The industrial sector apparently made enough profits to cause comment in the ghetto about such manifestations as the "gluttony" of the brush makers.[20] The black marketeers and their various middlemen and insurance underwriters, not to speak of leeches who demanded payments on threat of exposure, also became a significant economic force. At the same time, the Jewish Council, which had taxing powers, could not siphon off much money from these producers and traders. Too many transactions were unrecorded, and too many were pure barter. Nor was there all that much philanthropy. That is not to say that indifference reigned supreme. Thus Stanislaw Adler notes that apartments were sublet for very small sums, despite the considerable decrease in space or time for cooking, washing, or sleeping for the original tenants,[21] and another witness observed that even the hedonistic brush makers maintained an orphanage.[22]

Below the upper tier, a large number of Jews faced a daily struggle to make ends meet, and theirs was a long day, a drab day. In the main they were the laborers. Even outside or before the ghetto, Jewish employees were not in a good position. In Germany, they were not to receive subsidies, allowances, and various benefits.[23] In Poland the wages—primarily of significance in the early days prior to ghettoization—were set at 80 percent of the compensation paid to Poles.[24] Inside the ghetto, the situation was worse. Not much could be obtained for one's labor and not much could be bought with the money. The ghetto workshops in Lodz supplied laborers with meals and on rare occasions with shoes reconstituted from worn-out pairs that had been shipped in.[25] The Lodz laborer might go home in the evening to an unheated apartment without windowpanes.[26] For heavy laborers the food rations were dangerously insufficient. In the Warsaw Ghetto, there were self-employed men who pulled carts with as many as three passengers. The ricksha man received one zloty per person. For a kilogram of bread on the black market he paid eight to ten zlotys.[27]

Forced laborers assigned to various projects were in dire straits. Already in the early days, men returned from their work sites to the city of Lublin with blood oozing from their bodies. The Jewish Council appealed to the Germans to spare these men further beatings.[28] In the fall of 1942, many Minsk Ghetto laborers did not have shoes.[29] For a midday meal received by these laborers at work, the German city administration in Minsk expended ten pfennigs.[30]

People who did not earn enough tried to sell their possessions. In the Warsaw Ghetto, the sell-off began with valuables and continued with furniture, springs of mattresses, and finally pots and pans.[31] Peddlers stood in the street trying to sell locally produced wares or items that had belonged to needy families. Others slid into irremediable poverty.

There is no count of the people at the bottom. The ghetto leaders kept records of employment, rather than idleness. But the employment figures sometimes spoke for themselves. Adam Czerniakow in the Warsaw Ghetto noted in July 1942 a peak of 95,000 working Jews, including those employed by the council and its agencies, of a population nearly four times as large.[32] A smaller ghetto like Biala Podlaska in the Lublin District had 1,884 laborers of 8,500 inhabitants in May 1942.[33]

In his study of ghettos in Eastern Europe, Isaiah Trunk discovered a food pyramid in the Warsaw Ghetto. Council employees obtained 1,665 calories a day, independent artisans, 1,407, shop workers 1,225, and the population as a whole an average of 1,125.[34] The scientists in the ghetto, who counted everything, thus pointed only by implication to an amorphous group that consumed fewer than the 1,125 calories: the semi-starving and the starving.[35] Who were all these people?

Many had already been buffeted before the war. They had been marginalized during the depression of the 1930s when their employment became spotty or when they had lost jobs to become "independent" on the pettiest scale. Over the years these families had become increasingly dependent on charity, and by 1940 they had little to offer or to sell. Too unskilled to be readily absorbed in the ghetto economy and too weakened to perform its heavier menial labor, they lived shrinking lives, stretching their remaining resources to the utmost.

A second group consisted of refugees. In the west, the refugees from Germany and Austria were the new stateless people. In Slovakia, Bulgaria, and Romania, refugees were families who had been ousted from specific cities and who were looking for any housing they could afford. But in Poland, they had been poured from smaller ghettos into larger ones. A report of the Jewish Social Self-Help organization in the Warsaw Ghetto for January 1942 noted 2,977 refugees quartered in four buildings. A total of 539 had died in January. At Stawki Street No. 9, 1,100 were in 170 rooms "generally speaking, not heated." The water supply and toilets were not functioning. At Dzika Street No. 3, there were refugees with bleeding dysentery. They had to stay there.[36]

Stanislaw Adler notes that eventually bread in the Warsaw Ghetto was sold by the slice.[37] He also observed that the beggar population did *not* increase exponentially. The reason, he said, was the progressive dying off of beggars, who were then replaced by individuals who had reached the point of destitution in turn.[38]

16

THE UNADJUSTED

THE SALIENT CHARACTERISTIC of the Jewish community in Europe during 1933–1945 was its step-by-step adjustment to step-by-step destruction. In this respect there was no difference between the Jewish leaders and ordinary Jews. The basic strategy of minimizing losses, which was the maxim of the Jewish councils, was mirrored in the adaptations of Jewish households. Be it at the community or family level, reserves were husbanded to maintain stability. Appeals were made to authority for exemptions, extensions, or amelioration, but then pain and humiliation were accepted as the price of continued living. Some people, however, could not or would not make these adjustments. In one way or another they no longer cooperated with the perpetrator or with their own leadership. Although they differed in their deviations from the norm, they shared an essential attribute: they no longer played the prevailing game.

The principal manifestations of such non-conformist behavior were suicide, hiding, escape, and resistance. Most of these decisions were calculated, with or without extensive preparation, and many times they were the acts of individuals or of small groups of dissenters.

The radical act of killing oneself was usually prompted by a low tolerance of deprivation. For the emancipated Jews of Western Europe, sudden reversals were particularly traumatic, and in that environment suicide was most often the product of shock; in the ghettos and camps of the east, it was more commonly the outcome of weariness.

Konrad Kwiet, who made a study of suicide in the German Jewish community, suggests a conservative estimate of 5,000 self-inflicted deaths over the twelve years of Nazi rule—this in a population of little more than a half million that was steadily declining during that period. The standard measurement of suicide is an annual number per 100,000. Thirty or so would be high, 68—the number for Berlin Jewry in 1925—an epidemic. Kwiet believes that this high point was repeated or exceeded in 1933, and that in the course of the two deportation years from 1941 to 1943, there must have been at least 3,000 suicides in the remaining community, or about 1,500 per 100,000.[1]

When the Jews of Germany were buffeted by the compulsory wearing of the Jewish star and the onset of deportations, relatively many members of this community were past their prime, and many of the individuals who ended their lives could no longer look forward to anything. They wanted to stay in their apartments, surrounded by their books and phonograph records, to spare themselves an agony from which they had no hope of recovery. They also had the means to kill themselves with least suffering, usually with barbiturates that could still be obtained for a price that—however exorbitant—was going to be their last expense.

In a personal diary, a German woman, Ruth Andreas-Friedrich, tells a story of a Jewish friend, Mrs. Lehmann, who asked her to help pack. Mrs. Lehmann had been notified that she would be picked up on the following day. When Ruth Andreas-Friedrich arrived in Lehmann's apartment, she heard a Jewish subtenant pace back and forth behind a closed sliding door. "Isn't he packing?" she asked. "He doesn't want to go through this anymore," she was told in a whisper. "He made another decision." Soon the pacing stopped. No one opened the door. Even while the packing continued, Mr. Erichsohn was dying, "alone, considerate, and discreet."[2]

A survivor reports that there was also a substantial number of suicides in the transit camp of Drancy near Paris. He estimates that in a two-and-a-half-month period, about one hundred internees took their lives. Under these circumstances, however, the suicides were disapproved of, and the would-be suicides ostracized, for the simple reason that an individual who did not wait until the moment of departure was going to be replaced by another victim on the transport.[3]

The Polish Jews did not commit suicide in waves. They did not greet downturns and setbacks, however severe, with the sense of disbelief that was almost usual in Germany. Moreover they did not have so much access to barbiturates or other chemicals. Their self-inflicted deaths were therefore bound to be more violent. They would jump out of a four-story or even two-story window. They might walk to the ghetto wall or fence in the expectation of being shot by a guard, and sometimes the guard was reluctant to shoot. In the Lodz Ghetto, on July 14, 1944, Mindla Zarzewska, aged thirty-four, started to climb the fence early in the morning. The German Order Policeman reprimanded her and reasoned with her without success. At that moment, a higher-ranking police officer came by and also tried to deter her from setting foot on the fence. She persisted and was shot.[4]

In the death camps, the weary did not have to go out of their way to die. In Auschwitz, those who had given up were called *Muselmänner*, or Moslems, in Lublin (Maydanek) *Gamele*, or camels. They invited death by electrocution or shooting at the fence or they died passively, no longer eating, in their bunks.

For all those who did not want to go on anymore, there was a much larger number who did not want to die as yet. Prolongation of life was the main theme of ghetto thinking and the primary occupation of the ghetto inmate. So long as work certificates offered salvation they were grasped as a lifeline. Two processes, however, were simultaneously transforming the makeup of the Jewish community and the thinking of an increasing number of its people. One was the effect of the decimation caused by the deaths or deportation of weaker or more feeble individuals. This development, which was the exact opposite of the aging brought about by emigration in the German Jewish community, left the ghettos with significant if not preponderant shares of younger, healthier, and more resourceful men and women. The second impact was the growing doubt that the Nazi regime could be outlived by acts of accommodation. There was an unavoidable awareness that friends and family had disappeared without trace, and any optimistic fantasy about their fate was jarred from time to time by the thickening flow of rumors about shootings or gas. In short, the reduction of the Jewish communities was leaving a shrinking remnant composed of the most vigorous people, who had growing anxieties about their own future. The effect was seen first in simple acts of non-cooperation: Jewish families who no longer turned themselves in automatically and who tried to hide in place. Examples of such occurrences may be drawn from two small ghettos: Bilgoraj and Janow.

The Bilgoraj Ghetto in the Lublin District had no fence or wall. It contained barely 2,500 Jews. On March 22, 1942, 57 families with 221 persons, many of them ill, were transferred to Tarnogrod. The first major roundup followed in August. On that occasion, the Germans demanded 1,000 victims. As one platoon of German Order Police stood by, the Jewish Council met to decide who should be selected for labor in "the Ukraine." Inasmuch as almost half of the population was to be removed, the council's list included some people capable of work as well as women, children, and old people. Members of the council and skilled laborers, with their families, were to be exempt. The Jews marked for deportation were told to assemble in the marketplace to be transported to Ukraine. The Jewish police were present as the people were loaded on wooden carts. The column was met by another one from Tarnogrod. At the Zivierzyniec railway station, the Jews had to abandon their luggage. They were sent to the Belzec death camp and there were no survivors.

After the Jews who were left in Bilgoraj had no word from the evacuated people, they wondered whether Ukraine had been the real destination of the deportees. They started to ask questions of Polish railway men and found out that the train had gone to Belzec. One of the Polish drivers had actually taken the transport to the camp. Shortly thereafter, large quantities of clothing and prayer books were dumped in the Spolem cooperative to be sorted by Jews. This news spread quickly in the Jewish and Polish populations. At the end of

October the ghetto, diminished in size, was fenced, and during the early morning of November 2, two platoons of German gendarmerie arrived for the final roundup. Now there was much shouting and shooting. One thousand Jews were caught. The men had to walk to the train station, while the women and children were transported in carts. In the ghetto, two hundred Jews lay dead. Some others hid there, as yet undiscovered. Between seventy and eighty workers were set aside.[5]

Orderliness had broken down in Bilgoraj. To be sure, the Germans had not expected anything else, or they would not have doubled the police force for the second roundup and they would not have dispensed with the services of the Jewish council or with cover stories about Ukraine. In Janow, a ghetto in the Volhynian region, up to two thousand Jews faced a cavalry police squadron at the end of September 1942. The Volhynian Jews were the subject of massive shootings during that summer, and Janow was struck in the course of this operation. In the presence of the local Gebietskommissar and the mayor, a small detachment of Security Police, augmented by the squadron, which corresponded in size to a regular police company, moved into the ghetto, seizing Jews and saving one hundred to two hundred of them for work. It was apparent, however, that most of the intended victims were hiding in earth holes and bunkers. As a part of the squadron formed a cordon around the ghetto, other police entered it again. Unexpectedly the Germans encountered resistance of Jews using firearms and homemade explosives. Several ghetto houses were set on fire, either by the raiders or by the defenders. In the chaos that followed about fifty Jews broke through the cordon and escaped. The Germans in the ghetto withdrew to the perimeter, and the Jews were driven from their hiding places by heat, fire, and smoke. Unable to penetrate the police blockade, they were shot. Twelve hundred surrendered voluntarily and were killed in a ditch nearby. Four hundred charred bodies were removed on the following day in wooden carts.[6]

The recalcitrant Jews who hid in cellars, rooms, attics, or bunkers during roundups were still moored to the ghetto. They were bound to be targets of the German SS and Police armed with rifles, automatic weapons, and hand grenades. In the end only a handful of these Jews saved themselves. Completely different from this stationary reaction was a decision to flee.

The prospect of a successful escape from the trap of one's registered residence, or a ghetto, or a camp depended heavily on place, that is to say, one's entire cultural and physical environment. It was easier to be undetected in Rome than in Warsaw, easier for the small Greek-speaking community of Athens to blend with the surrounding population than for Ladino-speaking Jews to be anonymous in Salonika. In a western arc extending from Norway through Denmark, the Netherlands, Belgium, and France to Italy, hiding out was not even unusual, but in Germany, Poland, the Baltic area, and the occupied USSR, it was much more dangerous and difficult.

If location was one determining factor, then money was another. Almost everywhere, a Jew who had cash or salable possessions could start with an immediate advantage. Transportation, shelter, or a disguise could be expensive, especially when needed desperately. Finally, however, flight was a function of personality. The typical escapees, notably in Eastern Europe, were individuals who not only wanted to outlive the catastrophe but were prepared to abandon apartments and family members, to move from place to place, or to stay in a hole, surrounded by patrols, for an extended time.

Very few Jews in occupied Poland made an early decision not to wear the star and not to move into a ghetto, and if an escape was difficult at that point because of a lack of connections, money, or adaptability, it was going to be even more problematic thereafter. The presence of a fence or of guards was only part of the problem. There was also an invisible barrier: the fate of those who were going to be left behind. For a breadwinner with a wife and children, the drawback was obvious and usually decisive, but even for young, able-bodied people without dependents, there might still have been a dilemma. In a ghetto pursuing a strategy of salvation through work, the entire community depended on those who were most healthy and fit. It was precisely this issue that kept a prospective partisan force in the ghetto of Vilnius. Although it was possible for these young people to filter into the woods, the Ghetto chief, Gens, argued that their departure would spell out an erosion of the ghetto's economic base, dooming the non-working women, children, and old people.

In Eastern Europe, and in most of the Balkans as well, escape was also infrequent during roundups. Claude Lanzmann's film *Shoah* contains a scene in which survivors describe the deportation of eighteen hundred Jews from the Greek island of Corfu. It was June 1944 and the Italian-speaking Jews on Corfu were told that they would be transported for work in Poland. Then they saw that even the old and the sick were rounded up. For five days they were kept at a fort on the island. "No one," said Armando Aaron, "dared escape and leave his father, mother, brother. Our solidarity was on religious and family grounds." They were taken to the mainland on ferries made of barrels and planks, which were towed by small boats and manned by one, two, or three German armed guards, "but we were terrified," said Aaron. "You can understand, terror is the best of guards."[7]

The rarest escapes were those from trains and death camps. Almost invariably, this activity was the province of young people who did not have a close family by their side when they made their attempt. There was a major breakout from a western transport moving through Tarnowskie Gory to Auschwitz on February 7, 1943, when Jews had loosened the floorboards of a freight car. One woman was crushed under the wheels of the rolling train, another was shot, and subsequently six more escapees were caught.[8] When a mammoth transport from Kolomea and neighboring towns moved with 8,205 deportees to Belzec in the summer heat of September 1942, an undetermined number of Jews jumped out. The commander of the Order Police guard estimated that at least two-thirds of these jumpers had been killed.[9]

The quintessential escapee was the twenty-one-year-old Walter Rosenberg. Deported from Slovakia to Auschwitz in 1942, he worked on the ramp where the transports arrived from August 1942 to June 1943. During that time, six Czechoslovak Gypsies attempted to flee. Five were seized immediately and the sixth, Vruzen Vrba, was captured a week later. All were shot. Rosenberg worked himself up to the position of scribe. He had a small room with a bunk, chair, and table all his own. He was also aware of happenings in the camp.

One of the stranger occurrences was the presence of several thousand Czech Jews from Theresienstadt who had apparently been given a reprieve. In six months, they lost only about 20 percent of their people to the camps' privation—by Auschwitz standards, excellent treatment. Convinced that these Jews were going to be killed, Rosenberg looked for a leader among them to organize a revolt. He found Freddy Hirsch, a thirty-year-old man who was taking care of children and who had managed to organize a quasi-normal life for them. Explaining to Hirsch that a revolt and breakout would be the only hope of this Czech community, Rosenberg asked the thunderstruck Hirsch to lead it. On his part, Hirsch asked to think it over alone. Rosenberg gave him an hour. Returning to his hut, Rosenberg found Hirsch comatose from an overdose of pills. Hirsch could not be revived and the Czech Jews were gassed. After several months Rosenberg decided to plot his own escape. He knew that tracks were being built to enable the Germans to unload transports right in front of the gas chambers. He reasoned that only Hungary could still supply a large number of victims at this time. Memorizing much of the information that he had gathered, Rosenberg and another Slovak Jew, Alfred Wetzler, prepared a small covered ditch inside the camp perimeter in April 1944. There they waited for three days and three nights, while German guards were looking for them on both sides of the fence. Then they made their getaway. Walking across the mountains to Slovakia, they found representatives of the Jewish community in Zilina and revealed to them the accumulated facts. The Hungarian deportations began a month later, in May. Rosenberg did not rest. When a revolt broke out in Slovakia during the summer, he joined the partisans. After the war he migrated to Canada, where he became a professor of pharmacology at the University of British Columbia. He kept a name he had given himself after his escape: Rudolf Vrba.[10]

Resistance to destruction, in the sense of pitting oneself against the perpetrator, was an especially difficult undertaking. The potential resister was hemmed in not only by superior force but also by the stance of the Jewish community itself. Jewry, which had been without any arms even before the war, was committing itself to a strategy of accommodation. Nothing in this consensus was so inconceivable as an attempt to harm any perpetrator or to paralyze his actions. There were to be no "provocations." There was to be no semblance of revolt.

Self-restraint was strong enough to preclude any psychological warfare. In the Jewish councils, no pamphlets were composed and no arguments were made to show that any German action was hurtful and morally wrong. No ill will was expressed to the Germans. No threats were made to the life of any German. No rumors were started that the Allied powers would retaliate for the destruction of the Jews. One Jew once did write an anonymous postcard in Yiddish to a German journalist wishing that man's newborn child might die just as Jewish children were dying.[11] In the Jewish community such a man would be called primitive.

Sabotage was deemed more possible. It was covert and frequently untraceable. There were instances of damage inflicted by Jews in German labor camps on goods or equipment. Jewish furniture packers in the west made sure that the contents of apartments vacated by deported Jews would not arrive safely in Germany. More significant was the act of Communist Jews in Belgium who staged a raid on the Jewish community to destroy records. Later, the Comité de Défense des Juifs stopped a train already on its way to Auschwitz and liberated a number of victims.[12]

The final act of resistance was violent. The following incident took place in Kedainiai, Lithuania, on August 28, 1941. A small detachment of Security Police belonging to Einsatzkommando 3, aided by local civilian Lithuanians, killed 710 Jewish men, 767 Jewish women, and 599 Jewish children of that town on that day. The Jews were taken from a barn to a pit in groups of 200. According to the postwar testimony of one of the Lithuanians, a heavily built Jew, Slapoberskis, was told by a Lithuanian, Czygas, to undress. The Jew, fully realizing what was happening, said to the Lithuanian that he was a man like him. Czygas then tore the Jew's clothes off and drew his pistol. Slapoberskis grabbed Czygas and drew him into the ditch, holding him with one hand by the neck and firing the Lithuanian's pistol at the German commander with the other. Now the German jumped in to help Czygas, freeing him, only to be grabbed by Slapoberskis in turn. Another Lithuanian, Jankunas, who was heavy himself, jumped in, freeing the German, but found himself in the clutches of Slapoberskis. Jankunas drew a knife from his belt and killed the Jew. Czygas, gravely injured, died on the way to the hospital.[13]

What is notable about Slapoberskis is the rarity of his deed. Spot resistance even when objectively nothing could be lost anymore was an isolated act. The rhythm of compliant behavior, practiced over the centuries, was not about to break at the sight of a ditch. But what about physical resistance begun with more planning and fore-thought? There were three situations in which such fighting took place.

The first was a product of escape. In France, for example, young Jewish men, some of them members of the Zionist scout movement, others Communists, were living in illegality and, as a matter of conviction, opportunity, or necessity, found a path of action in the partisan movement. Similarly, but under more difficult circum-stances, Jews slipping out of ghettos or labor camps joined or formed their own partisan units in such areas as the wooded and marshy regions of Byelorussia. In Slovakia, many hundreds of inmates of a labor camp, finding themselves suddenly without guards during a Communist-led uprising, also became partisan fighters. One may find some Jews with weapons in hand in Italy and Yugoslavia, in-deed wherever some partisan activity took place, and their aggregate number is certainly more than a few thousand. Most of these Jews, however, had placed themselves under the command of a larger underground. They had become soldiers in the Allied cause.

A second circumstance was fighting in order to escape. It is note-worthy that such attempts were made in three of the six death camps in Poland. All three were relatively late. In Treblinka and Sobibor the revolts occurred in 1943. They were the work of plotters who took into consideration the decreased flow of new victims and who weighed the chances of success in a breakout against the im-probability that the guard forces would allow any inmate to go on living once the deportation program had been exhausted. In both Treblinka and Sobibor the planning evolved slowly and the revolts were costly, but at least a minority of the inmates reached freedom.[14] In Auschwitz, where an underground resistance organization was dominated by non-Jews, a revolt was carried out by the Jewish crematorium workers alone. The breakout attempt, in October 1944, was accompanied by heavy losses. It did not succeed.[15]

Escapees and inmates were most often individuals, banded together, acting for themselves. They made their decisions without calculating, or having to calculate, the possible consequences of their actions for an entire community of helpless people. The situation was different for those who wanted to fight in a ghetto, specifically to resist a roundup for deportation or shooting. The advocates of such resistance came from a variety of political movements, but they shared a basic philosophy. They wanted to make a stand in order to make a statement. Three conspicuous attempts of this nature were made in the ghettos of Vilnius, Bialystok, and Warsaw.

The Jewish community of Vilnius had been cut down by a series of mass shootings in 1941, so that by the end of the year, it was a remnant. On January 1, 1942, a proclamation was issued by an underground group telling the Jews to cast aside any illusions, informing them that those who had been seized were no longer alive, and calling upon them not to walk like sheep to the slaughter. This admonition was probably the earliest of its kind. One of the principal authors of the manifesto was a man in his early twenties, Abba Kovner. In essence, Kovner did not believe that one could rely on contracts or understandings with the Germans. He did not think that there was a viable major alternative to self-defense.

The aim of the underground clashed with the policy of the ghetto's Jewish police chief and, later, dictator, Jacob Gens, who combated any dissemination of news about the shootings and who strove to maintain a quiet, working ghetto. In October 1941 he had warned a woman who had escaped from the shooting site of Ponar not to say a word to anyone, and on January 4, 1942, he forbade "the spreading of false rumors and creating panic among the people." Gens was determined to hold the rumors and the underground in check.

The underground had another internal problem. It had formed a United Partisans Organization, with a Communist, Yitzhak Witenberg, in command. Unknown to the Jewish resisters in the ghetto, Witenberg was also a member of a Communist cell in the city. The

basic goals of the Jewish partisans inside and the Communist partisans outside the ghetto were not identical. The Jews were preparing
for a showdown when the time of the ghetto's liquidation might
come, and for this contingency they had Gens's guarded support.
The Communists, on the other hand, wanted young men to fight the
Germans in the woods then and there. One day, the Germans captured non-Jewish members of the cell in Vilnius and found out that
Witenberg belonged to this group, without, however, discovering
his dual role. They demanded his surrender, and Gens, with the
pained acquiescence of the Jewish partisan leaders, prevailed upon
Witenberg to give himself up. The United Partisans were now in
some disarray. There were more and more of them who favored a
departure to the woods, and after the Germans, full of suspicions
about Gens, also killed the Ghetto Chief, the partisans could not
dominate the ghetto. When the liquidation came, some Jews fought
inside and others broke out. The battle planned for so long was a
clash in which the Jews of the ghetto were largely passive. Abba
Kovner led one of the detachments into the woods. He survived, a
tormented witness.[16]

In the Bialystok District, which was traversed by Security Police
units in the summer of 1941, the ghettos were subsequently not
touched for a year. The largest ghetto, in the city of Bialystok, held
about thirty-five thousand Jews in October 1942. At the time, the
clear-sighted Ghetto Chief Barasz, who did not hesitate to speak
about annihilation, tried to maximize the ghetto's productivity as his
principal strategy to save the ghetto community. A young underground leader, Mordechaj Tenenbaum-Tamaroff, who began to
keep a diary on January 12, 1943, referred as early as January 19 to
nearby Treblinka as a death camp. Toward the end of that month
and the beginning of February, old clothes belonging to deportees of
extinct neighboring communities arrived to be made into rags.
Barasz himself sent some of the documents and photographs found
in the clothes to Tenenbaum-Tamaroff, who carried them, unable to
part with them for a minute, in his pockets all day long.

That month, Tenenbaum-Tamaroff drafted a manifesto, for "the
moment when we proclaim the counter-action," stating that 3 mil-

lion Jews had gone to their deaths in Kulmhof, Belzec, Auschwitz, Treblinka, and Sobibor, and warning the Jews that all deportees were going to their deaths. "We have nothing to lose anymore!" he went on. "Jews you are being led to Treblinka! They will poison us with gas like dogs with rabies and then they will burn us in ovens. We do not want to go like sheep to slaughter!"

German armament officials and the Security Police considered their next move against the Bialystok Ghetto in the light of the perennial labor shortage. It was agreed that the ghetto should be thinned but remain intact. Barasz was given a deportation quota of 17,000. Negotiating with the Germans, he obtained a reduction to 6,300. The Security Police, which had already procured eight trains with a capacity of 2,000 each, probably held to this goal in secret, but they did not hesitate to make promises to keep the ghetto quiet. The Jewish council started to compile a list of 8,500 undesirable people and unemployed families. On February 4, however, panic seized the ghetto, and when Barasz learned that the action was to begin at 3:30 A.M. of the next day, he sent his news to Tenenbaum-Tamaroff and at the same time passed the word that one should hide. Most Jews now began to conceal themselves in long-prepared hiding places. The Jewish Order Service largely refrained from cooperating in the roundup, and the Germans tried to rely on individual Jews who were promised safety for revealing where hidden Jews were located. One Jew tossed vitriol into the eyes of a German. The blinded man probably fired a shot that killed a Kriminaloberassistent. Between 8,000 and 10,000 Jews were transported to Auschwitz and Treblinka; hundreds more were shot on the spot.

For Tenenbaum-Tamaroff the foray into the ghetto removed any doubt about the closeness of the end. On February 27, he met with his associates of the Zionist Youth movement Dror and raised the question of whether resistance should be offered as soon as any Jews were seized in another roundup. Should anyone in the ghetto, he asked, be allowed to hide? The youth, he said, were on their own; their elders were not going to take care of anyone: "This is an orphanage." Hershel Rosental, in agreement, spoke of a choice between suffering a "beggar's death" and making the ghetto a chapter in history, as the Armenians had done in the First World War when they battled the Ottoman Turks at Musa Dagh. Sarah Koplinski said that "if it is a question of honor, we have already long lost it." She favored a breakout to the woods. But the sentiment of the group was against hiding or escape, and Tenenbaum-Tamaroff concluded that action had to begin "as soon as the first Jew is taken."

The end came for the Bialystok Ghetto in August 1943. For this action, the 26th Police Regiment, on its way from the Carpathian Mountains to the Eastern Front, was detoured to Bialystok. It contained German and Ukrainian units. At 4:00 A.M. of August 16, the Jewish Council was informed that all the Jews were to report at a collecting point with minimum baggage for a selection. The Jews assembled as ordered. Many families were torn apart as thousands of Jews had to remain on the grass in the summer heat for twenty-four hours. On the fourth day, youth groups still in the ghetto offered armed resistance. For several hours, the insurgents kept up the fire, almost exhausting their ammunition. Two detachments, one of them female under Mika Datner, concentrated on riddling the fence. When the two gaps had been created, the Germans fired into it. The rebels hoped that the Jews concentrated in the streets would break out en masse, but the bulk of the ghetto inhabitants still on the scene remained passive. As the Germans increased their counter-fire inside and outside the ghetto, nervous and frightened Jews voiced their reaction to the rebels, shouting, "Why are these bandits shooting? They bring misfortune upon us!" The battle was soon over. Among the dead insurgents, killed on August 20, 1943, was Mordechaj Tenenbaum-Tamaroff.[17]

Unlike Vilnius and Bialystok, the large Warsaw Ghetto was not subjected to deportations until a massive blow was struck on July 22, 1942. That is not to say that no one in the ghetto had any inkling of what was happening. Council Chairman Adam Czerniakow himself recorded his forebodings in a diary, and the historian Emmanuel Ringelblum was even more specific in his notes, mentioning Sobibor, "where Jews are choked to death with gases."[18] Dissemination of such news was, however, another matter. When a handful of resistance-minded Jews in the ghetto distributed some flyers in April

1942, several council members anxiously approached Czerniakow to tell him that the underground papers might bring "untold harm to the Jewish population."[19] Here, as elsewhere, information was not only not sought, it was to be smothered.

In the early spring of 1942, resistance in the Warsaw ghetto was little more than an idea discussed and disputed in underground meetings by representatives of various political parties. One of the participants was the young man who had arrived from Vilnius and later that year was going to be in Bialystok, Tenenbaum-Tamaroff. Another was the Zionist Menachem Kirszenboim, who considered the annihilation of the ghetto's 400,000 people unthinkable. The Socialist Bund leader Maurycy Orzech strongly believed that Jews should not fight a battle separate from the Poles; the time had not yet come. At a subsequent meeting in June, the historian Itzhak Szyper spoke out against self-defense, expressing his confidence that the core of the ghetto would be saved.[20] By the time the Warsaw deportations had run their course in September, that core consisted of seventy thousand Jews, half of them registered, the others hiding on both sides of the wall.

Complete unity was not going to be achieved. Each political party contributed small battle groups, and the Communists declined to serve with the right-wing Zionist Revisionists under the same overall command, with the result that the Revisionists fought as allies of the main Jewish Combat Organization. The Orthodox Agudath did not fight at all. The commanders were all very young, and on the whole they lacked military experience. The weapons, acquired or home made after the deportations, consisted of a few automatic weapons, some dozens of rifles, several hundred pistols, and a larger number of grenades and explosives. Stocks of ammunition were low. The fighting force may have numbered about 750.

Arrayed against the Jews were SS, police, army units, and Ukrainian collaborators, equipped with some armor and artillery, heavy and light machine guns, who outnumbered the defenders about three to one. Even so the battle lasted for three weeks in April and May 1943, and the Germans and their collaborators had sixteen dead and eighty-five wounded when it was over. In a letter written on April

23, 1943, the Jewish commander, Mordechaj Anielewicz, noted that the defense had become a reality and that the fighting was being observed beyond the walls. He was killed two weeks later. In these last moments of his life, he could not have imagined that his armed encounter with the Germans would be entered in the permanent pages of Jewish history.[21]

17

THE SURVIVORS

MORE THAN A MILLION JEWS who had lived under direct German control or in countries allied with Germany, and who had not fled to safety before or during the war, were still alive after May 1945.

The largest cluster in this remainder consisted of Jews who had not been engulfed in the final phase of the destruction process. Thus the Jewish communities of Old Romania and Bulgaria had been spared at the last moment by decisions of the governments in these countries. Also left were Jews living openly in cities where the Germans could no longer mobilize transport or police for deportations. Examples are Budapest, which had a ghetto during the winter of 1944–1945, and Paris, where quite a few Jewish families were still untouched in their apartments at the time of liberation. In addition, a sizable number of Jews were protected by their status, such as an effective foreign nationality or a mixed marriage.

A second major group had evaded death by hiding, resisting, or adopting a disguise. In Western Europe, many Jews found refuge in rooms, cellars, or attics of apartments or in monasteries or other institutions. In Yugoslavia, Greece, and Eastern Europe, some Jews were hiding in the mountains or woods, alone or with partisans. Almost everywhere, at least some Jews managed to obtain false papers to establish a false identity. In prisoner of war camps, where Soviet Jews were subject to shooting, some of the captives could pretend that they were non-Jews. Essentially these men concealed themselves, or were concealed, in the mass of other Soviet prisoners.

The third significant category in liberated territory or the conquered Reich were people who had been incarcerated to the very end. Among these individuals were the inhabitants of the Romanian-administered "colonies" between the Dnestr and Bug rivers, the men in the Hungarian labor companies, the Jews in the remnant ghettos of Cernauti and Theresienstadt, those in labor camps, those in the concentration camps of Dachau, Buchenwald, Mauthausen, and Bergen-Belsen, those debarked from ships that had left the concentration camp Stutthof, and those abandoned in marches from camps and labor sites. Many of the people in the camps had been transferred from other locations, particularly Auschwitz. The camp Jews and the marchers were found in particularly poor physical condition.

No ironclad definition of the term *Jewish survivor* was fashioned during the postwar period. The concept has no distinct boundaries. Yet there is an unmistakable rank order among the Jews who lived through the wartime Nazi years. In this hierarchy, the decisive criteria are exposure to risk and depth of suffering. Members of communities that were left intact and people who continued to live in their own homes are hardly considered survivors at all. At the other end of the scale, individuals who emerged from the woods or the camps are the survivors par excellence.

The idea that those who had reached bottom should be placed at the top is more than a matter of social restitution. They are elevated as possessors of a special kind of knowledge. Often enough survivors have spoken of such knowledge themselves. They have referred to it in expressions like "planet Auschwitz" and in such sentences as "Those who were not there cannot imagine what it was like." Clearly, *they* were there, and thus they are set apart or set themselves apart from anyone who did not share their fate. The outsider can never cross this divide and can never grasp their experience.

There is a corollary to this phenomenon. Survivors do not separate themselves from the dead. They assert that they belong to the dead and that they would have drowned with them in the cataclysm, were it not for an element of luck. Typically, when a Jewish Auschwitz survivor from Athens, Errikos Sevillias, wrote his memoirs, he alluded to inexplicable chance:

> I am one of the few who survived. What is strange is not that I withstood it, but that I wasn't destroyed. Seven times I saw death face to face and many other times strange circumstances drove it away from me suddenly, like lightning, without my knowledge or understanding. . . .[1]

Yet survival was not altogether random, and survivors who describe themselves as the few are not a sample of the many who died. In sheer physical terms, the veterans of camps, hideouts, and partisan units had two attributes. They were relatively young, concentrated in the age group from the teens to the thirties, and that is to say that those who were middle-aged were even fewer. They also had to be in good health at the start of the ordeal. Ghettos, let alone camps, marshes, and woods, were all prescriptions for illness, and anyone who was already burdened with a malady or disability usually had an insurmountable problem.

Social characteristics, although not as determinative as one's physical condition, were also important. The same advantages that favored people in ghettos, hiding or escape, also furthered ultimate survival. "We were scraping the bottom of our dwindling resources," states a survivor who was still in hiding in a Polish town during 1944.[2] He did not have to add that he had some resources to begin with. The Jewish physicians and carpenters were similarly able to prolong their existence, if not in freedom, then in a ghetto, and if not in a ghetto, then in a camp.

Most critical, however, was the psychological profile of the survivors. In this respect, they differed completely from the great mass of their fellow victims. The contrast may be glimpsed in three important traits: realism, rapid decision making, and tenacious holding on to life.

It was not common in the Jewish community to be realistic to the extent of observing one's environment soberly and drawing one's conclusions independently. It was not usual to be suspicious of explanations or assurances that demanded absolute trust in authority. Rudolf Vrba, who had already escaped from an internment camp in Slovakia and had been caught at the border of Hungary, was on a deportation train with Jewish families who had been promised "resettlement." When the train halted at Maydanek-Lublin, where he was pulled off with men aged sixteen to forty-five, he decided that from this moment, he would "trust nobody."[3] The realistic person did not rationalize steps into the unknown as benign. During a roundup in the Kaunas Ghetto in 1944, a woman, Liuba Daniel, "forbade" her husband to report. He did anyway and died. She survived.[4]

Presence of mind, coupled with the ability to make decisions instantly, was another rare characteristic. One woman, Mitzi Abeles, repeatedly escaped from pursuers who were within yards of her, at one point jumping in a nightshirt from a window in Zagreb, Croatia.[5] Errikos Sevillias, the Greek Jew in Auschwitz who ascribed his survival to incomprehensible fate, recalls a barracks selection in which he gave himself a poor chance of survival, because he had become emaciated. "In the instant," he writes, that "I saw the guard look elsewhere, I jumped and landed on the other side of the barrier," where the strong had already been separated from the weak.[6] The decision makers always took risks. Not always were their actions prompted by the appearance of a danger; sometimes they responded to an opportunity. When the teenager Isaac Rudnicki in the Swienciany Ghetto was assigned to work in a German weapons room, he removed two firearms and hid them in the ghetto. His family was petrified.[7] He eventually became a partisan and after his liberation fought in Israel's wars, rising in rank to Brigadier General with a new name: Yitzhak Arad.

The third component of the survivor's personality pattern was an absolute determination to live. One aspect of this tenacity was adaptability to the infliction of indignity, pain, cold, heat, and hunger. When Rudolf Vrba was transferred from Lublin to Auschwitz, he met two Poles, both of whom suggested laughingly that he should run for the wire—the guard would shoot and end things quickly. Vrba, angry, answered: "I'll be alive when you two are dead!" They died in fact a month later of typhus. Vrba, resolute, ate everything, "even if the bread contained sawdust, and the tea looked like sewer water."[8] Sevillias, much older than Vrba, was already over forty. His stamina was nevertheless exceptional. When the Soviet army liberated him, he weighed thirty-two kilograms, or seventy pounds. But he was alive.[9]

Sevillias, Vrba, Abeles, Daniel, and Arad are unusual people even among survivors. They epitomize the qualities that made survival possible in the most extreme situations. At the same time, they personify most clearly an essential truth that applied to everyone who surmounted the odds. They were lucky *after* they had tried to save themselves.

Almost all the Jews who were liberated at the end of the war had suffered a loss. For many, as in Old Romania, the damage was primarily material: savings, jobs, and apartments were gone. For some, including most of the camp survivors, the permanent hurt was the death of close family members. For still others, particularly those who were very young, the time in which one goes to school had slipped away.

Few of the survivors stepped into the postwar world with lasting physical illnesses or disabilities. They could not have survived in the first place if they had been crippled or blind. They were not, however, completely at peace. Those who were in their twenties or thirties, among them young widowers and widows, not infrequently married other survivors. Many who would normally have sought some advanced education did not pursue it. On occasion they would refer to themselves as "graduates" of Auschwitz or Bergen-Belsen.[10] They had great difficulty, like the refugees before the war, to say something about their experiences. The postwar societies of Israel and the United States were forward looking, and these countries were also confronted with new adversaries: Israel with the Arabs, the United States with the Soviet Union. The survivor had no audience and frequently felt the isolation of someone who cannot be understood. Many memoirs were written, but not for large audiences. Elie Wiesel wrote his story for Jewish readers in Yiddish under the title *And the World Was Silent*. The book was published in Argentina and only later, reduced in size, was it read everywhere under the title

Night. Primo Levi reports that his memoir was first published in an edition of twenty-five hundred copies and that six hundred, on the remainder list, were drowned in a Florentine flood.[11]

In Western Europe, the survivors returned to their homes. In two countries, Belgium and the Netherlands, the regenerated Jewish communities were fractions of their former size. In three, Denmark, France, and Italy, they were augmented by new immigrants: Polish Jews in Denmark, Algerian Jews in France, Libyan Jews in Italy. In Eastern Europe and the Balkans, however, the remnants either did not return or moved out in search of a new life in a Jewish state to come or in the United States. When the Soviet Union, long sealed, began to permit emigration, the outpour began also there, increasing in the 1980s and 1990s.

The survivors made their greatest impact on the Jewish community, not by anything they said or did, but by their presence as "irrepatriable displaced persons" in camps on German and Austrian soil between 1945 and 1948. The immigration laws of the Western countries and Palestine were those of 1939, and the semi-closed door of the British-ruled Palestinian mandate, permitting entry to only a trickle of those who languished in Germany, heated the sentiment of the Western Jewish communities, particularly in the United States, to a boiling point. Anti-Zionism in the Jewish community collapsed, and a consensus that Jewry, abandoned during the war, had to have a home of its own crystallized overnight. It was this pressure that induced the British government to abandon Palestine, and Israel was born, on May 14, 1948, three years almost to the day after the end of the catastrophe.

PART III

BYSTANDERS

"He says, it's this way:
if I cut my finger, it doesn't hurt him."
—A translator explaining an answer given to
Claude Lanzmann by Czeslaw Borowi,
a Pole who lived near the death camp Treblinka

18

NATIONS IN
ADOLF HITLER'S EUROPE

A POPULATION OF several hundred million non-Jews lived in areas controlled or influenced by the Nazi regime. Many of these people were remote from the scene of anti-Jewish activity; many others were neighbors of the victims. From those places where the view of the catastrophe was close, the news reverberated throughout Europe. Even if one looked away, asked no questions, and refrained from talk in public, a dull awareness remained. The disappearance of the Jews, or the appearance of their property, was a signal of what was happening. The event could not be stamped out completely.

At the same time, the rudimentary assessments of mood by German official observers indicate a prevailing sense of indifference, even of apathy, toward all events that did not immediately touch one's personal existence. As the war progressed, the preoccupation with one's own troubles increased. The Dutch were worried about their bicycles, the French about shortages, the Ukrainians about food, the Germans about air raids. All of these people thought of themselves as victims, be it of war, or oppression, or "fate."

Nevertheless, there were subtle, and sometimes not so subtle, variations in the attitudes among nations toward perpetrators and victims. In each nation, specific historic, cultural, and situational

factors shaped a characteristic reaction pattern, and even characteristic changes in this pattern, during the course of Jewry's destruction.

In the lineup of nations, one must begin with Germany itself. Here
the difference between perpetrators and bystanders was least pronounced; in fact it was not supposed to exist. The proposition was
spelled out most clearly by Reinhard Heydrich, Chief of the German
Security Police, at a conference chaired by Hermann Göring in November 1938. Göring suggested that ghettos would have to be created for Jews in all German cities, but Heydrich disagreed, stating in
no uncertain terms that he preferred control of the Jews through the
watchful eyes of the whole population.[1] That principle of universal
supervision was clearly based on the unarticulated presumption that
an army of ordinary German men and women was perpetually ready
to report anything suspicious in the Jewish community.

The isolation of the Jews in Germany was accomplished relatively
early. Before the compulsory middle names Israel and Sara were
decreed, and long before the mandatory star was instituted, Jews
were already stigmatized and sometimes shunned. In November
1934, a German attorney named Coblenzer, who lived in Bochum,
wrote a letter to the Justice Ministry, complaining that because of his
family name, which he did not wish to change, he was suspected of
being Jewish and was losing business to the point of approaching
poverty. A rumor that one was a Jew, he said, was equivalent to
financial ruin. He was a full Aryan with four years and four months
at the front in the First World War. In addition, he was in possession
of the Iron Cross First Class. Yet he was helpless, and so were, he
estimated, one tenth of all German businessmen in a similar predicament in his city.[2]

Whereas many Germans walked away from the Jews, they were
eager enough to acquire some Jewish property. After transports of
Jews began to move out of Leipzig to the "east," 118 suitcases, a
backpack, and a handbag were left behind with all their contents.
The representative of the Finance Ministry in the area handed over
these personal belongings to an auctioneer, who listed all the items,
their former Jewish owners, estimated yields, names of German purchasers, and realized prices. Virtually everything was sold.[3] All over
Germany, tens of thousands of Jewish apartments were taken over;

furniture from Jewish homes in Germany and the Western countries graced German offices and private German residences; and smaller objects were distributed to the needy, sometimes from the killing centers where they had been collected. The recipients did not ask many questions.

Relatively few Jews were able to hide in Germany. The statistics are scant, but a very high percentage of those few thousand who found refuge or help in German families were relatives of the rescuers by reason of a mixed marriage, or they were of partial German descent or converts to Christianity. Such are the findings of a survey made after the war in Vienna.[4] A similar result was obtained in a detailed study of Mönchengladbach and its vicinity. In this investigation, the period before the deportations was separated from the later, more dangerous time. The case histories for the first phase include a Jewish couple who dyed their hair blond, a Jewish woman with two children who changed hiding places frequently, and a number of Jews who pretended to be bombed-out Germans without papers. The later phase, which encompassed more individuals, included a half-Jew considered Jewish by official definition, a husband and wife in a mixed marriage, a Jewish woman in a privileged mixed marriage who—although safe—feared deportation, and so on.[5] In short, either the Jews were left to their own ingenuity or they depended largely on German relatives, if they had any.

Germany was the country in which the destruction process was launched. There was no cleavage between the German in the street and the perpetrators, who could be found in every agency. It was difficult to revolt against established order in a society where people were more likely to revolt against revolution, and it was doubly difficult, as well as doubly dangerous, to do so once all the decrees had been put into place and the trains had begun to roll. The helper in Germany was almost alone.

No country in Europe was like Germany. Not one was a carbon copy. The closest resemblance to the Reich in the near-totality of involvement must be sought in the Baltic region. And even there one may discern some important differences.

Estonia, Latvia, and Lithuania were anti-Communist. Their two decades of independence were ended by the entry of Soviet forces in

1940. A year later the Germans were welcomed as liberators. In their single year of rule, the Soviets had not only submerged the region, they had launched expropriations and deportations, incidentally also victimizing bourgeois Jews. The Baltic nationalists did not see Jews as fellow sufferers; they did, however, identify Jews in the Soviet police apparatus, and the new symmetry called for an alliance with Germany against the Soviet Union and against the Jews.

Lithuanians, Latvians, and Estonians by the tens of thousands stepped up first as civilians, then as auxiliaries, and finally as uniformed elements of the German police to seize, guard, and often shoot the Jews living in their midst. Within six months, during the second half of 1941, Baltic Jewry was annihilated save for remnants in ghettos. The Baltic police battalions went on to kill Jews transported into the region from Germany and then they ranged far outside their home bases to assist their German masters in the implementation of the final solution in Poland and the occupied USSR. Yet the Baltic peoples were not exuberant after their Jews had been killed.

Disappointments surfaced in the Baltic region as early as 1941. The fact that independence was not restored to the three countries was one major problem. Economic exploitation was another. Thus the Lithuanian leadership recognized immediately that the officially imposed exchange rate of one Reichsmark = 10 Rubles gave the Germans a great deal of currency with which to buy up everything.[6] The most vexing issue, however, was the sheer attitude of the German overlords toward the Baltic populations. For the Germans, Lithuanians and Latvians particularly were good-natured friendly folk, but essentially peasants. In SS circles, Lithuanians were considered mentally dull and filled with an incredible proportion of Slavic blood.[7] The German Stadtkommissar of Kaunas went so far as to call the Lithuanian people "primitive."[8] Even in higher-ranking Latvia, the Germans permitted themselves policies that rapidly caused resentment: corporal punishment of Latvian railway workers and segregation of Germans and Latvians on passenger trains, lest German travelers become infected with Latvian diseases.[9]

The Baltic volunteers had become tools. They had killed and many of their victims, their own Jewish neighbors, were buried in Baltic soil. The Jews of Germany were shipped out; they were not shot on the Rhine. The Jews of Riga or Kaunas, however, had been slain in the immediate vicinity of their homes. By the summer of 1942, there was an extensive search for mass graves in Lithuania. Officially the problem was the possibility of emerging diseases; unspoken was the likelihood of discovery.[10] In 1942 and again in 1943, anonymous Lithuanians passed out leaflets warning their fellow Lithuanians against continued shooting of Jews.[11]

In Latvia there was unease as well. As early as January 19, 1942. the SS and Police commander in the port city of Liepaja reported rumors to the effect that after the "execution" of the Jews, many Latvians would have to "travel the same way," especially if they had worked for German offices. When three German soldiers were found dead in Liepaja, there was a further rumor that one hundred Latvians would be shot, even though the soldiers had actually committed suicide.[12] In the southeastern area of Latvia, where Slavic populations were strong, it was whispered that after the Jews had been killed, Poles and Raskolniki (Old Believers, a schismatic group dissenting from the Russian Orthodox Church) would be shot. This impression was strengthened when an action to remove Poles and Russians was launched on May 4, 1942, in a manner, such as the encirclement of villages at night, that led people to expect the worst. A German gendarmerie lieutenant who observed the roundup thought that under the circumstances the reaction, however mistaken, was justified.[13]

In Ukrainian territory, Einsatzkommando 6 of the German Security Police noted in a report that hostility toward the Jews or—as the Kommando put it—an understanding of the Jewish question decreased from west to east.[14] The report, despite its impressionistic character, was not without foundation. The western regions of the Ukrainian SSR had been under Soviet rule for less than two years and the anger against the Communists, as well as the coupling of Jews and Communists, was probably as severe in this area as in the Baltic countries. In the old Soviet territory, on the other hand, the German conquerors were first greeted, then mistrusted, eventually feared, and finally rejected. These reactions surfaced despite the attempt of the German occupants to make a distinction between Ukrai-

nians and Russians, or more generally between Ukrainians and other
Slavs. In a valiant effort one German general signed an order stating
that Ukrainians were really Aryans, albeit with arrested development.[15] The theory remained a dead letter because of policies implemented in the occupied territories with respect to Russians,
Byelorussians, and Ukrainians alike. This leveling determined to a
considerable extent the similarity of the gray reactions of the eastern
Slavic peoples.

Whereas the Germans did not make many converts among Ukrainians living within the prewar boundaries of the Soviet Union, they
did not have to worry that the Ukrainians would aid the Jews. A
large number of young Ukrainian men were in the Red Army, or
prisoners of war, or evacuated as essential laborers by the retreating
Soviet authorities. Damaged cities and disrupted communications
had been left behind. A disoriented population, uncertain of its future under German occupation, scrambled for morsels to stay alive.
In this disintegration, the Jews were perceived as a different people
whose misfortune, deserved or undeserved, was not a Ukrainian
concern and still less a Ukrainian responsibility. Already at the end of
September 1941, Einsatzgruppe C, which was then operating in
northern Ukrainian territory, reported that Jews were considered a
burden, insofar as they consumed some of the food. Escaped Jews
were neither housed nor fed by Ukrainians. They were living in
earth holes or in crowded old huts.[16] Later, in Kharkov, where
almost all of the remaining Jews had already been shot, the attitude
toward Jewry of the civilian residents was reported to be, with isolated exceptions, still absolutely negative. Hidden Jews were seized
daily with the help of inhabitants who revealed the whereabouts of
the victims.[17]

In the area of Brest-Litovsk, which had a mixed population of
Ukrainians and Poles, the gendarmerie of the German police reported that during the mass shooting of Jews in October 1942, a
rumor was circulating to the effect that the Germans would go on to
shoot the Poles and Russians, and then the Ukrainians. These rumors, said the gendarmerie, had generated sympathy for the Jews,
but by November, the non-Jewish population, feeling secure again,
helped eagerly in the search for hidden Jews in the woods, and ex-

pressed gratitude for the opportunity to buy old Jewish furnishings from the emptied ghetto at bargain prices. At the same time, any Ukrainians who sheltered a Jewish person exposed themselves to an acute risk. Thus a German police company in the village of Samary, Volhynia, shot an entire Ukrainian family, including a man, two women, and three children, for harboring a Jewish woman.[18]

As in the case of the Baltic area, the Ukrainian Jews were annihilated rapidly. In the principal occupied Ukrainian cities east of Volhynia and Galicia, there were not even remnant ghettos at the end of 1941. Yet if the Ukrainians had separated themselves from the Jewish victims, they were now going to discover that in at least one respect the Germans were treating them almost like Jews and that their urban centers were about to acquire a crucial attribute of ghetto life: hunger. This problem was the direct result of a German policy to feed the invading armies with the produce and livestock of the invaded land.[19]

In the largest Ukrainian city, Kiev, where the Jews had been massacred in late September 1941, the Security Police reported on November 19 of that year that food was unobtainable for money and that it was traded only in barter.[20] Weekly rations in Kiev included two hundred grams of bread. Laborers were to receive an additional six hundred grams at work. Fat, meat, and sugar were not provided, and by December 1941 the Ukrainian mayor reported increasing hunger edema in the population.[21]

In the second largest Ukrainian city, Kharkov, where the German rulers judged the food situation to be catastrophic, they decided on December 16, 1941, to drive the urban population in foot marches of 10,000 weekly toward the front line and into the hands of the Red Army. The plan was abandoned, but there was no relief. For sixty miles, the Sixth Army's rear area had been "picked clean" (leergefressen). The city itself could not be rebuilt; it could only be "ripped apart" (ausgeschlachtet).[22] The plight of Kharkov is reflected in periodic reports of deaths to the German military government by the municipal statistical chief, Professor Siosnovy. With a population, as of July 1, 1942, of 446,073, the figures he sent are recapitulated in the table on page 202.

Like the Ukrainian SSR, all of Byelorussia was occupied during

DEATHS OF NON-JEWS IN KHARKOV*

1942	TOTAL DEATHS	DEATHS ATTRIBUTED TO HUNGER
January	1,603	552
February	2,133	1,283
March	2,699	1,821
April	2,953	2,101
May	3,161	2,237
June	2,426	1,375
July	1,966	1,089
August	1,365	725

* Population statistics for July 1, 1942, were enclosed in a report by Professor Siosnovy, Kharkov Oblast Archives, Fond 2982, Opis 1, Folder 232. Ukrainians were 69% of the population, Russians 28%. Biweekly death statistics from the second half of December 1941 through the first half of September 1942 are in a report by Siosnovy to Dr. Martin of the German Military Administration, September 28, 1942, Fond 2982, Opis 4, Folder 390a. The peak of 3,161 in May 1942 (0.7% of the entire city population) is close to half of the peak in the Warsaw Ghetto in mid-1941.

the war, and here too the Germans seized the wooden carts of the peasants, their livestock, and their harvests. Unlike Ukraine, the Byelorussian area was the scene of prolonged and sometimes intense partisan fighting, which the Germans countered with repeated expeditions in the course of which they turned villages into pyres and villagers into half-charred corpses.[23] A number of partisan detachments included Jews in their ranks, but in several cases the Jewish fighters thought it prudent not to disclose their identity to their non-Jewish comrades.[24] Those Jews who hoped to be protected by partisans were in a much more precarious situation. During one engagement, a large group of Jews, apparently unarmed, were abandoned by partisans who found themselves under attack by German and Slovak troops. A total of 113 Jews were massacred on that occasion upon capture.[25] In the end, quite a few Jewish escapees were on their own. They were not accepted by any partisan formation, because they were largely untrained and unarmed, or because they had with them women and even children. Banded together in Jewish units and camps, they could survive only by commandeering essential food and supplies from farms in their vicinity. Exposed to the ever present possibility of denunciation, they might also have had to threaten or use force against peasants, thereby widening the gulf between themselves and the surrounding population.[26]

The largest number of Jewish deaths occurred in occupied Poland. Most of the ghettos and all of the death camps were located in that country. In the camps, transports of Polish Jews were joined by deportation trains carrying Jews from northern, western, and southern Europe. Almost everywhere in Poland, Jewish death was proximate.

Prewar Poland was not a small country by European standards, but in economic terms, the strength and capacity of its people were limited. Foreign capital held most of Polish industry, especially oil, electrical, textile, chemical, and mining enterprises. The Polish population was overwhelmingly agricultural. Home construction was meager and housing density was nearly four per room, with separate kitchens, where available, counting as rooms.[27] Under the occupation, conditions deteriorated. The Polish intelligentsia was pursued and killed. Labor was abducted to Germany. The rates of alcoholism and tuberculosis rose precipitously. In the central portion of Poland, which the Germans called the Generalgouvernement, the black market dominated the food supply, and consumption dropped from 2,500–2,800 calories in 1940 to 2,050–2,400 in the winter of 1940–1941, to 1,700–2,200 by 1942.[28] If the Polish population as a whole did not starve like Jewish ghetto dwellers or Ukrainian city residents, the decrease of the food supply, particularly in urban areas, was beginning to endanger stamina and health.[29]

Polish attitudes toward Jews were embedded in a constellation of prewar sentiments that ranged from tolerance to animosity. Although Poles were the masters of the Polish republic that existed for two decades between the two world wars, they were only two-thirds of its population. There were sizable Ukrainian and Byelorussian minorities in the east and a substantial German minority in the west. Jews, relatively few in the west, were numerous in the central and eastern regions of Poland. Numbering about 3,350,000, or 10 percent of Poland's inhabitants, they were living mainly in cities and towns. Most Jews earned their living as self-employed individuals. Jewish wage and salary recipients were relatively few and almost entirely dependent on Jewish employers.[30] In the eyes of numerous Polish politicians, particularly in the right wing of the political spectrum, the Jews were simply too many. Polish society, its spokesmen and writers, were Catholic in religion and nationalist in outlook. Jewry was distinctly Jewish. The overwhelming majority of Jews spoke Yiddish as their first language, and notwithstanding the attendance of most Jewish children in Polish public schools, the Jews were not considered assimilable. Too many Jewish adults did not speak Polish well or at all. In the prevailing Polish view, the Jews could not, despite their protestations of loyalty to the Polish state, share the spirit and longings of the Polish people.

With the beginning of the occupation, the cleavage deepened. Polish peasants, for example, were relieved when their debts to Jews were cancelled,[31] and urban Poles were quick to improve their lodgings in the course of ghetto formation.[32] By the same token, when Jews, expelled from crowded cities, arrived in Kielce, the local Polish population "refused to receive them."[33] Perceptions were far apart as well. Thus the sociologist Jan Gross points out that in 1940 and 1941 there was a widespread belief among Poles that they were more exposed and more threatened than the Jews. The Jewish communities had a form of self-government in their councils; Jews were not shipped to Germany, and they were not arrested or tortured for political reasons. At the same time it was thought that Jews, unlike Poles, were docile and subservient to the Germans.[34]

During the period of ghettoization, the only significant activity shared by Poles and Jews was the black market trade, notably in Warsaw. In this exchange, the centuries-old congruity of the two communities emerged once more. In 1942, however, the deportations and killings of the Jews brought about a drastically altered situation for which neither the Poles nor the Jews were prepared.

For some of the right-wing Poles, who had always wanted the Jews to depart, the deportations came virtually as a wish fulfillment. The broader center, however, had more complex thoughts. Poles knew that they were not a favored group in German eyes, and the realization that the end had come for the Jews inevitably raised questions whether the Poles would be next. The reaction was observed in Volhynia,[35] and it surfaced again in the Lublin District, where the Germans followed their roundup of the Jews with a more benign, but forcible resettlement of Poles from one zone to another.[36]

There was also a sense that Jews, as victims of the German enemy, if not as Poles themselves, had to be helped. Two organized efforts, one civilian, the other paramilitary, were made in that direction. The civilian undertaking was carried out by a Council for Aid to Jews, Zegota. This organization was formed specifically to find hiding places for Jews and to help them in their prohibited existence. The work, carried out by Zegota members at the risk of their lives, included such tasks as preparing false documents, channeling money to Jewish escapees, placing Jewish children in orphanages, and contacting trusted Polish physicians to treat Jews who had become ill in their refuge.[37] Compared to the masses of Jews who died, very few people were saved by Zegota, but its resources were small and the dangers great, even while bounty hunters and blackmailers were on the track of Jews in hiding.

In the military sphere, Poland had three underground movements: the right-wing National Armed Forces (NSZ), whose hostility was extended to Germans, Ukrainians, Byelorussians, and Jews; the centrist Armia Krajowa, which reported to the Polish Government in Exile in London and was also the largest; and the Communist Armia Ludowa, the People's Army. In February 1942, the Armia Krajowa established a special section concerned with Jewish matters under Henryk Wolinski.[38] With its network of observers and couriers, the Armia Krajowa gathered information, which it sent to London. There the Polish Government in Exile made several statements cataloging these details, but in the absence of action on the part of Allied governments, the dissemination of the news could not alter the course of events.

Direct military assistance had more tangible effects, but it was neither automatic nor free of political calculations and complications. One chapter in this story is the Warsaw Ghetto battle, another the fate of Jewish partisan fighters in the woods.

In the Warsaw Ghetto, where mass deportations began on July 22, 1942, the representatives of the Jewish political parties were discussing resistance, but before the larger half of the ghetto population had disappeared they did not reach a positive decision. The first approach to the Armia Krajowa was therefore made either in August or September, that is to say, just before or just after the Warsaw Jewish community had shrunk from about 370,000 to barely 70,000.[39] The response to this initial request was meager. A handful of pistols were sent, most of them useless.

The Armia Krajowa was not yet convinced that the Jewish intention to fight was serious. In this respect, the leadership of the underground forces reflected a sentiment that was widespread in Poland. Two underground pamphlets, titled "Prezez . . . walke do zwyciestwa," illustrate this thinking with absolute clarity. The first, dated January 10, 1943, pointed out that

> The Jews gathered whither they were ordered, went whither they were led. Thus, within a few months, a few hundred Germans, Ukrainians, Latvians, and Lithuanians were able to destroy the Warsaw Ghetto with its population of nearly a half million.

Such happenings, the pamphlet went on, also occurred in the rest of the country. The occupation authorities might try to do the same to Poles, but in that case

> We believe that the Polish people will not choose to perish in a passive, glory-less, mass death.

On January 19–20, the SS and Police made a foray into the remnant ghetto to deport more Jews. This time, however, they were met with shots fired by Jewish resisters. The pamphlet issued by the same underground group on January 20, 1943, then said:

> It is worthy of note and the highest appreciation that during the "liquidation" of Jews the fighting underground organization resisted with arms.

The Germans, according to the pamphlet, had fled from the Jews and had left twenty dead.[40]

Polish supplies were indeed increased after the January incident. The deliveries, including a handful of machine guns, dozens of rifles and carbines, hundreds of pistols and revolvers, and thousands of grenades, were made by the Armia Krajowa and the Communist Armia Ludowa. Some arms were purchased by the Jews on the black market, and some explosives were home made with Polish help. The right-wing Jews in the ghetto procured arms separately from sympathetic members of the Armia Krajowa. The total weaponry in Jewish possession did not match the firepower of a single German infantry company. It was also paltry when measured against the stocks of the Armia Krajowa in the Warsaw area, which included 7 small anti-tank guns, 325 heavy and light machine guns, 6,045 rifles, 1,070 pistols and revolvers, and 7,651 grenades, plus a few airdrops from Britain.[41] But the Jews were newcomers to battle and the Poles were jealous of their arsenal.

An even more complicated problem arose when Jewish escapees in the woods attempted to join Polish partisans. Many members of the Armia Krajowa were civilians during the workday and underground soldiers only on weekends and at night. The Jews, on the other hand, did not and could not have regular jobs or occupations as fugitives. For the Armia Krajowa it was important to wait for a decisive moment of German weakness to seize portions of Poland, or at least Warsaw, and to secure such a foothold before Soviet forces could arrive. In the meantime, it hoarded its weapons with the thought that it had fewer arms than men. All too often the Jews presented themselves instead as additional men without rifles, pistols, or military training. If, in addition, they were poor speakers of Polish or recognizably Jewish, their handicaps made them a self-evident liability. The Polish Communists, fewer in number than the Armia Krajowa, were more hospitable. They wanted to act immediately to aid the Red Army, be it by sabotaging German supply lines or in other ways. Jews were accepted and Jewish Communists were doubly welcome in their ranks. The Armia Krajowa, in turn, looked upon the Communist Armia Ludowa as traitors to the Polish cause, and it did not rejoice when reinforcements reached Communist or Communist-dominated partisans.[42]

The escapees were not many and some of them had to fend for

themselves in small fighting detachments. Food, and everything else they needed, had to be acquired or taken somewhere. One German account noted that Polish peasants, about to be attacked by Jewish "bandits," had beaten thirteen of them to death.[43] What the peasants had done, some units of Polish right-wing formations, and even some of the Armia Krajowa forces, did more systematically, killing the diminishing fugitives without hesitation.[44]

In New York, on June 23, 1943, the Director of the Institute of Jewish Affairs of the World Jewish Congress, Jacob Robinson, bitterly castigated the Polish nation after he had learned that Treblinka had absorbed the Warsaw Ghetto Jews for all eternity. "How did it happen," he wrote in a memorandum, "that hundreds of thousands of Jews were deported and slaughtered during the course of four months without the slightest reaction on the part of the Polish population, the Polish underground, and the Polish Government in Exile?" Could such a thing have happened in any other country? No, he concluded, the Nazis were sure that the Poles would not budge, and the Poles in their blind hatred of the Jews were co-responsible for the slaughter.[45] Two days later, one of Robinson's colleagues, Arie Tartakower, met with Polish Ambassador Jan Ciechanowski in Washington. The Poles, said the ambassador, were trying to save as many Jews as possible, although they were not in favor of enlarging the scope of the Warsaw Ghetto battle, since the moment for an open uprising had not arrived. Ciechanowski realized that neither the supply of arms nor the attempts to hide the Jews in Polish homes were sufficient. Tartakower then summarized the ambassador's final remarks in the following words:

> The only effective way of saving the Polish Jews would be a declaration on the part of the United States and British governments that for every Jew killed, a German would be killed. Unfortunately, no such declaration was made so far, despite the many attempts of the Polish Government to convince these two governments on this point. Ciechanowski spoke about this problem with great bitterness.[46]

German power was not only established in the east. It radiated into an area extending from Norway through France and Italy to the

Balkans. Some of the nations in this sphere had at least a modicum of independence. Most were allies of Germany, with their own governments and laws. Four of the conquered nations, the Norwegians, Danes, Dutch, and, among the Belgians, the Flemish-speaking population, were considered Germanic. In the German scheme, these northwestern European peoples stood racially and culturally higher than Germany's allies in southern and southeastern Europe. As members of the Germanic family they were recruited into the SS, and if they were foreign workers in Germany, they had the highest privilege Germany could bestow on them: the freedom of sexual relations with German women. There was, however, an anomaly in this relationship. The vast majority of Germany's kinsmen maintained a reserve toward Germany. They did not forget for a moment that their independence had been compromised or extinguished under German control, and their democratic traditions stood in opposition to the Führer idea and all its derivatives. They looked toward London, dreaming of liberation. They also had accepted their Jews as part of their national fabric. In Norway, half of the small number of Jews were lost, because there were enough collaborators in the Quisling regime. In Belgium, the loss was also a half, and it was a much larger total, but a great many of the victims were foreign Jews and helpless refugees whose roots in the country were still shallow. Denmark retained internal independence until October 1943. It then saved almost all of its seven thousand Jews in an organized exodus across water to Sweden. The relatively small number was manageable, but the operation was nevertheless unique, because it had been assembled by all sorts of people spontaneously in haste, and because there were neither Danish police upon whom the Germans could rely for help nor an appreciable number of informers who were prepared to betray the undertaking.

The Netherlands, too, was a peaceful, democratic, tolerant country. Before the war, 140,000 Jews lived there, but in 1945, almost three quarters of them were dead. The ratio was the worst of Western Europe. Moreover, the Dutch Jews were a relatively old community; they had been in the country for hundreds of years. Rembrandt had painted them. Unlike the Jews who spoke Yiddish in Warsaw, or the Jews who spoke Ladino in Salonika, the Jews of

Amsterdam and all the other Dutch cities conversed in the language of their neighbors. Yet they died in proportions that recall the fate of Eastern and Balkan Jews.

The annihilation of Netherlands Jewry troubled the contemplative Dutch Christians for decades after the war. These retrospective and introspective thinkers transformed the general question, How could it have happened?, into a specific one: How could it have happened to such an extent on Netherlands soil? Even more pointedly: Allowing for the stranglehold of the Austrian Germans who ruled the Dutch domain during the war, or the geography of a flat country of cities and pastures, what role, active or passive, was played by Dutch administrative agencies and the population as a whole in this upheaval?

The Dutch people valued stability. It is for this reason that the ministerial bureaucracy, along with the entire business sector, had remained in the Netherlands under the occupation, and it is this goal that also dictated a policy of accommodation. That the Dutch administration was an exceptionally efficient apparatus only worsened the situation. As an example, the Dutch historian J. C. H. Blom cites "the almost perfect registration of the civilian population and the forgery-proof identity cards." Nor was this the only institutional problem. Blom calls attention to the segmentation of Dutch society into columns, or *zuilen*, of Catholic, Protestant, and non-denominational social-democratic communities that maintained self-contained political parties, trade unions, schools, clubs, medical institutions, and so on.[47] Thus the Jews were hemmed in by administrative controls from above and by social walls that limited their access to established lifelines in a crisis.

The Dutch population did regard the Jews as fellow citizens, and in February 1941 there was a general strike to express solidarity with them.[48] Such open opposition, however, was not manifested again.[49] When the deportations started, the principal means of help extended to the Jews was shelter in hiding. In this conspiratorial activity the Dutch developed some expertise. Helpers were encouraged and subsidized by the Dutch underground. If caught, they did not have to fear an automatic death penalty. Thousands were arrested for hiding Jews or Jewish belongings,[50] but it was German policy to detain such people only for a relatively short time in a camp within the country, and in serious cases to confiscate their property.[51] Judging from Security Police reports the Dutch became bolder as Germany's prospects for victory waned. Sturmbannführer Wilhelm Zoepf, who dealt with deportations in the Netherlands, complained in 1944 that many of the Dutch rescuers were looking for an "alibi" with which they could prove their anti-German stance, once the war was over.[52] In an undated report, the Security Police pointed out that arrested individuals were "decidedly not dismayed." They considered it an honor, the report went on sarcastically, to be placed in custody at the last moment.[53]

More, however, was involved than alibis. Many of the Dutch rescuers were desperately attempting to save people. In this war of attrition between the Dutch and the Germans, more Jews in hiding were lost than saved.[54] The Dutch were well aware that a seizure meant not only the burden of an arrest for a Dutch man or woman, but the death of the Jews in their care. Thus the Dutch protectors did not shy away from attempts to assassinate Dutch policemen who were aiding the Germans in the search for Jews.[55] The following story is told by a woman, the daughter of a Dutch judge, who was caring for three small children and their father in a small village from 1943 to 1945:

> I stayed with them until the end of the war. The more attached I became to them, the more scared did I become that we would be found out. One night they did come; four Germans led by a local policeman, a Dutchman, whom I had known for years. They could not find the hiding place, and finally left. Then after we had gone back to bed and tried to sleep, the Dutchman came back, by himself. The only solution at that time was to kill him, which I did.[56]

19

HELPERS, GAINERS, AND ONLOOKERS

IN THE COURSE OF THE ONSLAUGHT on European Jewry, some people in the non-Jewish population helped their Jewish neighbors, many more did or obtained something at the expense of the Jews, and countless others watched what had come to pass.

Help was by and large scarce and it was rendered most often at the last moment, after the start of roundups or deportations. Even then, the helpers seldom took the initiative. Sometimes the Jews were warned of danger, as in the French city of Clermont-Ferrand, where telephone calls or personal messages, some of them from gendarmes or secretaries, reached prospective deportees.[1] In Denmark there was an actual search for people in need, but in the usual case throughout Europe, the potential rescuer was approached by a victim or by someone already engaged in assisting stranded people. In short, most of the helpers were initially passive and most recipients of their kindness had already taken the critical step of leaving an apartment, ghetto, or camp.

There were two kinds of help. One was occasional, transitory, and relatively risk-free, such as alerting an unsuspecting victim of planned arrests, giving directions to fleeing Jews, diverting pursuers, or providing destitute individuals with small amounts of food, clothing, or money. The second was the more durable help, particularly shelter over time. Often enough payment was tendered for such protection, but that is not to say that the helper acted solely for profit or even that, all things considered, there was a business deal. For Poles or Ukrainians, a German discovery of their acts could be lethal.

What kind of persons were helpers? Basically, one may distinguish between people who wanted to save specific individuals or categories of individuals and those who willingly assisted almost any Jews, including total strangers. The selective helpers included first of all friends, relatives by intermarriage, and former business associates, employers, or employees. In all these situations a relationship or bond had been formed before the war, and there might have been some expectation of assistance in times of trouble. Sometimes, a gentile household was prepared to harbor a Jewish child. This kind of decision was considered when Jewish parents were in dire circumstances. There were also occasions when a non-Jewish man was attracted to a Jewish woman or when a gentile woman was drawn to a Jewish man. Probably, most of these encounters were brief or even casual. When relationships developed, they were obviously complicated, especially for a Jewish woman, even if no compulsion was exercised by the man. Of this, little is said in memoirs.[2]

The less discriminating helpers were motivated either by opposition to the German regime or by feelings of pure sympathy or humanitarian obligation. The oppositionists were sometimes political, like Oskar Schindler, who filled a plant with Jewish workers in order to save them, or Polish sanitation workers who helped Jews hiding in the sewers of Lvov, or several left-wing or Communist German civilians in the Bialystok area who actually supplied Jewish resisters in the ghetto with weapons.[3] The humanitarians have been the subject of an extensive literature.[4] They have been called altruists, righteous gentiles, and good samaritans, but there is little that they outwardly had in common. They were men or women, older or younger, richer or poorer. Like the perpetrators, whose exact opposites they were, they could not explain their motivations. They would characterize their actions as ordinary or natural, and after the war some of them were embarrassed by praise. Often they were members of a community, like the Protestants of Le Chambon in

France, who sheltered many Jews in a small area, or they were at least in touch with like-minded people in a loose network of helpers. Many of them had to make their decisions instantaneously. In this sense, they shared a personality characteristic with the Jewish fugitive who also acted rapidly. Finally, they had to have the inner flexibility to alter or abandon personal routines, particularly if a promise of three days of safety had to be extended to three weeks or three months.[5] They might indeed have been reluctant to make concession after concession, and there might have been tension between them and their lodgers, but they were still in a special category by virtue of the choice they had made.

Gainers outnumbered givers in the Jewish catastrophe. In many instances, little or nothing had to be done by the beneficiaries to enjoy the largesse. When Jewish enterprises were liquidated, the non-Jewish manufacturers and distributors automatically gained market shares. Jewish emigration, followed by ghettoization and deportation, freed well over 1 million apartments, although sometimes, as in Minsk, ghetto dwellings were rejected by dissatisfied ethnic Germans.[6] Levies imposed on Jewish communities were occasionally distributed to local inhabitants, as in Tunisia, and so on.

Active profiting was not eschewed either. Already in 1933 German medical students persecuted their fellow Jewish students to rid themselves of the competition.[7] German enterprises and their agents in banks, coveting a Jewish business, would take over their prey in unequal negotiations, assisted by regulations of the state. In black market trading in occupied Poland, the Polish suppliers were in a position to siphon off cash and valuables from the victims. Some individuals turned in escaping Jews for monetary rewards, and some extorted money or possessions from victims trying to live in hiding or disguise. When the Jews were already dead, the looters became busy. In the Radom District they rummaged in emptied ghettos tearing out everything they could. In Riga, they broke into piled-up suitcases, and on the site of Belzec, where the Germans had shut down a death camp, they searched for gold in the ashes.[8] Non-German takers making use of their various opportunities, as in Slovakia, were heard to say: "Better we than the Germans."[9]

During the stages of concentration, deportations, and killings, the perpetrators tried to isolate the victims from public view. The administrators of destruction did not want untoward publicity about their work. They wanted to avoid criticism of their methods by passers-by. Their psychic balance was jeopardized enough, especially in the field, and any sympathy extended to the victim was bound to result in additional psychological as well as operational complications. Voyeurs were not welcomed either. Such watching, especially by Germans, was considered an indecency. But regardless of whether the spectacle repelled or attracted the viewer, any rumors and stories carried from the scene were an irritant and a threat to the perpetrator.

Precautions were consequently plentiful. In Germany, Jews were sometimes moved out in the early morning hours before there was traffic in the streets. Furniture vans without windows were used to take Jews to trains. Loading might be planned for a siding where human waste was collected. In Poland, the local German administrators would order the Polish population to stay indoors and keep the windows closed with blinds drawn during roundups of Jews, even though such a directive was notice of an impending action. Shooting sites, as in Babi Yar in Kiev, were selected to be at least beyond hearing distance of local residents.

Not all of these measures were totally successful. To begin with, the actuality could not be hidden in any case. The non-Jewish population did not have to view the proceedings to realize that the Jews were disappearing. In the small railroad station at Sobibor, a Polish switchman just outside the camp became aware of the silence. "Forty cars had arrived and then—nothing."[10] Beyond inference, there were glimpses of the action itself. Some of these discoveries were made by people who stumbled upon the occurrence. Thus in occupied Poland, a German army inspector complained that soldiers had become inadvertent witnesses of an operation in which blows with rifle butts were delivered to the bodies of Jewish women in advanced stages of pregnancy.[11] Often enough the onlookers could not be barred. In 1943 on the island of Corfu they gathered to watch from street corners and balconies.[12] In the Hungarian city of Szeged, where Jews were marched, flanked by Hungarian gendarmes, to the train one morning in 1944, people stood in the street and laughed.[13] The hanging of two Jews in Zhitomir during 1941 was watched by a crowd of soldiers from rooftops.[14]

In Munich an SS lieutenant was on trial before the highest SS and Police court for photographing shootings he had ordered. He had the film developed in two private shops in southern Germany and then showed the photographs to his wife and various acquaintances, risking the spread of their contents across the border into neutral Switzerland. The SS court could not condone such behavior.[15]

The observers had gained access to a secret. Some of them indicated to the victims that they knew something, but without sharing their insight with clarity. Once, unsuspecting Jewish deportees on their way to Sobibor heard Polish voices utter the incomprehensible words: "Jews, you are going to burn!"[16] Another time, Polish peasants gestured to Jews on their way to Treblinka that their throats would be cut.[17] And that is where they left it, between a warning and a taunt.

20

MESSENGERS

THERE WERE PEOPLE who brought the dire news of annihilation to the outside world. These messengers were not necessarily sent by someone on an errand, nor did they always have an address where they could report. The effectiveness of their message therefore depended a great deal on who they were and what sort of impression they made, but even more so on the extent to which their listeners were prepared to absorb and accept the substance of the information itself.

Messengers were not altogether rare. The majority, however, remained inside German-dominated Europe. They delivered their disturbing discoveries to Jews who had not yet been taken out to be killed. Sometimes, for example, early escapees made their way back to Jewish communities or ghettos with word of shootings or gas. To the Jews still living in their apartments with their daily but familiar worries, the informants talked of events unimaginably worse than anything the hearers had yet experienced. It was easy to disbelieve or reject such disclosures. A famous depiction in literature of that kind of messenger is Moshe the Beadle in Elie Wiesel's *Night*. As a stateless person, the beadle was deported with his family during the summer of 1941 from the largely Jewish town of Sighet in Greater Hungary to a newly occupied area in the USSR where he witnessed

the shooting of his wife and children, as well as the deaths of countless other Jews. After he had managed to return to Sighet, those who
heard him tended to turn away from him, and when he repeated his
story, they considered him a madman. In 1944, it was their turn, and
during the roundup by a handful of Germans and Hungarian gendarmerie, hardly any of the victims tried to run away.[1]

The Jews of Sighet had not built an intelligence system and they
did not try to make discoveries. The same omission applies to Jewish
organizations and Allied governments outside the arena of destruction. They too had failed to focus their attention systematically on
the dynamic of destruction, and they were equally unprepared for
any revelation.

Among the messengers who reached Allied or neutral territory
were Germans and Poles. By and large they were active individuals
with confidence in themselves. They were also risk takers and non-
conformists, sometimes dissenters and resisters. Above all, they were
driven to speak. They were seldom casual informers; they spoke
almost always with a motive, and in some cases even with a recom-
mendation for ways to stop the killings. Their desire to give information was, however, no guarantee of accuracy. More than one of
them would report not only what they had seen but also what they
had heard without distinguishing between observation and rumor. If
they were not sure of themselves, they did not automatically point to
their lack of clarity. Given a listener who had only a weak factual
background to build on, they could be believed even though they
were describing something that had not happened, or conversely
they could be ignored even when they were precise.

For Jews and other non-German informants a major difficulty was
reaching a destination outside German control. The German re-
porter, on the other hand, had a problem finding an appropriate
contact and, having found one, maintaining anonymity. Psychologically, the German was isolated, unsupported at home and mistrusted
by the people he was trying to convince. This problem was accen-
tuated if he was a part of the regime that he opposed and exposed.

The German messenger who achieved the greatest fame after the
war was an SS lieutenant, Obersturmführer Kurt Gerstein. By the
end of the 1960s several articles and three books had been written

about him.[2] Of all the messengers, Gerstein was closest to the scene, and probably of all of them he was the least believed. He was born in 1905, one of seven children in a Protestant upper-middle-class family in Westphalia. His father was a judge, an older brother fell in battle at the close of the First World War, and two more were killed in the Second. The family had money. Nationalist by conviction, the father and the brothers had turned to the Nazi regime. Gerstein's father mainly missed the old imperial flag. Because a number of Jews had the name Gerstein, the father was at pains to emphasize the purely German ancestry of his family.

As a young man, Kurt Gerstein had already acquired a small reputation as a prankster, maverick, and rebel. He would walk into a church all the way to the front, turn around, and ask the congregation whether everyone had a ticket. When he was in the SS, he would stick a brush into his pistol holster and greet ladies by raising his cap. Much to the consternation of his father, he seemed to reject all authority. Irreverent if not irreligious, young Gerstein stood at the edge of the established church, conducting Bible classes in a camp for boys. Undisciplined but not anti-chauvinist, he embraced Nazism as a resurgence of the German spirit and joined the Nazi party in 1933. Twice arrested and once expelled from the party, he climbed back in at the insistence of his father. Obsessed with time, he moved constantly and attempted a multitude of tasks. He was a mining engineer and pursued medical studies but was impatient enough to try to heal patients before he was fully trained. Upon the outbreak of war he wanted to become a soldier but was referred to the SS, which eventually accepted him. He was six foot one in height. After the war he asserted that he was strongly motivated to probe the secrets of the Nazi system. The impelling factor, he said, was his discovery of the euthanasia program in which a sister of his brother-in-law had become a victim.

During the war, Gerstein was a married man and the father of three small children. Much of the time he was away from his wife, a parson's daughter who remained loyal to him throughout his SS career. Gerstein lived in a Berlin apartment, cared for by a middle-aged housekeeper. His SS position was in the Hygienic Institute, where his training in engineering and medicine, combined with his inventiveness, was put to use for disinfection. He designed some delousing equipment and was promoted to officer rank.

Gerstein discovered the annihilation of the Jews firsthand in August 1942, when he was ordered to travel to Poland with a shipment of hydrogen cyanide (Zyklon B) to investigate the possibility of substituting this gas for the fuel engines used in several of the death camps. He visited Belzec in the Lublin District and Treblinka in the Warsaw District. While in Belzec he timed a gassing operation delayed by a malfunctioning engine. He recalled that his host, Hauptsturmführer (Captain) Christian Wirth, had asked him whether it was better to have the lights on or off during the gassings. He remembered two women, a lovely girl in front of the line and a forty-year-old, cursing her murderer, who was whipped in the face. He noticed a five-year-old girl lose a necklace and a three-year-old boy pick it up with delight. Prodded by Wirth, who did not want to adopt the cyanide, Gerstein buried the gas he had with him.[3]

On a night train from Warsaw to Berlin on August 20, 1942, a thirty-five-year-old Swedish consul, Baron Göran von Otter, who had been unable to obtain a sleeping berth, stood in the corridor of the car. An SS officer glanced at him and during a stop followed him to the station platform, where the Swede stretched his legs. The SS officer asked him for a light. It was Gerstein. When von Otter produced the matches, the cover of which was marked "Swedish Consulate," Gerstein said, "Yesterday I saw something horrible." Von Otter, sensing the subject, asked whether it had something to do with Jews. The two men sat on the floor in the car's corridor as the train moved through the night. Gerstein cried and smoked incessantly. He named names and showed von Otter a requisition for the gas. He wanted the Allies to drop millions of leaflets on Germany to disclose the operation. Then the two men, still on the floor, fell asleep.[4]

Von Otter reported the meeting to the acting head of the Swedish legation in Berlin, but apparently the message was not passed on to the Allied authorities until after Germany's surrender.[5] Gerstein went on talking. He spoke to the Protestant bishop, Otto Dibelius, who considered the church itself to be a prisoner of the Nazi regime, and to the Papal Nuncio, Monsignor Cesare Orsenigo, who showed him the door. He also contacted someone in the Dutch underground, to have the message relayed by radio to London, but the underground begged Gerstein not to imagine stories about atrocities.[6]

Gerstein remained in the SS, continued in his job, and delivered Zyklon B to SS users in 1943 and 1944. Among these recipients was the administration of the Auschwitz camp, where the Jews were killed with the gas en masse.[7] Shortly after the end of the war, he wrote a long statement in French and a similar account in German. He was also interrogated by French officers. In these recollections, there are errors in rendering ranks and names, and there is an account, based on a fictitious story told to him, of a visit by Hitler to Lublin, complete with a conversation that was supposed to have taken place between Hitler and the SS and Police Leader in the Lublin District, Odilo Globocnik. There was no opportunity to hear Gerstein in a court. His French captors moved him to a Paris prison and held him there as a suspected war criminal. Distraught, Gerstein apparently hanged himself in his cell at the end of July 1945.[8]

One messenger was able to talk to dozens of high officials in the West. Indeed he became widely known while the war was still on. His name was Jan Karski and he was a courier between the Polish underground and the Polish Government in Exile. Inasmuch as his missions were official, he did not speak for himself, but there was an element of choice in the extent to which he reported the Jewish fate and the number of times he mentioned it.

Born in 1914, Karski entered first the Polish army and then the Polish diplomatic service. During the opening campaign against Poland in 1939, he was taken prisoner by the Soviets, who had joined Germany with an invasion of their own from the east. Pretending not to be an officer, he was released and began his hazardous career as a carrier of messages. Caught once, he tried to commit suicide, but he survived and was whisked out by the underground. In October 1942, at a time when deportations had already swept away most of Polish Jewry, but when it was still hard for outsiders to fathom the full measure of what was happening, Karski was in Warsaw, preparing to go to London again.[9]

With the consent of, and by arrangement with, the Polish underground he met with two Jewish leaders outside the remnant ghetto of Warsaw. They did not give their names, but one was the socialist Leon Feiner, the other a Zionist, either Adolf Berman or Menachem Kirszenbaum. They took him to the depopulated ghetto, where he saw "a people expiring, breathing its last before my eyes."[10] They told him what sort of message he should deliver to the Jewish leaders abroad. Those leaders should be advised to refuse food until something was done. The Allied governments should be asked to retaliate against the Germans in their own countries. German cities should be bombed and leaflets should be dropped explaining that the reason for the air raids was the continuing annihilation of European Jewry. The Jewish leaders requested Karski to see this annihilation for himself. He agreed and, accompanied by a guide, left Warsaw. What followed he described on many occasions, not only in the reports he made, but also in a book that appeared in 1944 and became a best-seller.[11]

Karski arrived in Britain in November 1942 and then went on to the United States, where he remained. When he reported to the Polish ambassador, Jan Ciechanowski, in Washington, his news was so electrifying that the Polish emissary arranged for a meeting between Karski and President Roosevelt. Ciechanowski describes the White House interview in his memoirs. Embedded in details about the mood in the Polish underground, Karski had given a "nerve-shattering description of his own visit—disguised as a policeman—to the two murder camps, Treblinka and Belzec, where Jews were gassed in railway trucks." Karski had also relayed to Roosevelt the Jewish request for bombers and leaflets.[12]

In a meeting shortly afterward with Polish Jews in the United States, Karski stated that he had visited Belzec in the uniform of a Latvian auxiliary. He described a scene of some five thousand Jews from Warsaw, one thousand of them under the open sky and the others in barracks, who were packed into freight cars over a period of eight hours. The floors of the cars were piled thick with quicklime. At this meeting, Karski mentioned a demand of the Jewish leaders in Warsaw for retaliation against Germans in England, the United States, and other countries, for holding disloyal Germans as hostages, and for bombing German cities with accompanying leaflets.[13]

In his book, published in 1944, Karski stated that he wore an Estonian uniform. The camp, still Belzec, he described as very small, with Ukrainian, Latvian, and Estonian guards. Karski stated that he kept as far away as possible from the Estonians to avoid any exchange of words. He recalled that the Jews, still from Warsaw, had left the camp on the day they came, and that they had been dumped as corpses.[14]

In fact, Jewish transports from Warsaw were routed to Treblinka, not Belzec. No transport left Warsaw in October. The guards in Belzec were mainly Ukrainian, although a few Baltic nationals may have been among them. The same composition applies to the guard force in Treblinka. Above all, trains did not leave Belzec or Treblinka so that the passengers could die in the cars. Belzec and Treblinka were death camps with gas chambers, and these facilities were not mentioned in Karski's account.

The politicians, however, whom Karski was addressing were in a poor position to judge details. Most of them had not even heard of Belzec or Treblinka. They could believe him and then decide to take no action, or they could be suspicious of him but realize that the moment of truth had come. For Szmuel Zygielbojm, the truth could not be evaded anymore.

Zygielbojm had been active in the Jewish trade union movement in Poland. A socialist, he had been named to the Warsaw Jewish Council established under the German occupation. After a few months he left, and later he became a member of the National Council of the Polish Government in Exile in London. There, he received ominous reports about the Jewish fate from the Jewish Socialist Bund in Poland. In October 1942 he met Karski. The Polish courier, who had been a diplomat and an officer, described Zygielbojm as a self-made man of proletarian origins who demanded facts and who asked Karski many questions, including inappropriate personal questions. Karski finally told Zygielbojm that the Jewish leaders in Warsaw had demanded a hunger strike. Zygielbojm dismissed the suggestion, saying he would be carried out before he could starve himself. In Washington a half-year later, Karski received a message that Zygielbojm had killed himself by turning on the gas in his apartment. After a moment of numbness, Karski felt the shock, the grief, and the guilt. "I felt as though I had personally handed Zygielbojm his death warrant, even though I had only been the instrument," he wrote in 1944. "Zygielbojm's death," he added, "did not have a shadow of consolation. It was self-imposed and utterly hopeless."[15]

At a liberators' conference sponsored by the United States Holocaust Memorial Council in October 1981, Karski, still tall, lean, and dignified, addressed a large group of delegates from several countries about his experience. He referred to himself as a "tape recorder." But now, he said, the curtain was drawn. The theater was empty. He had always remained a practicing Catholic, but after the war, he said, "I became a Jew like the family of my wife, who is sitting in this audience—all of them perished in the ghettos, in the concentration camps, in the gas chambers, so all murdered Jews became my family."[16]

21

THE JEWISH RESCUERS

DURING THEIR DISPERSION, the Jewish communities of the world had acquired a patina of timelessness. History and destiny were merged in a chain of generations. Diaspora Jewry also maintained an identity across boundaries and oceans. A bond of familiarity connected Jews everywhere.

Seven million Jews were subject to German domination or the rule of one of Germany's satellite states. Nine million were outside this sphere, fewer than twenty thousand in pivotal neutral Switzerland, somewhat more than 2 million in territories of the Soviet Union not overrun by the invaders, a few hundred thousand each in Britain and Palestine, and the largest number, near 5 million, in the United States.

The Soviet Jews were not, and could not be, independent actors on the political scene. They were cut off from the rest of the world and voiceless in their own country. With the onset of the German assault, the Soviet Jews were entirely dependent on their own individual initiative and on the possibilities provided by the Soviet government for flight.

The Jewish community of Great Britain had much more freedom than the Soviet Jews, and by the 1930s British Jewry numbered more than 300,000, but many of these people were immigrants or the children of immigrants from Eastern Europe. Jews did not arrive in Britain with the Romans. They came after William the Conqueror, and under the Angevin kings they were only thousands, engaging in moneylending, speaking French at home, and maintaining connections with the Continent. By the end of the thirteenth century they were expelled. But for a handful of Spanish Jews who set foot in Britain after 1492, Jews did not return to the British Isles until the middle of the seventeenth century. The newcomers were mainly Sephardic, that is to say, Spanish, Portuguese, or Italian in origin. One of their sons, Benjamin Disraeli, was the convert who became an empire builder in the nineteenth century. Nevertheless, the Jews were still few. In 1880, they were about 65,000, and only in the next sixty years did they increase fivefold. By and large, the absorption of the new immigration wave had been a successful venture, and during the First World War British Jewry could demonstrate its allegiance with the deaths of thousands of Jewish men in the British army. In this sense, British Jews acted just like the Jews in the German, Austro-Hungarian, Bulgarian, and Ottoman armies who patriotically shot at Britons, Christian or Jewish.

Unlike several Jewish communities on the Continent, British Jewry had not suffered from a regime of legal discrimination, save for the prohibition of officeholding. This near-equality was achieved without upheavals or revolutions. Yet there were apprehensions. In the old established portion of British Jewry, anxiety was created by the Zionist movement. In the community as a whole, during the time of high unemployment in the 1930s, there was fear of reactions to a sudden influx of refugees. It was important not to dilute the public perception that British Jews were thoroughly British, and nothing was to be done that might fan any latent anti-Semitism or give circulation to overtly poisonous speeches of Nazi sympathizers.

The principal organizations of British Jewry were the Anglo-Jewish Association and the Board of Deputies of British Jews. The former was predominantly non-Zionist or even anti-Zionist. The board, which supported Zionism, was headed by the historian Neville Laski, brother of the political theorist Harold Laski. In 1939, Selig Brodetzki, a professor of mathematics with Zionist credentials, became the board's president. In its earlier days, two Montefiores had presided over the board.

The Anglo-Jewish Association and the Board of Deputies were associated in a standing committee, the Joint Foreign Committee, which addressed itself to the oppression of Jews in non-Western European countries. The committee broke apart in the middle of the war, when the board was captured by the Zionists.

After the Nazis had come to power, the British Jewish organizations assumed that a few thousand Jews in Germany would try to reach Britain. The organizations undertook a guarantee that the Jews would not become a public charge. The Jewish leaders thought that the stay of the refugees would be temporary, pending a further migration to other destinations. Later, there were, however, unexpected increases in the number of immigrants, and immediately after the November 10, 1938, pogrom in Germany, there was a refugee crisis. At this point, the Home Secretary, Sir Samuel Hoare, declared at a Cabinet meeting that the Jewish organizations did not want an inundation of Jews, lest anti-Semitism increase. They also did not wish publicity about the number of refugees admitted, lest the Jewish leadership become the target of criticism that there were either too few or too many.[1] From this moment, Britain's Jewish organizations no longer played a major, let alone leading, role in the rescue of the European Jews.

A second substantial Jewish community under the British flag was Palestinian Jewry. By 1939, numbering 400,000, it was larger than the British, but eight years earlier its size had only been 175,000. The Jewish migration into Palestine during the 1930s had its origins mainly in Poland and Germany. Under regulations issued by the British High Commissioner of Palestine, "capitalists," professionals, and artisans were admitted if they could show specified sums of money in Palestine pounds, whereas laborers were allowed entry only within quota limits set twice yearly in the High Commissioner's office. The indigenous governing body of the Palestinian Jewish community, the Jewish Agency, had the residual task of distributing immigration certificates under the labor schedule.

Laborers immigrating to Palestine had to be young, and overall the Jewish population of Palestine, in contrast to the European Jews, was a young community. The Palestinian Jews were also preoccupied with building a completely self-sufficient Jewish society, speaking the Hebrew language, performing all economic tasks by themselves, and aiming at statehood. Immigrants were needed for the realization of this vision, but there was open Arab opposition to more Jewish immigration and to more Jewish acquisitions of Arab land. In the end the Jewish community was blockaded by two British decisions: one, the White Paper of May 1939 sharply curtailing immigration; the other, the Palestine Land Transfers Regulations of February 1940, which restricted land purchases.

Palestinian Jewry was not only frustrated; it was conscious of its short reach of power. The lightly armed Jewish settlers were mainly an underground force, and the Jewish Palestinian military units were at the disposal of the British Mandatory Power. In the middle of 1942, when the killing of Jews on the European continent was reaching its height, Palestinian Jewry became concerned by the closeness of German forces, which simultaneously invaded Egypt and the Caucasus. The Palestinian Jews were now absorbed with their own survival.

American Jewry was free and safe. It had grown from a small community of Portuguese Jews in the seventeenth century. In the middle of the nineteenth century, there was a noticeable immigration, mainly from Germany. Between 1881 and 1932, the Eastern European Jews arrived. The number of Jewish immigrants who settled in the United States during those five decades was over 2,300,000, and many of these Jews were still alive when the Second World War broke out. They had left parents, siblings, nephews, nieces, and cousins in Europe, although few had ever seen their relatives since youth.

The immigrants in the United States were almost invariably poor. Those who had preceded them tried to help. Aid societies were formed, employment was offered, albeit on the lowest rung of the economic ladder, and the newcomers were "integrated." Assistance was also extended to the needy Jews abroad and already in the nineteenth century, American Jews enlisted the Department of State to protest the persecution of Jews in Russia. By 1919 liberation had come to Jews everywhere, save for some communities in the Moslem world. Long-standing discriminatory measures against Jews had been dismantled in Russia and Romania. In Europe the Middle Ages were over at last.

Absolute equality was another matter, even in the United States. American Jewry was hemmed in geographically, economically, and psychologically. In the nineteen thirties, when the U.S. Jewish population was approximately 4,800,000, nearly 2,000,000 Jews lived in New York City. All over the United States, Jews were effectively barred from living in many neighborhoods. Quotas for Jews were established in colleges and medical schools. By and large, Jews were excluded from management and employment in heavy industry, the large banks, and the major insurance companies. Jewish business activity gravitated to the retail trade, the manufacture of clothing, and communications. The trade unions of the Jews were the International Ladies Garment Workers Union, the Amalgamated Clothing Workers, and the Fur Workers. The vast majority of the Jews did not own their own homes and struggled to pay rent. Even as their income rose to the levels of non-Jews in the cities, their capital and net worth were still relatively low. Moreover, American Jewry was uneasy about its status. The Jews read and listened nervously to open anti-Semitic statements that seemed to multiply in number and intensity of tone even as the situation of the European Jews was worsening. The American Jews were on the defensive and they proclaimed their undivided loyalty to America. There was to be no conflict between an American interest, such as the restrictive immigration laws adopted in the 1920s, and a Jewish need. America would always have priority.

As officeholders Jews were not numerous. The Secretary of the Treasury, Henry Morgenthau, Jr., was a Jew. The House of Representatives contained nine Jews, and after the election of 1940, just six. No Jew served in the Senate. As voters, American Jews overwhelmingly backed the Democratic party of Franklin Roosevelt in 1932, 1936, 1940, and 1944. Roosevelt—articulate reformer and trusted liberal—was Jewry's greatest hero. Like America, Roosevelt came first.

Two major political organizations had been formed by American Jews before Hitler came to power. The older of the two was the

American Jewish Committee, which was established in 1906, literally as a committee of individuals, and which was dominated by German Jews successful in business activities. In the 1930s it was headed by one of its founders, the Arkansas-born Cyrus Adler, then in his seventies. Trained as an Assyriologist, Adler went on to a career as cataloger of collections, co-founder of the Jewish Publication Society, and President of the Jewish Theological Seminary as well as Dropsie College. From 1941 to 1943, the committee was headed by Maurice Wertheim, an investment banker, and thereafter by the Alabama-born Judge Joseph Proskauer, who had immersed himself in New York Democratic party politics. The American Jewish Committee was anti-Zionist before and throughout the Second World War. In asserting Jewish rights or protesting against injustice, its style was always restrained. The committee did not organize public demonstrations.

The second political grouping was the American Jewish Congress and its outgrowth, the international World Jewish Congress. Originally an assembly of Jewish organizations, the American Jewish Congress became in the 1930s a society of individual members. The World Jewish Congress, founded in 1936, was formed of delegations from Jewish organizations and communities around the world, with sections in Great Britain, Latin America, and so forth. The principal figure in the American Jewish Congress and the World Jewish Congress was Stephen Wise, a Reform rabbi who was also a Zionist. Wise was born in 1874 in Budapest but was brought to the United States as a small child. His Zionist activity began early. As a young man he knew the founder of modern Zionism, Theodor Herzl, and helped organize the Zionist movement in the United States. Between 1936 and 1938 he also served as President of the Zionist Organization of America. Wise, perhaps more than any other Jewish public figure, identified himself with Roosevelt, whom he backed unreservedly and to whom he wrote letters addressing him as "Dear Chief."

In their base of support as well as style of leadership, the forces of Stephen Wise offered a contrast to the American Jewish Committee. When the World Jewish Congress sought to enlist a nominal advisory council for its newly created Institute of Jewish Affairs in 1941, one of the gentiles, Robert S. Lynd, Professor of Sociology

at Columbia University, wrote to the General Counsel of the
Institute:

Dear Mr. Levy:
You may add my name to the Advisory Council of the Institute of
Jewish Affairs. In thus agreeing, I do so with the understanding
that your organization is prepared to be bolder and less timid than
the American Jewish Committee. I get a very bad impression of the
tendency of the latter organization to follow an anxious "Hush!
Hush!" policy that looks as tho they are prepared to throw other
Jews to the wolves so long as their own well-to-do group gets by.
Any decent non-Jew wants to work with and for Jews in a world
like this, but he wants to work with democratic Jews, not upper
class folk who want to save their personal skins.
   And, of course, the tragedy of you Jews' being divided amongst
yourselves these days.

                                              Cordially
                                              Robert S. Lynd[2]

Not everything, however, was different in the approaches of the
American Jewish Committee and the American Jewish Congress.
Both organizations had opposed a resolution introduced by Representative Samuel Dickstein in 1933 to liberalize the immigration law,
preferring the less conspicuous approach of lobbying for more permissive applications of existing legal provisions.[3] When the Jewish
War Veterans of America and other small groups organized a boycott of German goods during the same year, the leadership of the
American Jewish Committee and the American Jewish Congress
again had similar reactions. Adler and Proskauer were dismayed,
while Wise hesitated to support the movement in the absence of "the
sanction of our government." Wise understood that the pressure was
rising in the Jewish community and therefore he wrote to a colleague
that he was trying to "resist the masses." In the end, his own administrative committee overruled him.[4] By November 1938 the deterioration of Jewry's position in Germany prompted the representatives
of the American Jewish committee, the American Jewish Congress,

the fraternal organization B'nai B'rith, and the Jewish Labor Committee to weigh the advisability of advocating a change in the immigration law and of organizing protest parades in the streets. Once again, the decision was in favor of restraint and inactivity.[5]

Both the American Jewish Committee and the World Jewish Congress built staffs. The World Jewish Congress in particular expanded its apparatus, adding a department of relief activities and creating the Institute of Jewish Affairs to collect information and engage in long-range planning. Among the new personnel were men who had only recently migrated from Europe, where they had been closely concerned with the Jewish situation. One of them was Jacob Robinson, born in Lithuania and a specialist in international law, who had served in the Lithuanian Parliament and as counsel in the Lithuanian Foreign Office. Speaking a multitude of languages, he was quick to perfect his English. Having arrived in December 1940, he took charge of the newly formed institute two months later. Another was Arie Tartakower, who had been an alderman in the Polish city of Lodz as late as 1938–1939. Specialized in the sociology and demography of Jews, he migrated with his knowledge in 1939 and became the head of the Relief Department of the World Jewish Congress and Deputy Director of the Institute of Jewish Affairs. A third was Arye Leon Kubowitzki, like Robinson Lithuanian-born but from childhood a resident of Belgium, where he participated in Jewish politics. Kubowitzki emigrated to the United States in 1940, joined the institute, and became the head of the World Jewish Congress European Department. Still another recent immigrant in the institute was Jakob Lestschinsky, who had spent his life gathering statistics about European Jewish communities.[6]

The combined experience of these men did not prepare them for an evaluation of the events on the Continent. They were not political scientists, and their expertise was concentrated on Jewish matters, not Nazi Germany. When Tartakower drafted the outline of an address that he was to deliver on March 29, 1941, to the Jewish Writers Club, he asked himself why the institute had been established in the midst of the war. His answer: the institute was to concern itself with rebuilding of Jewish life, so that "the day after the close of the war, every Jew should know what is his position in the world and what he is expected to do."[7] Ten months later, on January 24, 1942, the agenda for a meeting of the Executive Committee of the Institute's Board of Trustees contained proposals for "conservative" and "dynamic" solutions of the Jewish problem. The conservative approach included the reintegration of Jews in European economic life, restoration of their property, and equality of rights. The dynamic strategy comprised migration to Palestine, mass colonization, and transfers of populations.[8] All attention was riveted, in one way or another, on a reconstituted, normalized postwar world.

Several Jewish organizations established offices in Switzerland. When these outposts were created, before the German march across Europe, Switzerland was not considered an important location. The offices were to distribute some relief and gather some basic information. Their budgets were small and their personnel sparse.

The Jewish Agency in Palestine appointed as its representative in Switzerland the Berlin-born Richard Lichtheim, whose career in Jewish politics was marked, and sometimes interrupted, by a streak of independence. He had served as the Zionist Organization's representative in Constantinople during the First World War, and for two years, from 1921 to 1923, he had been a member of the Jewish Agency's Executive, which at this point did not yet have all of its departments in Palestine. Lichtheim was in charge of organization, but he resigned from that office in protest against the widening of the agency to include non-Zionists. Later he joined the nationalistic Revisionists led by Vladimir Jabotinsky, but when Jabotinsky left the Zionist Organization to found his own movement, Lichtheim did not follow him, just as earlier he had not followed the Zionist leadership.[9] In 1933 Lichtheim migrated to Palestine, and six years later, at the age of fifty-four, he set up his post in Geneva. There he began with a financial struggle to pay for postage stamps and telephone calls.[10]

Lichtheim's letters from Geneva are replete with warnings. Seeing darkness with every glance, he noted as early as October 1939 that in the newly occupied western portion of Poland, "we shall have to face the fact that under German rule 2,000,000 Jews will be annihilated in not less a cruel way, perhaps even more cruel, than 1,000,000 Armenians have been destroyed by the Turks during the last war."[11]

By November 1941, after the beginning of deportations of German Jews to Poland, he was full of forebodings. The fate of the Jews from Germany, he wrote, would be even more dreadful than that of the Polish Jews shut off in the ghettos, because the deportees did not have money, food reserves, or bedding. In the same letter he observed the "curious" fact that President Roosevelt never mentioned Jews in remarks about German oppression. The "studied silence" of the democracies was not making it easier for the victims.[12] On February 11, 1942, he wrote: "The number of [Jewish] dead after this war will have to be counted not in the thousands or hundreds of thousands but in the several millions,"[13] and on May 13, 1942, he reiterated his demand that the persecutions be given publicity in the British and American press and over the radio.[14] Two weeks later he predicted flatly that at the end of the war, two or three million Jews would be "physically destroyed."[15]

The World Jewish Congress placed its office in Geneva under the direction of Gerhart M. Riegner. In 1939, Riegner was twenty-eight years old. He was also energetic, sober, and outspoken. Originally from Berlin, where he had studied law, Riegner emigrated to Paris to continue his studies at the Sorbonne. Unable to practice in France, he moved on to Geneva, where he went to the university to study international law under such men as the refugee jurist Hans Kelsen and the Swiss-born Paul Guggenheim. Both Kelsen and Guggenheim recommended Riegner for the World Jewish Congress post.

Guggenheim, who was in his early forties, had been concerned with refugee matters and subsequently became involved with the politics of the Swiss Jewish community. He remained close to Riegner and the work of the Geneva post. The World Jewish Congress also operated a small rescue organization (Relico) in Geneva, which was headed by Adolf Silberschein, a former member of the Polish Parliament. In a letter to Nahum Goldmann, Chairman of the World Jewish Congress Executive Committee, Riegner described Silberschein as "a little bit retiring from his office work." Silberschein's health, he said, had not been good and a brother of Silberschein's in a Croatian concentration camp had not been heard from. All this affected Silberschein psychologically.[16] Silberschein on his part pointed out in a letter to Tartakower in New York that he had objected to Riegner as a representative of the World Jewish Congress. Riegner did not tell him much of what was going on. Referring to the Lichtheim-Guggenheim-Riegner group, he said that the trio was trying to oust the president of the Swiss Jewish community, Saly Mayer, and replace him with Guggenheim. It was, said Silberschein, a war between the intelligentsia and the establishment.[17]

Both Riegner and Silberschein had a problem with money. On March 1, 1942, Riegner wrote to Tartakower that the financial situation had become desperate, and that no funds had been received over a period of four months. "If you want us to continue work you must settle this immediately."[18] On March 28, Riegner and Guggenheim sent a cable to New York, protesting "your cutting the budget." The ordinary monthly budget was $975, and New York wanted documentation of expenses. On June 30, 1942, Wise and Goldmann cabled Riegner that Silberschein was to transfer relief activity to the Swiss Jews to be in compliance with U.S. law, and that the new budget was $500 for Riegner, Silberschein, two secretaries, and other expenses.[19]

At first, the information obtained by Riegner was the sort that could be culled from legal gazettes and newspapers. When the shootings in Eastern Europe and deportations from Germany began in 1941, the contents of his messages changed radically. The first deportations of the German Jews were mentioned in a telegram on October 16, 1941, and by March 23, 1942, Riegner sent a cable to Wise, Rabbi Maurice Perlzweig, and Rabbi Irving Miller in the World Jewish Congress headquarters in New York stating:

GRAVEST POSSIBLE NEWS REACHING LONDON PAST WEEK, SHOWS
MASSACRES NOW REACHING CATASTROPHIC CLIMAX PARTICULARLY
POLAND ALSO DEPORTATIONS BULGARIAN ROMANIAN JEWS ALREADY
BEGUN STOP EUROPEAN JEWS DISAPPEARING. . . .[20]

Riegner had only pieces of information, some inaccurate, but he collected them. On June 17, 1942, he wrote to Goldmann that "some weeks ago" Silberschein had received a telephone call from a German Red Cross representative in Kolomea (eastern Galicia). The man, with whom no one in the Geneva office had ever been in contact, had even introduced himself by name. He informed Silberschein that the situation of the Jews in Kolomea had become catastrophic. A great many men had died a violent death, and women and children needed help. The caller said that his human feelings moved him to contact the Geneva office to alleviate his conscience.[21] During the following month Riegner sent word that thirty thousand of forty thousand Jews in Vilnius were gone, that some of the Bialystok Jews had been deported, and that in eastern Galician villages serious "pogroms" had taken place in March and April.[22] By June and July reports of this nature were increasing in frequency and volume, but they still did not trigger a suspicion that Nazi Germany had embarked on a final solution.[23]

During July 1942, however, several Germans crossed into Switzerland with fundamental revelations. One of them was Ernst Lemmer, a founder of the German Democratic party in 1918 and Minister in West Germany during the 1950s and 1960s. Lemmer spent the wartime years as a newspaper correspondent in Budapest, Brussels, and Switzerland. According to Walter Laqueur, who made a search of these messengers, Lemmer met with several Swiss public figures in Zurich that July and told them about "gas chambers, stationary and mobile, in which Jews were killed." He wanted this news to be disseminated, but he was somewhat mistrusted and no one was inclined to do as he asked.[24]

On or about July 27, 1942, a German lieutenant colonel, Artur Sommer, who was an economist and Deputy Director of the "Allied and Neutral States" Group in the Economy Office of the Armed Forces High Command, traveled to Switzerland on official business. Sommer had been in Switzerland before and had visited another economist, Professor Edgar Salin, at the University of Basel. On those occasions Sommer had freely talked about German behavior in the USSR, once leaving packets of photographs showing emaciated and dead Soviet prisoners of war. This time Salin found a note without an envelope in his box. It stated:

In the East camps are being prepared in which all the Jews of Europe and a large part of the Soviet prisoners of war are to be gassed. Please send messages immediately to Roosevelt and

Churchill. If the BBC will warn daily against the gas ovens, their use may be prevented, since the criminals will do everything to make sure that the German people will not find out what they are planning and what they can surely carry out as well.[25]

The information in Sommer's note was already old. Gas had been considered for the European Jews during the early fall of 1941. The program was to be implemented in the Baltic area and Byelorussia, partly in camps prepared for roundups of Communists, but it was subsequently shifted to Poland, where it was in full swing by summer 1942. Evidently Sommer had learned of the early plans several months late. His suggestion that the British Broadcasting Corporation paralyze the perpetrators psychologically was not altogether new either. The BBC had already made some broadcasts, albeit not the plenary, forceful daily announcements that he had in mind.[26] Nevertheless, Sommer's message has considerable significance, first because it was sent by someone in Berlin who was likely to be close to the truth, and second because it was an unambiguous statement to the effect that European Jewry was to be gassed to death.

Salin was a convert to Christianity from Germany and he was sensitive to the unfolding events across the border. Nevertheless he did not know how to reach Roosevelt and Churchill. He contacted the American President of the Bank for International Settlements, Thomas H. McKittrick, in Basel, who subsequently assured Salin that he had gone to the American Minister in Bern immediately and that the Minister had cabled the news to "Roosevelt."[27] No cable containing the contents of Sommer's communication from the American Minister to any Washington address has been found in any archives.[28]

For a British connection, Salin contacted Chaim Pozner, without, however, revealing Sommer's name. Pozner, like Sommer a former student of Salin's, handed out Palestine immigration certificates for the Jewish Agency in Switzerland. Pozner claimed after the war that he had rendered voluntary services to V. C. Farrell, then in charge of British passport control in Switzerland but, according to Pozner, actually an intelligence officer. Pozner stated later that he had spoken to Farrell and that Farrell had promised to relay the message to London,[29] but no record of such a note has been found in British archives.[30] By way of insurance, however, Pozner had also sent the news to Chaim Barlas, a Jewish Agency representative who had once been stationed in Switzerland and who was now in Istanbul, Turkey.[31] On August 29, Pozner wrote again, wondering why a month had passed without a reaction from Palestinian Jewry.[32] Sommer's testimony was dissipated in the winds.[33]

A third informant was Eduard Schulte, who was an industrialist in Breslau, where he headed a large mining concern, Bergwerksgesellschaft Georg von Giesche's Erben. His connections in Germany included a German colonel and a Giesche manager who was close to Gauleiter Karl Hanke of Lower Silesia. Like Sommer, Schulte had previously been in Switzerland on business and had given information to various people about German policies and plans. This time, his visit was prompted by something he had heard about the Jews: they were going to be annihilated. On July 30, 1942, he talked to a business associate, Isidor Koppelmann, who contacted the press officer of the Swiss Jewish community, Benjamin Sagalowitz. Schulte wanted his message to be transmitted to America and Britain, and Sagalowitz turned to Riegner in Geneva. Riegner consulted Professor Guggenheim. The choices were few. One could not simply fly to London or New York and deliver the message personally. Communication through the mail or telegrams risked Swiss censorship. An approach to Allied representatives in Switzerland, however, offered the possibility of speed and security, as well as help in gathering additional information. On the morning of August 8, Riegner set out to meet with the British and American consuls in Geneva.[34] Riegner, who had not met Schulte and had not been given his name, drafted a notice containing the substance of Schulte's statement. It was addressed to Sydney Silverman, a member of the World Jewish Congress in London and member of Parliament, and to Wise in New York. Its text is as follows:

RECEIVED ALARMING REPORT STATING THAT IN FUEHRERS
HEADQUARTERS A PLAN HAS BEEN DISCUSSED AND BEING UNDER
CONSIDERATION ACCORDING TO WHICH TOTAL OF JEWS IN
COUNTRIES OCCUPIED CONTROLLED BY GERMANY NUMBERING

THREEANDHALF TO FOUR MILLIONS SHOULD AFTER DEPORTATION AND
CONCENTRATION IN EAST BE AT ONE BLOW EXTERMINATED IN ORDER
TO RESOLVE ONCE FOR ALL JEWISH QUESTION IN EUROPE STOP
ACTION IS REPORTED TO BE PLANNED FOR AUTUMN WAYS OF
EXECUTION STILL DISCUSSED STOP IT HAS BEEN SPOKEN OF PRUSSIC
ACID STOP IN TRANSMITTING INFORMATION WITH ALL NECESSARY
RESERVATION AS EXACTITUDE CANNOT BE CONTROLLED BY US BEG
TO STATE THAT INFORMER IS REPORTED HAVE CLOSE CONNECTIONS
WITH HIGHEST GERMAN AUTHORITIES AND HIS REPORTS TO BE
GENERALLY RELIABLE

> WORLD JEWISH CONGRESS
> GERHARD RIEGNER[35]

The words "all necessary reservation" were suggested by Guggenheim.[36]

By the end of July, gassings were already under way in Kulmhof,
Auschwitz, Belzec, Sobibor, Treblinka, and Maydanek (Lublin).
Only Treblinka had just begun its operations. The subject was no
longer under discussion and the Jews were not going to be killed "at
one blow." The message, however, contained not only the overwhelming truth of annihilation, but some telling details. Thus there
was a stockpiling of deportees from Germany and Slovakia in a number of eastern ghettos, pending organized shootings or gassings, and
prussic acid, the active ingredient in Zyklon, *was* the gas already
introduced in Auschwitz, the death camp in Upper Silesia, next door
to Lower Silesia.

When Vice Consul Howard Elting met with Riegner in the American consulate, he found the World Jewish Congress representative in
great agitation. Riegner brought up the prussic acid and Elting interjected that the report seemed fantastic to him. Riegner replied that
it had struck him the same way, but that he had to consider the recent
mass deportations from Paris, Holland, Berlin, Vienna, and Prague.
The report was so serious and alarming that he felt it his duty to
request that the Allied governments and Rabbi Wise be informed and
the governments "try by every means to obtain confirmation or
denial."[37]

For Riegner the pieces were already falling into place. They were not so convincing to the Allied governments. The Department of State decided that, pending corroboration of the information, the message should not be delivered to Rabbi Wise.[38] In the British Foreign office, the telegram was considered for seven days before it was passed on to Sydney Silverman.[39] Wise received the message from Silverman on August 24.[40]

In the meantime there were more and more witnesses and informants, albeit not all of them reliable. On August 14, 1942, a non-Jewish Pole, repeating a rumor circulating inside Europe, reported that bodies were disinterred for the production of soap and fertilizer. In this connection, however, the informant pointed to an actual death camp: Belzec.[41]

The geographic extent of the catastrophe was confirmed day after day. On August 31, 1942, Riegner reported to Miller details about a roundup in Paris. Abandoned children "were crying, weeping, calling for 'mother' across deserted and dark streets."[42] A week later he notified Goldmann, "deportations all countries growing daily."[43]

By October Riegner and Lichtheim had pooled their information. They met with the American Minister in Switzerland, Leland Harrison, and handed him an aide-mémoire, dated October 22, in which they pointed out that the "prominent German industrialist" (Schulte) who had originally conveyed the message of an intended annihilation was now in possession of a new report indicating that at the end of July Hitler had signed an order to destroy the Jews of Europe. The informant, according to the memoire, had stated that he had seen this order himself. He even had details, such as the attribution of the annihilation plan to State Secretary Herbert Backe of the Food Ministry and opposition to it from Generalgouverneur Hans Frank in Poland.[44]

No order of this nature, signed by Hitler, has been found in archives, and no reference to such a document has been spotted in the wartime German correspondence, but Hitler's veiled oral utterances had been quoted by his underlings on more than one occasion. The roles ascribed to Backe and Frank were suppositions drawn from a chain of rumors. These inferences too were far removed from the bedrock of the facts, but the food officials and Frank had discussed in

1941 the crucial question of how the ghettos were going to be kept alive for another winter.

Soon, two additional reports were received from German sources by Carl Burckhardt of the International Red Cross. According to this news, which Burckhardt transmitted through Guggenheim to Consul Squire and Minister Harrison, there existed a Hitler order for the "extermination" (*Ausrottung*) of all Jews by December 31, 1942.[45] Again, there is no record of such a plenary order by Hitler, but the deadline, fixed by Himmler and circulated widely, did apply to the Generalgouvernement.

Riegner and Lichtheim had already come to the conclusion that European Jewry was in the grip of annihilation. The indefatigable Riegner, a bachelor, spent many hours with the reports, interpreting them and thinking about their implications. The profoundly pessimistic Lichtheim had sent his own stream of warnings to the Jewish Agency.[46] Lichtheim was not immediately informed about Schulte's message, but as early as August 27 he had convinced himself that Hitler had killed or was killing 4 million Jews in continental Europe, that not more than 2 million had a chance of surviving, and that every month even this chance was becoming smaller.[47] In their joint memorandum of October 22, Lichtheim and Riegner pointed out that 4 million Jews were on the verge of complete destruction. They went on to make a distinction between Jews under direct German control and those in satellite countries. They urged that measures be taken to save the Jews still living in the "semi-independent" states of Hungary, Italy, Romania, Bulgaria, and Vichy France. They indicated that the Jewish population in these countries was 1,300,000.[48]

Outside continental Europe, the Jewish leadership was slow in assessing the import of the messages it received. The "mandarins" of the Zionist movement, Lichtheim wrote on September 9, 1942, to Nahum Goldmann of the Jewish Agency, were "shirking from the unpleasant task."[49] The Jewish Agency's Izhak Gruenbaum had in fact been receiving Lichtheim's detailed reports with some skepticism.[50] During the first half of October he did request one hundred pounds for cables with Lichtheim. The Jewish Agency's Treasurer, Eliezer Kaplan, allotted fifty.[51] Again, when the Jewish Agency Executive in Jerusalem met on October 25, 1942, it discussed the situation of the Jews in Europe along with such topics as the compensation of its employees, the government committee on wages, and a new constitution for employment bureaus.[52] A few weeks later, however, a group of Palestinian nationals arrived from various cities in Germany and German-occupied Europe in exchange for Germans. In the words of Moshe Shertok, who headed the Jewish Agency's Political Department, they told "tales of horror," including "harrowing" details about poison gas chambers. "Confess if not reported by persons coming from the spot would not have believed," he said in his telegram to London.[53]

In Jerusalem there was no room for doubt anymore. At a meeting of November 22, 1942, the Jewish Agency devoted its entire attention to European Jewry. No other item was on the agenda, and the conferees decided to make the news public.[54] On the next day, banner headlines appeared in the Hebrew press, and the Jewish population was stunned and paralyzed. "The entire reaction," wrote the American Consul in Jerusalem, "is pathetic in its helplessness."[55]

Within the Jewish Agency there were some reservations about this publicity. The legal adviser of the Agency's Political Department, Bernard Joseph, was concerned about "publishing data exaggerating the number of Jewish victims," lest a question be asked "where the millions of Jews are for whom the national home was to be created in Palestine."[56] Complications also arose from attempts to organize expressions of protest and sorrow. A general strike had been ruled out by the Jewish Agency Executive on November 22 as detrimental to the war effort. For rock-hard Zionists the lamentations were reminiscent of the weakness that had been displayed by European Jews over the centuries. The Chairman of the Jewish Agency Executive, David Ben-Gurion, felt that the public grieving was ineffective and—directed as it was toward the Europe that had been left behind by the settlers—not sufficiently Zionist in character. The entertainment industry, which served Allied soldiers on furloughs, became impatient with curtailments and shutdowns.[57] Finally, the weeping and fasting could not be continued indefinitely.

The Yishuv, as the Jewish community in Palestine called itself, was a Zionist enterprise. The president of the World Zionist Organization, the biochemist Chaim Weizmann, was a man in his late sixties who lived in Britain. In February 1942, he had been informed of a son's death aboard a British bomber on U-boat patrol. "A broken man," he went to the United States in April and stayed there for fifteen months, busying himself in the laboratory with butadiene and isoprene. His voluminous published correspondence during this period contains only minor references to the Jewish catastrophe.[58]

Ben-Gurion was not broken. He did not walk away from the news, but he could not deal with it either. "With almost cruel clarity," Dina Porat says of him, "he realized that the Yishuv could save only a limited number of people, and he kept the full significance of these conclusions to himself."[59] The principal burden of rescue had to be assumed in America.

New York had its mandarins too. They as well had difficulty grasping the developments in Europe. At summer's end in 1942, the possibility of physical destruction was still not accepted or even explored. Thus, on September 23 the demographic expert in the Institute of Jewish Affairs, Jakob Lestschinsky, wrote a summary report of what he considered to be the deficit of European Jewry. His overall figure was 1,600,000, and in his breakdown he estimated 200,000 refugees no longer in continental Europe, 200,000 dead of bombardments in cities, and 100,000 killed in combat. The remaining 1,100,000 he believed to comprise 500,000 dead of natural causes and 600,000 in "mass slaughter." The primary aim of Hitler's policy, he said, was "extermination," but then he added that even Hitler could not achieve this goal "in a few years' time." Hence, Hitler's primary method was the establishment of such hygienic conditions for Jews as would encourage them to die more rapidly.[60] The assumption that the deportees were still alive is reflected also in a telegram sent on October 16, 1942, by Rabbi Miller to Riegner, asking Riegner whether it was possible to obtain the present addresses of some of the people caught in the maelstrom.[61]

Publicizing what had been learned was another agonizing process. When Rabbi Wise of the World Jewish Congress had received the Riegner telegram through London at the end of August, he agreed with the State Department to withhold the information until it could be substantiated. Together with the heads of other Jewish organizations, he had "succeeded" in keeping his promise.[62] At the end of

November he finally approached the press with State Department concurrence, but the news was buried in the inside pages.[63] Wise and four colleagues did manage to see President Roosevelt. To this meeting, which took place on December 8, 1942, the Jewish delegation brought two memoranda, one with a summary of events, the other with recommendations. The compilers of the factual recapitulation had evidently not jettisoned Lestschinsky's evaluation. They said that almost 2 million Jews had died, an estimate that was half of the actual number at that time. They mentioned "mass murder, planned starvation, deportation, slave labor and epidemics in disease-ridden ghettos, penal colonies and slave reservations," but not gas. They named Mauthausen, Oswiecim (Auschwitz), and Chelmno (Kulmhof), but they did not identify Belzec, Sobibor, or Treblinka. They still referred to mass shootings in Kiev and other cities as "pogroms." In the recommendations there were only two requests: (1) warnings to be issued to Nazi Germany and its allies and (2) a commission to be created by the government to collect more information. There was no list of individuals to be warned, and there was no listing of questions about Jewry's fate to which answers might have been sought.[64]

At the end of the half-hour meeting, the five Jewish leaders left without even a promise that the government would establish a fact-finding agency. Yet Wise was satisfied. In a letter to Tartakower on December 15, 1942, he wrote that the President had received him, together with Maurice Wertheim of the American Jewish Committee, Henry Monsky of B'nai B'rith, Adolph Held of the Jewish Labor Committee, and Rabbi Israel Rosenberg of the Union of Orthodox Rabbis. To be sure the State Department had vetoed a suggestion that representatives of the Synagogue Council, the American Federation of Polish Jews, and the Orthodox Agudath Israel join the delegation, but the five visitors "were all moved by the earnestness and vigor with which the President reacted to our pleas for his help." It was evident, Wise went on, that the President and the State Department "comprehend the magnitude of the crime against our brother Jews throughout the land occupied by Hitler, and that our Government is determined to avert by all possible means the continuance of the wrong which has been and is being done the Jewish people."[65]

Not all of the five delegates formed such an impression of the meeting. Adolph Held of the Jewish Labor Committee noted in a memorandum that the President had received them in a buoyant mood, listened to the recommendations, and told the delegation that he already had most of the facts, with confirmations from many sources. He assented to the warning proposal and asked whether the delegates had other recommendations. When the Jewish leaders could not think of anything, Roosevelt switched to other topics. In this way he used up 80 percent of the allotted half-hour.[66]

The Jewish leadership in New York had no additional cards to play. Mass meetings had been organized and days of mourning proclaimed, but there was no program for going on. The reports, on the other hand, continued to arrive. In January a description of the remnant ghetto of Warsaw was received: debilitated women in dilapidated houses. "One speaks with stubborn certainty about gassings." In Berlin, working parents returned home to discover that their children had been seized. Two thousand Berlin Jews were in hiding. Many committed suicide with veronal, but inasmuch as this product was expensive, some victims had used poisonous mushrooms.[67] The Polish ambassador, Ciechanowski, wrote to Tartakower on March 24, 1943, enclosing a note from a "Jewish National Committee" in Poland addressed to Wise, Goldmann, and the American Jewish Joint Distribution Committee:

The remnants of the Jewish communities in Poland exist in the conviction that during the most terrible days of our history you have not brought us help. Respond at least now in the last days of our life. This is our final appeal to you.[68]

Shortly thereafter, when the Jews of Bulgaria were threatened with deportation, Wise and the American Jewish Committee's Proskauer, backed by the State Department, made an unsuccessful appeal to the British Foreign Secretary, Anthony Eden, in Washington to join with other Allied nations in a declaration calling upon Hitler to let the Jews leave occupied Europe.[69] After the Warsaw Ghetto battle was fought in April and May, the American Jewish Committee's Executive Vice President, Morris Waldman, pronounced the Jews of Europe doomed.[70] In a similar vein, Jacob Robinson predicted on June 25 that the number of Jews who would survive would be small. Momentarily dejected, he asked what should be done for the European Jews *after* the war.[71]

The Institute of Jewish Affairs was still cautious in its numerical conclusions. In a book published August 20, 1943, it estimated 3,000,000 Jews dead and 3,000,000 still alive.[72] That very month, Riegner and Lichtheim prepared their own remarkably accurate figures. The number of victims, they said, had reached 4,000,000. Excluding the Soviet Union, only 1,500,000 to 2,000,000 remained in continental Europe: several hundred thousand in Poland and Germany, 750,000 in Hungary, 250,000 in Romania, 200,000 in France, 60,000 in the Romanian-administered zone across the Dnestr in Ukraine, 50,000 in Italy, 50,000 in the Netherlands, 45,000 in Theresienstadt, 25,000 in Belgium, and another 50,000 in other occupied areas.[73] The Lichtheim-Riegner statistic jarred Robinson. It contradicted the findings of his own institute. Then he thought of another "harmful result": The higher estimate of the Jewish dead would reinforce the belief that Hitler had already solved the Jewish problem and that therefore nothing had to be done anymore to save the remaining Jews.[74]

After this correspondence, more information was received from the Polish Government in Exile about Oswiecim (Auschwitz). Tartakower was asked to evaluate the communication and on November 23, 1943, rendered this opinion:

> If we can accept as true the horrible figure that out of 520,000 Jews who were killed by poison gas in the camp at Oswiecim no more than 20,000 were Polish Jews and the remainder Jews from France, Belgium, Holland, Yugoslavia, and other countries, it would confirm the previous reports of the Polish Government about mass deportations of Western European Jews to Poland. However, I have some doubts whether this figure, which we find here for the first time, can be accepted as correct.[75]

The Auschwitz report, like Lichtheim and Riegner's compilation, was much closer to the truth than Tartakower's assessment, but

Tartakower was still extrapolating conclusions from the institute's earlier underestimates. There was an important consequence of this practice. Tartakower had missed the significance of Auschwitz as a place to which transports were being directed from all parts of western and southeastern Europe. He could not imagine its capacity. Nor was he alone in this oversight. Right up to the beginning of June 1944, the Jewish Agency Executive was unaware of the meaning of Auschwitz as a death camp.[76]

During a six-month period beginning in mid-May 1944, nearly 600,000 Jews were taken to Auschwitz, mainly from Hungary, but also from Lodz, Theresienstadt, Slovakia, France, Italy, Greece, and remnant labor camps in Poland. Except for a brief reopening of Kulmhof, Auschwitz was the only remaining German killing center. Its gas chambers were clustered within a small area, a possible target for Allied bombers based on airfields in Italy. Because of major industrial installations under construction in the Auschwitz complex, Allied reconnaissance aircraft began to take photographs of the area in April 1944. The Allied interest, however, was confined to the plants and the photo interpreters paid no attention to the gas chamber–crematorium units.

Bombing requests did come from Jewish organizations in Budapest, Hungary, and Bratislava, Slovakia, but these communications were slow and late. Chaim Weizmann and Moshe Shertok presented the requests to the British Foreign Office at the beginning of July, but without a sense of urgency.[77] In the United States, the bombing pleas from inside Europe were channeled by the War Refugee Board to the War Department. Eventually, all these requests were turned down both in London and in Washington. The bombing idea could not be forwarded with emphasis and conviction, because the Jewish leaders had not focused their attention on Auschwitz and because they could not visualize either the potentiality or the complexities of aerial interdiction. Indeed some of them had qualms. Leon Kubowitzki, who headed the Rescue Department of the World Jewish Congress, opposed the bombing of the installations because Jews would be killed in such a raid.[78]

One more possibility arose in 1944, one which was a more familiar tool than aircraft. Just when the deportations from Hungary began, the Germans themselves allowed an emissary of a Jewish rescue organization, Joel Brand, to carry a message to the Jewish Agency in Palestine for the ransoming of the remaining Jews. The price was ten thousand trucks. Brand met with Chaim Barlas, the Jewish Agency representative in Istanbul, before boarding a slow train across Turkey to British-occupied Syria, where he was held for many days. Shertok saw him there. Hearing the figure "6 million" for the first time from Brand, he sat in disbelief. Travel to London was not simple, even for Shertok. Eventually he arrived there and, accompanied by Weizmann, presented the proposal along with the bombing suggestion to the British Foreign Office. He had done his duty and the British refused the request. There was not to be even a simulated attempt to negotiate with the Nazis, and the Jews were not saved. [79]

22

THE ALLIES

FOR THE SOVIET UNION, Great Britain, and the United States, the rescue of Jewry was not a priority. From 1941 to 1945, all three were concerned with the war, including their losses and gains in combat and their respective spheres of influence after the surrender of Germany. The task of strategic intelligence was the assessment of enemy plans and capabilities in the various theaters of operations. The entire territory behind enemy lines was viewed primarily as a complex of production, mobilization, and supply. Very little else invited Allied curiosity. The veritable decimation of populations subjugated by Germany and its partners was at best a subordinated interest. The same disparity of attention characterized also the propaganda activities of the Allies. The Soviet Union gave more publicity to the limited exploits of armed partisans harassing the Germans behind the battle front than to the mass dying of Soviet prisoners of war in German captivity. The Western Allies were moved to lavish more sympathy on the underground Poles who struck out in a vain attempt to free Warsaw in 1944 than on the many young Polish men shot in reprisals or languishing in concentration camps. The currency of the Second World War was the bullet, shell, and bomb; those who did not have these means were the war's forgotten poor. With weapons one could obtain praise and often additional arms; with plight one could buy neither care nor help.

The Soviet Union had 5 million Jewish inhabitants on the eve of the German invasion, counting just over 3 million of them within the prewar boundaries of August 1939 and another 2 million in the areas acquired during 1939 and 1940. In the old region, the Jews were integrated into the life of the country. Jews, alongside a number of other non-Russians, had taken a leading part in the Communist Revolution. Freed of the restrictions of tsarist rule, the Jews surged forward, not only in the party apparatus, but in industry, universities, the arts, and even the military. In the mid-1930s, however, Stalin's purges caught up with several Jewish power figures. Some of them were not only removed and shot but accused of pro-Fascist activities.[1] These charges, to be sure, were only a ritual. Soviet leadership was Russified. When Stalin thought in 1939 of a rapprochement with Nazi Germany, he removed without explanations the Jewish Foreign Commissar, Maxim Litvinov, as a matter of course.

For the nearly 2 million Jews in the newly seized Polish, Baltic, and Romanian areas, the Soviet experience was brief. In a number of ways the Jews in these territories benefited from the full equality bestowed upon them under Soviet rule, but thousands of "bourgeois" Jews were rounded up as equals of bourgeois non-Jews and deported to the Soviet interior. Unwittingly, the Soviet Union had saved precisely these counter-revolutionary Jews from the German destruction process.

Jewry was not permitted to organize itself in the Soviet Union. It was recognized as a nationality in the census and on the internal passports that had to be carried by all Soviet adults, but there was no freedom of advocacy. When two Polish Jewish refugees from the German-occupied zone, the Socialists Henryk Erlich and Victor Alter, attempted to form a Jewish Anti-Fascist Committee in the wake of the German invasion, they were charged with urging the Soviet soldiers to surrender to the Germans. Both Erlich and Alter were shot. The committee, found to be a good idea after all, was established as a propaganda agency after their deaths.

The crisis for Jewry in the Soviet Union began on the day of the German assault, June 22, 1941. Some 4 million Jews were living in the path of the German advance. For all of these people effective rescue was possible only before the German armies arrived. In the westernmost regions, the vast majority of the Jews were trapped by the sheer speed of the German arrival. Thus German forces occupied Grodno on June 23, Kaunas, Vilnius, and Slonim on June 24, Brest-Litovsk and Daugavpils on June 26, Bialystok on June 27, Lvov on June 30, Riga on July 1, and Pinsk on July 4. During the hasty and sometimes confused retreat of the Red Army in these opening battles, civilians had few opportunities to flee by truck or train. Moreover, the silence of the Soviet Union about German anti-Jewish measures between 1939 and 1941 had left many Jews uncertain or in darkness about the Germans.[2] Later on, however, the possibilities and incentives for escape were considerably greater. Thus the German-Romanian offensive in Bessarabia was delayed, and the Bessarabian capital, Chisinau (Kishinev), although close to the starting line, did not fall until July 17. By then most of the Jews of the city had fled.[3] German forces were in the vicinity of Kiev in mid-July but did not capture the city until September 18. Again, most of the Jews were gone. Odessa, under Romanian siege, fell on October 16. Probably, a majority of the Odessa Jews were able to leave. There is clear indication in German reports that Jews in Kiev and Kharkov had departed in relatively larger numbers than non-Jews.[4] The question that may be asked about such departures is the extent to which they were caused or influenced by decisions of Soviet authorities.

Two principles appear to have shaped Soviet policy with respect to evacuations of populations from urban areas. One was the prevention of a hasty flight of people. Their production was needed until the very last moment,[5] and a premature abandonment was going to have a deleterious effect on morale.[6] In some locations, leaving required a permit.[7] The second guideline was applied in cities whose fall was imminent. In these situations, priority for evacuation was usually given to skilled workers, managers, party functionaries, civil servants, students, intellectuals, and various professionals.[8] Jews were well represented in these categories, and Jewish workers in particular were a sizable component of the eligible evacuees in the industrial cities, but there is little evidence of any Soviet attempts to evacuate Jews as such. One German Security Police unit moving from Smolensk toward Moscow in the fall of 1941 reported that a "planned evacuation" of Jews had taken place in its area,[9] but in most invaded regions Jews were often on their own.[10]

Soviet Jews, directly threatened but effectively muted, could not pressure the Soviet government to do anything, and that government was not going to take any overt steps to assist Jews as Jews. As a house of nationalities, the Soviet Union was fragile enough, and it was not about to differentiate between Jews and anyone else.[11] By contrast, Britain and the United States were not invaded, and the Jewish communities there had the freedom to approach high officials for help. Moreover, in the democracies some official answers had to be given to the petitioners. The only problem for the Jews was that the replies did not have to be positive. The Western Allies, for reasons of their own, did not wish to make distinctions either.

Between 1933 and 1939, when Jewish petitions were barely audible, Britain and the United States had to consider mainly the acceptance of refugees. The attitude of both countries in this matter was reserved. Both had many unemployed, and both were thinking in terms of small numbers. For the British government the advent of the Nazi regime at first appeared to be an opportunity to attract some outstanding individuals. During the middle of the 1930s there was a willingness to admit nurses and domestic servants, a policy whose result was that several thousand young middle-class Jewish women from Germany became maids overnight. In 1939 thousands of children were permitted entry. Britain, however, was not going to have an open door. Refuge was to be temporary, and the refugee was expected to re-emigrate to farther destinations. When the stream became an overflow and it was difficult for the majority to move on, the Home Office and the Colonial Office found themselves at opposite ends of a debate, the former in favor of more generous admissions to Palestine, the latter opposed.

After the outbreak of war, Great Britain was reluctant to be a haven for additional refugees. There was a fear of "spies" and an even greater fear of "dumping," if Britain should declare herself willing to accept any or all Jews. After the fall of the Netherlands, Belgium, and France, Britain interned thousands of refugees, and for some time any refugees who wanted to enlist in the army were barred from virtually all branches except the pioneers (the counter-part of the American engineers).[12]

By 1933 the United States already had an elaborate system for the admission of immigrants, based on quotas by country of birth. The German quota, merged with Austria's in 1938, was large enough until that year, but the Polish quota, which covered Jews born within the boundaries of prewar Poland but resident in Germany or Austria, was very small. In addition, regulations adopted by President Hoover during the economic depression provided that visas were to be given only to persons not likely to become a public charge. In most cases the applicant therefore had to have an affidavit promising support, if needed on arrival, from a family member. If the affidavit was made out by a friend or stranger, the intentions as well as the resources of the promisor were probed by consular officials more deeply. Much also depended on changing instructions from the State Department as well as the good will or prejudice of consuls, some of whom worked overtime, while others became experts in delay, creating "paper walls" that kept the victims inside the perimeter of Germany's reach.[13]

The news of annihilation received in the summer of 1942 created a much larger dilemma for the Western Allies. Fundamentally, they wanted to turn away from this development. They did not want to deal with it. Soon after Gerhart Riegner had brought the report about prussic acid to the attention of the American Consul in Geneva with the request that the message be transmitted to Rabbi Stephen Wise, two officials in the State Department, looking over the document, expressed unease. Paul Culbertson, Assistant Chief of the European Division in the department, could not see why the American legation in Bern had sent the telegram, but at the same time he was concerned that Wise would discover the contents sooner or later on his own and that then the Jewish leader would "react." Accordingly, he drafted a note to Wise. It was crossed out by his chief, Elbridge Dubrow, with the instruction "Do not send, ED." Dubrow then wrote a memorandum explaining that passing on the message was undesirable in view of the "fantastic nature of the allegation" and the "impossibility of being of any assistance."[14]

When Wise, with a delegation of Jewish leaders, met with President Roosevelt on December 8, 1942, asking only for more fact finding by the government and an official warning to the Germans, Roosevelt declared that he already had enough facts, that the warning would be issued, and that the Jews had his sympathy.[15] The patrician President could afford to be lofty. He was secure in his office, at the height of his power, and in full possession of his political instincts. So complete was his mastery of the situation that he never had to receive another Jewish delegation.

There was one more time when the State Department cut off dispatches sent by Riegner through U.S. diplomatic channels, inasmuch as private communications transmitted in this manner were a violation of Swiss neutrality laws.[16] As late as August 1943, the British Government insisted on the deletion of a phrase mentioning gas chambers in a proposed Allied declaration, on the ground that the evidence for killings in the chambers was still insufficient.[17] At the beginning of 1944, a detailed report from Auschwitz, transmitted by the Polish underground, was distributed to the Office of Strategic Services, the War Department, and the United Nations War Crimes Commission. It was buried in all three.[18]

William J. Casey, a naval lieutenant in the Office of Strategic Services stationed in London from October 1943, observes in his memoirs:

> I'll never understand how, with all we knew about Germany and its military machine, we knew so little about the concentration camps and the magnitude of the holocaust. We knew in a general way that Jews were being persecuted, that they were being rounded up in occupied countries and deported to Germany, that they were brought to camps, and that brutality and murder took place at these camps. But few if any comprehended the appalling magnitude of it. It wasn't sufficiently real to stand out from the general brutality and slaughter which is war. There was little talk in London about the concentration camps except as places to which captured agents and resistants were deported if they were not executed on the spot. And such reports as we did receive were shunted aside because of the official policy in Washington and London to concentrate exclusively on the defeat of the enemy.[19]

The dilatory treatment of the Jewish catastrophe evolved into a steady practice. The uncoordinated and piecemeal requests of the Jewish leaders were negated, even though the requested actions were within the realm of the possible, from safe havens for escaping Jews, evacuations of Jews from Romania and Bulgaria, and bombing of the Auschwitz gas chambers, to negotiations for ransoming the Hungarian Jews. Even when the U.S. Secretary of the Treasury, Henry Morgenthau, Jr., threw his weight into the battle for rescue, he had to overcome the reluctance of the State Department and the British Government in such a matter as licensing the American Jewish Joint Distribution Committee to move funds into Switzerland for the relief of Jews in German dominated Europe.[20]

The Western Allies did not want the war to be perceived by their own populations as an effort for the deliverance of Jewry. There was to be no hint or implication that Allied soldiers were mercenaries in a Jewish cause. It was hard enough to explain to a Briton or an American why the war was being fought, hard enough to make clear to an American why it was fought in Europe. For all of the emphasis on One World or the admonition that no man was an island, the ordinary Briton was very conscious of being on an island, albeit for a brief period in 1940 an endangered one. The American, on a much larger island, was an ocean away. Accordingly Britain and the United States fought a carefully controlled war, minimizing their casualties and simplifying their words. Given this stance, any liberation of the Jews could only be a by-product of victory.

23

NEUTRAL COUNTRIES

THE SECOND WORLD WAR engulfed the large majority of countries in Europe. Germany's expansion left little room for neutrality and by 1942 only five countries, aside from city states, had not been drawn into the conflict. The five were Portugal, Spain, Turkey, Sweden, and Switzerland.

Neutrality sometimes required effort. Only Portugal was not adjacent to any region under German control. Spain was entreated by the Germans to join their coalition and, failing to declare war, sent a division of volunteers to the Eastern Front. Turkey was cajoled by Britain and, seeing no gain, waited until June 1944 to close the Dardanelles to German shipping and until a safe moment in 1945 to declare war on Germany. Sweden, friendly with Finland, which fought on the German side, was also tied to Norway and Denmark, which were occupied by Germany. Switzerland was surrounded by Germany, Italy, and France. Both Sweden and Switzerland emphasized their traditional neutrality, and both permitted private trading with Germany. Thus Germany received iron ore and ball bearings from Sweden and a large variety of products from hundreds of firms in Switzerland. Sweden also allowed German military transports across its territory from and to Finland and Norway, while Switzerland tolerated the transit of coal.

The policy of the non-belligerent countries toward the plight of the Jews was shaped not only by a guarded strategy that took into account geography and the progress of the war, but also by such deeply rooted factors as their institutions and the nature of their relations with Jewry. Spain had expelled its Jews in 1492, and they had not returned 450 years later. The Spanish dictator, General Francisco Franco, had won a civil war with German and Italian help in 1939, and not much could be expected from him in Jewish matters. A few hundred Spanish Jews were repatriated to Spain from Salonika, and a total of about seventy-five hundred crossed into the country from France.[1] When Spain at one point barred escaping Jews and Allied prisoners of war, Churchill protested to the Spanish ambassador in London and the border was reopened.[2] By that time, in April 1943, the German army in Stalingrad had surrendered, and German-Italian forces in Tunisia were fighting with their backs to the sea.

Many of the Jews who had left Spain at the end of the fifteenth century had found refuge in the Ottoman Empire, but Turkey, the remnant of the empire after three defeats during the second decade of the twentieth century, was another entity. It had become a smaller country, politically nationalistic, and ethnically more homogeneous.

Turkey provided no permanent refuge and it was not going to offer itself as a stopping place if the Jews could not go on. The famous illustration is that of an unseaworthy ship, the SS Struma, which arrived on December 16, 1941, in Istanbul with 769 Romanian Jews fearing deportation to the Romanian-occupied USSR. The Jews had no permission to land in Palestine, and on February 24, 1942, the Turkish Government ordered the ship to move. It was towed to the Black Sea and sunk, apparently by a torpedo fired mistakenly by a Soviet submarine. There were two survivors.[3] The Balkan area had a large Jewish population, and henceforth the Turkish Government needed no confirmation of Britain's policy to frustrate the immigration of these Jews to Palestine.[4]

Unlike Turkey, Sweden was not a place that many Jews could

reach. Only Norway and Denmark were nearby, and their combined Jewish populations were less than ten thousand. Sweden offered sanctuary to both, saving about half of Norwegian Jewry and almost all the Danish Jews. In 1944, Sweden involved herself more heavily in the heart of Europe, particularly in Budapest, where, along with Switzerland, Portugal, and the Vatican, the Swedish legation issued "protective passports," established safe houses, and generally attempted to restrain the German occupants and their Hungarian puppets from killing more Jews on Hungarian soil in the final hours of the war. Upon the liberation of Jews in concentration camps in the spring of 1945, Sweden accepted thousands of victims for medical treatment and rehabilitation.[5]

Sweden and Switzerland were both highly developed democratic countries, but their responses to the Jewish catastrophe were somewhat different. In 1938, Switzerland became the first and only neutral country to initiate a German anti-Jewish decree. Dr. Heinrich Rothmund of the Federal Swiss Police insisted that Jews carrying German passports be specially identified, because Jews, unlike German tourists, were not likely to return home. The presence of only about 7,100 Jewish and non-Jewish refugees in Switzerland on September 1, 1939, attested to Rothmund's success. From that date to May 8, 1945, a total of 295,381 persons found temporary or long-term sanctuary in the country. Many were military deserters, escaped prisoners of war, and foreign children taken to Switzerland for medical care. A minority consisted of 9,909 emigrants and 55,108 civilian refugees. Jews were 6,654 of the emigrants and 21,858 of the refugees. To stem the tide of escapees seeking entry at the French border, the Federal Police issued instructions on August 13, 1942, to turn back civilian refugees. On August 30, a federal councillor, Eduard von Steiger, made a speech referring to Switzerland as a crowded little lifeboat.[6] In Bern the American minister, Harrison, cited three factors that in his view motivated Swiss policy: the growing number of foreigners—already 10 percent of the population; the "fear of giving anti-Semitism encouragement"; and the belief that "Swiss neutrality might be compromised" by the admission of an increasing number of refugees who were "enemies of the Nazi regime."[7] Not before July 12, 1944, were Jews admitted without question, and toward the end of the year, Rothmund protested against foot marches of Hungarian Jews to Germany.[8] Now he could clearly see that his problems had been caused by the Germans in the first place.

Switzerland was not only reluctant to admit more Jews, it was also reticent to condemn Germany for their fate. When the International Committee of the Red Cross, which as a private organization nevertheless mirrored Swiss policy, debated the issuance of a veiled but public declaration about "certain categories of nationalities" suffering "attacks on their lives for acts they did not commit," one member of the committee, Philippe Etter, a federal councillor and former Swiss Foreign Minister, persuaded the group to refrain from adopting the resolution.[9]

24

THE CHURCHES

THE CHURCHES, ONCE A POWERFUL PRESENCE on the European continent, had reached the nadir of their influence during the Second World War. In the secular state they had become an anachronistic remnant of their former selves. In Communist Russia, the church had all but disappeared. In Nazi Germany, the SS man who entered "believing in God" on his personnel record conveyed in this phrase his lack of affiliation with any church. Even in the democratic West, churches were subordinate structures, regulating the lives of citizens mainly on Sundays, and then only in a ceremonial manner. The churches could not pit themselves against the dominant political order. They could not preach that materialism was evil in an age that was materialistic to the core. They could not condemn nationalism or imperialism at a time when the nation state was triumphant. They could not brand any official killing as murder without risking the forcible closing of their doors by the state officials.

At the same time, the churches were trying to survive as an institution. They had budgets, owned real estate, and maintained visibility during holidays and state functions. They were timekeepers, marking the life span of individuals on such occasions as birth, marriage, and death. When war broke out they attempted to fortify the

spirit, and when the fighting was over they offered solace and pre-
served a memory of the dead.

The churches shared a fundamental belief in the divinity of Jesus
Christ, and with regard to Jewry, which they had persecuted for so
long because of its rejection of this divinity, they all knew at least in
principle that they could not sacrifice the baptized Jews without
abandoning a sacrament, and that they could not remain silent about
the destruction of the Jewish community without implying impotence, let alone indifference or consent. At the same time, the
churches had no mechanism for unity, and Catholic, Protestant, or
Eastern Orthodox leaders could not readily fuse their articulated
views into a common stand. What the various churchmen were going to do or fail to do now was, therefore, in no small measure the
consequence of where they were and who they were.

The defense of baptized victims was difficult enough, and in Germany it was compromised from the start. When the German civil
service law specifying ineligibility for appointment or retention of non-
Ayrans was promulgated in 1933, a great many individuals had to
prove their Aryan status by showing that all four of their grandparents
were Christian. The churches were the custodians of baptismal
records and marriage registrations going back several generations.
They supplied the required information as a matter of course, even
printing forms labeled "Certificates of Aryan Descent" to serve their
clients.[1] Later, when baptized Jews along with all other Jews were
marked with a star, Adolf Cardinal Bertram of Breslau agonized over
the question of separate services for baptized Jews, and the Evangelical
Lutheran churches in seven provinces expelled their star wearers.[2] No
battle had to be fought over a compulsory dissolution of mixed marriages. The Propaganda Ministry, weighing the fact that for the Catholic Church a marriage performed by a priest was a sacrament,
opposed the measure and it was not adopted.[3]

When a number of governments outside Germany were expected
to define the concept of "Jew" on the basis of the German model, a
number of churches fought a rear-guard action to save at least some
of the Jewish Christians, and the several different definitions in states
allied with Germany attest to that struggle. In the occupied Netherlands, where the German administration instituted sterilization of

Jewish partners in mixed marriages as a condition for their exemption from deportation, the Catholic and Protestant churches joined in protesting this violation of the admonition "Be fruitful and multiply" in Genesis 1/28, and when they thought that a compulsory divorce decree might be issued, they wrote to the Reichskommissar, citing Matthew 19/6, "What therefore God hath put together, let no man put asunder."[4] Ghettos were largely out of reach. The pastoral care of the Catholic Church extended to the Warsaw Ghetto, where the Jewish Catholics were visited by Polish priests, but in Theresienstadt, which was filled with deportees, some thousands of whom were Christians, there was no priest for the Catholics and until November 1944 no minister for the Protestants.[5]

If the protection of baptized people was problematical, any attempt to help professing Jews was to be even less promising. The introduction of anti-Jewish measures in the Netherlands generated protests of Protestant churches, but these expressions of disapproval were not always unanimous or public.[6] When the Vichy Government in France made an inquiry through its Ambassador at the Vatican to discover whether decrees contemplated in Vichy were exceeding the bounds of Catholic teaching, the reply specified that economic measures or those that would isolate the Jews were not breaches of traditional lines drawn by the Church.[7] No one, however, needed clarifications about the difference between old-style discrimination and plain annihilation.

Did the churches know what was happening when the Jews began to disappear? Did they have special sources of information—in the case of the Catholic Church, confessions—through which early and accurate knowledge could be obtained? And did they, in any case, grasp what they were able to discover? In most instances, the churches were not more familiar with the transformation or more insightful about it than Jewish bodies, or any underground organization, or any Allied government. At times, the clergy learned about deportations or massacres at the last moment from Jewish representatives who approached them with frantic appeals for help.

Neither the Protestant nor the Catholic churches presented a uniform response to the catastrophe. In Germany the Lutheran churches were quiescent, whereas in Denmark the Lutheran Bishop Fuglsang-

Damgaard did not hesitate to issue a proclamation affirming the need to preserve the freedom of Jewish brothers and sisters.[8] In the Netherlands, where Protestant and Catholic churchmen had already met periodically to discuss policy, the Germans offered them an enticing concession: Jewish Christians would not be deported, if the churches refrained from publicizing a protest against the deportation of the Jewish community. The Dutch Reformed Church accepted this condition, breaking ranks with the other churches.[9]

In Switzerland, the Protestants were also vocal, and this willingness to express opinions pitted them to a certain extent against the cautious neutrality of their government. In 1941, protest leaders emphasized the word of John 4/22 that salvation comes from the Jews. In 1942 they cited the Swiss theologian Zwingli that the church was the watchman of conscience. The Jews were at the bottom now and the church recited Matthew 25/40: "Inasmuch as ye have done it unto one of the least of these my brethren ye have done it unto Me." The Swiss objectors fought against the strict Swiss censorship law that precluded the news of the Jewish fate from becoming a public issue, but they accomplished very little.[10] In Britain the Archbishop of Canterbury rose in the House of Lords on March 23, 1943, to call upon the British Government to end its procrastination, and to move that temporary refuge be given to persons in danger who were able to leave enemy and enemy-occupied countries. The Jews, he said, were being slaughtered at the rate of tens of thousands a day on many days. And then he concluded: "We have discussed the matter on the footing that we are not responsible for this great evil, that the burden lies on others, but it is always true that the obligations of decent men are decided for them by contingencies which they themselves did not create and very largely by the action of wicked men."[11] The motion was agreed to and then forgotten.

The Christian denominations that did not answer to Rome were fragmented among the countries of Europe, and they spoke with many voices or not at all. But what about "monolithic" Catholicism? Here again, there was variety. That there should have been no single manifest Catholic message is a consequence in large part of the attitude of Pope Pius XII.

The Pope held three chairs. He was first of all the head of his church, in direct communication with bishops everywhere and through them with all Catholics. Second, he was a chief of state, the Vatican, with a diplomatic corps accredited to Catholic and non-Catholic countries. Third, he was the Bishop of Rome. In each of these positions, he had a channel for expressing his thoughts.

As the head of the Church, speaking for the Church, he was reluctant to make any gesture. On October 6, 1942, Harold Tittmann, Assistant to the U.S. President's Personal Representative at the Vatican, speculated that the Pope's disinclination to issue a public statement about Nazi "atrocities" in Poland was rooted in a fear that the German people would reproach him, just as they had accused Pope Benedict XV of pro-Allied sentiments during the First World War. Moreover, Pius XII had had many years of "conditioning" in Germany when he had represented the Vatican there.[12] Tittmann nevertheless attempted to enlist the Papacy's support of an Allied declaration dated December 17, 1942, "German Policy of Extermination of the Jewish Race." Luigi Cardinal Maglione, the Vatican's Secretary of State, then declared that the Pope could not publicly denounce particular atrocities.[13] Pius XII thereupon delivered a Christmas message with only a veiled reference to hundreds of thousands killed or dying only because of their race. When Tittmann expressed his disappointment, the Pope stated plainly that he could not name the Nazis without including the Communists.[14]

In the multitude of documents published by the Vatican about the diplomatic activity of the Pope and his envoys, the nuncios, there are very few instructions to raise the subject of the Jews. When the nuncios spoke, they seem to have followed their own dictates. Monsignor Cesare Orsenigo in Berlin was especially feeble in this attempt. Addressing Staatssekretär Ernst von Weizsäcker in the German Foreign Office about the so-called hostage shootings in Serbia—mass killings that at the time were aimed at Jews and Gypsies—he first asked whether the German official was amenable to such a discussion and, when given a negative reply, promptly withdrew his request.[15] In Slovakia, the young Monsignor Giuseppe Burzio was much more forceful. The Slovak state was highly visible in its Catholicism. Its president was Monsignor Josef Tiso, and priests sat in the Slovak parliament, participating in votes that resulted in anti-Jewish legislation, including a deportation statute. After talking fruitlessly to the Slovak Prime Minister Voytech Tuka, he wrote in an exasperated mood to the Vatican, pronouncing the Slovak as "demented."[16] The Abbot Giuseppe Marcone in Croatia, a satellite state no less Catholic than Slovakia, reported on July 17, 1942, a conversation with Eugen Kvaternik of the Croatian police to the effect that 2 million European Jews had already died and that Croatian Jewry would probably suffer the same fate. Many thousands of Jews had already died at the hands of Croatians within the country, and when deportations to Auschwitz began, Marcone made small piecemeal appeals, now for baptized Jews, now for Jews in mixed marriages, now for children.[17]

The officials of the Vatican's Department of State, like those in Washington, did not put their pieces of information together. When Myron Taylor, the American President's representative at the Vatican, asked on September 26, 1942, whether the Vatican could confirm reports of mass killing, Cardinal Maglione noted in his file that he had no confirmation of such grave news.[18] Much later, in May 1943, an unsigned memorandum for the record in the office of the Vatican Secretary of State hinted at discovery and dismay. "Jews, horrendous situation," the writer began, and went on to describe the disappearance of Polish Jewry, special camps for death, including Treblinka (which he placed near Lublin), and gas.[19] In September 1943, the German army occupied Rome and during the following month, Jews were seized in the Italian capital, the city where the Pope himself was the bishop.

After the first transport had left Rome with just over a thousand Jews, Weizsäcker, now the German envoy at the Vatican, noted the remarkable failure of the Pope to say something. There was only an indistinct report in the Vatican newspaper, *Osservatore Romano*, this after a deportation that had taken place "under the windows of the Pope."[20] Weizsäcker's language was not a mere figure of speech. Many of the Jewish victims had been captured in a poor quarter of the city, Trastevere, on the same side of the Tiber River as the Vatican, within a few minutes' walking distance from it.[21]

The Pope could not resolve his dilemma. For him the criticism of one side meant the endorsement of the other. Many of the bishops in

Europe had balancing problems as well. For some, the scale was weighted toward silence or inactivity, for others toward speech and action.

Auxiliary Bishop Vincentas Brizgys in Lithuania welcomed the Germans. He was a young man, carrying on the day-to-day business of the church in place of the ailing Archbishop Juozapas Skvireckas. In the small area of Lithuania Brizgys could not remain unaware of the massive participation of Lithuanians in the shootings of Jews. It is at the height of these massacres that he forbade the Lithuanian clergy to assist the Jews in any way.[22] Yet a diarist who was the Secretary of the Jewish Council in Kaunas notes that as early as July 1941, Brizgys would talk to Rabbi Shmuel Abba Snieg, a former Lithuanian army chaplain. In the spring of 1943, when Lithuanian enthusiasm for Germany had waned considerably, Brizgys talked to Snieg again, this time confirming a recent mass shooting near Vilnius, but at the same time expressing the belief that nothing further would happen in Kaunas. When Rabbi Snieg inquired about sheltering Jewish children in monasteries, the bishop replied that these institutions were for practical purposes autonomous and their abbots and priors did not excel in mercy and love.[23]

In Lvov, the Ukrainian Metropolitan Andrej Septyckyj, whose domain was the Catholic Church of the Eastern Rite in the region, also welcomed the Germans. Septyckyj was a thoroughly political man. Although old and confined to a wheelchair, he fervently wanted Ukrainian independence and dreamt of extending his church to the large Ukrainian heartland that had been dominated by Christian Orthodoxy before the Russian Revolution. The sudden arrival of the German army in 1941 opened this opportunity and during the following years he received and had cordial conversations with German officials, especially the Gouverneur, Otto Wächter. Septyckyj, a count, had been a cavalry officer in the Austro-Hungarian Army before he became a priest, and Wächter was the son of a nobleman who had been a general in Catholic Austria. Yet Septyckyj was not untroubled. He did not overlook the German killing of Jews in Galicia and in the Ukrainian territories to the east. He was profoundly disturbed by the participation of Ukrainian militia in these operations, and his temperament did not allow him to rest.

In August 1942, Septyckyj wrote about these events to Himmler himself. Shortly thereafter he dispatched a lengthy handwritten letter dated August 29–31, 1942, to the Pope, in which he referred to the government of the German occupants as a regime of terror and corruption, more diabolical than that of the Bolsheviks. The number of Jews killed in his region had passed two hundred thousand. There had been massacres in Kiev and Ukrainian villages of men, women, and children. He had protested against this homicide in pastoral letters, but "naturally" they were confiscated, and then he had written his letter to Himmler.

The Pope did not have to compose a reply. He had already done so on August 26 as if anticipating Septyckyj's consternation. In the Papal letter, which arrived in Lvov after several weeks, Pius XII quoted from Psalm 27: "Dominus illuminatio mea, et salus mea, quem timebo? Dominus protector vitae meae, a quo trepidabo?" (The Lord is my light and my savior; whom should I fear? The Lord is the protector of my life; whom shall I dread?) Then he counseled Septyckyj to bear adversity with serene patience. The Metropolitan, who could not tolerate such conditions with serenity, later spoke to a Ukrainian who had collaborated with the Germans in France, expressing his outrage once again.[24]

Monsignor Alois C. Hudal was the titular bishop of the German community in Rome. His church in the heart of the city was the Santa Maria dell'Anima. Born in Graz, Austria, in 1885 as a son of a shoemaker, Hudal became a priest in 1908 and pursued theological studies, eventually writing books about current as well as ancient topics. In these works there is much that mirrors the Nazi description of the Jews as materialistic self-seeking people whose presence in the universities, the professions, the cinema, the press, and the theater was preponderant and truly calamitous. Now, as he said in the nineteen thirties, the condominium between Germany and Jewry was rescinded. Hudal's attitude was so well known to the Italian Church leaders that one day at Christmas 1939 he received a letter from the Vatican addressed on the envelope "Al Collegio ariano dell'Anima." During the war he never ceased to pray for Germany's victory, and when Italy surrendered to the Allies, he considered the armistice treason. After Germany itself was defeated, he helped more than a few fleeing Nazis with false papers, and Gouverneur Wächter, in hiding, died in his arms.

Yet it is to Hudal that a nephew of the Pope, Carlo Pacelli, went one morning in October 1943 to inform him that arrests of Italian Jews had just begun in Rome. Hudal immediately wrote to the German army commander of the city, General Rainer Stahel, beseeching him to order the immediate cessation of this roundup, lest the Pope intervene publicly, bringing harm to Germany.[25]

In Berlin itself, an ailing priest in his sixties, Bernhard Lichtenberg, who served as Prior of St. Hedwig's Cathedral, was entrusted by Bishop Konrad von Preysing with the task of giving material and spiritual help to persecuted people, particularly Jewish converts to Catholicism. Lichtenberg worked without ledgers or receipts, collecting clothes and food ration cards. From the time of the November 10, 1938, pogrom, he prayed aloud every evening for non-Aryan Christians and Jews. His marginal notes contained such phrases as "Do not delude yourselves" (*Täuschet euch nicht*) and "This must be said" (*Das muss gesagt werden*). On August 29, 1941, he was overheard by two young women in his prayer and denounced to the Gestapo. Arrested on October 23, 1941, he was then interrogated for thirteen hours. He denied nothing but defended himself: He had prayed, not preached, and in his morning prayers he had included Hitler. He also offered to accompany the Jews who were being deported to the Lodz Ghetto in order to minister to the Catholics among them. The cup did not pass from him. Indicted for endangering the public peace from the pulpit and sentenced to two years, he was sent to prison on May 29, 1942. There his weight declined from 188 pounds to 124. Promptly, on October 23, 1943, he was discharged, not to go home but to be incarcerated in Dachau. On the way he became ill and was delivered to a hospital. His hour had come. He was given last rites and died at 6 A.M. on November 3, 1943.[26]

NOTES

PART I: PERPETRATORS

1: ADOLF HITLER

1. Ernst Deuerlein, ed., *Der Aufstieg der NSDAP in Augenzeugenberichten* (Munich, 1974), pp. 67–70. Ludwig Wittgenstein, the philosopher, who also was born in 1889, also attended the Realschule in Linz with less than sterling success. See Kurt Wuchterl and Adolf Hübner, *Ludwig Wittgenstein* (Reinbek bei Hamburg, 1979). Wittgenstein, who had Jewish ancestry on his father's side, attended the Realschule from 1903 to 1905, Hitler from 1900 to 1904. There is no indication that they met. Wittgenstein went on to higher education and became a lieutenant in the Austro-Hungarian army during the First World War.

2. On Hitler's Viennese years, see J. Sydney Jones, *Hitler in Vienna* (Briarcliff Manor, N.Y., 1983).

3. For the years 1913–1919 in Hitler's life, see particularly Deuerlein, *Der Aufstieg*, pp. 74–95. The text of Hitler's letter is on pp. 91–94.

4. See the letter from the Chief of the Reich Chancellery, Heinrich Lammers, to Staatssekretär Franz Schlegelberger, April 19, 1937, enclosing a memorandum by Dr. Gerhard Wagner containing Hitler's views. German Federal Archives, R 43 II/733. Dr. Bloch, who was still living in Austria when the country was occupied in 1938, emigrated without hindrance.

5. Jones, *Hitler in Vienna*, pp. 185–89.

6. Gerhard Engel, *Heeresadjutant bei Hitler 1938–1943*, ed. Hildegard von Kotze (Stuttgart, 1974), pp. 31–32.

7. Deuerlein, *Der Aufstieg*, pp. 95–97.

8. Initially, the book appeared in two parts. The first half was published in July 1925, the second in December 1926. *Ibid.*, pp. 424–25.

9. *Ibid.*, pp. 424, 426.

10. For an analytical essay about the rise of the party to power and

Hitler's style of leadership, see Hans Mommsen, *Der Nationalsozialismus und die deutsche Gesellschaft* (Reinbek bei Hamburg, 1991), pp. 11–101.

11. The auditing generated a stream of correspondence about his tax liabilities over a period of years. Oron James Hale, "Adolf Hitler: Taxpayer," *American Historical Review,* vol. 60 (1955), pp. 830–42.

12. Eberhard Jäckel, *Hitler's Weltanschauung* (Stuttgart, 1981), pp. 137–59, 175.

13. Not a few books in Hitler's private library were devoted to architectural subjects, and in his *Mein Kampf* he refers to his architectural talents, that, he says, were recognized even by the art professors who rejected his application to the academy.

14. The text of the speech was reproduced in the German press.

15. On stocks, see Bernard P. Bellon, *Mercedes in Peace and War* (New York, 1990), p. 221. The rent receipts survived in the cases holding his private library at the end of the war.

16. Leonard Heston and Renate Heston, *The Medical Casebook of Adolf Hitler* (Briarcliff Manor, N.Y., 1979), pp. 29–31.

17. Engel, *Heeresadjutant,* pp. 42, 46, and 33–34.

18. The painting, about the First World War, by Elk Eber, is reproduced in Georg Schorer, *Deutsche Kunstbetrachtung* (Munich, 1939), p. 172.

19. See the correspondence in the National Archives of the United States, Record Group 242, T 175, Roll 69.

20. See Heston and Heston, *The Medical Casebook,* particularly pp. 38–55, 136–42.

21. Uwe Adam, *Judenpolitik im Dritten Reich* (Düsseldorf, 1971), pp. 58–61.

22. See the text of the exchange of letters between Hindenburg and Hitler, April 4 and 5, 1933, in Walter Hubatsch, *Hindenburg und der Staat* (Göttingen, 1966), pp. 375–78. The text of the law signed by Hitler on April 7, 1933, is in the *Reichsgesetzblatt* I, 175.

23. See the *Reichsgesetzblatt* I, 188, 217, and 275.

24. Rudolf Schottlaender, ed., *Verfolgte Berliner Wissenschaft* (Berlin, 1988), p. 85, citing an excerpt of Max Planck's essay "Mein Besuch bei Adolf Hitler," in *Physikalische Blätter* (1947), p. 143.

25. See the decree of November 14, 1935, *Reichsgesetzblatt* I, 1333.

26. Chief of the Party Court Walter Buch to Göring, February 13, 1939, Nuremberg trials document PS-3063.

27. Testimony by Göring, International Military Tribunal, *Trial of the Major War Criminals,* vol. 9, pp. 276–78.

28. On the "fine," see *ibid.* On the star veto, see Wilhelm Stuckart (Interior Ministry) to Lammers, August 14, 1941, Nuremberg trials document NG-1111.

29. Order by Hitler, September 1, 1939, Nuremberg trials document PS-630.

30. Engel, *Heeresadjutant,* pp. 94–95.

31. See Christopher Browning, *Fateful Months* (New York, 1985).

32. Himmler's speech of June 21, 1944, Nuremberg trials document NG-4977.

33. *Kriegstagebuch des Oberkommandos der Wehrmacht (Wehrmachtführungsstab) 1940–1945,* ed. Percy Schramm and Hans-Adolf Jacobsen (Frankfurt am Main, 1965), vol. 1, pp. 340–42.

34. Summary of conference chaired by Frank, March 25, 1941, Frank Diary, Nuremberg trials document PS-2233.

35. Lammers to Martin Bormann (Chief of the Party Chancellery), June 7, 1941, Nuremberg trials document NG-1123.

36. Göring to Heydrich, July 31, 1941, Nuremberg trials document PS-710.

37. Adolf Eichmann, *Ich, Adolf Eichmann* (Leoni am Starnberger See, 1980), pp. 178–79, 229–33, 479.

38. The two cases of requests for a prior Führer authorization are Himmler's in October 1941 with respect to the deportation of the Jews in Salonika, noted by Engel, *Heeresadjutant,* p. 111, and General Otto von Stülpnagel's for the deportation of one thousand Jews from France, transmitted by General Quartermaster of the Army Eduard Wagner to Ambassador Karl Ritter in the Foreign Office, December 12, 1941, Nuremberg trials document NG-3571.

39. See the text of the summary of the conference of January 20, 1942, Nuremberg trials document NG-2586-F.

40. See the facsimile of a notation by Himmler in his telephone log, in David Irving, *Hitler's War* (New York, 1977), p. 505.

41. Gertrude Schneider, *Journey into Terror* (New York, 1979), pp. 14–15, 155. On Hitler's intention to deport the Jews, see Himmler's letter of September 18, 1941, to Gauleiter Arthur Greiser, who governed an incorporated area in occupied Poland, with respect to an intended dumping of sixty thousand Jews in the Lodz Ghetto as a kind of interim solution: Himmler Files, Folder 94, Library of Congress. See also Bormann's letter to Gauleiter Baldur von Schirach, November 2, 1941, on Vienna's housing problems, passing on Hitler's suggestion that relief be provided by means of

deportations rather than new construction: German Federal Archives, R 43 II/1361a.

42. See the summary of the Hitler-Horthy meeting of April 18, 1943, Nuremberg trials document D-736.

43. Hauptsturmführer Bohrsch (Security Service) to Reich Security Main Office/III-B (Standartenführer Hans Ehlich), May 18, 1944, National Archives Record Group 242, T 175, Roll 583.

44. Text of the order dated April 8, 1940, by Field Marshal Wilhelm Keitel, in H. G. Adler, *Der verwaltete Mensch* (Tübingen, 1974), p. 295.

45. Reich Security Main Office/I-A-5 (signed Sturmbannführer Schwinge) to BdS (Befehlshaber der Sicherheitspolizei—Commander of Security Police) in Krakow, April 24, 1943, enclosing a directive by Bormann, citing Hitler, of November 14, 1942, National Archives Record Group 242, T 175, Roll 484.

46. See the correspondence, November–December 1944, in the German Federal Archives, R 43 II/599.

47. Hitler's political testament, April 29, 1945, Nuremberg trials document PS-3569.

2: The Establishment

1. See *Wer ist Wer,* 1967.

2. Statement by Werner Dubois, November 29, 1962, in the Sobibor case, filed by West German prosecutors under 45 Js 27/61, document books, vol. 8, pp. 1597–1603.

3: Old Functionaries

1. See Case No. 11 (the Ministries Case) in Nuremberg Military Tribunals, *Trials of War Criminals 1946–1949,* 15 vols. (Washington, D.C.) vol. 14, pp. 216 ff., 291 ff., 671 ff., and 1004.

2. Case No. 3 (Judiciary Case), *Trials of War Criminals,* vol. 3, pp. 941, 1081–87, 1200, 1203–4.

3. See the summary of the conference chaired by Kühnemann on May 29, 1942, YIVO Institute document G-59, and *Wer ist Wer,* 1962.

4. See the short biography in Wolf Keilig, *Das deutsche Heer 1939–1945* (Bad Neuheim, 1957), alphabetical looseleaf.

5. *Ibid.,* entry for Otto von Stülpnagel. The decrees may be found in the *Verordnungsblatt des Militärbefehlshabers in Frankreich.* The conversation between Frank and Rosenberg of October 13, 1941, is recorded in summary in the Frank Diary, October 14, 1941, National Archives of the United

States, Record Group 238, T 994, Roll 4. Rosenberg rejected von Stülpnagel's request. The subsequent correspondence about the one thousand Jews is in Nuremberg trials document NG-3571. Von Stülpnagel's suicide occurred on February 6, 1948.

6. See Case No. 6 (I. G. Farben Case), in *Trials of War Criminals*, vol. 7, p. 354, and vol. 8, pp. 787–802, 1076–79, 1363.

7. Jean-Paul Pressac, *Auschwitz: Technique and Operation of the Gas Chambers* (New York, 1989), particularly pp. 93–104, 183–249, 355–76.

8. Personnel Record of Max Montua in the Berlin Document Center. Montua's order of July 11, 1941, to the 307th, 316th and 322d Police Battalions in the Military History Archives (Prague), Collection Polizei Regiment Mitte A-3-2-7/1 K. 1. By October 19, 1941, the early impressions had probably worn off. On that day, the regiment assisted the Security Police in the shooting of 3,726 Jews "of both sexes and every age" in Mogilev. Reich Security Main Office/IV-A-1, Operational Report No. 133 (60 copies), November 14, 1941, Nuremberg trials document NO-2825. On Mogilev, see also Ruth Bettina Birn, *Die Höheren SS- und Polizeiführer* (Düsseldorf, 1986), p. 171n. The Higher SS and Police Leader was Erich von dem Bach.

9. Indictment of Gustav Laabs, Alois Häfele, and others at a court in Bonn, July 25, 1962, 8 Js 180/61; judgment of the court in Bonn, March 23, 1963, and revised judgment of the court in Bonn, July 27, 1965, 8 Ks 3/62. Häfele fought against French troops in 1945 but was not captured. He held odd jobs after the war and was pensioned in 1951. His arrest took place ten years later. He was sentenced to thirteen years. The Karlsruhe police official was Polizeirat Fritz Wimmer. The Higher SS and Police Leader was Wilhelm Koppe. Two chains of command led from Koppe to the Kulmhof camp:

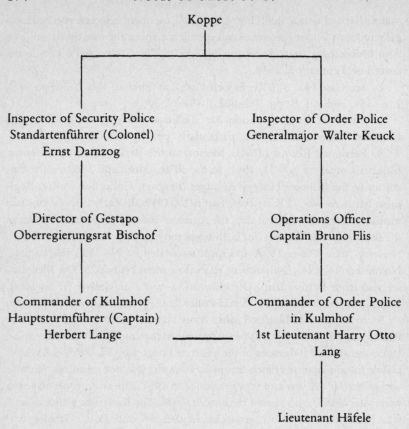

Koppe

Inspector of Security Police
Standartenführer (Colonel)
Ernst Damzog

Inspector of Order Police
Generalmajor Walter Keuck

Director of Gestapo
Oberregierungsrat Bischof

Operations Officer
Captain Bruno Flis

Commander of Kulmhof
Hauptsturmführer (Captain)
Herbert Lange

Commander of Order Police
in Kulmhof
1st Lieutenant Harry Otto
Lang

Lieutenant Häfele

4: Newcomers

1. See the title page in Adolf Hitler's *Mein Kampf,* listing the sixteen men by name and occupation.

2. See Matatias Carp, *Cartea Neagra—Suferintele Evreilor din Romania 1940–1944,* 3 vols. (Bucharest, 1946–48), vol. 3, pp. 202, 227.

3. See Auschwitz strength reports, some undated and some for December 1944, National Archives of the United States Record Group 242, T 580, Roll 321.

4. For short biographies of incumbents in the party and government, see Robert Wistrich, *Wer ist Wer im Dritten Reich?* revised and expanded by Hermann Weiss (Frankfurt am Main, 1979). For capsule biographies of Generalgouvernement personnel, see Werner Präg and Wolfgang Jacobmeyer, eds., *Das Diensttagebuch des deutschen Generalgouverneurs in Polen* (Stuttgart, 1975), pp. 945–55.

5. *Wer ist Wer*, 1967–68. For some of Vialon's activities in the Ostland, see National Archives Record Group 242, T 459, Roll 3 and Roll 24.

6. On Müller, see Wistrich, *Wer ist wer im Dritten Reich?*

7. See Bradley F. Smith, *Heinrich Himmler: A Nazi in the Making, 1900–1926* (Stanford, Calif., 1971), and Peter Loewenberg, "The Unsuccessful Adolescence of Heinrich Himmler," *American Historical Review*, vol. 76 (1971), pp. 612–41, particularly p. 632.

8. See Eichmann's Argentinian memoirs, *Ich, Adolf Eichmann* (Leoni am Starnberger See, 1980), and the transcript of his trial in Jerusalem. An English Language mimeographed copy of the transcript is located in the library of the University of Vermont.

9. See Katzmann's extensive personnel record in the Berlin Document Center. Katzmann's report to Higher SS and Police Leader Friedrich Krüger of June 30, 1943, on the Galician operation is in Nuremberg trials document L-18.

10. Oberg's personnel record, Berlin Document Center.

11. Personnel record of Dolp in Berlin Document Center. The line to which Dolp was assigned was to close the gap between the Bug and San rivers. On conditions in the Belzec labor camp, see the report of Major Braune-Krickau, operations officer of the Oberfeldkommandantur 379 in Lublin, September 23, 1940, National Archives Record Group 242, T 501, Roll 213. The 19th SS Grenadier Division, commanded by Bruno Streckenbach, former personnel chief of the Reich Security Main Office, was Latvian.

12. On Ohlendorf, see Wistrich, *Wer ist Wer im Dritten Reich?*

13. Personnel record of Ernst Weinmann in Berlin Document Center. In Serbia, Jewish men were shot by the German army, and Jewish women and children were gassed by the Security Police. Weinmann, not the commander at this point, concerned himself mainly with resettling ethnic Germans and combating the early, non-Communist partisans.

14. Personnel record of Erwin Weinmann in Berlin Document Center. Erwin Weinmann, not found after the war, was officially presumed dead in 1949.

15. Personnel record of Max Thomas in Berlin Document Center.

16. Personnel record of Edinger Ancker in Berlin Document Center. Details about the Netherlands assignment and the Walraven family, with the text of Hitler's order, are in another personnel record of Ancker, in the Deutsches Zentralarchiv in Potsdam, 15.01. The Potsdam Archives were incorporated into the German Federal Archives after the annexation of the German Democratic Republic. The summary of the conference of March 6, 1942, is in Nuremberg trials document NG-2586-H.

17. Personnel record of Otto Wächter in Berlin Document Center. On Wächter's death, see Alois Hudal, *Römische Tagebücher* (Graz and Stuttgart, 1976), p. 298.

18. Generalgouvernement/Interior Main Division/Population and Welfare to Lublin District/Interior/Population and Welfare, February 10, 1942, referring to a directive of Staatssekretär Bühler of December 16, 1941, in Centrana Zydowska Komisja Historyczna w Polsce, *Dokumenty i materialy do dziejow okupacji niemeckiej* (Warsaw, Lodz, and Krakow, 1946), vol. 2, pp. 4–6.

19. Remarks by Frank in the Generalgouvernement conference of May 30, 1940, Frank Diary, Nuremberg trials document PS-2233.

20. Krüger to Himmler, June 5, 1940, German Federal Archives, R 70, Polen/189.

21. Memorandum by Himmler, March 25, 1942, Nuremberg trials document NG-3333.

22. Präg and Jacobmeyer, *Das Diensttagebuch*, p. 949.

23. KdS (Kommandeur der Sicherheitspolizei) III A 4 (Security Service) in Galicia to Reich Security Main Office III-A (Obersturmbannführer Karl Gengenbach, Security Service), June 20, 1943, National Archives Record Group 242, T 175, Roll 575.

24. Frank's remarks in the Generalgouvernement conference of December 16, 1941, Frank Diary, PS-2233.

25. Frank's remarks in a Generalgouvernement meeting of January 25, 1943, Frank Diary, PS-2233.

26. Entry by Frank in his diary, September 1, National Archives Record Group 238, T 992, Roll 6.

27. Summary of discussion among Frank, Bühler, and Higher SS and Police Leader Koppe (Krüger's successor), September 15, 1944, Frank Diary, PS-2233.

28. Testimony by Frank, International Military Tribunal, *Trial of the Major War Criminals*, vol. 12, p. 198.

29. *Ibid.*, p. 13. Frank was convicted and hanged.

30. Hugo Wittrock, *Erinnerungen* (Lüneburg, 1979). On Jeckeln, see p. 37. Wittrock ordered the registration of Jewish property on October 11, 1941, and the formation of a ghetto on October 23, 1941. Texts in National Archives Record Group 242, T 459, Roll 23.

5: ZEALOTS, VULGARIANS, AND BEARERS OF BURDENS

1. See, for example, Rauter's report to Himmler, September 10, 1942, Nuremberg trials document NO-2256.

2. See, for example, Luther's jealous safeguarding of Foreign Office jurisdiction in his memorandum of August 2, 1942, Nuremberg trials document NG-2586-J, or his urging that Jews of Belgian nationality be deported from Belgium, in his letter to Werner von Bargen (Foreign Office representative in Belgium), December 4, 1942, Nuremberg trials document NG-2519.

3. Amtsgerichtsrat Erhard Wetzel (Ministry for Eastern Occupied Territories and the party's Race Political Office) to Amtsgerichtsrat Weitnauer and Oberregierungsrat Walter Labs (both in the ministry), January 5, 1942, enclosing summary of a discussion between Gross and Chief of the Reich Chancellery Lammers, Nuremberg trials document NG-978.

4. Statement by Karl Heim, April 18, 1969, in vol. 18, pp. 98–103, of the prosecution document books in the case against Albert Ganzenmüller before a Düsseldorf court, 8 Js 430/67.

5. Statements by Karl Reelitz, April 26, 1967, and by Otto Purschke, April 28, 1967 (Ganzenmüller Case), vol. 14, pp. 84–90 and 96–97.

6. Hauptsturmführer (Captain) Theodor Dannecker to Standartenführer (Colonel) Helmut Knochen and Obersturmbannführer (Lieutenant Colonel) Kurt Lischka, May 15, 1942, in Serge Klarsfeld, ed., *Die Endlösung der Judenfrage in Frankreich* (Paris, 1977), p. 56.

7. Judgment of a German court in Munich against Johannes Schlupper and others, March 29, 1944, 115 Ks 6/71.

8. Judgment of a German court in Darmstadt against Georg Dengler, July 14, 1950, 2a Ks 1/49.

9. Report by a German army inspector (signed Neuling) for July 6–August 21, 1942, Yad Vashem Microfilm JM 3499.

10. Filip Müller, *Eyewitness Auschwitz* (Briarcliff Manor, N.Y., 1979), pp. 140–41.

11. Franciszek Piper, "Extermination," in Danuta Czech et al., *Auschwitz*, 2d. ed. (Warsaw, 1985), p. 99. The prisoner was Josef Engel.

12. Investigative report by an Oberkriminalassistent (signature illegible), October 16, 1942, from the Düsseldorf Archives through the courtesy of Professor Konrad Kwiet.

13. See Werner Präg and Wolfgang Jacobmeyer, eds., *Das Diensttagebuch des deutschen Generalgouverneurs in Polen* (Stuttgart, 1975), p. 948.

14. Entry by Czerniakow in his diary on May 21, 1941, in Raul Hilberg, Stanislaw Staron, and Josef Kermisz, eds., *The Warsaw Diary of Adam Czerniakow* (Briarcliff Manor, N.Y., 1979), p. 239.

15. Summary of the meeting, October 14–16, 1941, in the Frank Diary, National Archives of the United States, Record Group 238, T 992, Roll 5.

The controlling voice of the Generalgouvernement's Main Division Food and Agriculture in the matter of food supplies to the ghetto is specifically mentioned in the memorandum of a conference held on February 3, 1941, signed by the German Warsaw city administration's Direktor Hans Makowski on February 3, 1941, Yad Vashem Microfilm JM 1113. The peak month of ghetto deaths was reached in August 1941, when the figure was 5,560. Summary report by Ghetto Kommissar Heinz Auerswald, September 26, 1941, Yad Vashem Microfilm JM 1112. It is likely that this number was the last at Fischer's disposal. In Kaufmann's one-hundred-page book, Jews are not mentioned. Theodore Kaufmann, *Germany Must Perish* (Newark, N.J., 1941).

16. Diary entry by Abraham Lewin, May 24, 1942, in Anatoly Polansky, ed., *A Cup of Tears* (Oxford and New York, 1988 and 1989), pp. 95–96. The shooting, according to Lewin, took place during the preceding week in front of 11a Pawia Street.

17. See the judgment of a Berlin court against Alfred Filbert, June 22, 1962, 3 Pks 1/62. Filbert commanded Einsatzkommando 9 in the central sector.

18. Notation of the Mounted Battalion of the 2d SS Cavalry Regiment, August 1, 1941, National Archives Record Group 242, T 354, Roll 168.

19. Report of the Mounted Battalion, August 12, 1941, Military History Archives (Prague), Collection Kdo Stab RFSS Ia/2/2 Kr. 10.

20. The documents, originally in the possession of the Groscurth family, were handed to Helmut Krausnick, the director of the Institute of Contemporary History in Munich, and were first published by Krausnick and Harold Deutsch, eds., in *Helmuth Groscurth: Tagebuch eines Abwehroffiziers* (Stuttgart, 1970), pp. 88–91, 534–42. Some of the documents, as well as the testimony of the officer candidate and August Häfner, were printed in Ernst Klee, Willi Dressen, and Volker Riess, eds., *"Schöne Zeiten"* (Frankfurt am Main, 1988), pp. 131–45. On Groscurth's life, see the introduction in Krausnick, *Groscurth,* pp. 1–95. Groscurth long smarted from Reichenau's rebuke. See his correspondence with Lieutenant Colonel Kleikamp (intelligence officer of Army Group South) and the letter to his brother Reinhard: *Groscurth,* pp. 541–42, and 526. Groscurth was captured with the Sixth Army in Stalingrad and died in captivity: *Groscurth,* p. 95.

21. The basic story of Lechthaler's background and experiences is contained in two judgments of a German court in Kassel, the first rendered on April 25, 1961, the second after review on January 9, 1963, both filed under 3a Ks 1/61, and the indictment, January 3, 1961, 3a Js 72/160.

22. A table of organization of the 707th Division may be found in National Archives Record Group 242, T 501, Roll 15.

23. Order by the Kommandant in Weissruthenien/Ia (operations officer), signed by Bechtolsheim, October 2, 1941, in the files of the Railway Directorate in Minsk. U.S. Holocaust Memorial Museum Archives Record Group 22.03 (Belarus Central State Archives), Roll 2, Fond 378, Opis 1, Folder 698. *White Ruthenia* was the German designation for the civilian-controlled area of western Byelorussia.

24. Order signed by Bechtolsheim, October 8, 1941, *ibid.*

25. See the court decisions, 3a Ks 1/61, and Lechthaler's consecutive statements, April 8–July 4, 1960, in 3 Js 72/60 document books, vol. 1, pp. 129–40; vol. 2, pp. 340–45; and vol. 4, 679–82. Lechthaler misidentified the operations officer as "Hartmann." The actual operations officer, von der Osten, was no longer alive in 1960. See also the statement by Bechtolsheim, July 6, 1960, vol. 4, p. 706 ff. The general had no recollection of Lechthaler, but he did remember the presence of the police battalion.

26. See the orders of October 10 and 16, 1941, U.S. Holocaust Memorial Museum Archives Record Group 22.03 (Belarus Central State Archives), Roll 2, Fond 378, Opis 1, Folder 698.

27. Order of October 10, 1941, *ibid.*

28. Order of October 16, 1941, *ibid.*

29. The action in Slutsk is vividly described in the written protest addressed by Gebietskommissar Heinrich Carl to Generalkommissar Wilhelm Kube, October 30, 1941, Nuremberg trials document PS-1104. Kube also wrote a letter about the action to Reichskommissar Hinrich Lohse, November 1, 1941, PS-1104. Kube noted that, although the Reserve Police Battalion 11 was directly subordinated to the armed forces, he wanted its officers prosecuted. See also Carl's statement of December 15, 1959, in 3a Js 72/60, vol. 1, pp. 51–61, and two statements by Willy Papenkort, May 12 and 16, 1960, vol. 2, pp. 356 ff. and 85 ff. Papenkort's outburst about the Lithuanians is recalled by a member of the police battalion, Erwin Bagdonat, in a statement of May 20, 1960, vol. 3, pp. 421–24. The battalion physician, Dr. Walter Philipzig, recalls "three or four" actions, one in Molodeczno. See his statement of June 30, 1960, vol. 3, pp. 633–37. The intelligence officer of the 707th Division noted in his monthly report for October 11 to November 10, 1941, that in the course of a "cleansing action" the battalion had shot 5,900 Jews in the Slutsk-Kletsk area. German Federal Archives—Military Archives (Freiburg), RH 26-707/2.

Lechthaler was sentenced to three and a half years after the first trial. The sentence was reduced to two years in the second. Upon appeal by the prosecution, the second sentence was overruled on May 6, 1963, 2 StR 467/63. By then, Lechthaler was almost seventy-three years old.

In his order of October 20, 1941, Bechtolsheim complained that Jews were reappearing in localities where they had been completely annihilated. The order of November 10 states that the police battalion had left on November 6, but that the Lithuanian units had remained. On November 13, another divisional order noted the increased participation of Jews in the partisan movement and admonished the troops to ensure that the Jews disappear from the villages. On November 24, an order over the typed signature of Bechtolsheim, certified by von der Osten, reiterated that Jews had to disappear from the countryside and that the Gypsies also had to be annihilated. In this order, however, there is a retreat. Evidently stung by the repercussions of Slutsk, Bechtolsheim states that the implementation of "major" actions against the Jews was not the task of the division, but that Jewish groups encountered in the open could still be "finished off" or taken to a ghetto. See U.S. Holocaust Memorial Museum Archives Record Group 22.03 (Belarus Central State Archives), Roll 2, Fond 378, Opis 1, Folder 698.

6: PHYSICIANS AND LAWYERS

1. Robert Jay Lifton, *The Nazi Doctors* (New York, 1986), pp. 14–18. The geneticist Benno Müller-Hill points out interestingly that doctors have always been ready for "small annihilation measures," such as amputations and abortions. See his *Tödliche Wissenschaft* (Hamburg, 1984), p. 91.

2. Michael Kater, *Doctors under Hitler* (Chapel Hill, N.C., 1989), pp. 17–19, 54–74, 177–221.

3. See the law of April 7, 1933, *Reichsgesetzblatt* I, 188.

4. Notation by Friedrich Kritzinger (Reich Chancellery), April 12, 1938, citing Staatssekretär Franz Schlegelberger of the Justice Ministry, German Federal Archives R 43 II/1535. See also Schlegelberger's testimony in the Justice Trial, *Trials of War Criminals 1946–1949*, 15 vols. (Washington, D.C.) vol. 3, pp. 718–19.

5. Müller-Hill, *Tödliche Wissenschaft*, pp. 21, 23, 38–39, 152–57.

6. See Verschuer's detailed report about Liselotte Milisch (wife of Regierungsassessor Willy Bukow) to Ministerialdirektor Schellen (Prussian Ministry of the Interior), September 20, 1933, enclosed by Staatssekretär Stuckart to Heinrich Lammers of the Reich Chancellery, November 17, 1944, German Federal Archives R 43 II/599. Part of the problem was the determination of whether Mrs. Bukow had inherited her narrow high-set convex nose from her father's or her mother's side. In this particular case,

the judgment was favorable for Mrs. Bukow. In 1953, Verschuer continued his career as Professor of Anthropology at the University of Münster.

7. Robert N. Proctor, *Racial Hygiene* (Cambridge, Mass., 1988), pp. 95–117.

8. See the report of Dr. Carl Clauberg (Auschwitz) to Himmler, June 7, 1942, Nuremberg trials document NO-212.

9. See the summary report (undated and unsigned) in National Archives of the United States, Record Group 242, T 1021, Roll 18.

10. Lifton, *The Nazi Doctors,* pp. 270–84, 384–414.

11. *Ibid.,* pp. 194–95.

12. Reich Security Main Office IV-A-1, Operational Report 132, November 12, 1941, Nuremberg trials document NO-2830.

13. See Christopher Browning, "Genocide and Public Health: German Doctors and Polish Jews, 1939–41," *Holocaust and Genocide Studies,* vol. 3 (1988), pp. 21–36.

14. Trude Maurer, "Medizinalpolizei und Antisemitismus," *Jahrbücher für die Geschichte Osteuropas,* vol. 33 (1985), pp. 205–30.

15. Wilhelm Hagen, "Krieg, Hunger und Pestilenz in Warschau 1939–1945," *Gesundheitswesen und Desinfektion,* vol. 65 (1973), pp. 115–43, particularly pp. 117, 129, 133–35.

16. See the photograph with the sign *Seuchensperrgebiet* in Jüdisches Historisches Institut, *Faschismus—Getto—Massenmord* (Berlin, 1961), p. 105.

17. Hagen to Stadtkommandant Ludwig Leist, September 22, 1941, Yad Vashem Microfilm JM 1112.

18. Hagen to Hitler, December 7, 1942, and subsequent correspondence in National Archives Record Group 242, T 175, Roll 38.

19. Hagen, "Krieg," *Gesundheitswesen* (1973), vol. 65, on pp. 122–25.

20. The text of the decree is reproduced in Jüdisches Historisches Institut, *Faschismus—Getto—Massenmord,* pp. 128–29.

21. Large portion of the verbatim transcript of the conference of November 12, 1938, in Nuremberg trial document PS-1816.

22. Circular letter by Stuckart of June 2, 1942, German National Archives, R 43/422a.

23. For an analysis of these cases, see Ingo Müller, *Furchtbare Juristen* (Munich, 1987), pp. 97–123.

24. *Ibid.,* pp. 123–27.

25. Announcement by the Rector of Freiburg University (Martin Heidegger) in the *Freiburger Studentenzeitung,* November 3, 1933, reprinted in Guido Schneeberger, ed., *Nachlese zu Heidegger* (Bern, 1962), p. 137.

26. Report by Glehn for the month of March 1942, April 18, 1942, Archives of the Main Commission for the Investigation of Nazi War Crimes in Poland, Trial of Josef Bühler, vol. 285, pp. 17–23.

27. Uwe Adam, *Judenpolitik im Dritten Reich* (Düsseldorf, 1972), pp. 111, 245–46.

28. On Jewish estates, see Generalkommissar in White Ruthenia to Reichskommissar/Trusteeship (Special Representative for Seizure of Jewish Property in the Ostland) Bruns, March 4, 1942, National Archives Record Group 242, T 459, Roll 3. See also the forms used by the Stadtkommissar/ IIIe of Minsk in 1943, U.S. Holocaust Memorial Museum Archives Record Group 22.04 (Minsk Oblast Archives), Roll 2, Fond 688, Opis 5, Folder 6.

29. Indictment of Erhard Kröger before a Stuttgart court, January 30, 1968, 18 Js 139/66.

7: NON-GERMAN GOVERNMENTS

1. See Samuel Abrahamsen, *Norway's Response to the Holocaust* (New York, 1991), pp. 115–35.

2. Report by the German Security Police in the Netherlands, No. 87, March 31, 1942, National Archives of the United States, Record Group 242, T 175, Roll 670.

3. See, in general, Jacob Presser, *The Destruction of the Dutch Jews* (New York, 1969), pp. 349–55.

4. Guus Meershoek, "De Amsterdamse hoofdcommissaris en de deportatie van de joden," in *Oorlogsdocumentatie '40–'45. Derde jaarboek van het Rijksinstituut voor Oorlogsdocumentatie*, ed. N. D. Barnouw et al. (Zutphen, The Netherlands, 1992), pp. 9–43. Tulp died suddenly in October 1942. Before the involvement of the Amsterdam police, the Germans relied heavily on voluntary Jewish reporting for deportation. In 1943, a Jewish Order Service from the Westerbork transit camp was employed in Amsterdam roundups.

5. G. L. Durlacher, *Streifen am Himmel* (Reinbek bei Hamburg, 1988), pp. 30–32, 43.

6. See the correspondence in National Archives Record Group 242, T 175, Roll 485.

7. Robert Paxton, *Parades and Politics at Vichy* (Princeton, 1966), pp. 176–77.

8. *Ibid.*, p. 238.

9. On the Vichy regime, see Jean-Pierre Azéma, *From Munich to the Liberation, 1938–1944* (Cambridge, England, 1984), and Milton Dank, *The*

French against the French (Philadelphia, 1974). For Vichy's anti-Jewish role, see Michael Marrus and Robert Paxton, *Vichy France and the Jews* (New York, 1981), and Serge Klarsfeld *Vichy-Auschwitz*, 2 vols. (Paris, 1983 and 1985). Bichelonne died in Germany, November 1944, after surgery; Pucheu, in Algeria after serving as Interior Minister, was shot there by the Free French, March 1944. Bousquet, sentenced to national degradation, remained a free man.

10. On Laval and the Jewish children, see Marrus and Paxton, *Vichy France and the Jews*, pp. 263–69. Laval escaped France at the end of the war, then was returned and tried there, unsuccessfully attempted suicide, and was shot in October 1945.

11. See Frederick B. Chary, *The Bulgarian Jews and the Final Solution, 1940–1944* (Pittsburgh, 1972).

12. Quoted in Radu Ioanid, *The Sword of the Archangel Michael* (New York, 1960), p. 114.

13. On Romania, see in the main Matatias Carp, *Cartea Neagra—Suferintele Evreilor din Romania 1940–1944*, 3 vols. (Bucharest, 1946–48), and Jean Ancel, ed. *Documents Concerning the Fate of Romanian Jewry during the Holocaust*, 12 vols. (New York, 1986). Ion Antonescu was executed in 1946.

14. On Hungary, see Randolph Braham, *The Politics of Genocide*, 2 vols. (New York, 1981).

8: NON-GERMAN VOLUNTEERS

1. The first commander was sixty-year-old Colonel Roger-Henri Labonne, described by Jean-Pierre Azéma as a "chocolate soldier." Jean-Pierre Azéma, *From Munich to the Liberation, 1938–1944* (Cambridge, England, 1984), pp. 142, 144. He was quickly replaced by the more professional Colonel Edgar Puaud.

2. Report by Gendarmerie Lieutenant Egger of the gendarmerie post at Training Camp "Center" (Truppenübungsplatz "Mitte") in Radom to Commander of Truppenübungsplatz "Mitte" in Radom and Commander of Truppenübungsplatz in Kruszyna, December 19, 1942, and subsequent correspondence, Yad Vashem Microfilm JM 3499.

3. Claude Lévy and Paul Tillard, *Betrayal at the Vel d'Hiv* (New York, 1969), pp. 9, 25. Doriot was killed in Germany during an aerial strafing attack.

4. Paul Jankowski, *Communism and Collaboration: Simon Sabiani and Politics in Marseilles, 1919–1944* (New York, 1989), pp. 93–120, particularly pp. 95 and 113 ff. Sabiani was the party's chief in the Marseilles region.

5. Michael Marrus and Robert Paxton, *Vichy France and the Jews* (New York, 1981), p. 335. Darnand was shot for treason in October 1945. Azéma called him a prototype of "plebeian fascism": *From Munich to the Liberation*, pp. 142–43.

6. Susan Zuccotti, *The Italians and the Holocaust* (New York, 1987), pp. 148–53, 189–208.

7. See Liliana Picciotto Fargion, *Il libro della memoria: Gli Ebrei deportati dall'Italia (1943–1945)* (Milano, 1991), p. 30.

8. Eugene Levai, *Black Book on the Martyrdom of Hungarian Jewry* (Zurich and Vienna, 1948), pp. 335–421.

9. German Security Service report in Bratislava, September 22, 1944, National Archives of the United States, Record Group 242, T 175, Roll 583. About four thousand Hlinka guards were serving as of February 1945. Memorandum on Slovak forces by German Armed Forces Operational Staff (Wehrmachtführungsstab/Op H), February 26, 1945, National Archives Record Group 242, T 77, roll 1419.

10. Raul Hilberg, Stanislav Staron, and Josef Kermisz, eds., *The Warsaw Diary of Adam Czerniakow* (Briarcliff Manor, N.Y. 1979), *passim*. Czerniakow's entry of September 23, 1941, about an impending memorandum by the municipality opposing boundary changes, is on pp. 281–82.

11. Report by Ortskommandantur I/853 in Mariupol, October 2, 1941, National Archives Record Group 242, T 501, Roll 56.

12. Reich Security Main Office IV-A-1, Operational Report No. 156, January 16, 1942, Nuremberg trials document NO-3405. The mayor was Senitsa Vershovsky.

13. Reports by Ortskommandantur I/853 in Nikolaev, September 15 and 25, 1941, National Archives Record Group 242, T 501, Roll 56.

14. Poster of the Kharkov indigenous municipal administration in Kharkov Oblast Archives. The archives also hold the registration books. See two typical volumes with interspersed yellow sheets in Fond 2982, Opis 6, Folders 13 and 35.

15. Reich Security Main Office IV-A-1, Operational Report No. 164, February 4, 1942, Nuremberg trials document NO-3399, and the account by the Kharkov survivor Maria Markovna Sokol in Ilya Ehrenburg and Vasily Grossman, eds., *The Black Book* (New York, 1981), pp. 51–56.

16. Excerpt from the statement by David Davidovich Egoff (a Volga German), February 28, 1947. U.S. Holocaust Memorial Museum Archives, Record Group 22.03 (Belarus Central State Archives) Roll 6, Fond 845, Opis 1, Folder 206. Stylistically, the statement is filled with accusatory and self-accusatory language of the sort imposed by Soviet interrogators on

their captives in those days. There is, however, no reason to doubt the veracity of the substance of the account.

17. For insurgent activity against the Soviets, see Algirdas Martin Budreckis, *The Lithuanian National Revolt of 1941* (South Boston, 1968), and *I Laisve* (To Freedom), a newspaper published by the Lithuanian National Front, June 24, 1941. The newspaper issue reveals sharp anti-Jewish sentiments. For Lithuanian killings of Jews during the first few days and the meeting of the Security Police with Jewish leaders, see Reich Security Main Office IV-A-1 Operational Report No. 19, July 11, 1941, Nuremberg trials document NO-2934, and the report by Brigadeführer Walter Stahlecker, Commander of Einsatzgruppe A, covering activities to October 15, 1941, Nuremberg trials document L-180. The confirmation of the mayor's ordinance is contained in Public Proclamation No. 2, signed Cramer, July 31, 1941, *Amtsblatt des Generalkommissars in Kauen,* vol.1, no. 2, November 1, 1941, pp. 1–2. Correspondence and records of meetings between Jewish leaders and Lithuanian municipal officials, including the memorandum by Rozenbliumas of July 22, 1941, are contained in Yad Vashem Document 0-14/12-4. The Lithuanian Provisional Government was dissolved by the German civil administration in early August, but Palciauskas continued as mayor. Palciauskas, who was born in 1907, emigrated to the United States after the war without revealing his official position in 1941 and 1942. Long afterward, he faced a U.S. court. See *United States v. Kazys Palciauskas,* 559 F. Supp. 1294 (1983).

18. Municipality of Vilnius/Housing Office (signed by Mayor Karolis Dabulevicius and housing chief A. Bockus) to Gebietskommissar of the city of Vilnius (Hans Hingst), September 17, 1941, Lithuanian Central State Historical Archives, Fond 643-s, Opis 3, Folder 4083.

19. A figure of 14,297 Polish police in the Generalgouvernement at the end of 1942 was given by Order Police Chief Kurt Daluege in a report dated February 1, 1943, Nuremberg trials document NO-2861. In Poland, the right-wing extremists belonged to a *resistance* group. Their treatment of Jewish escapees in the woods is another matter.

20. For the presence of Polish police at the Warsaw Ghetto wall, see the discussion between Heinz Auerswald (Ghetto Commissar) and Waldemar Schön (Warsaw District Interior Division), November 8, 1941, Yad Vashem Microfilm JM 1112. For the countryside, see the report of the Kommandeur of Order Police in the Lublin District, June 6, 1943, noting that Polish police of Karczmiska patrolling the area had spotted a group of fifty Jews who had escaped from the Poniatowa labor camp, killing two

men and wounding a woman. Archiwum Panstwowe w Lublinie, Collection Ortskommandantur I/524, sygn. 14.

21. See Himmler's instructions to Higher SS and Police Leaders Hans Adolf Prützmann, Friedrich Jeckeln, and Erich von dem Bach, and SS and Police Leader Odilo Globocnik (Lublin), July 25, 1941, National Archives Record Group 242, T 454, Roll 100.

22. Order by the Commander of Army Group Center Rear Area/Chief of the General Staff, signed by Colonel Freiherr Rüdt von Collenberg, February 12, 1942, National Archives Record Group 242, T 501, Roll 15.

23. A Soviet estimate of the number of Ukrainians as of early 1939, within an area bounded by the postwar frontiers of the USSR, was 35,611,000. Joint Economic Committee, Hearings on "Dimensions of Soviet Power," December 10 and 11, 1962, 87th Cong., 2d sess., pp. 586–87. In addition, several hundred thousand Ukrainians were living in the adjacent Lublin area, which became a district of the Generalgouvernement, and which was neither prewar nor postwar Soviet territory. Under German occupation, the Ukrainian SSR was divided as follows: Galicia (Polish territory before September 1939) to the Generalgouvernement; Volhynia (also former Polish territory) and other western Ukrainian regions (including Kiev) to the civilian Reichskommissariat Ukraine; eastern Ukraine (including Kharkov) to German military control; and the area between the Dnestr and the Bug (including Odessa) to Romanian civil administration.

24. A German compilation of September 15, 1942, indicated 3,247,353 Ukrainians and 955,821 Poles in the Galician District. Lvov Oblast Archives, Fond 35, Opis 9, Folder 47. Just then, the third largest group, the Jews, were undergoing annihilation.

25. Presentation by Katzmann at a meeting with Generalgouverneur Frank in Lvov, October 21, 1941, Frank Diary, National Archives Record Group 238, T 992, Roll 5.

26. Correspondence of Ukrainian police in Lvov, April–June 1942, in Lvov Oblast Archives, Fond 12, Opis 1, Folder 38. See also Michael Hanusiak, Lest We Forget (Toronto, 1976), particularly facsimiles of documents showing the involvement of Ukrainian precinct police in Lvov, pp. 146, 148, 178, and 202. For the background and career of a Ukrainian policeman in Stanislavov, see United States v. Bohdan Kozij, 540 F. Supp. 25 (1982).

27. Order by Feldkommandantur 551 in Gomel (signed Lieutenant Laub) to mayors, September 4, 1941, National Archives Record Group 242, T 315, Roll 1671. Report by Major Münchau, following an inspection tour of Army Group South Rear Area, October 23, 1941, noting that the Mayor of

Solotoshna had set up a Ukrainian militia: National Archives Record Group 242, T 501, Roll 6. On December 18, 1941, Feldkommandantur 197 reported that six hundred Jews had been killed in Solotoshna: T 501, Roll 6.

28. See the order of the Commander of Army Group South Rear Area, July 11, 1941, German Federal Archives RH 22/5, and his order of July 22, 1941, National Archives Record Group 242, T 501, Roll 5.

29. Order by Higher SS and Police Leader Jeckeln (then in the area of Army Group South), July 6, 1941, German Federal Archives, RH 22/5, and the correspondence, with detailed regional statistics, in German Federal Archives R 19/121 and R 19/122, starting with the proposal of the *Befehlshaber* (Commander) of the Order Police in Ukraine, Generalmajor (Brigadier General) Ott. von Oelhafen, to the Main Office Order Police, October 12, 1941, R 19/121.

30. Report of the numerical strength of the Schutzmannschaft as of July 1, 1942, German Federal Archives R 19/266.

31. In all, 49 officers and 459 non-commissioned officers in the cities; 230 officers and 2,128 non-commissioned officers on the land: *ibid.*

32. Gendarmeriegebietsführer in Brest-Litovsk (Lieutenant Deuerlein) to Kommandeur of Gendarmerie in Lutsk, October 6, 1942, National Archives Record Group 242, T 454, Roll 102.

33. Reich Security Main Office IV-A-1, Operational Report No. 106, October 7, 1941, Nuremberg trials document NO-3140. The shooting took place on September 18, 1941.

34. Reich Security Main Office IV-A-1, Operational Report No. 80, September 11, 1941, Nuremberg trials document NO-3154.

35. Report by Sonderkommando 11a for the period August 22–September 10, 1941, Nuremberg trials document NOKW-636.

36. Reich Security Main Office IV-A-1, Operational Report No. 88, September 19, 1941, Nuremberg trials document NO-3149. The shooting occurred on September 6, 1941.

37. Ortskommandantur in Kakhovka to Rear Army Area 553, with a copy to Feldkommandantur 810, October 20, 1941, Nuremberg trials document NOKW-1598.

38. Reich Security Main Office IV-A-1, Operational Report No. 119, October 20, 1941, Nuremberg trials document NO-3404.

39. This reasoning was supplied by Einsatzkommando 6. Reich Security Main Office IV-A-1, Operational Report No. 81, September 12, 1941, Nuremberg trials document NO-3154.

40. See the reports of Lieutenant Deuerlein in Brest-Litovsk, October 6 and 10, 1942, National Archives Record Group 242, T 454, Roll 102.

41. Strength report of July 1, 1942, German Federal Archives R 1/266. The total manpower of the 18½ battalions was 6,671, including 115 officers and 779 non-commissioned officers. The 2d (Nachtigall) Battalion, recruited in the Generalgouvernement before the invasion of the USSR, was also Ukrainian. Eventually, the number of battalions was doubled. See Hans-Joachim Neufeldt, Jürgen Huck, and Georg Tessin, *Zur Geschichte der Ordnungspolizei: 1936–1945* (Koblenz, 1957), part II (by Tessin).

42. Judgment of a German court in Koblenz against Carl Zenner and Hans-Hermann Remmers, June 12, 1961, 9 Ks 1/61. Reich Security Main Office IV-A-1, Operational Report No. 140, December 1, 1941, Nuremberg trials document NO-2831. Generalkommissar Wilhelm Kube of the Generalbezirk "White Ruthenia" objected to the presence of armed Ukrainians in his domain. His reservations were conveyed by Gauleiter Alfred Meyer of the Ministry for Eastern Occupied Territories to Reinhard Heydrich: summary, dated October 4, 1941, of their discussion in National Archives Record Group 242, T 976, Roll 28.

43. Adalbert Rükerl, *NS-Vernichtungslager* (Munich, 1977), pp. 122–23, 207, and statements by former German guards in the Belzec Case, 1 Js 278/60, vol. 7, pp. 1254–88, 1311–31, 1409–35, and in the Sobibor Case, 45 Js 27/61, vol. 3, pp. 520–23.

44. See the report by SS and Police Leader Jürgen Stroop, commander of the forces deployed against the ghetto, to Higher SS and Police Leader Krüger, May 16, 1943, Nuremberg trials document PS-1061. By the winter of 1943–1944, the morale and reliability of some of the Ukrainian units had declined. See the correspondence, with lists of names, about a hundred men of the 60th (Ukrainian) Battalion in a penal labor camp, in U.S. Holocaust Memorial Museum Archives, Record Group 22.03 (Belarus Central State Archives), Roll 3, Fond 389, Opis 1, Folder 2.

45. The stationary Byelorussian Schutzmannschaft numbered 4,580 in mid-1942. Strength report of the Schutzmannschaft, German Federal Archives R 19/266.

46. Lieutenant Max Eibner via Gendarmerie Hauptmannschaft to Kommandeur der Gendarmerie in White Ruthenia (area of Byelorussia under civil administration), November 4, 1942, U.S. Holocaust Memorial Museum Archives Record Group 22.03 (Belarus Central State Archives), Roll 4, Fond 389, Opis 1, Folder 3.

47. Report by Gendarmerie Commander Eibner (unsigned) via Gendarmerie Hauptmannschaft to Kommandeur der Gendarmerie, August 26, 1942, Zentrale Stelle der Landesjustizverwaltungen in Ludwigsburg, Collection UdSSR 245c, pp. 90–91.

48. See, for example, his report of February 5, 1943, U.S. Holocaust Museum Archives, Record Group 22.03 (Belarus Central State Archives), Roll 4, Fond 387, Opis 1, Folder 3. In the areas east of Byelorussia, there was a Russian stationary auxiliary police under army jurisdiction. See the report of Security Division 221/Operations (Sicherungsdivision 221/Ia) to the Commander of the Army Group Center Rear Area, October 27, 1941, mentioning Russian police guarding Jews in Klintsey: National Archives Record Group 242, T 315, Roll 1668. The areas between Byelorussia and Moscow were more sparsely inhabited by Jews, and the large majority of these Jewish residents had departed with the Red Army.

49. The Soviet estimate of nationalities of 1939, within a territory comprising the postwar USSR, included 1,143,000 Estonians, 1,628,000 Latvians, and 2,032,000 Lithuanians. Joint Economic Committee, Hearings on "Dimensions of Soviet Power," pp. 586–87. *Baltic* as a term for the three nationalities is a concept of political geography. Only Lithuanian and Latvian are Baltic languages, whereas Estonian is related to Finnish. During the Middle Ages, German orders dominated the area; in early modern times Catholic Lithuania was joined with Poland, and farther north, Sweden and Denmark had seized territory. In the eighteenth century the entire Baltic became a part of the Russian Empire.

50. The utilization of members of pro-German nationalist organizations and of former Baltic soldiers who had not fought against Germany at the outbreak of war was recommended by the Eighteenth Army. See the order by the Eighteenth Army/Ic AO (Intelligence) Qu 2, July 9, 1941, National Archives Record Group 242, T 315, Roll 574.

51. By July 1, 1942, the total strength of the Baltic Schutzmannschaft (not including five battalions assigned to armies) was 115,034, compared to 435,469 in the Ukrainian Schutzmannschaft (not including one battalion assigned to the military). If firemen and temporary so-called *Hilfsschutzmannschaften* are subtracted, the Balts numbered 34,229 and the Ukrainians 34,595. Included in these numbers are 54 Estonian, Latvian, and Lithuanian battalions and the 18½ Ukrainian, but not those under military command. Of the Baltic Schutzmannschaft as a whole 3 percent were officers, compared to less than 1 percent in the Ukrainian. Strength report of the Schutzmannschaft, July 1, 1942, German Federal Archives R 19/266.

52. Order by General Franz von Roques, September 20, 1941, extending an earlier prohibition of August 3, 1941, aimed only at Latvia, to his entire area. U.S. Holocaust Memorial Museum Archives, Record Group 22.03 (Belarus Central State Archives), Roll 4, Fond 389, Opis 1, Folder 3. Von Roques had already complained on July 8, 1941, to the Commander of

Army Group North, Field Marshal Wilhelm Ritter von Leeb, about Lithuanian killings of Jews in Kaunas. In that meeting von Roques doubted the efficacy of such killings altogether and suggested sterilizations of all Jewish men. Leeb's diary, as cited by Helmut Krausnick, in Helmut Krausnick and Heinrich Wilhelm, *Die Truppe des Weltanschauungskrieges* (Stuttgart, 1981), pp. 207-208.

53. Reich Security Main Office IV-A-1, Operational Report No. 111, October 12, 1941, Nuremberg trials document NO-3155. See also the testimony of Sandberger before the U.S. Military Tribunal, Case No. 9, November 12-17, 1947, English transcript pp. 2213-20, 2348-49, 2381-92. Estonians are not mentioned as participating in the shootings at Pskov. A total of 963 Estonian Jews were reported killed, and Estonia was claimed to be free of Jews, in a draft report of Einsatzgruppe A (February 1942), Nuremberg trials document PS-2273.

54. The transports from Theresienstadt and Berlin are noted in the schedules set up in a railway conference of the Generalbetriebsleitung Ost, August 6, 1942, U.S. Holocaust Memorial Museum Archives, Record Group 22.03 (Belarus Central State Archives), Roll 2, Fond 378, Opis 1, Folder 784. They were due to leave September 1 and 10, respectively, for Raasiku. H. G. Adler notes in *Theresienstadt* (Tübingen, 1960), pp. 52-53, that forty-five young women survived. The killings are described in testimony, an abridged text of the indictment against Mere, March 10, 1961, and the text of the judgment by the Estonian Supreme Court (no date), in Raul Kruus, *People, Be Watchful* (Tallin, 1962). Kruus also includes a facsimile of the organization plan of Sonderkommando 1a, complete with German and Estonian components, as of July 1, 1942, *ibid.*, pp. 202-203.

55. See statements of survivors in Ilya Ehrenburg and Vasily Grossman, eds., *The Black Book* (New York, 1981), pp. 390-98. See also photographs of bodies in Klooga. Kruus, *People,* p. 196. The nationality of the shooters, except for several Germans, was not identified.

56. The Lithuania that was taken over by the USSR in 1940 did not include the port of Klaipeda (Memel), which was German until the end of the First World War and which was retaken by Hitler in March 1939. Vilnius (Vilna) was Polish between the two world wars. It was acquired by the Soviet Union in September 1939. After the Soviet Union annexed Lithuania in June 1940, Vilnius was incorporated into the Lithuanian SSR.

57. Reich Security Main Office IV-A-1, Operational Report No. 12, July 4, 1941, Nuremberg trials document NO-4529.

58. Reich Security Main Office IV-A-1, Operational Report No. 8, June 30, 1941, Nuremberg trials document NO-4543. Report by the Com-

mander of Einsatzgruppe A (Stahlecker), October 15, 1941, Nuremberg trials document L-180.

59. Reich Security Main Office IV-A-1, Operational Report No. 19, July 11, 1941, Nuremberg trials document NO-2934.

60. Lithuanian Central State Historical Archives, Fond 689, Opis 1, Folder 20.

61. Reich Security Main Office IV-A-1, Operational Report No. 88, September 19, 1941, Nuremberg trials document NO-3149.

62. See B. Baranauskas and K. Ruksenas, eds., *Documents Accuse* (Vilnius, 1970), particularly pp. 161–67, 216–23. A contemporary Jewish view of Lithuanian collaboration is contained in a letter written by Khone Boyarski while in hiding. Boyarski lived in Butremonys, south of Kaunas, and neither he nor his family survived. His letter was found after the war and copied twice. The copies were collated, and the collation was translated and published with annotations in Nathan Cohen, "'The Destruction of the Jews in Butremonys as Described in a Farewell Letter from a Local Jew," *Holocaust and Genocide Studies*, vol. 4 (1989), pp. 357–75. The letter refers to Lithuanians involved in roundups and shootings as "partisans" (in quotation marks) wearing white armbands and as "bandits" (not in quotation marks). Stylistically, the letter is reminiscent of a medieval Hebrew chronicle.

63. War Diary of the 403d Security Division/Ia, July 25, 1941, National Archives Record Group 242, T 315, Roll 2206. See also Budreckis, *The Lithuanian National Revolt,* pp. 79–82.

64. Reich Security Main Office IV-A-1, Operational Report No. 21, July 13, 1941, Nuremberg trials document NO-2937.

65. Antanas Iskaukas to Kommandeur of Order Police, September 9, 1941, Lithuanian Central State Historical Archives, Fond 689, Opis 1, Folder 20.

66. Final report by Higher SS and Police Leader Jeckeln on "Swamp Fever," November 6, 1942, Nuremberg trials document PS-1113. The battalions were the 3d and the 15th. Also participating were one Ukrainian and four Latvian battalions.

67. As of July 1, 1942, it was the 2d Lithuanian Battalion. Strength report of the Schutzmannschaft, July 1, 1942, German Federal Archives R 19/266. Later it was the 252d Battalion. Krüger to Himmler, July 7, 1943, Himmler Files, Folder 94, Library of Congress.

68. See the paper by Andrew Ezergailis, "Who Killed the Jews of Latvia?" presented at a conference on anti-Semitism at Cornell University, April 8–10, 1986, and the article by Margers Vestermanis, "Der lettische

Anteil an der 'Endlösung,' " in Uwe Backes, Eckhard Jesse, and Rainer Zitelmann, eds., *Die Schatten der Vergangenheit* (Frankfurt am Main, 1990), pp. 426–49.

69. Lieutenant Colonel Voldemars Veiss (Acting Director of the Section of Internal Security in the Latvian General Directorate of Internal Affairs) to the SS and Police Leader in Latvia (Schröder), January 7, 1942, German Federal Archives, R 92/519.

70. On Arajs, see the judgment against him by a Hamburg court, December 21, 1979 (37) 5/76. See also the paper presented by Andrew Ezergailis, "Sonderkommando Arajs," at the Ninth International Conference of Baltic Studies in Scandinavia, Stockholm, June 3–4, 1982.

71. Reich Security Main Office IV-A-1, Operational Report No. 24, July 16, 1941, Nuremberg trials document NO-2938.

72. Testimony by Reinhard Wiener (in the German navy at the time), December 15, 1969, in the case against Erhard Grauel (Einsatzkommando 2) before a Hannover Court, 2 Js 261/60. Wiener, who made a short clandestine film of these shootings, saw about two hundred spectators at the site.

73. Reich Security Main Office IV-A-1, Operational Report No. 24, July 16, 1941, Nuremberg trials document NO-2938.

74. Security Division 281/VII (Military Government), signed in draft by Generalleutnant Friedrich Bayer, to Commander of Army Group North Rear Area, July 27, 1941, National Archives Record Group 242, T 315, Roll 1871. The toll as of that date was three thousand to four thousand.

75. Reich Security Main Office IV-A-1, Operational Report No. 40, August 1, 1941, Nuremberg trials document NO-2950.

76. Stahlecker report, October 15, 1941, Nuremberg trials document L-180.

77. Undated draft report by Stahlecker (February 1942), Nuremberg trials document PS-2273.

78. Indictment of Arajs, May 10, 1976, 141 Js 534/60, and judgment, December 21, 1979 (37) 5/76. Petitions by Latvian Riga precinct and harbor policemen to receive Jewish Ghetto furniture, National Archives Record Group 242, T 459, Roll 2. Several of the policemen indicate that they had participated in the "Jewish action."

79. Account by Benjamin Edelstein (undated) in the collection of evidence prepared for the Arajs indictment, 141 Js 534/60, pp. 6075–6097.

80. See, for example, the report by Hauptwachtmeister Schultz in Baranovichi, October 18, 1942, acknowledging the help of a company of Latvians in the killing of two thousand Jews in the ghetto of Stolpce. Zentrale

Stelle der Landesjustizverwaltungen in Ludwigsburg, UdSSR 245c, pp. 79–80. The 18th Latvian Police Battalion was stationed in Stolpce at the time.

81. The 22d and 272d Battalions. Tessin in Neufeldt, Huck, and Tessin, *Zur Geschichte der Ordnungspolizei*, part II, pp. 102, 107.

82. See the article on the Latvian Legion in *Latvju Enciklopedija* (Stockholm, 1952), vol. 34, pp. 1288–1322, and Visvaldis Mangulis, *Latvia in the Wars of the 20th Century* (Princeton Junction, 1983). Most Riga policemen were evacuated by sea.

83. Complaint by R. Saulis, February 24, 1942, and subsequent correspondence, including Lobe's letter of April 24, 1942, in Latvian Central State Historical Archives, Fond 82, Opis 2, Folder 1. Lobe is reported to have found refuge in Sweden after the war. Osis is reported to have arrived, via Sweden, in Britain.

PART II: VICTIMS

9: THE JEWISH LEADERS

1. Report by Waldemar Schön (Director of Resettlement in the Warsaw District, with responsibility for the creation of the Warsaw Ghetto), January 20, 1941, German Federal Archives, R 102 1/2.

2. Order by Heydrich, September 21, 1939, Nuremberg trials document PS-3363. In Galicia, many Jewish councils had been formed by the Jews themselves. The Germans decided to demand lists of the memberships with a view to removing unsuitable persons. Summary of an assembly of heads of local districts (Kreishauptmannschaften) in Galicia, September 2, 1941, Glowna Komisja Badania Zbrodni Hitlerowskich w Polsce, Trial of Josef Bühler before the High People's Tribunal, sygn. 286, p. 104.

3. A list of council chairmen and their deputies in fifteen towns of the rural Kreishauptmannschaft Lublin-Land (adjacent to the city of Lublin) reveals a median age of thirty-seven. This group was even younger, if the three largest communities (Piaski, Belzyce, and Brzeziny) are subtracted: see the list dated November 28, 1939, in Archiwum Panstwowe w Lublinie, Collection Kreishauptmann Lublin-Land, sygn. 101, karta 9–10. The middle-aged Belzyce Judenrat was dismissed for incompetence, that is, failure to support unpaid forced laborers employed in a river regulation project. Lublin District/Wasserwirtschaftsinspektion (signed by Inspekteur Woltheimer) to Kreishauptmann Lublin-Land (attention Dr. Polzer), August 26, 1940, *ibid.*, sygn. 102, karta 6.

4. Essays about several Jewish councils in eastern and western regions

of Europe may be found in Yisrael Gutman and Cynthia Haft, eds., *Patterns of Jewish Leadership in Nazi Europe* (Jerusalem, 1979). On the formation of the councils in Poland, see Isaiah Trunk, *Judenrat* (New York, 1972), pp. 1–60.

5. Baeck's life before 1933 is described in detail by Leonard Baker, *Days of Sorrow and Pity* (New York, 1978).

6. See mainly the Reichsvertretung collection in the Leo Baeck Institute Archives in New York, AR 221.

7. On the wartime period see the Leo Baeck Institute Microfilm Roll 66.

8. On this transition, see Herbert Rosenkranz, *Verfolgung und Selbstbehauptung* (Vienna and Munich, 1978), pp. 1–72.

9. Text of Eichmann's letter to Herbert Hagen, May 8, 1938, *ibid.*, pp. 71–72.

10. See the entries by Czerniakow of February 20, 1940, and October 5, 1941, in his diary. Raul Hilberg, Stanislaw Staron, and Josef Kermisz, eds., *The Warsaw Diary of Adam Czerniakow* (Briarcliff Manor, N.Y., 1979), pp. 119–20, 285.

11. On Rumkowski's background and rule, consult Leonard Tushnet, *The Pavement of Hell* (New York, 1972), pp. 1–70, and Shmuel Huppert, "King of the Ghetto," *Yad Vashem Studies,* vol. 15 (1983), pp. 125–57. There is a chronicle of approximately 1 million words written in the ghetto under Rumkowski's direction. See the substantial selections in Lucjan Dobroszycki, ed., *The Chronicle of the Lodz Ghetto* (New Haven, 1984). Texts of Rumkowski's speeches and small excerpts from various diaries of Lodz Ghetto inmates were published by Alan Adelson and Ralph Lapides, eds., *Lodz Ghetto* (New York, 1989).

12. Transcript of the celebration session on the first anniversary of the establishment of the Bialystok Judenrat, June 29, 1942, in Yitzhak Arad, Yisrael Gutman, and Abraham Margaliot, *Documents on the Holocaust* (Jerusalem, 1981), pp. 264–66.

13. The history of Jewish upheavals in Vilnius is vividly portrayed by Yitzhak Arad, *Ghetto in Flames* (New York, 1982).

14. Gens is described by Tushnet, *The Pavement of Hell*, pp. 139–99, and Arad, *Ghetto in Flames*, pp. 125–27 and *passim*.

15. See Joseph Michman, "The Controversial Stand of the *Joodse Raad* in the Netherlands," *Yad Vashem Studies*, vol. 10 (1974), pp. 9–68.

16. See Jacques Adler, *The Jews of Paris and the Final Solution* (New York and Oxford, 1987), and Cynthia Haft, *The Bargain and the Bridle* (Chicago, 1983). Adler notes Mayer's attitude with regard to foreign Jews on p. 84.

17. On Lambert, see Richard J. Cohen, *The Burden of Conscience* (Bloomington, Ind., 1987); Adler, *The Jews of Paris*; and Haft, *The Bargain*.

18. See in the main Adler, *The Jews of Paris*. The conversation between Lambert and Helbronner, which took place in early August 1942, is recounted in Lambert's diary. Richard Cohen, ed., *Carnet d'un témoin* (Paris, 1985), entry of September 6, 1942, p. 180.

19. On the creation of the Centrala and Gingold's role, see Bela Vago, "The Center of the Jews in Romania," in Gutman and Haft, eds., *Patterns of Jewish Leadership*, pp. 287–309. On Filderman's expectations of hard currency reimbursement, see the memorandum of Gustav Richter in the German Legation, January 31, 1944, and Jewish correspondence intercepted by the Germans, National Archives Record Group 242, T 175, Rolls 659 and 660.

20. Gingold summarized his philosophy in an undated report, the text of which is in T 175, Roll 661.

21. On Gens, see Arad, *Ghetto in Flames*, pp. 342–51, and Tushnet, *The Pavement of Hell*, pp. 176–77.

22. Excerpts from the speech by Barasz in the judgment of a German court in Bielefeld against Wilhelm Altenloh and others, April 14, 1967, 5 Ks 1/65. The reference by Barasz to Bialystok as a newly conspicuous ghetto, second in size only to Lodz, was based on the mass deportation of Warsaw Jews during the preceding few months.

23. Text of Rumkowski's speech, February 1, 1942, in Adelson and Lapides, *Lodz Ghetto*, pp. 208–211.

10: The Refugees

1. See the bar chart and the statistics of the Reichsvereinigung, Leo Baeck Institute Microfilm Roll 66.

2. There is a considerable literature about the refugees. The intellectuals are the subject of Laura Fermi, *Illustrious Immigrants*, 2d ed. (Chicago, 1971), and many of them are listed in the *Encyclopaedia Judaica*. The immigrants in England are described by Marion Berghahn, *German Jewish Refugees in England* (New York, 1984). More or less successful immigrants in the United States are the focus of Herbert Strauss, ed., *Jewish Immigrants of the Nazi Period in the USA*, 6 vols. (New York and Munich, 1978–87). Intellectuals from Vienna appear in the pages of Paul Hofmann's *Viennese* (New York, 1988).

3. Fritz Haber, who had left the Jewish faith, was exempted from automatic dismissal by reason of his service as gas officer in the First World War, but he chose emigration because his Jewish assistants could not remain

in his laboratory. He died in 1934. One half-Jew, Gustav Herz, severely wounded in 1915, continued to work in Siemens & Halske. Another, Niels Bohr, escaped from Denmark in 1943. Otto Warburg returned to Germany after the war. Albert Einstein had already emigrated in 1932. The impact of refugee physicists, chemists, and mathematicians on the atomic bomb project in the United States is described by Richard Rhodes, *The Making of the Atomic Bomb* (New York, 1986).

4. Facsimile of Bloch's letter to the University of Leipzig Philosophical Faculty in Manfred Unger and Herbert Lang, eds., *Juden in Leipzig* (Leipzig, 1988), no pagination.

5. *Matter of Marburg v. Cole*, Court of Appeals of New York, 1941, 286 NY 202, 36 N.E. 2d 113. In the matter of tests imposed on refugee physicians, see Eric Kohler, "Relicensing Central European Physicians in the United States, 1933–1945," *Simon Wiesenthal Center Annual*, vol. 6 (1989), pp. 3–32.

6. Wolfgang Benz, ed., *Das Tagebuch der Herta Nathorff* (Frankfurt am Main, 1988).

7. Berghahn, *German-Jewish Refugees in England*, p. 84, citing a memoir by Dr. Stephen Westman.

8. Nathan Reingold, "Refugee Mathematicians in the United States of America, 1933–1941, Reception and Reactions," *Annals of Science*, vol. 38 (1981), pp. 313–38.

9. On Tucholsky, see German Information Center, *The Week in Germany*, January 19, 1990.

10. Berghahn, *German-Jewish Refugees in England*, pp. 119–20.

11. Renate Bridenthal in "Fragment of a German-Jewish Heritage in Four 'Americans,' " *American Jewish Archives*, vol. 40 (1988), pp. 365–84. Bridenthal, then a child in this family of four, became a professor of history.

11: MEN AND WOMEN

1. Konrad Kwiet, "Nach dem Pogrom: Stufen der Ausgrenzung," in Wolfgang Benz, ed., *Die Juden in Deutschland 1933–1945* (Munich, 1988), p. 611. Kwiet cites a memoir by Joel König, whose mother made the remark.

2. Undated report of Einsatzgruppe A/Staff/II in Byelorussia, Latvian Central State Historical Archives, Fond 1025, Opis 1, Folder 3.

3. Felix Gruenberger, "The Jewish Refugees in Shanghai," *Jewish Social Studies*, vol. 12 (1950), pp. 329–48.

4. Yitzhak Arad, *Ghetto in Flames* (New York, 1982), pp. 147–48.

5. Lucjan Dobroszycki, ed., *The Chronicle of the Lodz Ghetto, 1940–1944*

(New Haven, 1944), entry of January 10–13, 1942, pp. 120–21. The rabbinate was "authorized" to grant the divorces.

6. Liebman Hersch, "Jewish Population Trends in Europe," in Jewish Encyclopedic Handbooks, *The Jewish People Past and Present* (New York, 1948), vol. 2, p. 2. Data for Germany in *Jüdisches Nachrichtenblatt* (Berlin), November 10, 1939.

7. Adam Czerniakow (Chairman of the Jewish Council in the Warsaw Ghetto) to Heinz Auerswald (Ghetto Kommissar), February 18, 1942, enclosing a statistical report for 1941, Zentrale Stelle der Landesjustizverwaltungen in Ludwigsburg, Akten Auerswald, 365e.

8. Statistical report apparently prepared by the Jewish Council in the Lodz Ghetto for the period covering May 1, 1940, to June 30, 1942, YIVO Institute, Lodz Ghetto Collection No. 58.

9. Dobroszycki, *Chronicle of the Lodz Ghetto*, after p. 103.

10. *Ibid.*, entry of June 28, 1942, pp. 214–15.

11. Statistical report, YIVO Institute, Lodz Ghetto Collection No. 58.

12. Yisrael Gutman, *The Jews of Warsaw, 1939–1943* (Bloomington, Ind., 1942), p. 271, citing *Wiadomosci* of December 1942.

13. Statistical report, YIVO Institute, Lodz Ghetto Collection No. 58.

14. Men were 57 percent of all the deportees from France: Serge Klarsfeld, *Le mémorial de la deportation des Juifs de France* (Paris, 1978). In Italy, 53 percent of the deportees ascertained by name were men: Liliana Picciotto Fargion, *Il libro della memoria* (Milan, 1991), p. 27. On the transports from Belgium men were 51 percent: Serge Klarsfeld and Maxime Steinberg, *Mémorial de la deportation des Juifs de Belgique* (New York, 1982). Among the much larger number of victims in Central and Eastern Europe, women must be assumed to have outnumbered men. Precise ratios, however, are difficult to calculate. The Soviet Union, for example, had a census in January 1939 showing a Jewish population of 3,020,000, including a surplus of 142,000 women. In 1959, there were 2,269,000 Jews, including some survivors in annexed regions. In terms of proportions only, the surplus of women should have been 110,000. Actually it was 207,000: see Mordechai Altshuler, *Soviet Jewry since the Second World War* (New York, 1987), pp. 89–90. This result does not mean that the toll of the men in the catastrophe was disproportionately heavy. It does mean that one must take into account a considerable but as yet undetermined number of men who died in the Red Army and in postwar Soviet labor camps.

15. On Auschwitz, see Danuta Czech, "Kalendarium der Ereignisse im Konzentrationslager Auschwitz-Birkenau," *Hefte von Auschwitz*, particu-

larly vols. 7 and 8 (1964). Alexander Donat compiled a list of Treblinka survivors: see his *Treblinka* (New York, 1979), pp. 284–91. On Sobibor, see the statement of Abraham Margulies in Miriam Novitch, ed., *Sobibor* (New York, 1980), p. 64.

12: MIXED MARRIAGES

1. Definitions of mixed marriages vary. The criterion for Nazi Germany was descent. For the Soviet government it was nationality, and for other countries religion. In prewar Poland, those areas that had been Russian or Austro-Hungarian in 1914 were covered by legal provisions allowing only religious marriage ceremonies. A conversion by one of the prospective partners to the religion of the other was, therefore, a prerequisite for the marriage, and the resulting union was not regarded as "mixed." Early intermarriage rates in central and western Europe are listed by Felix Theilhaber, *Der Untergang der deutschen Juden* (Munich, 1911), pp. 103–110. Some of these rates for 1926–1927 are tabulated by Arthur Ruppin, *Soziologie der Juden* (Berlin, 1930), vol. 1, p. 213. For the USSR in the interwar period there are some data in Mordechai Altshuler, *Soviet Jewry since the Second World War* (New York, 1987), pp. 24–26. Mixed marriage statistics for Germany (within the frontiers of 1937), Austria, and Bohemia-Moravia, as of December 31, 1942, are in the report by SS statistician Richard Korherr to Heinrich Himmler, April 19, 1943, Nuremberg trials document NO-5193. Netherlands statistics are in reports of the Security Police in the Netherlands, March 20, 1943, and January 15, 1944, National Archives of the United States, Record Group 242, T 175, Roll 671. On Denmark in October 1943, see Hugo Valentin, "Rescue and Relief Activities in Behalf of Jewish Victims of Nazism in Scandinavia," *YIVO Annual of Jewish Social Science*, vol. 3 (1953), p. 239. An overall figure for German-dominated Europe is difficult to estimate, but it is likely to have exceeded 100,000.

2. Charles Cruikshank. *The German Occupation of the Channel Islands* (London, 1975), pp. 197, 203–204.

3. Annual report of the Elder of the Jewish Council Josef Löwenherz in Vienna, January 22, 1945, Yad Vashem Document O 30/5. Circular signed by Karl Oppenheimer (Steward of the remnant Jewish community in Frankfurt), February 8, 1945, in Kommission zur Erforschung der Geschichte der Frankfurter Juden, *Dokumente zur Geschichte der Frankfurter Juden 1933–1945* (Frankfurt, 1963), p. 531.

4. Befehlshaber (Commander) of Security Police in the Netherlands Wilhelm Harster, to offices under his jurisdiction, May 6, 1943, Eichmann trial Israel Police document 1356.

5. Kurt Jakob Ball-Kaduri, "Berlin wird Judenfrei: Die Juden in Berlin in den Jahren 1942/1943," *Jahrbuch für die Geschichte Mittel- und Ostdeutschlands*, vol. 22 (1973), pp. 196–241, particularly pp. 212–14, 221–22. Clandestine photographs of the demonstrations were taken by a Jewish photographer, Abraham Pisarek. Sybil Milton, "The Camera as Weapon: Documentary Photography and the Holocaust," *Simon Wiesenthal Center Annual*, vol. 1 (1984), pp. 45–68, on p. 54.

6. Judgment against Friedrich Bosshammer in a Berlin court, April 11, 1972 (500) 1 Ks 1/71 (RSHA) (26/71).

7. Situation report of the Kommandeur of Security Police in Lithuania for January 1943, Lithuanian Central State Historical Archives, Fond 1399, Opis 1, Folder 32.

8. Text of the unsigned and undated letter to the German Party/FS, in the original Hungarian and German translation, in the file of the German Security Service in Vienna, National Archives Record Group 242, T 175, Roll 583.

9. Diary of Sarra Gleykh, entry of October 18, 1941, in Ilya Ehrenburg and Vasily Grossman, eds., *The Black Book* (New York, 1981), pp. 70–76, on p. 72. Gleykh describes the death of a Jewish woman and her half-Jewish child.

10. Judgment of a court in Bonn against Gustav Hermann Sorge and Wilhelm Schubert, February 6, 1959, 8 Ks 1/58.

11. Judgment of a Hamburg court against P. and his sister-in-law for denunciation, May 11, 1948 (50) 17/48, in Adelheid L. Rüter-Ehlermann and C. F. Rüter, eds., *Justiz und NS-Verbrechen*, vol. 2 (Amsterdam, 1969), pp. 491–97.

12. Philip Mechanicus, *Year of Fear* (New York, 1968).

13. Slottke to Zoepf, July 29, 1942, and notation of August 4, 1942, National Archives Record Group 242, T 175, Roll 671.

14. H. G. Adler, *Der verwaltete Mensch* (Tübingen, 1974), pp. 337–39.

15. Ibid., pp. 697–98.

16. Max Wagner's letter to Interior Minister Frick, August 5, 1942 (typewritten date changed in handwriting to September 26, 1942), and subsequent Gestapo correspondence, in the Düsseldorf Hauptstaatsarchiv through the courtesy of Konrad Kwiet.

17. The natural children of a German father were protected, even if they were Jewish, so long as they lived with him. See the circular by Eichmann's deputy, Rolf Günther, February 20, 1943, Israel Police document 1282.

18. Jochen Klepper, *Unter dem Schatten Deiner Flügel* (Stuttgart, 1956–1959). The book is a slightly shortened version of his diary from April 1932

to December 10, 1942, edited by Benno Mascher. The meetings with Frick and Eichmann are described on pp. 1129–33. Frederick William I (1688–1740), who built the Prussian army, was the father of Frederick the Great.

13: CHILDREN

1. See Arthur Ruppin, *The Jews in the Modern World* (London, 1934), pp. 100–102.

2. Statistical report in the YIVO Institute, Lodz Ghetto Collection No. 58.

3. Organization chart of the Lodz Ghetto, August 20, 1940, Wi/ID 1.40. Original once located in the former Federal Records Center in Alexandria, Virginia.

4. Lucjan Dobroszycki, ed. *The Chronicle of the Lodz Ghetto* (New Haven, Conn., 1984), entry for June 8, 1942, pp. 214–15.

5. Rumkowski's speech, October 17, 1943, *ibid.*, pp. 399–400.

6. Adam Czerniakow (Chairman of the Jewish Council of Warsaw) to Heinz Auerswald (Ghetto Kommissar), February 12, 1942, enclosing a statistical report for 1941, Zentrale Stelle der Landesjustizverwaltungen in Ludwigsburg, Akten Auerswald, 365 e.

7. Raul Hilberg, Stanislaw Staron, and Josef Kermisz, eds., *The Warsaw Diary of Adam Czerniakow* (Briarcliff Manor, N.Y., 1979), entry for September 5, 1941, p. 277.

8. Czerniakow to Auerswald, report for January 1942, February 6, 1942, Zentrale Stelle, Polen Red No. 3650, pp. 546–559.

9. Marian Fuks, ed., *Adama Czerniakowa dziennik getta Warszawskiego* (Warsaw, 1983), facsimile on p. 252.

10. Hilberg, Staron, and Kermisz, eds., *Warsaw Diary*, entries for September 5 and November 8, 1941, pp. 276–77; June 1 and 7, 1942, pp. 361, 363–64; April 20 and May 22, 1942, pp. 345, 357–358.

11. Diary of a nurse from the Warsaw Ghetto underground archives "Oneg Shabbat" in Joseph Kermish, ed., *To Live with Honor and to Die with Honor* (Jerusalem, 1986), pp. 405–406.

12. Natan Kosinski, "The Profile of the Jewish Child," November 1, 1941, *ibid.*, pp. 370–91. Kosinski was an educator.

13. Report of the Jewish Association for Self-Help (JSS) for February 1942, *ibid.*, pp. 326–31.

14. Kosinski, "Profile," *ibid.*, p. 377.

15. Statistical report by Czerniakow, February 12, 1942, Zentrale Stelle, Akten Auerswald 365 e.

16. Hilberg, Staron, and Kermisz, eds., *Warsaw Diary*, entry for July 1942, pp. 375–77.

17. *Ibid.*, entry for October 11, 1941, p. 287.

18. H. G. Adler, *Theresienstadt* (Tübingen, 1960), pp. 553–59.

19. Yitzhak Arad, *Ghetto in Flames* (New York, 1982), p. 319.

20. See, for example, the report of the Slovak Jewish Council/Division for Special Tasks in the Novaky transit camp, June 12, 1942, Yad Vashem Document M-5(18)7.

21. Statement by Martha Mosse (Director of the Housing Office), July 23–24, 1958, Leo Baeck Institute, AR 7183.

22. Serge Klarsfeld, *Memorial to the Jews Deported from France* (New York, 1983), p. xv.

23. Hillel Kieval, "Legality and Resistance in Vichy France: The Rescue of Jewish Children," *Proceedings of the American Philosophical Society*, vol. 124 (1983), pp. 339–66, on pp. 357–58.

24. Klarsfeld, *Memorial to the Jews Deported from France*, p. xxv.

25. Serge Klarsfeld and Maxime Steinberg, *Mémorial de la deportation des Juifs de Belgique* (Brussels and New York, 1982).

26. Testimony of Dr. Aharon Peretz, May 4, 1961, English transcript of the trial of Adolf Eichmann before the District Court in Jerusalem, mimeographed, sess. 28, pp. Nn1, OO, OO2. Dr. Peretz estimated that thirteen hundred children were caught.

27. Dobroszycki, *The Chronicle of the Lodz Ghetto*, entry of July 2, 1942, p. 218.

28. *Ibid.*, entries for September 1 and 14, 1942, pp. 248–55. Rumkowski's speech of September 4, 1942, is in Alan Adelson and Robert Lapides, eds., *Lodz Ghetto* (New York, 1989), pp. 328–31.

29. *United States v. Bohdan Kozij*, 540 F. Supp. 25 (1982).

30. Klarsfeld and Steinberg, *Mémorial de la deportation des Juifs de Belgique*.

31. Elie Wiesel, *Night* (New York: 1969), pp. 40–42.

32. Claude Lanzmann, *Shoah* (New York, 1985), pp. 3–5, 96, 103–105.

33. Report by Standartenführer (Colonel) Karl Jäger, December 1, 1941, Institut für Zeitgeschichte, Munich, Fb 85/2.

34. Testimony by Dr. Peretz, May 4, 1961, Eichmann trial transcipt, sess. 28 p. Nn1.

35. Testimony of the mother, Mrs. Rivka Yosselevska, May 8, 1961, Eichmann trial transcript, sess. 30, pp. L1–N1. Mrs. Yosselevska, wounded, crawled out of the pit. Small children, also wounded, escaped from the grave as well but, not knowing where to go, were rounded up and shot.

14: CHRISTIAN JEWS

1. For Hungary, see *Donauzeitung* (Belgrade), August 15, 1944, p. 3. For estimates respecting Germany and Austria, see the memorandum by the Jewish Reichsvereinigung of November 11, 1941, and the letter by Josef Löwenherz (Jewish Community in Vienna) to Paul Eppstein (Reichsvereinigung in Berlin), November 14, 1941, both in Leo Baeck Institute Microfilm Roll 66. The Bohemian-Moravian figure is reported by the American Jewish Committee, *The Jewish Communities in Nazi Europe*, reprint of 1944 edition (New York, 1982), section on Czechoslovakia. The Romanian figure, which is a precise 4,631, is taken from a census of the Jewish population in Old Romania and reported by the Jewish Centrala in Yad Vashem Document M-20. On the Netherlands, see the Security Police report of March 20, 1943, noting 1,572 Protestants (following the deportation of 96 of them in the previous year), National Archives of the United States, Record Group 242, T 175, Roll 671. Catholic Jews in the Netherlands numbered about seven hundred: Henry L. Mason, "Testing Human Bonds within Nations: Jews in the Occupied Netherlands," *Political Science Quarterly*, vol. 99 (1984), pp. 328–29. On Italy, see Sergio della Pergola, "Appunti sulla demografia della persecuzione antiebraica in Italia," *La Rassegna di Mensile*, vol. 18 (1981), pp. 120–37.

2. During the nineteenth century, conversions numbered 85,000 in Imperial Russia, 45,000 in Austria-Hungary, and 23,000 in Germany. Arthur Ruppin, *Soziologie der Juden*, vol. 1 (Berlin, 1930), p. 297.

3. See the discussion and planning concerning the Evangelical Jews in the Security Police report of March 20, 1943, National Archives Record Group 242, T 175, Roll 671.

4. Security Service in Vienna to Reich Security Main Office III-B (Standartenführer Ehlich), August 1942, T 175, Roll 583.

5. Files of the Reich Association of non-Aryan Christians in the Staatsarchiv Leipzig (German Democratic Republic), Collection Polizeipräsident Leipzig V, Folders 4537 and 4538.

6. Raul Hilberg, Stanislaw Staron, and Josef Kermisz, eds., *The Warsaw Diary of Adam Czerniakow* (Briarcliff Manor, N.Y., 1979), entry of May 29, 1940, containing the text of the letter from Aleksander Mietelnikow to Norbert Goldfeil, chief of the Jewish Community's Labor Battalion, p. 155.

7. Alexandre Safran, *Resisting the Storm* (Jerusalem, 1987), on Nandor Gingold, p. 87.

8. Randolph Braham, *The Politics of Genocide* (New York, 1981), pp. 450–51, 462–66.

9. The German Minister in Hungary, Edmund Veesenmayer, to the Foreign Office in Berlin, November 21, 1944, Nuremberg trials document NG-4987.

10. See the unsigned report of an agent in German service (Matei Grünberg-Willman, a functionary of the Jewish Centrala) in the files of Hauptsturmführer Gustav Richter (Eichmann's representative in Bucharest), September 1, 1942, and Richter's memorandum of the same date, National Archives Record Group 242, T 175, Roll 657. Von Neumann, principal shareholder of the textile firm Aradana, was thirty-one years old. When he was arrested after the war, the Jewish leader Wilhelm Filderman requested Chief Rabbi Safran to intercede for him: Safran, *Resisting the Storm*, p. 87.

11. Yisrael Gutman, *The Jews of Warsaw* (Bloomington, Ind., 1982), p. 62, citing the *Gazeta Zydowska* of May 12, 1941.

12. Stanislaw Adler, *In the Warsaw Ghetto* (Jerusalem, 1982), p. 169.

13. *Ibid.*, pp. 171–72. For living conditions of prominent converts in the ghetto, see portions of Ludwik Hirszfeld's memoirs in Wladislaw Bartoszewski and Zofia Lewin, eds., *Righteous among the Nations* (London, 1969), pp. 332–37.

14. Bartoszewski and Lewin, *Righteous*, pp. 332–37.

15. On Hirszfeld and Stein, see Hilberg, Staron, and Kermisz, *Warsaw Diary*, passim.

16. Adler, *In the Warsaw Ghetto*, pp. 90, 169–72, 176, 263. Hilberg, Staron, and Kermisz, *Warsaw Diary*, entries by Czerniakow of July 2, 1941, p. 254, and July 27, 1941, pp. 262–63.

17. On Szerynski's career, see Adler, *In the Warsaw Ghetto*, pp. 23, 50, 52, 62, 107, 108, 110, 203, and Hilberg, Staron, and Kermisz, *Warsaw Diary*, passim. The incident with the porters is described in Stefan Ernest, "Treci front," pp. 143–45, unpublished ms., through the courtesy of Lucjan Dobroszycki.

18. Cordelia Edvardson, *Gebranntes Kind sucht das Feuer* (Munich, 1987). See also her *Die Welt zusammenfügen* (Munich, 1991).

15: THE ADVANTAGED, THE STRUGGLERS, AND THE DISPOSSESSED

1. Isaiah Trunk, *Judenrat* (New York, 1972), p. 357.

2. Stanislaw Adler, *In the Warsaw Ghetto* (Jerusalem, 1982), pp. 91–216, particularly 104, 144–49, 183–84, 191–95. Adler wrote this memoir while still in hiding. He handed the manuscript to a Jewish woman who had survived with him and who had decided to emigrate. Adler, alone, re-

mained in Poland, where he held a relatively high position in the pre-Communist Polish Government. On July 11, 1946, he shot himself. See the introduction by Ludmilla Zeldowicz, a neurologist, pp. xi–xviii.

3. Samuel Willenberg, *Surviving Treblinka* (Oxford, 1989), p. 129.

4. For Germany, see the correspondence in the Zentrales Staatsarchiv Potsdam, Collection Reichsvereinigung 75 c Re 1, Folder 50. For the Netherlands, see Jacob Presser, *The Destruction of the Dutch Jews* (New York, 1969), pp. 202–211.

5. Report by Martha Mosse, June 8, 1942, Collection Reichsvereinigung 75 c Re 1, Folder 50.

6. Lilienthal to Eppstein, June 7, 1942, *ibid.*

7. Korherr to Otto Hunsche (Eichmann section in the Reich Security Main Office) and Walter Stock (Berlin Gestapo), June 12, 1943; Korherr to Himmler, June 12, 1943; Korherr to Rudolf Brandt (Himmler's Adjutant), June 19, 1943; all in National Archives Record Group 242, T 175, Roll 68. Korherr was prepared to go to Theresienstadt to continue his collaboration with Simon but was told that such a trip was impossible.

8. Y. H. Grabski, T. Katchinski, and M. Alter to Yitzchak Giterman (local representative of the Joint Distribution Committee), February 5, 1942, in Joseph Kermish, ed., *To Live with Honor and Die with Honor* (Jerusalem, 1986), pp. 417–18.

9. Security Service in Slovakia (signed Wahl) to Security Service in Vienna (Hauptsturmführer Herrmann), April 12, 1943, National Archives of the United States, Record Group 242, T 175, Roll 583.

10. Report by Feldkommandantur 239 for October 15–November 5, 1941, dated November 24, 1941, in J. J. Kondufor et al., eds., *Die Geschichte Warnt* (Kiev, 1986), p. 63.

11. See the population statistics in the files of the Generalkommissar White-Ruthenia, dated January 1, 1943, U.S. Holocaust Memorial Museum Archives, Record Group 22.03 (Belarus Central State Archives), Roll 12, Fond 370, Opis 1, Folder 1432. Statistics of physicians, in Gebietskommissar Baranowicze/Sozialamt to Generalkommissar/IIb, February 13, 1942, and instructions for reduction of Jewish physicians at liberty, in Hauptkommissar Baranowicze/IIe (signed Dr. Wiechmann) to Gebietskommissar Baranowicze, March 12, 1942, in *ibid.*, Roll 11, Fond 370, Opis 1, Folder 138. The Hauptkommissariat Baranowicze contained several Gebiete, including the Gebiet Baranowicze.

12. H. G. Adler, *Theresienstadt* (Tübingen, 1960), pp. 504, 509.

13. Text in large excerpt of a presentation to a ghetto medical seminar by Dr. Josef Reiss, March 4, 1943, *ibid.*, pp. 497–99. Later, "prominent" per-

sons were to receive special attention. See the directive of the Theresienstadt Ghetto Health Division, February 19, 1944, in H. G. Adler, ed., *Die verheimlichte Wahrheit* (Tübingen, 1958), pp. 210–11.

14. Abraham Lewin, *A Cup of Tears* (Oxford, 1988), p. 101.

15. Adina Blady Szwajger, *I Remember Nothing More* (New York, 1990), pp. 52–58. The author was a courier for the underground in 1943–1944. During the time in hiding she performed euthanasia on a woman who had run, shouting in Yiddish, into the street; *ibid.*, p. 150. After the war, the author finished her studies and practiced medicine in Poland, where she remained. She wrote her memoirs in the late 1980s.

16. Robert Jay Lifton, *The Nazi Doctors* (New York, 1986), pp. 214–21.

17. *Ibid.*, pp. 221–22.

18. On Warsaw, see Adam Czerniakow, Chairman of the Jewish Council, to Ludwig Leist, German Stadtkommandant of the City of Warsaw, May 21, 1940, Yad Vashem Microfilm JM 1113. On Lublin, see the annual report of the Jewish Council for September 1939–September 1940, Archiwum Panstwowe w Lublinie, Collection Judenrat, sygn. 8, karta 705–65. See also Trunk, *Judenrat*, pp. 379–80.

19. See the Romanian General Staff memorandum signed by General N. Mazarini and Colonel Borcescu, February 7, 1942, National Archives Record Group 242, T 175, Roll 663.

20. Contemporaneous written comments by Henryk Rosen for the Jewish underground archives, in Kermish, *To Live with Honor*, pp. 747–52, on p. 749.

21. Adler, *In the Warsaw Ghetto*, p. 53.

22. Rosen in Kermish, *To Live with Honor*, p. 749.

23. Staatssekretär Friedrich Syrup of the Labor Ministry to the Interior Ministry, January 3, 1941, Nuremberg trials document NG-1143.

24. See the detailed figures, fixed for age and training, as of March 1941, in the files of the Lublin Judenrat, Archiwum Panstwowe w Lublinie, Judenrat, sygn. 6, karta 80.

25. Lucjan Dobroszycki, ed., *The Chronicle of the Lodz Ghetto* (New Haven, Conn., 1984), entry for October 20, 1942, p. 272.

26. *Ibid.*, entry for November 9, 1942, p. 287.

27. Adler, *In the Warsaw Ghetto*, p. 253.

28. Undated report by the Jewish Council (1940), Archiwum Panstwowe w Lublinie, Judenrat, sygn. 6, karta 288.

29. Report by the Fifth Police Precinct in Minsk, September 23, 1942, U.S. Holocaust Museum Archives, Record Group 22.03 (Belarus Central State Archives), Roll 11, Fond 370, Opis 1, Folder 480. The Hauptwach-

mann (Police Sergeant) thought that in the winter many Jews would not be able to work without shoes and that delivery of wooden shoes might be appropriate.

30. Order by Wehrmachtsortskommandantur Minsk (signed Generalmajor Sperling), December 5, 1942, U.S. Holocaust Memorial Museum Archives, Record Group 22.03 (Belarus Central State Archives), Roll 11, Fond 379, Opis 2, Folder 45. The Jews referred to in the order were working for the German army, which paid wages to the German city administration and deducted the ten pfennigs from the wages.

31. Lewin, A Cup of Tears, entry of May 27, 1942, p. 100.

32. Hilberg, Staron, and Kermisz, eds., Warsaw Diary, entry of July 11, 1942, p. 378.

33. Report by the Lublin District/Population and Welfare, May 5, 1942, German Federal Archives R 102 II/24.

34. Trunk, Judenrat, pp. 356, 382.

35. For the implications of living with insufficient food, see Leonard Tushnet, The Uses of Adversity (New York, 1966), p. 62 ff. The author was a physician.

36. Report by Jewish Social Self-Help, February 1942, in Kermish, To Live with Honor, pp. 326–31.

37. Adler, In the Warsaw Ghetto, p. 254.

38. Ibid., pp. 116–17.

16: THE UNADJUSTED

1. Konrad Kwiet, "The Ultimate Refuge—Suicide in the Jewish Community under the Nazis," Leo Baeck Institute Yearbook, vol. 19 (1984), pp. 136–67.

2. Diary of Ruth Andreas-Friedrich, entry of September 2, 1942, in Gerhard Schoenberner, ed., Zeugen sagen aus (Gütersloh, n.d.), pp. 284–85.

3. Testimony by Georges Wellers, May 9, 1961, trial of Adolf Eichmann before a Jerusalem court, English transcript, sess. 32, p. M1.

4. Lucjan Dobroszycki, ed., The Chronicle of the Lodz Ghetto 1941–1944 (New Haven, Conn., 1984), entries of July 17 and 18, 1944, pp. 529–30.

5. Judgment of a German court in Hannover against Johannes von Dollen, Johannes Friedrich Rathje, and others, April 10, 1978, 1 Ks 1/75. The movement of the fifty-seven families is noted by Richard Türk, Director of the Population and Welfare Division of the Lublin District, in his report of April 7, 1941, Jüdisches Historisches Institut Warschau: Faschismus—Getto—Massenmord (Berlin, 1961), p. 271.

6. West German investigative report about Police Battalion 306, Police Regiment 16, Cavalry Police Battalion (Abteilung) II (including squadron in Janow), and Security Police Post in Pinsk, 4 Js 901/62.

7. Claude Lanzmann, *Shoah* (New York, 1985), pp. 128–32.

8. Communications by the Regierungspräsident Springorum of Katowice, February 24, 1943, and General of Order Police Otto Winkelmann, April 6, 1943, in the files of the Order Police in Latvia, Latvian Central State Historical Archives, Fond 83, Opis 1, Folder 117.

9. Report of Police Battalion 24/Company 7 to the Kommandeur of Order Police in Galicia, September 24, 1942, Zentrale Stelle der Landesjustizverwaltungen, Collection UdSSR, vol. 410, pp. 508–10.

10. See Rudolf Vrba and Alan Bestic, *I Cannot Forgive* (New York, 1964), and Vrba's account in Lanzmann's *Shoah, passim*. On the escape and death of Vruzen Vrba, see Danuta Czech, *Kalendarium der Ereignisse im Konzentrationslager Auschwitz-Birkenau 1939–1945* (Reinbek bei Hamburg, 1989), entries of May 7 and 14, 1943, pp. 487, 494–95. Rudolf Vrba's escape is noted by Czech in the entry of April 7, 1944, *ibid.*, p. 751.

11. The postcard, written in Yiddish, is contained in German translation in the report of the Propaganda Division of the Radom District, October 3, 1942, YIVO Institute, Document Occ E 2-2. It was highly disturbing to the German recipients.

12. The destruction of the records in Belgium occurred at the end of July 1942. Maxime Steinberg, "The Trap of Legality: The Association of the Jews of Belgium," Proceedings of the Third Yad Vashem Historical Conference, *Patterns of Jewish Leadership in Nazi Europe 1933–1945* (Jerusalem, 1979), pp. 353–76, on pp. 363–65. The interception of the train on Belgian soil, April 19, 1943, is noted by Serge Klarsfeld and Maxime Steinberg, *Mémorial de la deportation des Juifs de Belgique* (Brussels and New York, 1982), no page numeration.

13. Excerpt from a statement by the witness Vladislovas Silvestravicius, a truck driver who transported older and infirm Jews to the shooting site, in *Judgment of United States v. Kungys*, September 28, 1943, 571 F. Supp. 1104, on 1117–19. The killing operation in Kedainiai was recorded in a report by Einsatzkommando 3, signed by Standartenführer Karl Jäger, December 1, 1941, Institute für Zeitgeschichte, Fb 85/2.

14. See in the main Yitzhak Arad, *Belzec, Sobibor, Treblinka* (Bloomington, Ind., 1987), pp. 270–364.

15. Jadwiga Bezwinska, ed., *Amidst a Nightmare of Crime* (Auschwitz Museum, 1973), pp. 66, 154–78.

16. See the basic story in Yitzhak Arad, *Ghetto in Flames* (New York, 1982). The reaction to the proclamation by Gens is noted by Leonard Tushnet, *The Pavement of Hell* (New York, 1972), p. 177.

17. For the fate of the Bialystok Ghetto, see the detailed description in the judgment of a German court in Bielefeld against Wilhelm Altenloh and others, April 14, 1967, 5 Ks 1/65. The eight trains projected for the February 1943 deportations are listed in the circular by Karl Jakobi of the German Railways' Generalbetriebsleitung Ost/PW, January 16, 1943, in U.S. Holocaust Memorial Museum Archives, Record Group 22.03 (Belarus Central State Archives, Roll 2, Fond 378, Opis 1, Folder 784. The text of Tenenbaum-Tamaroff's proclamation is in Jüdisches Historisches Institut Warschau, *Faschismus—Getto—Massenmord*, pp. 558–59, and in Bronia Klibanski, "The Underground Archives of the Bialystok Ghetto," *Yad Vashem Studies*, vol. 2 (1958), pp. 295–329, on pp. 328–29. The institute dates the proclamation August 16, 1943, but Klibanski notes that the document was drafted by Tenenbaum-Tamaroff in January 1943 and that it was not published. Her text contains the words indicating that it was to be used when the moment came. Excerpts from Tenenbaum-Tamaroff's diary are in the judgment and in Klibanski's article. Verbatim excerpts from the discussion of February 27, 1943, are in Yitzhak Arad, Yisrael Gutman, and Abraham Margaliot, eds., *Documents of the Holocaust* (Jerusalem, 1981), pp. 296–301. The description of the fighting at the fence is taken from the testimony of Liza Czapnik and others, in *Faschismus—Getto—Massenmord*, pp. 562–64.

18. Raul Hilberg, Stanislaw Staron, and Josef Kermisz, eds., *The Warsaw Diary of Adam Czerniakow* (Briarcliff Manor, N.Y., 1979), entries from October 27, 1941, noting anxiety with increasing frequency to July 1942. Ringelblum's entry for June 1942, in Joseph Kermish, "Emmanuel Ringelblum's Notes hitherto Unpublished," *Yad Vashem Studies*, vol. 7 (1968), pp. 173–83, on p. 178.

19. Hilberg, Kermisz, and Staron, *Warsaw Diary*, entry of April 19, 1942, pp. 344–45.

20. Report by Tenenbaum-Tamaroff, April 1943, on the meeting in Warsaw a year earlier, and excerpt from Hersh Berlinski's memoirs summarizing the meeting of June 1942, in Ber Mark, *Uprising in the Warsaw Ghetto* (New York, 1975), pp. 100–103.

21. Text of Anielewicz's letter in Arad, Gutman, and Margaliot, *Documents of the Holocaust*, pp. 315–16. German forces and casualties are described by the German commander, SS and Police Leader Jürgen Stroop, in his report to Higher SS and Police Leader Krüger, May 16, 1943, Nuremberg trials document PS-1061. The genesis of the revolt is described in detail

by Yisrael Gutman, *The Jews of Warsaw 1939–1945* (Bloomington, Ind., 1982).

17: The Survivors

1. Erikkos Sevillias, *Athens-Auschwitz* (Athens, Greece, 1983), pp. 1–2.

2. Samuel L. Tenenbaum, *Zloczow Memoir* (New York, 1986), p. 255.

3. Rudolf Vrba and Alan Bestic, *I Cannot Forgive* (New York, 1964), p. 52.

4. Statement by Liuba Daniel, November 1965, Yad Vashem Oral History Collection, 2568/74.

5. Statement by Mitzi Abeles, 1958, Yad Vashem Oral History Collection, 530/32.

6. Sevillias, *Athens-Auschwitz*, p. 56.

7. Yitzhak Arad, *The Partisan* (New York, 1979), p. 53 ff.

8. Vrba, *I Cannot Forgive*, p. 78.

9. Sevillias, *Athens-Auschwitz*, p. 78.

10. One should note two Nobel Prize winners in the sciences among the survivors: the biologist Rita Levi-Montalcini, who belongs to an older generation and who continued her research privately even during the German occupation of Italy, and the chemist Roald Hoffmann, born 1937 in Zloczow, who survived with his mother in hiding, lived in Krakow and displaced persons camps, immigrated to the United States in 1949, and rapidly advanced there to a peak of academic success. In a totally different endeavor, Aaron Lustiger, an adolescent who was hiding in France, adopted the Catholic faith and eventually became Jean-Marie Cardinal Lustiger, Archbishop of Paris.

11. Several survivors became Holocaust researchers. They include H. G. Adler, Philip Friedman, Yitzhak Arad, Yisrael Gutman, Lucjan Dobroszycki, and Nechama Tec.

PART III: BYSTANDERS

18: Nations in Adolf Hitler's Europe

1. Minutes of the conference of November 12, 1938, Nuremberg trials document PS-1816.

2. Coblenzer (signed without first name) to Justice Ministry, November 22, 1934, German Federal Archives in Potsdam, Collection 15.01 Reich Interior Ministry, Folder 27405. His letter was passed on to the Interior Ministry.

3. Hans Klemm, auctioneer, to Oberfinanzpräsident in Leipzig, May

16, 1942, Staatsarchiv (State Archives) in Leipzig, Collection Hans Klemm Versteigerung, Folder 21. A transport of some 625 had left on January 21, 1942, a smaller one of 300 on May 10, 1942. See the correspondence in the Stadtarchiv (City Archives) Leipzig, Collection Sonderregelung für Nicht-arier/Ernährungsamt 6. The suitcases were probably left behind by the January deportees.

4. C. Gwyn Moser, "Jewish *U-Boote* in Austria 1938–1945," *Simon Wiesenthal Center Annual*, vol. 2 (1985), pp. 53–61.

5. Günter Erckens, *Juden in Mönchengladbach* (Mönchengladbach, 1989), vol. 2, pp. 420–33. See also the individual experiences of persons in hiding recorded by Wolfgang Benz, "Überleben im Untergrund," in Volker Dahm et al., eds., *Die Juden in Deutschland 1933–1945* (Munich, 1988), pp. 660–700, 730–32.

6. Generalkommissar Theodor Adrian von Renteln via Reichskommis-sar Lohse to Minister Rosenberg, September 27, 1941, enclosing the mem-orandum of Lithuanian activists of September 15, 1941, YIVO Institute Document Occ E3b-92.

7. Memorandum by Gottlob Berger (SS and Ministry for Eastern Oc-cupied Territories) summarizing a conference attended by Heinrich Himm-ler, Karl Wolff, Hans Adolf Prützmann, Ulrich Greifelt (all in the SS), Alfred Meyer (East Ministry), and Wilhelm Stuckart (Interior Ministry), August 17, 1942, National Archives of the United States, Record Group 242, T 175, Roll 68. The topic was Germanization. Estonians were deemed eligible, Lithuanians not.

8. Speech by Stadtkommissar Cramer of Kaunas at an official gather-ing, February 18, 1944, Nuremberg trials document PS-204.

9. The whipping was quickly discontinued. SS and Police Standortführ-er in Liepaja to Kommandeur of Order Police in Latvia, March 3, 1942, Latvian Central State Historical Archives, Fond 83, Opis 1, Folder 22. Correspondence on segregation of Latvians on trains in June 1942, *ibid.*, Fond 69, Opis la, Folder 1.

10. See the letter by the Lithuanian District physician in Trakai to the German Gebietskommissar in Wilna-Land, July 8, 1942, Lithuanian Central State Historical Archives, Fond 613, Opis 1, Folder 10.

11. See a leaflet attributed by the German Security Police not to Com-munists (who were very few) but to nationalists, in Reich Security Main Office IV-A-1, Operational and Situation Report No. 155, January 14, 1942, Nuremberg trials document NO-3279. A 1943 leaflet with sim-ilar language is included in the monthly report of the Kommandeur of Security Police in Lithuania to the Reich Security Main Office, May 31,

1943, Lithuanian Central State Historical Archives, Fond 1399, Opis 1, Folder 26.

12. SS and Police Standortführer in Liepaja to Kommandeur of Order Police in Latvia, January 19, 1942, Latvian Central State Historical Archives, Fond 83, Opis 1, Folder 22.

13. SS and Police Standortführer in Daugavpils (signed Gendarmerie Leader Wimmer) to Commander of Gendarmerie in Latvia, *ibid.*, Fond 82, Opis 2, Folder 1.

14. Reich Security Main Office IV-A-1, Operational and Situation Report No. 81, September 12, 1941, Nuremberg trials document NO-3154.

15. Order by General der Infanterie (Lieutenant General) Erich Friderici, Commander of Rear Area Army Group South, December 14, 1941, National Archives Record Group 242, T 501, Roll 6.

16. Reich Security Main Office IV-A-1, Operational and Situation Report No. 49, September 25, 1941, Nuremberg trials document NO-3146. See also the report by Section VII (Military Government) of the army's Security Division 213, signed by division commander von Courbiere, August 27, 1941, National Archives Record Group 242, T 501, Roll 34.

17. Reich Security Main Office IV-A-1, Operational and Situation Report No. 191, April 10, 1942, Nuremberg trials document NO-3256.

18. The Gendarmerie-Gebietsführer in Brest-Litovsk (signed by Lieutenant of the Gendarmerie Deuerlein) to the Gendarmerie-Hauptmannschaft in Kobryn, December 5, 1942, German Federal Archives, R 94/7. The action in Samary is reported by the 9th Company of the 15th Police Regiment in Volhynia, November 1, 1942, Zentrale Stelle der Landesjustizverwaltungen, Collection UdSSR 412, pp. 841–42.

19. The principle is enunciated in a circular of the Wirtschaftsstab Ost, the economic agency covering the area under military administration in the occupied USSR, March 1942, Belarus Central State Archives, Fond 393c, Opis 1, Folder 321.

20. Reich Security Main Office IV-A-1, Operational and Situation Report No. 135, November 19, 1941, Nuremberg trials document NO-2832, and Operational and Situation Report No. 191, April 10, 1942, Nuremberg trials document NO-3256.

21. The Mayor of Kiev to the German Stadtkommissar, December 1941, in J. J., Kondufor et al., eds., *Die Geschichte Warnt* (Kiev, 1986), p. 77.

22. Reports by the Economic Inspectorate Ukraine, December 16, 1941; Sixth Army to High Command of the Army/General Staff, December 16, 1941; and Generalmajor (Brigadier General) Nagel (High Command of the Armed Forces/Economy-Armament Office), December 31, 1941, National

Archives Record Group 242, T 77, Roll 1070. The description of the land and the city is in Nagel's report.

23. See, for example, the report by Johann Bölt (undated, probably June 1943), about his trip to the Begomel area, following the anti-partisan operation "Cottbus," U.S. Holocaust Memorial Museum Archives, Record Group 22.03 (Belarus Central State Archives), Roll 4, Fond 359, Opis 1, Folder 8.

24. See the testimony by Alexander Abugov in Nusan Porter, ed., *Jewish Partisans* (Lanham, Md., 1982), vol. 1, pp. 135–51, on p. 136.

25. Reports by the 727th Regiment of the 707th Division, April 2 and 4, 1942, National Archives Record Group 242, T 501, Roll 15. The division was located in the eastern half of the Byelorussian SSR.

26. Such units were sometimes spotted by the Germans. See, for example, a report by Armed Forces Commander White Ruthenia/Ic (Intelligence), September 26, 1942, about a Jewish group numbering 100 to 150 in the woods south of Orla, in U.S. Holocaust Memorial Museum Archives Record Group 22.03 (Belarus Central State Archives), Roll 2, Fond 378, Opis 1, Folder 789. There is a large survivors' literature about these units.

27. See Joseph Marcus, *Social and Political History of the Jews in Poland, 1919–1939* (Berlin, New York, and Amsterdam, 1983).

28. Jan Tomasz Gross, *Polish Society under German Occupation* (Princeton, 1979), particularly pp. 97–103.

29. See the discussion in the Generalgouvernement food conference of September 5, 1941, Frank Diary, National Archives Record Group 238, T 992, Roll 5. Also, Joanna K. M. Hanson, *The Civilian Population and the Warsaw Uprising of 1944* (Cambridge, London, and New York, 1982), pp. 8–43.

30. Marcus, *Social and Political History*, pp. 35 ff., 64 ff., 437 ff.

31. Gross, *Polish Society*, pp. 103–4.

32. Despite gains of space as result of ghetto formation, the Poles were still crowded. Polish Warsaw (population 1 million) was lacking 70,000 apartments. Remarks by Hermann Fribolin (German administration in Warsaw) in the Generalgouvernement meeting in Warsaw on October 14–16, 1941, Frank Diary, National Archives Record Group 238, T 992, Roll 5. In the city of Radom, the norm was a room density of six for Jews, and three for Poles. Remarks by Stadthauptmann Rudolf Pavlu in construction conference of the Generalgouvernement in Krakow, March 19, 1942, Frank Diary, *ibid.*, Roll 6.

33. Report by the Kreishauptmann in Kielce, March 6, 1941, Yad Vashem Microfilm JM 814.

34. Gross, *Polish Society*, pp. 184–86.

35. See the report of Captain Helmut Saur (Commander, 10th Company, 310th Battalion, 15th Police Regiment), October 26, 1942, Zentrale Stelle der Landesjustizverwaltungen, UdSSR 412, pp. 839–40.

36. See the correspondence, December 1942–April 1943, in National Archives Record Group 242, T 175, Roll 38; and the Police conference in the Generalgouvernement, January 25, 1943, Frank Diary, Nuremberg trials document PS-2233.

37. See Wladislaw Bartoszewski and Zofia Lewin, eds., *Righteous among Nations* (London 1968), specifically Bartoszewski's introduction on pp. xliv–l, memoirs on pp. 41–108, and documents on pp. 690–715. See also Yisrael Gutman and Shmuel Krakowski, *Unequal Victims—Poles and Jews during World War Two* (New York, 1986), pp. 252–99.

38. On Wolinski, see Gutman and Krakowski, *Unequal Victims, passim.*

39. *Ibid.*, pp. 143–71.

40. English translation of the texts of the two pamphlets in Jacob Robinson to Stephen Wise and others, November 22, 1943, American Jewish Archives in Cincinnati, World Jewish Congress Collection/IJA Files, Box 2. The estimate of twenty dead was an exaggeration.

41. Gutman and Krakowski, *Unequal Victims*, p. 161. Small detachments of the Armia Krajowa and the Armia Ludowa were fighting at the wall outside. Several Poles were killed in these engagements. There was apparently no coordination between the two Polish forces. The Poles also assisted Jewish fighters escaping from the ghetto at the end of the battle.

42. See the analysis by Richard C. Lukas, *The Forgotten Holocaust: The Poles under German Occupation 1939–1945* (Lexington, Ky., 1986), pp. 76–80, 176.

43. Report by the Kommandeur of the Order Police in the Lublin District, November 4, 1943, Archiwum Panstwowe w Lublinie, Collection Ortskommandantur I/524, sygn. 19. The incident took place in Rechta on November 1, 1943.

44. Note the report by the Order Police in Lublin, June 6, 1943, *ibid.*, sygn. 14, describing an attack by twenty armed "bandits" on a band of twelve Jews in Izbica on June 4. Ten Jews were killed. For a recapitulation of extortions, informing, hunts, and killings, see Gutman and Krakowski, *Unequal Victims*, pp. 204–25.

45. Robinson to officials in the World Jewish Congress, June 28, 1943, American Jewish Archives, World Jewish Congress Collection/Institute of Jewish Affairs—Jacob Robinson Files, U 320, No. 4.

46. Tartakower to World Jewish Congress officials, with a copy to Robinson, July 1, 1943. In the talk, Ciechanowski also stated that he did not

blame the Jews for fighting or for "having at least an illusion of fighting the Germans" in eastern Poland under auspices of the Russians, but he did not think these guerrilla activities very "desirable." *Ibid.*

47. J. C. H. Blom, "The Persecution of the Jews in the Netherlands: A Comparative Western European Perspective," *European History Quarterly*, vol. 19 (1989), pp. 333–51. See also Götz Aly and Karl Heinz Roth, *Die restlose Erfassung* (Berlin, 1984), pp. 64–67.

48. Armament Inspectorate Niederlande/WS to High Command of the Armed Forces/Economy-Armament Office, March 11, 1941, Wi/IA 5.12, folder once located in the Federal Records Center in Alexandria, Virginia. Memoranda by Ernst Wörmann (Foreign Office), February 25 and 26, 1941, Nuremberg trials document NG-2805.

49. In August 1942, a call for demonstrations was unheeded. Report by the intelligence officer of the LXXVIII Army Corps, September 7, 1942, National Archives Record Group 242, T 314, Roll 1614. The occasion, the Queen's birthday on August 31, was to be used for a strike and the closing of shops. Nothing happened.

50. As of August 13, 1944, the number interned for assisting Jews, but not yet charged, was 1,997. Report by Befehlshaber (Commander) of Security Police in the Netherlands, August 15, 1944, National Archives Record Group 242, T 175, Roll 670.

51. Report of the Commander of Security Police for 1942, *ibid.*

52. Report by Zoepf, April 15, 1944, National Archives Record Group 242, T 175, Roll 671.

53. Undated report of the Security Police in the Netherlands, *ibid.*

54. Otto Bene (Foreign Office Representative in the Netherlands) to the Foreign Office, September 11, 1942, March 20 and June 25, 1943, and February 11, 1944, Nuremberg trials document NG-2631.

55. Unsigned report (by Zoepf), April 15, 1944, enclosed in a briefing of the Befehlshaber of Security Police, June 15, 1944, National Archives Record Group 242, T 175, Roll 671. A Dutch policeman, Wilhelm (*sic*) de Groot, who had discovered hidden Jews, was killed in Leiden.

56. Marion P. Pritchard, "It came to pass in those days. . . ," *Sh'ma*, April 27, 1984, pp. 97–102. The half-Jewish mother of the three children had left her family after she could no longer bear the strain.

19: Helpers, Gainers, and Onlookers

1. John F. Sweets, *Choices in Vichy France* (Oxford and New York, 1986), p. 132.

2. In the Galician area of Poland, German private company managers

kept Jewish women as sexual slaves. Report by the Security Service in Galicia (Kommandeur of Security Police/III-A-4) to Obersturmbannführer (Lieutenant Colonel) Karl Gengenbach and Obersturmbannführer Willi Seibert in Berlin and to Standartenführer (Colonel) Heim in Krakow, July 2, 1943, National Archives of the United States Record Group 242, T 175, Roll 575. See also the novel about a Pole and a Jewish woman by Hermann Field and Stanislaw Mierzenski, *Angry Harvest* (New York, 1958).

3. On Schindler, see Thomas Keneally, *Schindler's List* (New York, 1982). On Lvov, see Philip Friedman, *Their Brothers' Keepers* (New York, 1957), p. 207. On Bialystok, see the statement by Liza Czapnik in Jüdisches Historisches Institut Warschau, *Faschismus—Getto—Massenmord* (Berlin, 1961), pp. 500–502.

4. See in particular Nechama Tec, *When Light Pierced the Darkness* (New York and Oxford, 1986); Samuel P. Oliner and Pearl M. Oliner, *The Altruistic Personality* (New York, 1988); and the earlier work by Friedman, *Their Brothers' Keepers*.

5. See Jacob Presser, *The Destruction of the Dutch Jews* (New York, 1969), pp. 381–405.

6. Stadtkommissar Wilhelm Janetzke to Generalkommissar Wilhelm Kube, November 17, 1942, enclosing report by city inspector Herbert Löbel and city employee Werner Plenske, November 16, 1942, and Kube's reply expressing annoyance, November 20, 1942, U.S. Holocaust Memorial Museum Archives, Record Group 22.03 (Belarus Central State Archives), Roll 11, Fond 370, Opis 1, Folder 486.

7. Michael Kater, *Doctors under Hitler* (Chapel Hill, N.C., 1989), pp. 169–72.

8. War Diary, Armament Command Radom, August 24, 1943, Wi/ID 1.37, folder once located in the Federal Records Center in Alexandria, Virginia. Neuendorff in Generalbezirk Latvia to Reichskommissar Ostland/IIh (Finance), December 4, 1941, National Archives Record Group 242, T 459, Roll 21. Large excerpt from the report of a Polish court in Zamosz, October 10, 1945, investigating Belzec, in Adalbert Rückerl, *NS-Vernichtungslager* (Munich, 1977), pp. 143–45.

9. Thirteenth Situation Report of the German Security Service in Žilina, Slovakia, covering events of May 1942 in the Žilina transit camp, National Archives Record Group 242, T 175, Roll 584. The culprits, according to the report, were members of the Slovak Hlinka Guard who mistreated the captive Jews and took from them valuables, clothes, underwear, and shoes.

10. Statement by Jan Piwonski in Claude Lanzmann, *Shoah* (New York, 1986), p. 67.

11. Report by an army inspector in the Generalgouvernement of Poland for July 6–August 21, 1942 (signed Neuling), Yad Vashem Microfilm JM 3499.

12. Statement by Armando Aaron in Lanzmann, *Shoah*, p. 129.

13. Statement by Tibor Vago in Lea Rosh and Eberhard Jäckel, *Der Tod ist ein Meister aus Deutschland* (Hamburg, 1990), p. 289.

14. See the photographs and related German testimony in Ernst Klee, Willi Dressen, and Volker Riess, eds., *"Schöne Zeiten"* (Frankfurt am Main, 1988), pp. 106–8.

15. Judgment of the SS and Police court in Munich against Max Täubner, May 25, 1943, reprinted in large excerpt in *ibid.*, pp. 184–90.

16. Statement by Itzhak Lichtman in Miriam Novitch, *Sobibor* (New York, 1980), pp. 80–85.

17. Statements by the Treblinka survivor Richard Glazar and by several Polish witnesses in Lanzmann, *Shoah*, pp. 34–45, 37.

20: MESSENGERS

1. Elie Wiesel, *Night* (New York, 1969), pp. 15–16, 31–32.

2. The first book was written by Gerstein's friend Helmut Franz, *Kurt Gerstein* (Zurich, 1964). It was followed by two works, originally in French: Saul Friedlander, *Kurt Gerstein—The Ambiguity of Good* (New York, 1969), and Pierre Joffroy, *A Spy for God—The Ordeal of Kurt Gerstein* (New York, 1970). Friedlander relies mainly on documents and letters, Joffroy on interviews. Gerstein's family life and early experiences are described in detail by Joffroy.

3. For Gerstein's descriptions of Belzec, see Friedlander, *Gerstein*, pp. 102–14; Joffroy, *Spy*, pp. 278–99; and Nuremberg trials document PS-1153, containing one of Gerstein's texts. Professor Wilhelm Pfannenstiel, who went to Belzec with Gerstein, confirmed in two postwar statements of his own some of the details related by Gerstein. See Pfannenstiel's statements of June 5, 1950, and November 9, 1952, in the files of the Belzec case tried in Germany, 1 Js 278/60, vol. 1, pp. 41–44, 135–41.

4. Von Otter told the story on several occasions. See Friedlander, *Gerstein*, pp. 122–27; Joffroy, *Spy*, pp. 111–17; and "A tale of horror on the Berlin express," *The Sunday Times* (London), March 29, 1981, p. 14.

5. See the comment by Hans Rothfels, the text of a memorandum sent by the Swedish legation in London to the British Foreign Office on August 7, 1945, and a letter from the Swedish Foreign Office to Leon Poliakov of the

Centre de Documentation Juive Contemporaine in Paris, November 10, 1949, in *Vierteljahrshefte für Zeitgeschichte*, vol. 1 (1953), p. 192. Apparently, von Otter reported only orally, on August 23, 1945, to the acting head of the Swedish legation, Eric von Post. An extant aide-mémoire, with some details of the Gerstein–von Otter meeting, is dated August 7, 1945. See Steven Koblik, *The Stones Cry Out* (New York, 1988), pp. 58–59, with the text on pp. 198–200.

6. See Friedlander, *Gerstein*, on Dibelius, p. 136, and Joffroy, *Spy*, on Orsenigo and the Dutch underground, pp. 172–73, 290.

7. Gerstein's customer account in the Deutsche Gesellschaft für Schädlingsbekämpfung (DEGESCH), Nuremberg trials document NI-7278, and Gerstein to Gerhard Peters (DEGESCH), May 24, 1944, Nuremberg trials document NI-9908.

8. Joffroy, *Spy*, pp. 246–66.

9. A biographical sketch of Karski, whose original name was Kozielewski, is in Martin Gilbert, *Auschwitz and the Allies* (New York, 1981), p. 347.

10. Jan Karski, *Story of a Secret State* (Boston, 1944), pp. 323–26. For the names of the Jewish leaders and additional details, see Walter Laqueur, *The Terrible Secret* (Boston, 1980), pp. 119–20, 229–31.

11. The book was *Story of a Secret State*.

12. Jan Ciechanowski, *Defeat in Victory* (Garden City, N.Y., 1947), p. 182.

13. Minutes of the meeting between Karski and representatives of Polish Jewry, chaired by Arie Tartakower, August 9, 1943, American Jewish Archives, World Jewish Congress Collection/Alphabetical Files—Poland, 205 A-1. Belzec had already been connected with the Warsaw Ghetto in a report taken to Switzerland by a Pole in mid-August 1942. See Gerhart Riegner to Irving Miller, August 28, 1942, American Jewish Archives, World Jewish Congress Collection/Alphabetical Files—Switzerland, 184-A, No. 1.

14. Karski, *Secret State*, pp. 339–51.

15. *Ibid.*, p. 338.

16. Verbatim remarks by Karski in Brewster Chamberlin and Marcia Feldman, eds., *The Liberation of the Nazi Concentration Camps 1945* (Washington, D.C.: U.S. Government Printing Office, 1987), pp. 176–81, 190–91, on p. 191.

21: THE JEWISH RESCUERS

1. On the reactions of the Jewish organizations in 1933 and 1938, see A. J. Sherman, *Island Refuge: Britain and Refugees from the Third Reich 1933–1939* (Berkeley, Calif., 1973), pp. 29–33, 173–79.

2. Robert S. Lynd to Beryl Harold Levy, December 22, 1941, American Jewish Archives in Cincinnati, World Jewish Congress Collection/Institute of Jewish Affairs—Jacob Robinson Files, U 230, Box 2.

3. See Rafael Medoff, *The Deafening Silence* (New York, 1987), p. 22–27, and the *American Jewish Year Book 1935–1936*, vol. 37, pp. 427–30. Under the law, the annual maximum number of European immigrants was sharply limited, and the annual maximum percentage of all immigrants originating by birth in any particular European country was to be proportional to the percentage of white Americans whose ancestry could be traced to that country. Although the quota assigned to German-born immigrants was not filled until the fiscal year July 1, 1938, to June 30, 1939, when it was oversubscribed, there was a prior difficulty in that prospective immigrants had to prove that they would not become a public charge. Few refugees had sufficient dollar funds or a guaranteed job on arrival. Therefore, they depended initially on support from friends or relatives. Representative Dickstein, who chaired the House Committee on Immigration, proposed that Jewish refugees related to American citizens be allowed entry outside the quota limits.

4. Medoff, *The Deafening Silence*, pp. 28–32. Interestingly enough, Palestinian Jewry took the pragmatic course not only of refraining from a boycott but of increasing German imports in the context of an agreement under which Jews could depart from Germany for Palestine, leaving their money in blocked funds in Germany and receiving the equivalent amount in Palestine pounds from the Jewish Agency. The agency was compensated with shipments of German goods financed with blocked funds of the emigrants. On the origins and impact of this agreement, which weakened the boycott movement, see Francis R. Nicosia, *The Third Reich and the Palestine Question* (Austin, Tex., 1985), pp. 29–49.

5. Medoff, *The Deafening Silence*, p. 51 ff.

6. See their short biographies in the *Encyclopaedia Judaica*.

7. Outline of Tartakower's address to the Jewish Writers Club, March 29, 1941, American Jewish Archives, World Jewish Congress Collection/Institute of Jewish Affairs—Organization Files, U 249, Box 4.

8. Agenda for the meeting of the Executive Committee of the Board of Trustees of the Institute of Jewish Affairs, January 24, 1942, American Jewish Archives, World Jewish Congress Collection/Institute of Jewish Affairs—Jacob Robinson Files, U 320. Box 3.

9. For his various appointments, see Adolf Böhm, *Die Zionistische Bewegung 1918 bis 1925*, vol. 2 (Jerusalem, 1937), *passim*. His politics and relationship with Jabotinsky are described by Francis Nicosia, "Revisionist

Zionism in Germany (I)—Richard Lichtheim and the Landesverband der Zionisten-Revisionisten in Deutschland 1926–33," *Leo Baeck Institute Year Book* (1986), vol. 31, pp. 209–40.

10. Lichtheim to Joseph Linton (Financial and Administrative Secretary of the World Zionist Organization in London), October 12, 1939, in Henry Friedlander and Sybil Milton, eds., *Archives of the Holocaust*, vol. 4, ed. Francis Nicosia (New York, 1990), pp. 1–4. The correspondence in this volume is culled from the Central Zionist Archives in Jerusalem.

11. *Ibid.*

12. Lichtheim to Linton (then Political Secretary of the World Zionist Organization in London), November 10, 1941, *ibid.*, pp. 34–37.

13. Lichtheim to Arthur Lourie, Secretary of the Emergency Committee for Zionist Affairs in New York (formerly with the Jewish Agency in London), February 11, 1942, *ibid.*, pp. 43–45.

14. Lichtheim to Leo Lauterbach, Organization Department of the Jewish Agency in Jerusalem, May 13, 1942, *ibid.*, pp. 49–50. Also, Lichtheim to Linton, May 20, 1942, *ibid.*, pp. 51–52.

15. Lichtheim to Lauterbach, May 29, 1942, *ibid.*, p. 53.

16. Riegner to Nahum Goldmann, June 17, 1942, American Jewish Archives, World Jewish Congress Collection/Alphabetical Files—Switzerland, 186 A, Box 1.

17. Silberschein to Tartakower, September 22, 1943, American Jewish Archives, World Jewish Congress Collection/Institute of Jewish Affairs—Polish Documents Wartime, 170 A, Box 1.

18. Riegner to Tartakower, March 10, 1942, American Jewish Archives, World Jewish Congress Collection/Alphabetical Files—Switzerland, 186 A, Box 2.

19. *Ibid.* Also subsequent correspondence in the same box.

20. Telegrams in American Jewish Archives, World Jewish Congress Collection/Alphabetical Files—Switzerland, 184 A, Box 1. Perlzweig was Chairman of the British Section of the World Jewish Congress until 1942, when he became the head of the Department of International Affairs in New York. Miller was Secretary General of the World Jewish Congress from 1942 to 1945. Romanian deportations to Poland did not materialize and Bulgarian deportations had not begun. News from Poland, however, continued to pour in. A report received in London from the Jewish Socialist Bund in Poland in May 1942 noted for the first time the gassing of Lodz Jews in a "special automobile" (gas van) near the village of Chelmno (Kulmhof). Text of the Bund report in Yehuda Bauer, "When Did They Know?" *Midstream*, April 1968, pp. 57–58.

21. Riegner to Goldmann, June 17, 1942, American Jewish Archives, World Jewish Congress Collection/Alphabetical Files—Switzerland, 184 A, Box 1.

22. Riegner to Miller (received July 17, 1942), American Jewish Archives, World Jewish Congress Collection/Alphabetical Files—Switzerland, 186 A, Box 2.

23. See the report of the Institute of Jewish Affairs to the Installation Conference of the Advisory Council on European Jewish Affairs, June 6–7, 1942, American Jewish Archives, World Jewish Congress Collection/Alphabetical Files—Switzerland, 184 A, Box 1. The first subheading of this report was "Pogroms, murder, torture," and references were made to Vilnius, Kaunas, Vitebsk, Minsk, and Kiev. Note also the letter of Gisi Fleischmann, an especially alert observer on the Jewish Council in Slovakia, to Silberschein, July 27, 1942, Yad Vashem Archives, M7/2-2, in which she discusses the deportation of 60,000 Slovak Jews, including old people, pregnant women, and infants, to the Generalgouvernement and to Auschwitz, District Sosnowitz, in Upper Silesia. She thought that the deportees were exposed to severe privation and asked Silberschein for clothing and food. She was not aware that the victims in the Generalgouvernement were channeled to Maydanek (Lublin) and Sobibor, both equipped with gas chambers, or that Auschwitz was a death camp.

24. Walter Laqueur, *The Terrible Secret* (Boston and Toronto, 1980), pp. 211–13.

25. Edgar Salin, "Über Artur Sommer, den Menschen und List-Forscher," *Mitteilungen der List Gesellschaft,* vol. 6 (1967), pp. 81–90. The approximate July 27, 1942, date was furnished to me in a telephone conversation on August 11, 1979, by Chaim Pozner (Pazner in 1979), who worked for the Jewish Agency in Geneva during 1942.

26. Martin Gilbert, *Auschwitz and the Allies* (New York, 1981), pp. 42–44, 46, and Monty Noam Penkower, *The Jews Were Expendable* (Urbana, Ill., and Chicago, 1983), pp. 59–60.

27. Salin, "Sommer," *Mitteilungen,* vol. 6 (1967), pp. 85, 86.

28. Walter Laqueur in Laqueur and Richard Breitman, *Breaking the Silence* (New York, 1986), p. 264.

29. Gilbert, *Auschwitz and the Allies,* p. 56. Penkower, *The Jews Were Expendable,* pp. 60–62, 317. Pozner also made this statement in his telephone conversation with me in 1979.

30. Samuel Scheps (Pozner's superior in the Geneva office of the Jewish Agency) to me, August 5, 1988, noting correspondence from the British

historian Martin Gilbert, whose search, at the request of Pozner, in the archives was futile.

31. Penkower, *The Jews Were Expendable,* pp. 61–62, 317.

32. *Ibid.,* pp. 66–67, 319. Penkower, who researched the Pozner connection exhaustively, found the August 29, 1942, letter in the Yad Vashem Archives in Jerusalem.

33. In his telephone conversation with me, Pozner insisted that he had actually overheard a conversation between Sommer and Salin while hiding in the room in which it took place. Pozner, however, did not know Sommer's name until after its publication in Salin's article. See Penkower, *ibid.,* p. 317, citing two letters from Salin to Pozner, dated April 22, 1969, and December 20, 1972, in which Salin disclosed the name to Pozner "for the first time." In several statements to Penkower, Pozner asserted that he had been in touch with the press officer of the Swiss Jewish Community, Benjamin Sagalowitz, *ibid.,* pp. 61–62, 317, and in his telephone call to me he stated that the information had reached Riegner. After I had reproduced the substance of Pozner's call in a footnote of my *La destruction des Juifs d'Europe* (Paris, 1988), pp. 964–65, Riegner wrote to me on July 18, 1988, characterizing Pozner's story as completely invented and pointing out that there was "no reason why he should have passed on the message to me through Sagalowitz in Zurich, while we were both in Geneva and knew each other quite well."

34. A portion of this story was first uncovered by Arthur Morse, *While Six Million Died* (New York, 1967), pp. 3–7. Schulte's identity was discovered years after his death by Monty Penkower and, independently, by Richard Breitman and Alan Kraut. See Penkower, *The Jews Were Expendable,* pp. 62, 317–18; Breitman and Kraut, "Who Was the 'Mysterious Messenger'?" *Commentary,* October 1983, pp. 44–47; Laqueur and Breitman, *Breaking the Silence* (New York, 1988); and Breitman in Breitman and Kraut, *American Refugee Policy and European Jewry 1933–1945* (Bloomington, Ind., 1987), pp. 148–57, 279–81. See also the correspondence by Penkower, Breitman, and others in *Commentary,* January 1984, pp. 4–10. The books co-authored by Breitman are more detailed about Schulte's background and the transmission of the message. There are some small discrepancies among the various accounts.

35. Memorandum by U.S. Vice Consul Howard Elting in Geneva, August 8, 1942, with attached draft of a telegram prepared by Riegner "giving in his own words a telegraphic summary of his statement to me"; National Archives of the United States, Record Group 84, American Legation Bern, Confidential File 1942, Box 7, 840.1 J. Riegner's first name was misspelled.

In subsequent transmissions, the language of the telegram was edited to conform to English usage. The message was discovered by Morse, who published it in one of its later formulations: *While Six Million Died,* p. 8. Schulte had requested anonymity, but in October 1942, the American Minister in Switzerland pressed Riegner for the disclosure of his name. Leland Harrison to Under Secretary of State Sumner Welles, October 24, 1942, National Archives Record Group 84, American Legation Bern Confidential File 1942, Box 7, 840.1 J. The American minister was then handed a sealed envelope containing a plain four-folded sheet of paper with the typed unsigned notation:

> Generaldirektor Dr. Schulte
> Montanindustrie (Bergbau)
> in engen oder engsten Kontakt mit den massgebenden
> Wehrwirtschaftskreisen
> Coal, iron, and steel industry (mining)
> in close or closest contact with the approprite
> armament-economy rings.

The envelope and paper are filed with Harrison's letter in the same box. Riegner apparently became aware of Schulte's name later on but respected Schulte's privacy. Schulte, who made one more trip to Switzerland in 1943, then stayed there. After the war, he divorced his wife, who had remained in Germany, and married a Jewish woman he knew in Switzerland.

36. Laqueur and Breitman, *Breaking the Silence,* pp. 146–47. Penkower, *The Jews Were Expendable,* pp. 63–64. Laqueur and Breitman state that Guggenheim also advised the deletion of a reference to a crematorium: *Breaking the Silence,* p. 146.

37. Memorandum by Elting, August 8, 1942, National Archives Record Group 84, American Legation Bern, Confidential File 1942, Box 7, 810.1 J.

38. J. Klehr Huddle (Counselor of the U.S. Legation in Bern) to Elting, August 21, 1942, *ibid.*

39. Bernard Wasserstein, *Britain and the Jews of Europe* (London and Oxford, 1979), p. 168. Gilbert, *Auschwitz and the Allies,* pp. 59–60.

40. Telegram from Silverman to Wise, August 24, 1942, American Jewish Archives, World Jewish Congress Collection/Alphabetical Files—Switzerland, 184 A, Box 1.

41. Lichtheim to Lauterbach, August 30, 1942, enclosing the report, in *Archives of the Holocaust,* vol. 4, ed. Nicosia, pp. 61–63. Also, Riegner to Miller, August 28, 1942, American Jewish Archives, World Jewish Con-

gress Collection/Alphabetical Files—Switzerland 184 A, Box 1. The report was channeled to Riegner from the Polish legation in Switzerland. See the unsigned "note" in the same box. See also Secretary of State Hull to U.S. Representative Myron C. Taylor at the Vatican, September 23, 1942, asking for possible confirmation from Vatican sources: National Archives Record Group 84, American Legation Bern Confidential File 1942, Box 7, 840.1 J. Bodies were first buried in mass graves then dug up and burned in Belzec. There was no production of soap or fertilizer in the camps.

42. Riegner to Miller, August 31, 1942, American Jewish Archives, World Jewish Congress Collection/Alphabetical Files—Switzerland, 184 A, Box 1. This letter was not received in New York until October 5, 1942.

43. Riegner to Goldmann, September 7, 1942, *ibid.*

44. Harrison to Welles, October 24, 1942, enclosing aide-mémoire and annexes, National Archives Record Group 84, American Legation Bern Confidential File 1942, Box 7, 840.1 J.

45. Paul Squire to Secretary of State, with copy to American Legation in Bern, October 29, 1942, enclosing affidavit by Guggenheim dated on the same day, *ibid.*

46. See *Archives of the Holocaust,* vol. 4, ed. Nicosia.

47. Lichtheim to Linton, August 27, 1942, *ibid.,* pp. 59–60.

48. Harrison to Secretary of State, October 24, 1942, enclosing the aide-mémoire, National Archives Record Group 84, American Legation Bern Confidential File 1942, Box 7, 840.1 J. The text of the aide-mémoire was received by the World Jewish Congress on November 24, 1942. American Jewish Archives, World Jewish Congress Collection/Alphabetical Files—Switzerland, 184 A, Box 1.

49. Lichtheim to Goldmann, September 9, 1942, *Archives of the Holocaust,* vol. 4, ed. Nicosia, pp. 380–86.

50. Dina Porat, *The Blue and the Yellow Stars of David* (Cambridge, Mass., 1990), pp. 35–36.

51. *Ibid.,* p. 36.

52. Yoav Gelber, "Moralist and Realistic Approaches in the Study of the Allies' Attitude to the Holocaust," in Asher Cohen, Yoav Gelber, and Charlotte Wardi, eds., *Comprehending the Holocaust* (Frankfurt am Main, 1988), pp. 107–123, on pp. 117, 123.

53. Shertok to Linton, November 20, 1942, in *Archives of the Holocaust,* vol. 4, ed. Nicosia, p. 168.

54. Dina Porat, "Palestinian Jewry and the Jewish Agency: Public Response to the Holocaust," in Richard Cohen, ed., *Vision and Conflict in the Holy Land* (Jerusalem and New York, 1985), pp. 246–73.

55. L. C. Pinkerton, U.S. Consul in Jerusalem, to Secretary of State, November 30, 1942, National Archives Record Group 59, Decimal File 1940–1944, Box 2917, 740.00116, European War 1939/673.

56. Yoav Gelber, "Zionist Policy and the Fate of European Jewry," *Yad Vashem Studies*, vol. 13 (1979), pp. 169–210, on p. 195.

57. See Porat, "Palestinian Jewry," in Cohen, ed., *Vision and Conflict*, p. 246 ff., particularly pp. 247 and 253. Ben-Gurion's comment was made on December 6, 1942: *ibid.*, note 28, p. 270. The continuing debate over demonstrative versus non-demonstrative reactions is described by Porat in "Al-domi: Palestinian Intellectuals and the Holocaust, 1943–1945," *Studies in Zionism*, vol. 5 (1984), pp. 97–124.

58. See Barnett Litvinoff, general editor, *The Letters and Papers of Chaim Weizmann*, series A, vols. 20 and 21, ed. Michael Cohen (New Brunswick and Jerusalem, 1979). See also Litvinoff's biography, *Weizmann* (New York, 1976), and Weizmann's autobiography, *Trial and Error* (New York, 1949). During the First World War, Weizmann was the Director of the British Admiralty Laboratories, working on acetone, a solvent useful in making cordite, which in turn was needed for naval ammunition. At that time Weizmann became acquainted with Winston Churchill, who was the First Sea Lord. Weizmann's Second World War research was in a sense a return to his life in 1916. Butadiene and isoprene were of interest in the production of synthetic rubber. The Allies, like Germany, were cut off from natural rubber in Malaya, which was occupied by the Japanese.

59. Porat, *The Blue and the Yellow Stars*, pp. 250–52. On Ben-Gurion's utterances and letters, see also Tuvia Frieling, "Ben-Gurion and the Holocaust," *Yad Vashem Studies*, vol. 18 (1987), pp. 199–232.

60. Summary report by Jakob Lestschinsky, September 23, 1942, American Jewish Archives, World Jewish Congress Collection/Alphabetical Files—Switzerland, 184 A, Box 1.

61. Miller to Riegner, October 16, 1942, with attached explanation to the censor, American Jewish Archives, World Jewish Congress Collection/Alphabetical Files—Switzerland, 186 A, Box 2.

62. Wise to Roosevelt, December 2, 1942, cited in excerpt by Medoff, *The Deafening Silence*, pp. 100, 203.

63. See *The New York Times*, November 25, 1942, p. 10. This article made mention, on the basis of information from the Polish Government in Exile, of the death camps Belzec, Sobibor, and Treblinka. On the following day, Wise was quoted on p. 16 with "before" and "after" figures.

64. Memorandum with summation submitted to Roosevelt on Decem-

ber 8, 1942, in American Jewish Archives, World Jewish Congress Collection/Alphabetical Files—Poland, 205 A, Box 3.

65. Wise to Tartakower, December 15, 1942, *ibid.*

66. David S. Wyman, *The Abandonment of the Jews* (New York, 1984), pp. 72–73, 365. In Britain, the Board of Deputies was received behind closed doors by Richard Law in the Foreign Office. The board had not succeeded in obtaining an interview with Foreign Secretary Anthony Eden: remarks by Selig Brodetsky during a London meeting of the Executive of the Jewish Agency, November 30, 1942, *Archives of the Holocaust,* vol. 4, ed. Nicosia, pp. 82–86.

67. Unsigned note in German, January 14, 1943, American Jewish Archives, World Jewish Congress Collection/Alphabetical Files—Switzerland, unmarked box, "Rescue-Warnings" 1941–43, I-K.

68. Ciechanowski to Tartakower, March 24, 1943, American Jewish Archives, World Jewish Congress Collection/Institute of Jewish Affairs—Jacob Robinson Files, U 320, Box 4.

69. Minutes of a March 29, 1943, meeting of the Joint Emergency Committee, Wise presiding, Archives of the American Jewish Committee, EXO-29, Waldman Files (Joint Emergency Committee).

70. Waldman to Proskauer, May 19, 1943, *ibid.*

71. Robinson to Wise and Goldmann, June 25, 1943, American Jewish Archives, World Jewish Congress Collection/Institute of Jewish Affairs—Jacob Robinson Files, U 320, Box 4.

72. Institute of Jewish Affairs, *Hitler's Ten-Year War on the Jews* (New York, 1943).

73. Sumner Welles to Wise, August 6, 1943, enclosing the memorandum, American Jewish Archives, World Jewish Congress Collection/Alphabetical Files—Switzerland, 184 A, Box 1. The memorandum had been submitted by Lichtheim and Riegner to Minister Harrison on October 22, 1942. National Archives Record Group 84, American Legation Bern, Confidential File 1942, Box 7, 840.1 J.

74. Robinson to Wise, Goldmann, and others, August 19, 1943, American Jewish Archives, World Jewish Congress Collection/Institute of Jewish Affairs—Jacob Robinson Files, U 320, Box 4.

75. Tartakower to Wise, Goldmann, and others, November 23, 1943, American Jewish Archives, World Jewish Congress Collection/Alphabetical Files—Switzerland, 184 A, Box 1.

76. Porat, *The Blue and the Yellow Stars,* pp. 212–16.

77. See the note, dated July 7, 1944, summarizing the meeting by Weiz-

mann and Shertok with Eden on July 6, with an attached aide-mémoire; Shertok to Ben-Gurion, July 6, 1944; a "note on the proposal for bombing the death camps," July 11, 1944; A. W. G. Randall (British Foreign Office) to Shertok, July 15, 1944; and Richard Law (British Foreign Office) to Weizmann, September 1, 1944, turning down the request. All documents in the Weizmann Archives, Rehovoth, Israel. In his published diary, Eden did not mention any meetings with the Jewish leaders. See his *The Reckoning* (Boston, 1965).

78. Herbert Druks, *The Failure to Rescue* (New York, 1977), pp. 65 ff., citing Kubowitzki's letter of July 1, 1944, to John W. Pehle, Director of the U.S. War Refugee Board.

79. For the Brand mission, see primarily the documents dated June 5 to November 2 in the Weizmann Archives, the testimony by Brand in the trial of Adolf Eichmann in Jerusalem, sess. 56, 57, and 59, May 29–31, 1961, and Eichmann's testimony, sess. 86, July 5, 1961.

22: THE ALLIES

1. Purged, among others, were Lev Kamenev, Grigori Zinoviev, and Karl Radek. Kamenev and Zinoviev were shot in 1936. Radek disappeared later.

2. Reichskommissar Ostland to Generalkommissar White Ruthenia, August 4, 1941, enclosing report by Sonderführer Schröter, YIVO Institute Occ E 3a-2.

3. The Jewish population of Kishinev in 1930 was 41,405. A Romanian count after the capture of the city was 11,252. Report by Romanian Investigation Commission of December 1941 in Matatias Carp, *Cartea Neagra— Suferintele Evreilor din Romania 1940–1944*, 3 vols. (Bucharest, 1946–48), vol. 3, pp. 61–65.

4. The total prewar population of Kiev was 846,290. On January 1, 1943, after the killing of the Jews and the loss of Ukrainians, it was 384,570. Jews were 140,000 in Kiev in 1926. A total of 33,771 were reported shot. Reich Security Main Office IV-A-1 Operational and Situation Report No. 128, November 3, 1941, Nuremberg trials document NO-3157. There was no ghetto in Kiev and it is likely that only a few thousand more were hiding in the city. Shootings, at any rate, were henceforth taking place only in small batches. In Kharkov the total prewar population sank from 833,430 to 456,639 in December 1941 before shootings and starvation. Jews were 81,000 in the city in 1926, and 10,271 during the registration of December 1941. The final registration figures are in the Kharkov Oblast Archives,

Fond 2982, Opis 1, Folder 232. No figures of Jewish populations in cities during the census of 1939 have been published.

5. See the recollections of Joseph Weingartner, a survivor of Kerch (Crimea), in Ilya Ehrenburg and Vasily Grossman, eds., *The Black Book* (New York, 1981), p. 273.

6. See the diary of Sarra Gleyckh of Mariupol, *ibid.*, p. 70.

7. Report by Moisey Samoylovich Everson about Kislovodsk in the Caucasus, *ibid.*, pp. 265–72. This city was taken by the Germans in the summer of 1942.

8. The Wirtschaftsstab Ost/Fü/I L (Economy-Armament Staff operating in the military area), in a biweekly report of December 31, 1941, noted that the Soviets had succeeded in drawing back their skilled labor. National Archives of the United States, Record Group 242, T 77, Roll 1093. Generalmajor (Brigadier General) Nagel of the Wirtschaftsstab reported after an inspection trip to Kharkov that the Soviets had forcibly "deported" all halfway useful labor forces: note by Nagel, December 31, 1941, National Archives Record Group 242, T 77, Roll 1070.

9. Reich Security Main Office IV-A-1, Operational and Situation Report No. 123, October 24, 1941, Nuremberg trials document NO-3239.

10. See the accounts of Jewish survivors in Ehrenburg and Grossman, eds., *The Black Book,* reporting that they were unable to leave Berdichev, p. 14; Khmelnik, p. 28; Odessa, p. 28; Minsk, p. 139; Rostov, p. 256; Yalta, p. 278; Daugavpils, p. 347; Borisov, p. 361; the Smolensk Oblast, p. 365; and Ordzhonikidze, p. 366. From Stalino, a German military government official reported that all the "well-to-do" Jews had fled: Report by Feldkommandantur 240/VII, December 4, 1941, National Archives Record Group 242, T 501, Roll 6. See also Dov Levin, "The Attitude of the Soviet Union to the Rescue of the Jews," in Yisrael Gutman and Efraim Zuroff, eds., *Rescue Attempts during the Holocaust* (Jerusalem, 1977), pp. 225–36. There were some local Soviet officials who recognized the special plight of the Jewish inhabitants. The biweekly report of the Wirtschaftsstab Ost Fü/I L for November 1-15, 1941, dated December 8, 1941, noted that Soviet Police ("GPU") in Dnepropetrovsk had given Jews whose appearance was not Jewish papers or passports legitimizing them as Russian or Ukrainian: National Archives Record Group 242, T 77, Roll 1093.

11. Noteworthy in this connection is the treatment of Hungarian Jewish forced laborers, organized in unarmed companies of the Hungarian army, after they were overtaken by the advancing Red Army. Many thousands of these Jews were kept in prisoner of war camps and waited for a long time

for their repatriation. See George Barany, "Jewish Prisoners of War in the Soviet Union during World War II," *Jahrbücher für Geschichte Osteuropas,* vol. 31 (1982), pp. 161–209.

12. A. J. Sherman, *Island Refugee—Britain and Refugees from the Third Reich 1933–1939* (Los Angeles, 1973). Louise London, "British Government Policy and Jewish Refugees 1933–45," *Patterns of Prejudice,* vol. 23 (1989), pp. 26–43. Louise London, "Jewish Refugees, Anglo-Jewry and British Government Policy, 1930–1940," in David Cesarani, ed., *The Making of Modern Anglo-Jewry* (Oxford, 1990), pp. 163–208. Miriam Kochan, *Britain's Internees in the Second World War* (London, 1983).

13. David S. Wyman, *Paper Walls* (Amherst, Mass., 1968). Henry L. Feingold, *The Politics of Rescue* (New Brunswick, N.J., 1970).

14. Notes by Culbertson and Dubrow, August 13, 1942, National Archives Record Group 59, Decimal File 1940–1944, Box 5465.

15. David S. Wyman, *The Abandonment of the Jews* (New York, 1984), pp. 72–73. Coincidentally, several Jewish women's organizations in Palestine appealed on December 4, 1942, to Eleanor Roosevelt for any help she might be able to give to save the shattered remnants. On December 10, 1942, President Roosevelt forwarded the plea to Under Secretary of State Sumner Welles with the note "Will you let Eleanor know what she can say in reply to the enclosed telegram?" National Archives Record Group 59, Decimal File 1940–1944, Box 2917, 740.0016 European War 193/727 PS/DLB.

16. The text of the cable, signed on February 10, 1943, by Welles, who was probably unaware of its contents, in Henry Morgenthau, "The Morgenthau Diaries," *Colliers,* November 1, 1947.

17. Secretary of State Cordell Hull to Ambassador William H. Standley in Moscow, August 30, 1943, *Foreign Relations of the United States 1943,* vol. 1, pp. 416–17.

18. Ferdinand Lammot Belin to William Langer (both in the Office of Strategic Services), April 10, 1944, National Archives Record Group 266, OSS 66059. Captain Paul M. Birkeland (U.S. Assistant Military Attaché in London) to War Department Military Intelligence, March 17, 1944, noting that a copy was also given to Herbert Pell of the United Nations War Crimes Commission, National Archives Record Group 165, Box 3138, Poland 6950.

19. William J. Casey, *The Secret War against Hitler* (Washington, D.C., 1986), p. 218. It is interesting to note that J. Edgar Hoover, Director of the Federal Bureau of Investigation in the Department of Justice, did not overlook signs of the Jewish catastrophe, even though his jurisdiction was lim-

ited to the Western Hemisphere. See his telegram to Assistant Secretary of State Adolf Berle, May 5, 1942, on deportations, National Archives Record Group 59, Decimal File 1940–1944, Box 5465, and his note to Berle, with copies to Naval Intelligence and Army Intelligence (Brigadier General Hayes P. Kroner), "LIQUIDATION OF THE JEWISH POPULATION OF EUROPE," September 9, 1942, National Archives Record Group 165.77, Box 1191. In the letter of September 9, Hoover states that he also informed Elmer Davis, Director of the Office of War Information. From the wording of the letter, it appears that Hoover had access to the August telegram sent by World Jewish Congress Representative Gerhart Riegner to London and New York.

20. In the summer of 1943, Roosevelt had given his permission in principle for the deposit of the funds. Stephen Wise to Roosevelt, July 23, 1943, thanking the "chief." National Archives Record Group 59, Decimal File 1940–1945, Box 5465. For the subsequent correspondence, see Morgenthau to Hull, November 24, 1943, and Hull to the American legation in Bern, January 5, 1955, *ibid*.

23: Neutral Countries

1. On the repatriation, see Nehemia Robinson, "Die Juden in Franco-Spanien," *Aufbau* (New York), September 11, 1953, p. 3. On escapes, see Haim Avni, *Spain, the Jews, and Franco* (Philadelphia, 1982), pp. 94–147.

2. Martin Gilbert, *Winston S. Churchill*, vol. 7 (Boston, 1988), pp. 377–78.

3. Ira A. Hirschmann, *Lifeline to a Promised Land* (New York, 1946), pp. 3–6, and Jürgen Rohwehr, *Die Versenkung der Flüchtlingstransporte Struma und Mefkure* (Frankfurt am Main, 1965).

4. On March 27, 1943, when Bulgarian Jewry was in acute danger of deportation, and when transports from Bulgarian-occupied Thrace and Macedonia were already rolling into Treblinka, Jewish leaders in the United States asked Foreign Secretary Eden for help to move the Jews out of Bulgaria. Eden replied, "Turkey does not want any more of your people," without having to add the word *either*. Minutes of the March 29, 1943, meeting of the Joint Emergency Committee, Stephen Wise presiding, Archives of the American Jewish Committee, EXO-29, Waldman Files (Joint Emergency Committee). In the end the Bulgarian Jews were not deported.

5. Sweden's role is described by Steven Koblik, *The Stones Cry Out* (New York, 1988).

6. Alfred A. Häsler, *The Lifeboat Is Full* (New York, 1969), pp. 30–53, 331–32, 115–16. A total of 9,751 Jews and non-Jews were excluded at the border between August 1942 and the end of the war. Clandestine crossers

were expelled the same way to prevent their immediate detection by the Germans. *Ibid.,* pp. 190–92, 329, 331.

7. Leland Harrison to Department of State, January 15, 1944, National Archives of the United States Record Group 84, American Legation in Bern 1942–1947, Box 42, 848 (Intergovernmental Committee on Refugees). Harrison based his assessment on a Swiss note of November 16, 1943.

8. Häsler, *Lifeboat,* pp. 285, 329.

9. Arie Ben-Tov, *Facing the Holocaust in Budapest* (Geneva and Dordrecht, 1988), pp. 131–37. The meeting took place on October 12, 1942. It should be recalled, however, that Carl Burckhart, a former Swiss Minister in Berlin and future President of the International Red Cross, was a conduit, in strict confidence, for information about the Jewish catastrophe to the Jewish community and the American Legation in Switzerland that very month. See correspondence in National Archives Record Group 84, American Legation in Bern, Confidential File 1942, Box 7, 940.1 Jews.

24: The Churches

1. See the filled out form of the Catholic Diocese Aachen, "Nachweis der arischen Abstammung," December 15, 1936, certifying the marriage of Peter Wilhelm Jansen and Agnes Kreitz on January 29, 1859, U.S. Holocaust Memorial Museum Archives. Also in 1936 the Evangelical-Lutheran Church in Berlin prepared an alphabetical card index of baptisms covering 1800–1874, with special references to baptized Jews and Gypsies: Götz Aly and Karl Heinz Roth, *Die restlose Erfassung* (Berlin, 1984), pp. 70–71.

2. On Bertram, see *Mitteilungen zur weltanschaulichen Lage,* April 15, 1942, pp. 13–17, EAP 250-c-10/5, at one time in the Federal Records Center in Alexandria, Virginia. On Lutheran expulsions see the announcement, with seven signatures, of December 17, 1941, in Helmut Eschwege, *Kennzeichen J* (Berlin, 1966), pp. 161–62.

3. See the summary of the conference held on March 6, 1942, Nuremberg trials document NG-2586-H.

4. See the texts of the letters dated May 19, 1943, and October 14, 1943, in Johan M. Snoek, *The Grey Book* (New York, 1970), pp. 131–33.

5. As to Theresienstadt, see H. G. Adler, *Theresienstadt 1941–1945* (Tübingen, 1960), pp. 308, 611.

6. Snoek, *The Grey Book,* pp. 123–25.

7. See the excerpt of the report by Ambassador Léon Bérard (accredited to the Holy See) to Marshal Pétain (August 1941) in Leon Poliakov, *Harvest of Hate* (Syracuse, 1949), pp. 299–301.

8. Jorgen H. Barford, *Escape from Nazi Terror* (Copenhagen, 1968), pp. 12–13.

9. Snoek, *The Grey Book*, pp. 125–31.

10. *Ibid.*, pp. 207–26. Also, Alfred A. Häsler, *The Lifeboat Is Full* (New York, 1969), pp. 115–18, 122–26, 140–44.

11. Parliamentary Debates, Fifth Series, vol. CXXVI, House of Lords, 8th Sess., 37th Parliament, 6 & 7 George VI, Vol. 2 of the session (London, 1943), pp. 813–60.

12. Tittmann to Secretary of State, October 6, 1942, *Foreign Relations of the United States 1942*, vol. 2, pp. 776–77.

13. Report by Tittmann enclosed by Harrison (U.S. Minister in Switzerland) to Secretary of State Hull, December 26, 1942, *ibid.*, vol. 1, pp. 70–71.

14. Harrison to Hull, January 5, 1943, enclosing report by Tittmann of December 30, 1942, *Foreign Relations of the United States 1943*, vol. 2, pp. 911–13. The text of the Christmas message appeared in *The New York Times*, December 25, 1942, p. 10.

15. Ernst von Weizsäcker to Ernst Wörmann and other officials in the German Foreign Office, December 5, 1941, Nuremberg trials document NG-4894.

16. Burzio to Maglione, April 10, 1943, in John F. Morley, *Vatican Diplomacy and the Jews during the Holocaust* (New York, 1980), pp. 239–43.

17. *Ibid.*, pp. 147–65.

18. Taylor to Maglione, September 26, 1943, enclosing a Jewish Agency memorandum of August 30, 1942, *Foreign Relations of the United States 1942*, vol. 3, pp. 775–76. Note by Maglione (probably September 27, 1942) in Secrétairie d'Etat de Sa Sainteté, *Actes et documents du Saint Siège relatifs à la seconde guerre mondiale*, vol. 8 (The Vatican, 1974), p. 665. The Jewish Agency memorandum, based on reports of Christian Poles, had mentioned mass deportations, the Belzec camp, and soap made from corpses. These reports Maglione could not confirm in particulars.

19. Note dated May 5, 1943, *Actes et documents*, vol. 9 (1975), p. 274.

20. Weizsäcker to Foreign Office, October 28, 1943, Nuremberg trials document NG-5027.

21. Robert Katz, *Black Sabbath* (New York, 1969), pp. 142–43, 173–91.

22. Reich Security Main Office IV-A-1, Operational and Situation Report No. 54, August 16, 1941, Nuremberg trials document NO-2849.

23. Avraham Tory, *Surviving the Holocaust—The Kovno Ghetto Diary*, ed. by Martin Gilbert with notes by Dina Porat (Cambridge, Mass., 1990),

entry of April 30, 1943, pp. 312–17. Tory, who could only recapitulate the rabbi's recollection of the meetings, thought that the bishop was understanding. On a subsequent occasion, the bishop apparently spoke in a balmy manner to Snieg: entry of September 28, 1943, pp. 484–86. The Jewish children were rounded up in 1944 and killed.

24. On Septyckyj's background, attitudes, and protests, see Hansjakob Stehle, "Der Lemberger Metropolit Septyckyj und die nationalsozialistiche Politik in der Ukraine," *Vierteljahrshefte für Zeitgeschichte,* vol. 34 (1986), pp. 407–425. Septyckyj's letter of August 29–31, 1942, to Pius XII in *Actes et documents,* vol. 3, part II, pp. 625–29, and Pius XII to Septyckyj, August 26, 1942, on pp. 622–23 of the same volume. Septyckyj's letter to Himmler has not been found. Septyckyj's outrage expressed to Vsevolod Frederic, in a memorandum by Frederic, September 19, 1943, Centre de documentation juive contemporaine, Document CXLVa 60. The Metropolitan, who wrote a welcoming letter to Stalin after Lvov was captured by the Red Army, died shortly afterward in 1944.

25. See Alois Hudal, *Die Grundlagen des Nationalsozialismus* (Leipzig and Vienna, 1937), and his *Römische Tagebücher* (Graz and Stuttgart, 1976). The *Tagebücher* are evidently an edited version of the original manuscript and do not follow a diary form. Hudal's letter to Stahel, October 16, 1942, was enclosed by Gerhard Gumpert (German diplomat in Rome) to the German Foreign Office on the same day; Nuremberg trials document NG-5027. Hudal included a slightly different, possibly draft version of the appeal in his *Tagebücher,* p. 215.

26. Otto Ogiermann, *Bis zum letzten Atemzug* (Leutesdorf, 1985). Lichtenberg's fate was noted in diplomatic correspondence. See Legationsrat Richard Haidlen (in charge of Vatican affairs in the Political Division of the German Foreign Office) to Weizsäcker, November 11, 1941, Nuremberg trials document NG-4447, and Pius XII to Preysing, *Actes et documents,* vol. 2 (1967), pp. 376–81.

INDEX